Keystone

William K. Durr
Vivian O. Windley
Mildred C. Yates

CONSULTANT   Paul McKee

Houghton Mifflin Company • BOSTON
Atlanta · Dallas · Geneva, Illinois · Hopewell, New Jersey · Palo Alto · Toronto

Acknowledgments

For each of the selections listed below, grateful acknowledgment is made for permission to adapt and/or reprint original copyrighted material, as follows:

"As I Walk Through the Water," by Ruben Marcilla from *Wishes, Lies, and Dreams: Teaching Children to Write Poetry*, by Kenneth Koch and the students of P.S. 61 in New York City. Copyright © 1970 by Kenneth Koch. Reprinted by permission of Random House, Inc. and International Famous Agency for Kenneth Koch.

"Ben and Me," adapted from *Ben and Me*, by Robert Lawson. Copyright 1939 by Robert Lawson, by permission of Little, Brown and Co.

"Call It Courage," from *Call It Courage* by Armstrong Sperry. Copyright 1940 by the Macmillan Company, renewed 1968 by Armstrong Sperry. By permission of the Macmillan Company and The Bodley Head.

"Camels: Ships of the Desert," an abridged and simplified version of "The Camel" from *The Wonderful World of Mammals: Adventuring with Stamps*, copyright © 1973 by Roger Caras. Reprinted by permission of Harcourt Brace Jovanovich, Inc. and Elaine Greene Ltd.

"A Cat Called Good Fortune," reprinted with permission of Macmillan Publishing Company from *The Cat Who Went to Heaven*, by Elizabeth Coatsworth. Copyright 1930 by Macmillan Publishing Co., Inc., renewed 1968 by Elizabeth Coatsworth Beston.

"The Cherub and My Sainted Grandmother," by Barbara Corcoran. From *American Girl*, copyright © 1973 by Girl Scouts of the U.S.A. By permission of McIntosh and Otis, Inc.

"City" by Langston Hughes. Copyright 1958 by Langston Hughes. Reprinted by permission of Harold Ober Associates Inc.

"The Clockmaker and the Timekeeper," from *Tales of Old China*, by Isabelle Chang. Copyright © 1969 by Isabelle Chang. By permission of Random House, Inc.

"The Computer Triumphs Again," from *Ollie's Team and the Baseball Computer* by Clem Philbrook. © 1967, Hastings House Publishers.

"Computers—Giant Brains?" by Malcolm Weiss and Anita Soucie. © 1968 by Scholastic Magazines, Inc., reprinted by permission from *Young Citizen*.

"Damon and Pythias," by Fan Kissen. Reprinted by permission of the author.

"A Day in the Life of Henry Reed," adapted from *Henry Reed, Inc.* by Keith Robertson. Copyright © 1958 by Keith Robertson. All rights reserved. Reprinted by permission of The Viking Press, Inc.

"Delicatessen," from *City Poems* by Lois Lenski. Copyright © 1971 by Lois Lenski. Used by permission of Henry Z. Walck, Inc.

"Drums," adapted by permission of William Morrow & Co., Inc. from *Drums, Rattles, and Bells* by Larry Kettelkamp. Copyright © 1960 by Larry Kettelkamp.

"Eat-It-All Elaine," from *Don't Ever Cross a Crocodile*, by Kaye Starbird. Copyright © 1963 by Kaye Starbird. Reprinted by permission of J. B. Lippincott Company.

"Elizabeth Blackwell, M.D.," from "Elizabeth Blackwell: America's First Woman Doctor," by Lynne Cheney. Copyright © 1973, Highlights for Children, Inc., Columbus, Ohio.

"Ellen Swallow and Rachel Carson," adapted from *American Girl*, February, 1974, by permission of *American Girl*, published monthly by Girl Scouts of the U.S.A.

"An Eskimo Boy's Courage," from *Tiktaliktak*, written and illustrated by James Houston, copyright © 1965 by James Houston. Reprinted by permission of Harcourt Brace Jovanovich, Inc. and Longman Canada Limited.

"Expedition from Arreol," by Michael C. Slaughter. © 1968 The Curtis Publishing Company, by permission from *Jack and Jill* Magazine.

"Federico Discovers the Sea," from *I Am from Puerto Rico*, by Peter Buckley. Copyright © 1971 by Peter Buckley. Reprinted by permission of Simon and Schuster, Children's Book Division; and Curtis Brown, Ltd.

"Flight to Freedom," from *Harriet Tubman: Flame of Freedom*, by Frances Humphreville. Copyright © 1967 by Houghton Mifflin Company.

"A Flying Tackle," by Rafe Gibbs. Used by permission of the author.

Copyright © 1979, 1976 by Houghton Mifflin Company

All rights reserved. No part of this work may be reproduced or transmitted in any form or by any means, electronic or mechanical, including photocopying and recording, or by any information storage or retrieval system, without permission in writing from the publisher. Printed in U.S.A.
ISBN: 0-395-26594-0

"Girls Can, Too!" from *Girls Can, Too!* by Lee Bennett Hopkins. Copyright © 1972 by Lee Bennett Hopkins. Reprinted by permission of Curtis Brown, Ltd.

"The Grasshopper," from *Every Time I Climb a Tree* by David McCord, copyright 1952 by David McCord. Used by permission of Little, Brown and Co.

"The Great Penobscot Raid," from *More Glooscap Stories*, by Kay Hill. Copyright © 1970 by Kay Hill. By permission of Dodd, Mead & Company, Inc. and Collins-Knowlton-Wing, Inc.

"Hinky Pinky," from *Arrow Book of Word Games*, by Murray Rockowitz, © 1964 by Scholastic Magazines, Inc.

"Hi-ya, Bird," from *Let the Balloon Go*, by Ivan Southall. Copyright © 1968 by Ivan Southall. By permission of St. Martin's Press, Inc., and Methuen Children's Books Limited.

"A Horse for Reg," from *Trust a City Kid* by Anne Huston and Jane Yolen. Copyright © 1966 by Anne Huston and Jane Yolen. Used by permission of Lothrop, Lee and Shepard Company.

"An Impossible Choice," from *The Bushbabies*, by William H. Stevenson. Copyright © 1965 by William H. Stevenson. Reprinted by permission of Houghton Mifflin Company and Hutchinson Publishing Group Ltd.

"Indian Boy Joins Sentinel Staff," adapted from *The Year of Small Shadow*, © 1961 by Evelyn Sibley Lampman. By permission of Harcourt Brace Jovanovich, Inc. and Curtis Brown, Ltd.

"In Time of Silver Rain," from *Fields of Wonder*, by Langston Hughes. Copyright 1938 and renewed 1966 by Langston Hughes. Reprinted by permission of Alfred A. Knopf, Inc.

"The Iroquois Steelworkers," adapted with permission of Macmillan Publishing Co., Inc. from *The Tuscaroras* by Shirley Hill Witt. Copyright © 1972 by Shirley Hill Witt.

"John Muir: Friend of the Forest," by Gerry Bishop. Reprinted from *Ranger Rick's Nature Magazine* by permission of the publisher, the National Wildlife Federation.

Jokes: "Al: Why does . . . ," "Bill: Speaking of . . . ," and "Customer: When I bought . . ." reprinted from *Children's Digest Magazine*.

Joke: "Fatty: Say, can . . ." from *Fun Parade* by Mark Riddell, © 1959 by Doubleday and Company, Inc. Reprinted by permission.

"Jumping Pennies," from *Fun and Play All the Way*, by Anne Blaine, copyright © 1961. Used by permission of Doubleday & Co., Inc.

"Keplik, the Match Man," from *The Witch of Fourth Street*, by Myron Levoy. Text copyright © 1972 by Myron Levoy. Used by permission of Harper & Row, Publishers, Inc.

"The King of the Frogs," adapted from *Tales Told Near a Crocodile*, by Humphrey Harman. Copyright © 1962 by Humphrey Harman. All rights reserved. By permission of The Viking Press, Inc. and Hutchinson and Co., Ltd.

"The Little Lizard's Sorrow," from *The Toad Is the Emperor's Uncle*, copyright © 1970 by Sung Ngo-Dinh. Reprinted by permission of Doubleday & Co., Inc.

"Lucy Speaks Out," from *Stand Up, Lucy* by Elizabeth Hall. Copyright © 1971 by Elizabeth Hall. By permission of Houghton Mifflin Company, the author, and McIntosh and Otis, Inc.

"Mary Cassatt: Child in a Straw Hat," by Marian King. Copyright © 1974, Highlights for Children, Inc., Columbus, Ohio.

"Matt Henson: A True Explorer," by Pat Robbins. Used by permission of the National Geographic School Bulletin, copyrighted by the National Geographic Society.

"The Memory of Beauty," from *Wind in My Hand* by Hanako Fukuda, copyright © 1970, published by Golden Gate Junior Book Department of Childrens Press, Chicago.

"Mummy Slept Late and Daddy Fixed Breakfast," from *You Read to Me, I'll Read to You*, by John Ciardi. Copyright © 1962 by John Ciardi. Reprinted by permission of J. B. Lippincott Company.

"My Friend in Africa," from *My Friend in Africa*, copyright © 1960 by Frederick Franck. By permission of the publisher, The Bobbs-Merrill Company, Inc. and Frederick Franck.

"Open Gate to Freedom," abridged and adapted by permission of the publishers from *Dangerous Journey* © 1959 by Laszlo Hamori; English translation © 1962 by Harcourt Brace Jovanovich, Inc. Permission also granted by Penguin Books Ltd.

"Our Friends, The Bees, Wasps and Hornets," reprinted from *Ranger Rick's Nature Magazine* by permission of the publisher, the National Wildlife Federation.

"Prairie Dog Town," adapted from *Prairie Dog Summer*. Copyright © 1972 by Faith McNulty. Used by permission of Coward, McCann & Geoghegan, Inc. and McIntosh and Otis, Inc.

"Purim Jester," from *All-of-a-Kind Family Downtown*, by Sydney Taylor. Copyright © 1972 by Sydney Taylor. Used by permission of Follett Publishing Company, a division of Follett Corporation.

"A Raccoon to Remember," from *Frosty, A Raccoon to Remember*, by Harriett E. Weaver. Copyright 1973 by Harriett E. Weaver. Used by permission of Chronicle Books, a Division of the Chronicle Publishing Company.

"The Race with Two Winners," adapted by permission of Random House, Inc. from *Great Flying Adventures*, by Sherwood Harris. Copyright © 1973 by Sherwood Harris.

"The River Bank," reprinted by permission of Charles Scribner's Sons from *The Wind in the Willows* by Kenneth Grahame. Copyright 1908 Charles Scribner's Sons.

"Salt to Timbuktu," from *Camel Caravan*, by Arthur Catherall, copyright © 1968 by the author, and reprinted by permission of the Seabury Press, New York.

"A Secret for Two," by Quentin Reynolds. Copyright © 1936 Crowell-Collier Publishing Company. By permission of Maxwell P. Wilkinson.

"The Sneaky Water-Stealer," from *How the True Facts Started in Simpsonville and Other Tales of the West* by William D. Hayes. Copyright © 1972 by William D. Hayes. Used by permission of Atheneum Publishers.

"Song of an Unlucky Man," from *A Crocodile Has Me by the Leg*, by Leonard W. Doob, published by Walker & Company, Inc., New York, N.Y. © 1966, 1967 by Leonard W. Doob.

"Thomas Jefferson: Dollars, Dimes, and Cents," from *Meter Means Measure*, by S. Carl Hirsch. Copyright © 1973 by S. Carl Hirsch. Reprinted by permission of The Viking Press, Inc.

"The Tunnel," abridged with permission of Macmillan Publishing Co., Inc. and the author from *The House of Dies Drear* by Virginia Hamilton. Copyright © 1968 by Virginia Hamilton.

"What Is Orange?" from *Hailstones and Halibut Bones*, by Mary O'Neill. Copyright © 1961 by Mary O'Neill. Reprinted by permission of Doubleday and Company, Inc. and The World's Work, Ltd.

"Witches and Onion Sandwiches," from *Jennifer, Hecate, William McKinley, and Me, Elizabeth*, by Elaine Konigsburg. Copyright © 1967 by E. L. Konigsburg. Used by permission of Atheneum Publishers and Macmillan, London and Basingstoke.

"The Women Were Digging Clams," from *Our Fathers Had Powerful Songs*, by Natalia Belting. Copyright © 1971 by Natalia Belting. Reprinted by permission of the publishers, E. P. Dutton & Co., Inc.

"Wondering," by Kelvin Windsor. Reprinted by permission of E. S. Richardson, Lincoln Heights School, Auckland, New Zealand.

Illustrators: PP. 12–25, LEN EBERT; PP. 26–36, BOB SCHULENBERG; P. 37, JOAN PALEY; PP. 38–49, ARVIS STEWART; PP. 52–62, LESLIE H. MORRILL; PP. 63–66 (*also* PP. 81, 160, 188, 262, 294, 382, 408, 496, 520), LOU CUNETTE; PP. 67–74, ROBERT ANDREW PARKER; PP. 79–80, ED EMBERLY; PP. 83, 85, ELAINE LIVERMORE; PP. 87–91, FRED GERLACH; PP. 92–97, MICHAEL HAMPSHIRE; PP. 98–99, WALLY NEIBART; PP. 100–113, TRINA HYMAN; PP. 118–129, CALVIN BURNETT; P. 131, ANCO; PP. 134–147, DOUGLAS GORSLINE; P. 148, LINDA CHEN; PP. 149–158, KINUKO CRAFT; P. 159, JARED D. LEE; PP. 161–162, ELAINE LIVERMORE; PP. 166–178, HAL FRENCK; PP. 179–186, BRUCE COCHRAN; P. 187, CALVIN BURNETT; PP. 189, 192, ELAINE LIVERMORE; PP. 194–201, ERIC VON SCHMIDT; PP. 202–204, GARY FUJIWARA, *designer;* PP. 206–207, DAVID S. ROSE; PP. 208–221, CHRISTINE CZERNOTA; PP. 226–232, BRAD HOLLAND; P. 233, ERROL LE CAIN; PP. 234–239, MARC BROWN; PP. 240–253, LANE YERKES; PP. 254–259, SAUL LAMBERT; PP. 260–261, DOROTHEA SIERRA; PP. 263, 266, ELAINE LIVERMORE; P. 283, JOHN HAM; PP. 284–293, CHRISTINE CZERNOTA; PP. 295, 299, ELAINE LIVERMORE; PP. 307–315, HILARY KNIGHT; PP. 318–333, GUY BILLOUX; PP. 338–349, DAVID S. ROSE; PP. 350–354, JEANETTE KEHL; P. 355, JEAN CALLAN KING/Visuality; PP. 357–370, GORDON LAITE; PP. 371–380, ROBERT BIRD; PP. 389–396, JAMES HOUSTON; PP. 397–407, FRED GERLACH; PP. 414–425, BILL MORRISON; P. 426, LEIGH GRANT; P. 427, Remington Rand Office Systems Division, Sperry Rand Corp.; PP. 430–441, ROBERT LAWSON; PP. 446–470, KAREN WATSON; P. 471, JOHN HUEHNERGARTH; PP. 472–480, BEATRICE DARWIN; PP. 482–493, GARY FUJIWARA; PP. 494–495, SUSAN SWAN; P. 497, LEN EBERT; P. 498, GUY BILLOUX; P. 499, ROBERT BIRD; PP. 502–515, DON PULVER; PP. 517–519, JEAN CALLAN KING/Visuality; P. 521, GORDON LAITE; P. 522, DAVID S. ROSE; P. 523, LANE YERKES; PP. 524–528, LINDA CHEN; PP. 529–536, FREDERICK FRANCK; PP. 538–551, JERRY PINKNEY.

Photographs: P. 51, ERIK ANDERSON; P. 75, A. REININGER/DeWys Inc.; P. 77, Stock, Boston; PP. 131–132, Ludwig Industries; P. 191 (*top r*) THIGPEN PHOTOGRAPHY; PP. 202, 204, COLLECTION OF MR. AND MRS. PAUL MELLON; P. 205, BILL SUMNER; PP. 268–281, PETER BUCKLEY; P. 282, JOHN MARTUCCI; P. 303 (*l to r*) EDWARD F. HUTCHINS, CHARLES S. HOFMANN; P. 304 (*top and bottom*) CHARLES S. HOFMANN, (*middle*) ELBERT R. JAYCOX; P. 305 (*top*) CHARLES S. HOFMANN, (*middle*) HAROLD V. GREEN; P. 306 (*l to r*) ALFRED RENFRO/National Audubon Society, RICHARD PARKER/Franklin; P. 338, Stock, Boston; P. 356, ERIK ANDERSON; P. 429, DATA 100 CORP.; P. 481, LARRY WEST; P. 516, VICTOR ENGLEBERT/Dewys, Inc.; PP. 517–519, Culver Pictures, Inc.

Book cover, title page, and magazine covers by MARTUCCI STUDIOS.

Contents

5

SPIRALS

COMPASS

CURRENTS

Beacon

Beacon

STORIES

ARTICLES

POEMS

JUST FOR FUN

SKILL LESSONS

The Cherub and My Sainted Grandmother

by Barbara Corcoran

When I was thirteen, I took on the job of breaking a pony for the Hagens up the road. They had sent to Colorado for this pony for their ten-year-old daughter, and after it came, nobody could do a thing with it. The pony cost a hundred and fifty dollars, and Mr. Hagen offered me a hundred to break it. That made a pretty expensive pony, it seemed to me, but I was glad of the chance to earn the money. There was a beautiful Mexican saddle that I had my heart set on, and it cost ninety-eight dollars and fifty cents.

My father always kind of bragged around about the way I could break horses. "My daughter," he told people when he thought I wasn't listening, "has got a way with horses."

What he didn't know was that I had found a book in the library, written by an easterner. It had all kinds of ideas about horse training that my father and the other ranchers would have died laughing at. This easterner believed in getting the horse to trust you, gentling it instead of "showing

it who's boss." I tried it on some of the range colts that my dad brought in, and it worked like a charm. Using patience instead of force turned out better horses, it seemed to me. Horses aren't as dumb as people sometimes think. They can learn a lot if you get them to trust you. Look at the Arabians or the Lippizans, for instance.

Anyway, my father hitched up the horse trailer, and we drove over to Hagens' one early September afternoon.

I saw the pony at the other side of the fenced pasture. He was a three-year-old Shetland, a pinto with a pretty face but too much fat. I looked him over. I had never worked with a horse that someone else had tried to break. But a little old pony shouldn't be too bad.

"What's his problem, Aaron?" my father asked.

"Nobody can stay on him; that's his problem," Mr. Hagen said. "He's fired off everybody that got on him. And they call him Cherub! Can you beat it?"

"He's not very big," I said. I have never understood why anyone wants to ride a pony anyway. I was riding horses when I was four.

"He's murder," Mr. Hagen said. "Big or not big. And I paid a hundred fifty cash for him."

I wanted to say that the pony probably didn't know that, but I didn't.

My father leaned on the rail fence and narrowed his eyes the way he does when he's sizing up stock. "Maybe he's just plain mean," he said. "Animals are like people; some are bad clear through and some are good clear through. Take my sainted mother. Not a bad bone in her body."

He always spoke of Grandma as "my sainted mother," although I knew for a fact that sometimes he got furious with her. She lived in a cabin up the river, and she wouldn't let him or anyone else "do" for her. She was as independent as you can get. I loved her.

Besides, I have never believed that about some being all good, some all bad. I knew, though, that Dad was giving me an out with the pony. He didn't want me to get hurt or take on a job I couldn't finish.

"Well, Maggie, what do you think?" he asked me.

"I'll give it a try," I said. It made me feel important to have grown men wanting my opinion. I started to climb the fence.

"Take it easy," Mr. Hagen said.

I started to walk slowly toward the pony. I expected him to shy off to the far end of the corral. Instead he ran straight at me.

I was too surprised to move. A horse will almost never run at a person, unprovoked. I kept waiting for him to stop, but he didn't. He charged right at me and bit my arm. I had on a heavy jacket, so it wasn't too bad, but it made me mad. I didn't have a rope, so I grabbed his mane and jerked his head down. He slewed around, kicking like mad, but I had a good grip and he couldn't get his head up. After a minute he quieted down, but I got a look at his eyes, and I knew he was figuring what to do next.

My father and Mr. Hagen came running. I thought I could use a tail rope to get him to the trailer, but when my father saw the blood on my jacket, he jerked that old pony around and tied him up like a side of beef. Then he and Mr. Hagen half dragged and half shoved him to the trailer, with the pony heaving and fighting all the way.

I felt sick. This was no way to begin. But Dad was too upset to reason with. All the way home he sputtered. He wasn't going to let me work with an evil monster like that one. He would take a hand at breaking the pony himself, since we had made a bargain with Hagen.

It wasn't until the pony was turned out into our corral, and Dad had taken me to the doctor for a tetanus shot, that I got to talk to him. I told him I'd said I would break the pony, and I didn't want to go back on my word. My father was

always impressed by that kind of statement. He was a great one for not going back on your word. Finally he agreed to let me try if I promised to be careful, and if I would go and stay with my grandmother for a couple of days till my arm healed. He knew me well enough to know that if I stayed around where the pony was, I'd be out there with him.

I liked to visit my grandmother. And I think she enjoyed me because she could talk to me and I wouldn't try to boss her around.

She was unloading her jeep when we got there. She had just been to town, and when Grandmother went to town, she bought almost a boxcar load of stuff, so she wouldn't have to go again in a hurry. Dad and I helped her unpack, and Dad gave her lots of advice about taking care of herself and getting in plenty of stovewood before snow, and things like that. She smiled and thanked him and patted him as if he were a little boy, and he went away happy.

"Now," she said. She settled down in the Boston rocker in the sunny living room. "To what do I owe the honor of this visit?" She had nice, twinkly, gray eyes, and she didn't look much older than my mother had before she died.

"I'm being kept out of the way." I told her about the pony. When I came to the part about Dad saying he had a sainted mother, she laughed hard, and her rocker squeaked back and forth, and her sneakers made little patting sounds on the floorboards.

"You and I know how sainted I am, don't we?" she said. I knew she meant about Great Uncle James. I knew the story by heart but I loved to hear it.

So she told me again about Grandfather's brother James. "A good man, James was, but he was never wrong in his life, and that can be a trying thing. He came out here to the cabin after your grandfather died, and he told me I could not live here alone. It wasn't fitting, he said, and people would criticize him if he let me.

"When he was all through, I said, 'James, you mean well, but I intend to live as I choose.' Well, he was stunned. God rest his soul, he was a good man." Grandma bit her lip and paused, as if she wasn't sure she should be repeating the story.

"I know," I said, so she wouldn't quit, "how important and successful Uncle James was." I did, too. There was a bank in town named for him, and my father had never failed to point it out to me.

"Well," she went on, "James did get bossy. He said he was going to force me out of here. And he said something not quite nice about your grandfather. And . . ." Her eyes sparkled wickedly as she remembered. "It just so happened that I had taken a key-lime pie out of the icebox, intending, you know, to offer him a piece. But when he said your grandfather was shiftless, which was not true . . ." Her pupils got very black, and I could almost see her, how pretty she must have looked, twenty years ago, glaring at Uncle James.

She gave a little contented sigh. "I just let it fly." Every time she told me, I practically rolled on the floor laughing. Great Uncle James died before I was born, but I had seen pictures of him, with a mustache like President Taft's and a cold face. In my mind's eye I saw that lovely fluffy pie spread all over that face.

"And that," Grandma said, "is your sainted grandmother." She went to get some oatmeal cookies, the kind with millions of raisins and nuts in them. "I ought never to have told you. It really makes me sort of ashamed when I think of it."

"Why?" I asked. "He deserved it."

She shook her head. "One shouldn't throw pie in the face of a man's dignity."

"But he was bossy. And mean about Grandfather."

"James was a stubborn and a self-righteous man, but still I shouldn't have done it. If a man counts so heavily on his dignity, one shouldn't attack him in that quarter."

Grandma's cabin was on the edge of the forest, ten miles from the nearest house. There were only three rooms, but it was as comfortable and gracious as a miniature southern mansion. Grandmother never ate, even alone, without a white linen tablecloth and the good silver.

I was truly sorry when my visit was over and I heard Dad's pickup down on the county road. But I was anxious, too, to start working with the Cherub.

When Grandma heard Dad coming, she said, "Margaret, you're growing up now, so I'll tell you a little secret."

I didn't feel grown up at all, but I was curious. "Fire away, Grandma," I said.

"You can succeed through love. Not force or power or always being right, just love. Do you understand me?"

"No, Ma'am," I said. I heard my father coming up the path. He always made a lot of racket coming up a path.

"Use love with your pony," she said. "I think he needs it."
She put a neat package of pralines in my pocket and kissed
me.

As soon as I got home, I went to work on the Cherub problem. I was out in the corral every morning right after sunup.
I tried every trick in the book. The trouble was, whoever had
begun to train him had done everything wrong. Cherub was
determined not to be broken.

For the first few days, he tried to charge at me again, but
I tried a crazy trick I had read about. I held up a stick, just
a little old stick, in front of his face. It worked.

To lead him, I used a long, soft rein at first, looped around
under his tail. It didn't work too well so I changed to a rope.
That has a little more bite but not enough to injure him.
Pretty soon I could guide him with light pulls on the halter.
There were setbacks, of course. Some days he wouldn't do

a thing I wanted him to, and one day he jerked suddenly, and I found myself sitting on the ground. He thought that was pretty funny. You let a horse think he's outsmarted you once, and it takes a long time to get him over it. Cherub has intelligent, dark eyes in that pretty little face of his, and I could swear he was laughing at me.

Day by day, though, he got a little better. He got so he'd let me lead him around the ring I had marked out for him. I usually use a whip to flick a horse on the legs, to direct him, but I couldn't use a whip with Cherub. The minute he saw it, he froze. Somebody must have tried to whip-break him.

One morning when things were going well, Dad came out to look us over. Cherub tore the line out of my hands and raced around the ring like a maniac.

"He's no good," Dad said. "I told you all along. We'll take him back to Hagen before you break your neck."

But it was more than earning the money now. I wanted to train Cherub and I knew I could. The next day, when the sun was spreading pink light all over the ground, I took the saddle I'd used when I was little, and I went out to the corral. A child's saddle is lightweight. I tied the stirrups to the horn, so they wouldn't bang against him. I walked up to him slowly and easily, talking all the time. He let me put the halter on, but he craned his neck around suspiciously while I put on the saddle.

The minute he felt its weight, he reared. He plunged and danced like a wild bronc. The saddle went sailing through the air and hit me in the head. It knocked me out for a minute. When I came to, Cherub was at the other end of the corral, still kicking up those wicked little heels. I had a thundering headache.

I took the saddle to the barn and went to the house to lie down. Dad hit the roof when he saw me. My head was a little bloody. So he went through the whole thing again of taking me to the doctor, swearing to take the pony back, and so on.

This time I couldn't talk him out of it, but luckily my grandmother happened to come by.

"Let her handle the pony her own way, Victor," she said
to my father. She seldom spoke to him in that stern way, but
when she did, he just said, "Yes, Ma'am."

She stayed overnight, and in the morning she went out
to look at Cherub. "He's too fat," she said. "No wonder he
won't take a saddle. Put him on a diet."

So Cherub went on a diet. It worked two ways; he lost
weight, and he got so hungry that he was glad to see me when
I came with his dinner. Once a week, to boost his morale,
I gave him half a candy bar. He doted on candy bars.

In a week he began to shape up. And he was getting better
about letting me touch him. I decided to try the saddle again.

I waited till he had his nose in a bucket of oats. He shied
a little, but he let me put the saddle on. As soon as he started
to pull away, I took it off. I did this about a dozen times that
morning, and by the time Dad whistled me up for lunch,
Cherub was taking the saddle with no fuss.

After that, I kept a saddle on him while I walked him

around and while he was eating. When I tightened the cinch, the strap that goes around a horse's body and holds the saddle on, he just peered at me to see what I was up to.

I put him on long reins then, and taught him commands. He was a smart little pony, and once he decided it was fun, he learned fast. The Cherub was no jughead.

I had decided on a Sunday morning to ride him for the first time. When I got up, I found it was raining, a slow, cold drizzle. But I had told Cherub I was going to ride him, and I'd begun to get crazy notions that he knew what I said to him.

In case he didn't take to the idea of somebody on his back, I took along a pair of hobbles and a rope. If I had to, I would use the "running W" trip rope. I had never seen it used, but I had read about it. The way it works is, if the horse gets out of hand, you pull on the rope that is attached to the hobbles. This trips him and brings him to his knees.

I led him out to the north pasture. He was acting sweet as honey. But sure enough, the minute I swung my leg over the saddle, he bucked. For a minute I tried to control him with my hands and my voice, but he wasn't having any of that. The rain was dripping down my neck, and I was cold and Cherub was jarring me in every bone. I pulled on the rope.

It was so easy and so fast, it almost caught me by surprise, too. I slid right up onto his neck, and he nearly fought his way back on his feet before I got the rope taut. I slid off and moved to his head. He was down on his knees and he looked foolish and sort of hurt—I mean hurt in his feelings. He gave me a look that said, "I thought we were friends."

"Well," I said, "you have to learn that crime doesn't pay." To complete the "running W," I was supposed to push him over on his side and pull his head around and tie the rope to the cinch. It doesn't really hurt the horse, but it is uncomfortable, and it makes him feel helpless. If there is one thing a horse is terrified of, it's losing his footing. I guess it's the way humans feel when their hands are tied.

I put my hand on Cherub's neck to push him over. But I couldn't do it. He was looking at me with those black eyes rolled back a little, and he looked scared and pleading. All of a sudden I knew what Grandma meant about the key-lime pie. It just doesn't feel right to destroy somebody's dignity.

I let up on the rope. Cherub struggled to his feet and stood still, his sides heaving. I patted him and gave him half a candy bar. He didn't even try to bite my hand. I got up on him again. He stood still. I touched him lightly with my heels, and he broke into a nice trot. I rode him for over an hour, and he acted as proud as punch.

When my father saw us ride up to the barn, he stood still, afraid of spooking Cherub, and also surprised, I guess. Cherub acted as if he had been a civilized horse all his life. No shenanigans. I rubbed him down and fed him.

At the end of the week my father said, "Hagen was asking after the pony. I told him you were about ready."

Cherub was ready, but I wasn't. I made excuses to keep him another week. It was ridiculous; he was riding perfectly. And Firefly, my own horse, was getting fat and lazy.

The day came when I couldn't put it off any longer. I rode Cherub to the Hagens', and my father came along in the pick-up. I felt like crying. I talked to Cherub all the way and gave him an extra candy bar.

Mr. Hagen said he looked fine. He gave me a check for a hundred dollars, and I led Cherub out to their pasture. The little girl was dancing up and down, eager to get on her pony. I never liked her much.

Mr. Hagen grabbed Cherub's bridle with his heavy hands and told his daughter to get on. She was carrying a fancy little whip.

"You'd better not carry the whip," I told her. "Cherub doesn't like a whip."

"I got it for my birthday," she said. As if that settled it.

Her father boosted her up, and she plunked down in the saddle. I held my breath. Cherub did a little sideways dance, and Mr. Hagen jerked hard on the reins. Cherub stood still. The girl took the reins. She dug her heels into Cherub's side, and at the same moment she moved the whip, and Cherub caught sight of it. He bucked, and the girl slid out of the saddle like a sack of grain. Her father grabbed her. Cherub headed for me.

There we stood, Mr. Hagen and his daughter glaring at Cherub and me. The kid wasn't hurt, but she was crying, and Mr. Hagen was furious.

"I thought you said that jughead was broke," he said.

"He is broke," my father said. He was mad too. "You saw Maggie ride him up here."

I handed Mr. Hagen his check. "I'll pay for the pony," I said. "One hundred dollars. Fifty dollars a month."

"Take him!" Mr. Hagen said. "He's a no-good outlaw."

So that's how I happen to have a fat and sassy pony on my hands. For about a year, until I got too big, I rode him once or twice a week, so neither of us would feel our work was wasted. After that I took him on a lead rein when I rode Firefly. They got to be good friends.

Cherub is pretty old now, and pretty plump, but he wanders around the pasture enjoying himself, usually sticking close to Firefly. And once a week my sainted grandmother brings him some cookies.

AUGHOR

AUTHOR

Barbara Corcoran writes about the West and the Northwest, but she did not always live there. She was born in Massachusetts and stayed there after she graduated from college. Then she discovered the West. When she was living in California, she made a few brief trips to the Northwest and soon began writing about it. "The Cherub and My Sainted Grandmother" was one of the results. Almost a dozen of her books for older children have a background in Montana, Colorado, or northwestern Canada. Now she lives in Montana when she's not traveling.

Among Ms. Corcoran's books about the West are *The Long Journey* and *Sasha My Friend*, a William Allen White Award winner. She has also written books, mostly about wild animals, under the pen name of Paige Dixon.

In addition to writing books and stories, she has had a wide variety of jobs, including university teaching, working in summer theaters as "crew," writing plays, and writing for television and radio. Recently she spent a few years in Europe.

EXPEDITION FROM ARREOL

BY MICHAEL C. SLAUGHTER

A low rumble of thunder rolled out of the foothills, and then the rain came down fast. Everybody took off in different directions. Rob Jacoby grabbed his mitt and bat, and ran home across the park. The warmth of the big old house felt good as he got out of his wet clothes. He thought tonight would be a good time to get started on his history term project.

Since his father was working late at NISI, he and his mother had dinner alone. Afterward Rob went back up to his room to study, but his mind wandered. He just sat with his papers spread out, listening to the rain against the window.

Later, Rob went to the window and stared out at the lights of the NISI installation on the ridge. The National Interplanetary Study Institute was a division of Blakemore Chemical Industries.

Rob's father had been a researcher at NISI since it had started four years ago. Sometimes his work kept him at the laboratory for days at a time. He didn't say much about his research, but he had told Rob that the United States would probably be traveling to other planets sooner than most people expected.

After the rain had almost stopped, Rob opened the window. There was a peculiar odor in the air, almost like the ozone smell made when electric sparks pass through the air. But, somehow, it reminded Rob of almonds. He leaned farther out the window to see if he could tell where it was coming from.

Suddenly his whole body jerked, and he heard a terrible crackling sound. He felt himself pulled off his feet and out through the window. He tried to yell but no sound came. He was suspended in air, a few feet from his upstairs window. The whole house was bathed in an eerie, blue glow. He had a sensation of numbness, of a slow falling. Then he was unconscious.

26

When he regained consciousness, Rob smelled that same odd odor. He tried to move his arms and legs, but he was enclosed in a plastic capsule, from which a heavy blue gas was being slowly exhausted.

Gradually the cover of the capsule was lifted away. Rob rubbed his eyes and stared into the face of the strangest man he had ever seen. The man's rubbery skin was bright orange, and his head was completely hairless. His large, shiny, green eyes looked back at Rob.

The orange man placed his big hand on Rob's head. "How do you feel, Robert?"

"How do you know my name?" Rob blurted out.

"We have been studying your family for some time. You were transported here by our special force. We had meant to take your father, but unfortunately you triggered the mechanism before we were ready."

"I don't understand."

"We created a force field about your house. We intended to draw your father into it and transport him to us, but you leaned out of the window and entered the field, activating it. At once you were transported into our receiver here in the spacecraft."

"Spacecraft!"

"We are from Arreol, a planet in the solar system beyond yours. Our expedition is composed of three ships. I am the captain."

Rob saw other strange men behind the captain. "Why do you want my father?" he asked.

"We have developed interplanetary travel to a high degree, but our efforts to explore the vastness of the universe are primitive," the captain said. "Your government's space program *seems* to be based on rocket propellants. But actually they've made grants to a private company, Blakemore Chemicals, which has discovered a method for isolating and reproducing energy in a pure form. Your father is the scientist who perfected the process. Because of

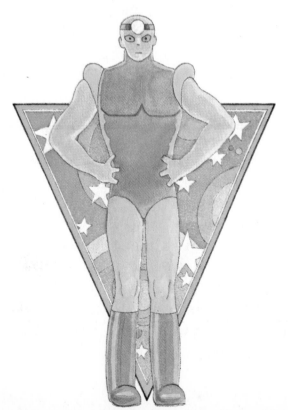

this, the United States will, in only a few months, be able to span this galaxy in days."

Rob stared with amazement. "What do you mean to do with my father?"

"We'll take him to Arreol to work in our laboratories."

"You can't do that!" Rob cried. "You can't take him away. My father wouldn't work for you, even if you did take him to Arreol!"

"We were afraid that might be true," the stranger answered coolly. "But since you are now in our possession, he cannot refuse. Harm might come to you. I'm sorry, but that is the way it must be."

Another orange man burst into the room, waving his arms. He was shouting wildly, but his sounds were not words. "Put on your sensor disc so the boy can understand you," the captain said.

Rob realized that all the Arreol men had small discs strapped to their foreheads. The man attached his and spoke again. "We've been discovered! A patrol has been sent out to intercept us."

"Lower the monitor screen!" said the captain. "Are they government soldiers or a NISI patrol?"

A large screen descended from a port just above Rob's head. It flickered and then showed a view of the edge of the woods behind the NISI installation. An odd doughnut-shaped object stood on angled legs like an enormous grasshopper.

The captain saw Rob's puzzled look. "That is our supply ship, but no one is on board. It carries provisions and equipment and is manned by remote control."

Rob looked back at the screen. A faint orange glow was becoming stronger.

"It's a NISI patrol," an Arreol man shouted. "Look at that light! They've already activated their weapons! We must prepare—"

"We can't defend ourselves against NISI weaponry!" the captain exclaimed. "Establish contact with them at once and tell them we have the boy. They won't fire at us if they think he might be hurt."

Just then the screen flared up with a brilliant white light, and Rob heard a rushing noise. The cabin shuddered so violently that he was thrown to the floor.

"It's too late," the captain cried. "We're being attacked!"

Rob covered his head with his hands as the spaceship was rocked by a violent explosion. He looked at the screen in time to see the supply craft swallowed in a bright ball of flame.

"Activate the engines," the captain yelled.

Men leaped to the instrument panel, and Rob felt the floor begin to hum and vibrate beneath him. "Where are we going?" he cried.

"To Arreol."

"We can't! You can't take me away with you."

The captain looked squarely at Rob. "You will be lucky if we get away, boy!"

The cabin rolled under another explosion, and Rob was thrown against the instrument panel. He could see most of the Arreol men sprawled on the floor. One pulled himself painfully to a control panel and moved a large lever forward. Rob felt as if an enormous weight were crushing him and pushing him down. Then, quite quickly, the weight was released. Everyone stood up with some effort.

"What happened?" Rob asked.

"We had to make an emergency takeoff," said the captain. "That last shot was much too close. The ship may have received some structural damage." He turned to the men at the controls. "Give me our course."

"It doesn't look good, sir. We are not accelerating at a proper rate. We have only barely broken the Earth's gravitational field, and now we are rapidly losing forward speed. I think we are operating on our suborbital cruising engines alone."

"Make contact with our sister ship." the captain ordered. "Have it rendezvous with us and survey our external damage."

"We can't, sir. Our radio has been knocked out."

"Fix it. Unless we can call the other ship to come to our aid," the captain said gravely, "it is going to take us a long, long time to travel through space to Arreol."

"How long?" Rob asked.

The captain said, "Oh, we'll be able to live. We have synthetic provisions and a water reclaiming plant on board."

"How long?" Rob repeated.

"About two thousand earth days," the captain answered sharply.

"Over five years!" gasped Rob.

"That's right. Five years at the speed we're traveling to navigate the billions of miles to Arreol." The captain sat down, quite dejected. "We've lost the race to develop interstellar travel. "We've kidnapped you for no purpose, boy."

Rob ran from the cabin. He didn't stop until he found himself in a part of the craft at the farthest point from the control room. He sat down, breathing heavily and shaking.

"Five years!" he said. "I can't spend five years out here in nowhere." A burning sensation spread through his throat.

Suddenly Rob saw a slim figure dart from behind a tall stack of crates toward another stack. Instinctively he leaped. They collided and fell together to the floor. Rob stared at the figure bewildered. It was a boy, an Arreol boy, about his own age. Rob noted that he was wearing a sensor translating disc.

"What are you doing on this

ship?" Rob asked. "You're a stowaway, aren't you?"

"I'm not a stowaway," the orange boy flashed back. "My father is the captain of the craft."

"The captain!"

"That's right. I know almost all there is to know about this ship."

"Then why are you sneaking around?" Rob persisted.

The boy stood silently and then said, "I know all about you, Rob. I've been listening."

"Why are you hiding here if your father is the captain?" Rob asked, growing more puzzled.

"I hardly know my father," the boy said. "On Arreol I'm enrolled in advanced technical classes and I study day and night. My father is always away on ex-

peditions. I decided to leave school and travel with him. It was easy to get aboard and hide, but I haven't the courage to tell my father what I've done." He paused for a moment. "My father will make me go back to school, but I don't want to learn to be a scientist. I want to go on expeditions, and I want to be with him."

He reached back under a cover and withdrew a glass tube with several wire filaments running its length. "I decided to prolong this trip for as long as possible," he said at last, "so I took this part out of the engine."

"What is it?" Rob asked excitedly.

"It's a 'revilator.' The engines can't run well without it."

Rob was astounded. "So that's

why we can't travel fast. You've sabotaged the spacecraft!"

"Yes. That was just after we landed, before I realized what the purpose of the expedition was and that you would be with us."

"What are you going to do now? You must return that part."

"I know. But I don't know how to put it back."

Rob was too excited to be angry. "Come on," he said. "Let's go find your father."

Suddenly the spacecraft veered off course. The boy tripped, and the revilator fell from his hands and smashed on the floor.

Rob stared at the shattered glass. "Five years! How could you have dropped the revilator?" Rob cried in desperation.

"I—I don't know. I just lost my balance," the Arreol boy answered. He tried vainly to piece together the shattered tube.

"Forget it. It's impossible," Rob said. He was disgusted. "Five years stranded in space," he repeated bitterly to himself. He grabbed the boy. "Come on. We're going to tell your father what's happened."

The boy nodded and they walked toward the control room.

The captain turned around sharply as they entered and stared at his son with amazement. The boy hesitated and then ran to his father's arms.

"What is this?" the captain asked, holding his son. "What are you doing here, and why are you with that boy?"

The Arreol boy hung his head. "I was not meant to be a scientist," he answered. "I want to be with you." He looked into his father's face and then slowly began to tell him about the revilator.

The captain stepped back and

held his son at arm's length. His face was pale. Finally he spoke with great difficulty. "Do you mean that you jeopardized this entire expedition just to be at my side?"

"I didn't think of the expedition," the boy answered. "I just thought of you."

The captain gestured to an aide and the man came over. After the captain spoke to him very softly, the aide hurried from the room. When he returned, Rob and the Arreol boy stared at him, disbelieving. He was holding a revilator in his hands.

The captain laughed. "Did you imagine that we didn't carry spare parts aboard the spacecraft? I thought that the engines were damaged from the outside attack. Now that we know what the real problem is, it can be repaired easily." He turned to the aide. "How long will it take to replace the revilator?"

"No more than twenty minutes, sir," the man answered. "However, we can't do it while the ship is in flight. The engines must be turned off."

The captain frowned. "Very well, then. We will have to return to Earth." He appeared thoughtful. "Perhaps there is another reason to land on Earth."

He looked at his son and at Rob. "It seems that I have forgotten what a son can mean to a father. Do you want to go home, Robert?"

"Oh, yes, sir," Rob answered quickly.

"I think that is the best place for you. It was a mistake to have taken you at all."

The captain turned aside to the communications desk. "Is the radio operating yet?"

"Negative, sir. We can't send word out. However, we have been able to receive a few weak signals from our sister ship. They discovered our absence and have made contact with us."

The captain appeared troubled. "If we can't send radio messages, we won't be able to let the NISI ground patrols know of our peaceful intention. They are certain to detect us before the engines are completely repaired. We can't prevent them from firing on us."

Rob spoke up. "Sir, if you can land near NISI, maybe I can get inside to tell them what has

happened. I know the guards, and I'll try to reach someone who can stop the attack!"

"We can't do that," answered the captain. "It would be too dangerous for you."

"It's your—our—only chance," Rob protested. Maybe I can stop an attack and allow you time for repairs."

The captain stood considering Rob's idea. He called the navigator to him and discussed their chances. Then he turned back to Rob. "The navigator says that we can get within a mile of NISI before their high energy equipment will interfere with our engines. Can you run that far in time?"

"I will have to," Rob answered.

In a short while, the spacecraft and its cover ship settled silently in a meadow behind the installation. Rob stepped from the door of the craft. The lights of the NISI project burned intensely through the dark night and created strange shadow patterns in the tall meadow grass. There was a light rain. It seemed odd to Rob that it should still be raining. It seemed like such a very long time ago that he had

been standing at the window of his room feeling the rain blow against his face. He stepped away from the spacecraft quickly, but stopped for a moment to look back at the captain and his son standing in the doorway. He felt a twinge within him which he didn't quite understand. Finally he waved, then turned, and ran as fast as he could across the meadow. The mile seemed farther than he thought. He was gasping for breath.

Suddenly he heard a rushing sound overhead, and the sky lighted up in a brilliant white glare. Rob was thrown to the ground, stunned.

"They're attacking the spacecraft!" he exclaimed numbly.

His heart pounded as he saw a bright ball of fire roll into the sky. But it seemed to be several hundred yards beyond where the two sister ships had landed. "There's still time," he said to himself. "They haven't found the range yet."

He picked himself up and began running desperately toward the buildings on the ridge. His sides ached as he ran, and the cuffs of his trousers were soaked from splashing through puddles. The firing continued. Each time it seemed closer to the spacecraft.

At last Rob reached the guard booth at the gate. "Halt!" the guard called. He lowered his rifle as he recognized the figure emerging from the darkness. "What are you doing out here?"

"Get me to the defense officer," Rob panted. "I know what's going on. I've been in the spaceship, and I've got to stop the attack."

The guard looked doubtful.

"Please, it's urgent!"

"I'll call your father. He's in the defense command center right now," the guard said finally, wondering how Rob even knew that the spacecraft existed.

Rob waited anxiously. The distant explosions became more frequent. At last the guard handed the phone to Rob. He blurted out the story to his father and pleaded with him to stop the attack.

"Stay there," his father ordered and hung up.

Very shortly the firing ceased. Rob sat down on an old wooden chair in a corner of the guard booth. At last his father appeared in the doorway. Rob ran over to him. His father put an arm on Rob's shoulder and spoke quietly. "What were they like, son?"

"Like us."

His father was quiet. At last he said, "We can't be sure, but one of the ships may have been destroyed in the attack."

Rob looked up at him in horror. "Which one?"

"We don't know. There's no way of knowing, but it's possible that only one of the two craft escaped."

Rob looked out of the windows of the booth. The dull glow of daybreak was on the horizon beyond the great meadow. He pictured the orange-skinned boy and his father standing in the doorway of their craft. There was an ache in his throat.

Suddenly his father pointed excitedly at the sky just above the woods. "Look, it's the spacecraft! Wait, wait, there's another. Two ships! They both made it."

Rob smiled and moved closer to his father. "The strangers are gone," he said. "My friends are flying toward home."

JUMPING PENNIES

Here's a tricky puzzle that you'll have lots of fun trying to solve. First, divide a piece of paper into twenty-five small boxes. Then arrange nine pennies in the center boxes as shown below.

Now, try to get rid of all the coins but one by jumping one penny over the other. You may jump across, up, down, or diagonally, as in a game of checkers. You may use the same penny to jump over more than one coin. Every time you jump a coin, take it off the board. The last coin *must* be left in the center square.

coin in the center square.
Finally, jump Penny 5 over Penny 6 to end up with a single
Penny 7 over Penny 4. Jump Penny 6 over Pennies 2 and 7.
jump Penny 5 over Pennies 8, 9, and 1. Then jump
First, jump Penny 5 over Pennies 8, 9, and 1. Then jump

Flight to Freedom

by Frances Humphreville

Harriet Tubman had as much courage, intelligence, and daring packed into her small body as any of the heroes you have read about. Born a slave on a Maryland plantation, she had a deep longing for freedom, not just for herself but for all her people. She was in her twenties when she made her own escape. During the next twenty years, she guided so many slaves to freedom that a $40,000 reward was offered for her capture. Many times her determination and her knowledge of woodlands saved her and her charges from being captured by slave hunters and their dogs. During the Civil War, she served the Union Army not only as a cook and a nurse, but also as a spy and a scout. She died in 1913, a tiny lady whose life spanned nearly a century of adventure.

This story, taken from Frances Humphreville's book HARRIET TUBMAN: FLAME OF FREEDOM, tells of Harriet's daring escape to freedom.

One day Harriet was working near the road. She had been sent to trim some of the hedges that screened the highway from the fields.

A carriage stopped near her and a woman got out. She was dressed in the clothes of a Quaker. Pretending to fix the harness on her horse, she stood very close to Harriet.

"How did you hurt your head?" she asked. Her voice was low and kind.

Harriet knew that Quakers did not believe in slavery. She told the woman about the accident, a bad blow on her forehead, which had happened while she was trying to protect a fellow slave who was escaping.

"Have you ever heard of the Underground Railroad?" asked the woman.

"I've heard the men talk to my father about it," Harriet answered. "I know it isn't a real railroad. It's made up of people who help the slaves to freedom, isn't it?"

"Indeed it is. Over three thousand people help run our railroad. We've taken almost one hundred thousand slaves to free states."

"Why, that's wonderful!" Harriet exclaimed.

The Quaker lady glanced around her and then got into her carriage. Looking straight ahead, she said quickly, "If I were to travel north, I would follow the Choptank River. I would go up to its beginning. That is just at the border between Delaware and Maryland. Then I'd go north by northeast. It's fifteen miles from the border to John Hill's farm in Camden, Delaware."

In a few minutes she was gone. Harriet repeated the directions to herself so she would not forget them. It was good to know that somewhere there were people who believed that the slaves should be helped to freedom.

Harriet had always loved the Bible story that told of how Moses led his people, the people of Israel, out of slavery in Egypt. One of her favorite songs was "Go Down, Moses," but the slaves were not allowed to sing it now.

Go down, Moses,
Way down in Egypt's land.
Tell old Pharaoh,
Let my people go.

Then one night when Harriet was bringing in her last basket of cotton as the full moon was coming up, her spirits rose with the beauty of the evening. With her sturdy back erect and her head high, she was humming softly "Go Down, Moses" when a big black whip came down in a searing lash across her shoulders.

"How many times do you have to be told not to sing that song?" the overseer demanded. "I'm in charge here now, and you are no longer wanted. I'm going to take care of you this week once and for all when the cotton's in." The whip cracked around her bare ankles. "Think about that while you wait for the trader!"

When slaves were traded, they had to go wherever they were sent. Harriet knew the time had come. She must make a break for freedom or forever be a slave.

Later that night, Harriet crept from her bed and made ready for the journey. She had planned the route she would follow and the food she would need. Now, in a small bag, she packed some corn bread and some scraps of pork. She took the few coins that were left from her earnings. Though she felt a pang of regret, she put the family's best hunting knife into her pocket.

She walked to the nearby cabins for two of her brothers, keeping carefully to the shadows. Benjamin and William Henry did not really want to go with Harriet. They talked in hushed whispers to her now. They reminded her of the bloodhounds that could track them down so easily. They talked about the unknown route and the cold weather of the North.

"You know the rewards are getting larger," William Henry said. "The punishment gets worse for each runaway. Let's wait and see what happens here."

Harriet was furious. "Stay here, then," she said, and her voice shook with anger. "It's now or never for all of us. The trader will be here again in the next few days."

"We'll go with you," Benjamin said after a moment.

So they moved out singly and met beyond the cornfields near the woods. They hadn't walked far before a fog shut down. Harriet was used to it, for mist and fog often hung over the land along Chesapeake Bay, but it made her brothers uneasy. They couldn't see ahead of them for more than a few feet. There were no stars to help tell directions.

After a while a light rain began to fall. The men fell into holes at the swamp edge. They walked into small bushes and briers that tore at their clothes. They were terrified of the many night noises. They pleaded with Harriet to turn back. They stumbled, fell, and argued with her about

the fast pace she had set and the direction she had taken.

Harriet moved as though guided by an unknown force. She seemed not to hear their pleading or their whining.

When they finally stopped for a short rest, her brothers declared they had decided to turn back.

Benjamin said, "We're going home. You'd better come, too. The dogs'll find you in an hour or so in the morning. We can't have walked very far. Come on back, Harriet. The risk is too great."

Harriet shook her head. "I want liberty," she said. "No man will ever take me alive. I don't intend to give up easily, now or later. I will fight for freedom as long as my strength lasts. What better way to go than that?"

Her brothers hugged her and turned away. William Henry's face was wet with tears. Harriet waited, hoping that her brothers might change their minds and return, but the fog swallowed them up, and she was alone.

As she started out again, the fog lifted. Soon the bright North Star was shining down to help her on her way. Harriet had a feeling of wild joy, as if this were a sign of approval for her lonely journey.

At the first sign of daylight, Harriet headed for one of the great swamps that ran behind many of the large plantations. She was almost frantic with fear as she saw two water snakes slither down into one of the swamp pools. At the next deep pool, she closed her eyes and waded in. Dogs could not track her if she walked through water.

Picking her way carefully, she kept to the sluggish pools. She walked around the hummocks, and traveled as fast as she could until the sun had risen higher. Now was the time of real danger. She found a small island in the tall swamp grass and lay down to rest. Twice during the day, she heard the distant shouts of men, but she forced herself to lie quiet and even managed to take short naps.

When it was almost dark, Harriet came out of the swamp and looked about her. Now was the time to follow the Quaker lady's advice. Harriet headed in the direction of the Choptank River.

Harriet walked at night and hid by day. She crawled into the thick underbrush and slept when she could. Once she awoke hearing voices. Three men on horseback had stopped not far from her. They were hunting for runaway slaves. She held her breath until they moved on.

Now she must try to keep her wits about her. She stopped often to check her direction by the stars. She limited herself to using only a part of her few supplies each day. She looked for and found wild grapes to eat and clean water to drink. She moved very carefully among the trees and hid whenever she heard voices or horses' hoofs. She made wide circles around farm buildings, for dogs might bark and bring out the owners to investigate.

When she reached the Choptank, she took off her shoes and waded in up to her waist. The sight of the river comforted her. The water was soothing to her tired feet. She sang softly. For the first time since she had left home, she felt a calm courage.

Harriet waded upstream until only a thin stream of water came down over the rocks. This, then, was the spot where the Choptank River began.

Now she would have to face the fifteen-mile walk to Camden. This part of the journey might prove the most dangerous of all, even at night. She would have to leave the river and the safety of the woods for the open fields and the highway.

It was almost daylight when she saw in the distance the buildings of a town. She stopped at a group of shacks that looked like the shacks slaves lived in. She dared go no farther lest she take a wrong path.

The black woman who answered Harriet's light tap on the door was already dressed in her cook's apron and cap. Before Harriet could ask a question, the woman said softly, "That's the Hill farm in the little hollow. Go to the haystack nearest the big barn. There's loose hay near the bottom. Crawl in and wait until about mid-morning. Then go to the door and give two short raps. That's the Underground's signal. Hurry!" The door closed.

Harriet followed the directions. The haystack was warm. She had a fine, safe view of the house and barns. She fell asleep. She was awakened by the sound of horses' hoofs. Two men were riding away from the farm. Much later, a woman dressed in the Quaker garb came out to feed the chickens. Harriet waited and watched until the woman went back into the house. When she felt sure that the woman was alone, she went quickly to the door and gave it two quick knocks. The lady who had been feeding the chickens drew her into the house at once.

"Welcome," she said. "I'm Mrs. Hill. You look as though you need some food and rest right away. And a good hot bath will make you feel better, too. We can talk later."

So Harriet bathed and ate. She slept almost all day in a hidden room behind a fireplace.

In the late afternoon Mrs. Hill came into the room and sat down in a chair by the bed. "Stay right where you are," she said as Harriet sat up in bed. "Travel has to be done after dark. There's no great hurry. You just rest as long as you can."

Then, from Mrs. Hill, Harriet learned the true meaning of the Underground Railroad. She liked Mrs. Hill and enjoyed talking with her.

"I know the Railroad is a way to help my people escape to the northern states," Harriet said, "but it's not very clear to me how it works."

"The Underground is not a railroad, and of course, it doesn't run under the ground," Mrs. Hill said.

"My father used to tell me about it when I was a little girl," Harriet told her. "For some time I thought he meant that trains really ran under the ground."

Mrs. Hill smiled. "It's called the Underground Railroad because of the fast and secret way it helps Negroes to travel north. We don't talk very much about the real facts. There's danger in too many people knowing the exact details."

"I understand," Harriet said. "I'm grateful for anything you can tell me to help me along the way. And I'm interested in having my own people help, too."

Mrs. Hill nodded her head to show that she agreed. "But many of the southern slaves do help," she said. "Even when they can't escape themselves, they help runaways. They give them food and clothing. They risk their own lives to take the runaways to safe hiding places."

"That's why I think all my people will be free someday," Harriet said proudly. "If the right spirit is there, we'll be able to help each other. I feel better already," she added.

"But you aren't safe yet," Mrs. Hill warned her. "You will be in constant danger until you're out of Delaware and into Pennsylvania or New York State." She waited a moment as though not sure of how much she should tell. "Philadelphia is our eastern headquarters. The city is a natural crossroads for our work. There are a great many workers there."

"What do they all do?"

"Well, some serve as guides or conductors," Mrs. Hill said. "Others make maps showing the stations. They draw skulls to mark the places to stay away from. They write travel routes in codes. Of course, whenever possible, we send fugitives on with a guide. When that's not possible, we give them a map. And we make them learn the directions by heart, in case they lose the map."

"I'd like to be a conductor someday," Harriet said.

"All the conductors are men," Mrs. Hill answered. "Very few of them get any praise, because they aren't known by name—except for Thomas Garrett in Wilmington. His fame for his work in helping escaping slaves has spread to all the northern states. He's been a fine example to all of us."

"He's a Quaker too, isn't he?" Harriet asked. "It was a Quaker lady who told me to come here and gave me such good directions."

"Yes, Quakers believe in freedom for everyone. But we aren't the only ones who help. Other stations along the way are kept by Methodists, German farmers, and many other people who are against slavery."

That night Harriet met Mr. Hill, who was as kind to her as his wife had been. He drove her in his wagon as far as he could along a back road. "I must be back by daylight to go about my business as usual," he said. "I've already been fined for helping slaves."

Harriet thanked him for herself and for her people.

"Follow this road to my brother's farm," Mr. Hill told her. "It's at the top of a hill. The house is white with a wide stone

wall around it. It has red barns exactly like mine. Meanwhile I will get word to Thomas Garrett to expect you in Wilmington."

Thomas Garrett! Harriet could hardly believe she would see the most famous conductor of them all.

James Hill was just as nice as his brother, Harriet decided. James warned Harriet to be very careful while traveling over the twenty-three miles to Wilmington and Thomas Garrett.

"There are posters everywhere offering five hundred dollars for your capture," he said. "Also, Thomas Garrett is very closely watched."

He drove Harriet part of the way and then turned her over to another conductor—a free black. This man had a plan to outwit the patrol stationed just outside the city of Wilmington.

He dressed Harriet in ragged overalls and a big old floppy hat. He gave her a rake and hoe to carry. Then, walking together as two black workmen, they passed by the guards and into Wilmington. In the early morning they crept through the streets to the shoe store of Thomas Garrett.

Thomas Garrett was a small, gentle old man. He and his wife, Sarah, were Quakers. They had moved to Wilmington, Delaware, about the time Harriet was born.

He was famous for his kindness to runaway slaves. He had been arrested a number of times for helping them to escape and fined so heavily that he had been left without a cent. At sixty he had opened a shoe store and gone on helping escaping slaves. Again he had been arrested and fined. He was criticized strongly by people who approved of slavery. Through it all, he kept his sense of humor.

Behind the shelves of shoes, Mr. Garrett had a secret room with no windows. "Rest here," he told Harriet. "Tomorrow you'll have new shoes and a ticket over the border." He smiled at her. "You are very close to being my two-hundredth passenger," he said. "Our work has spread. There's an Underground in all the northern states from Maine to Iowa."

After Harriet had rested, Mr. Garrett explained the route she must take. "Wilmington is only eight miles from the Pennsylvania border. Naturally the border is heavily guarded. Your best disguise is that of a working man. I'll take you as near to the crossing point as I can."

Very carefully he went over the directions and made Harriet repeat them until he was certain she knew them. "Head for Philadelphia as soon as you can," he advised her. "There'll be jobs there and other free Negroes to help you. You may want to visit the office of Mr. William Still. He's secretary to the committee that helps runaways. If he's very busy, you may not be able to see him, but one of his workers will help you with any problems you may have."

Harriet thanked him. She tried to put into words some of her gratitude and respect, but the words would not come.

Thomas Garrett seemed to understand. His farewell and his low bow were something Harriet would always remember.

It was only about a week after she left Maryland that Harriet crossed the border into Pennsylvania. She was tired out, the new shoes Mr. Garrett had given her hurt her feet, and she had no place to go, but she was free.

"I made it, Lord," she said aloud. "Now it's up to me to see that my family makes it, too—and all the others who want to be free."

AUTHOR

Dr. Frances Humphreville started writing short stories and poetry when she was only ten years old. By the age of seventeen, Mrs. Humphreville was teaching school and was having some of her short stories published. During her long career as a teacher, Mrs. Humphreville has taught every grade, from elementary school to high school to college. Despite her busy schedule, she has found time to do volunteer work with gifted, retarded, deaf, and blind children.

Mrs. Humphreville was born in Maine and now lives with her husband in a long, low ranch house in Shelton, Connecticut. There she is often visited by a variety of food-seeking animals which include a huge crow, a raccoon family, and many birds. The Humphrevilles have a pet cat who has learned to meow over the telephone. Besides her writing, Mrs. Humphreville enjoys swimming, taking pictures, and playing the piano, violin, and tenor saxophone.

What Is Orange?

Orange is a tiger lily,
A carrot,
A feather from
A parrot,
A flame,
The wildest color
You can name.
Orange is a happy day
Saying good-by
In a sunset that
Shocks the sky.
Orange is brave
Orange is bold
It's bittersweet
And marigold.
Orange is zip
Orange is dash
The brightest stripe
In a Roman sash.
Orange is an orange
Also a mango.
Orange is music
Of the tango.
Orange is the fur
Of the fiery fox,
The brightest crayon
In the box.
And in the fall
When the leaves are turning
Orange is the smell
Of a bonfire burning. . . .

Mary O'Neill

PRAIRIE DOG TOWN

by Faith McNulty

Paul was delighted when his Uncle Joe, a zoologist, invited him to help with a field study of prairie dogs in South Dakota. Paul had always wanted to camp out in the country, where he could hunt. But Joe insisted that Paul leave his BB gun behind. "I study living animals, not dead ones," Joe said. Paul began to see things Joe's way after making friends with Sam, the very first prairie dog they caught and marked.

For the next few days Joe and Paul went on catching and marking prairie dogs. Sometimes they caught a prairie dog they had already marked. The one that turned up most often was number one, the pup that Paul had named Sam. Perhaps he was greedier than the others or had less fear of strange things. Each time he was caught, Paul held him for a moment and stroked him. Each time Sam put up less of a fight. Other pups screamed in fear when they were picked up, but Sam only chuckled and chattered.

"Sam, you're getting to be a pest," Joe said as Paul turned him loose for the third time in a day. Sam ambled away. He no longer bothered to run.

When enough prairie dogs had been marked, Joe settled down to serious watching. He made notes of every tiny event among the prairie dogs: how they behaved while they ate, played, and so on. Paul spent a good deal of time watching with him. From time to time Joe talked about the meaning of what they saw.

Joe made notes on how the prairie dogs kept in touch with

each other. Every few minutes one prairie dog would run to another. They touched their mouths together. It looked as though they were kissing. They stroked each other with their front paws and nibbled each other's fur. Prairie dogs, Joe said, love to be petted by another prairie dog. It is called grooming. They stay close to each other in order to be groomed.

One afternoon a hawk circled high over the town. An alert prairie dog gave a special hawk-warning cry, and all the prairie dogs ran for safety. One small pup was slow. The hawk swooped on it with amazing speed. It tumbled the pup over but failed to pick it up. Flapping its large wings, it swooped again. This time it got a firm grip with its claws and carried the pup away.

Paul had wanted to rush out to save the pup, but it all happened too fast.

"Don't let yourself feel bad about it," Joe said. "Hawks must eat meat. They have no choice. It is not useless and cruel when that happens naturally. It has to happen. Animals need food, the same as we do."

Joe explained that there are

two large groups of animals: those that eat plants and those that eat meat. The meat-eaters must kill other animals for food. They are called predators. They live by catching plant-eaters. Because they must work so hard to get their food, they have small families. Food is easy for plant-eaters to get, and they have big families. Even though many are killed and eaten by predators, there are always many left. If some plant-eaters were not killed by predators, there would be too many. They would eat up all the food and starve. So that's how the two kinds of animals live together. The plant-eaters provide food for the predators, and the predators keep the plant-eaters from outgrowing their supply of food.

There are big meat-eaters, such as lions and wolves, and small ones, such as cats and owls. There are big plant-eaters, such as cows and deer, and small ones, such as rabbits and prairie dogs. Each kind of animal gets its food in its own way, and each depends on the way of life of other animals. A prairie dog town, for instance, provides food for many animals in many ways.

"I'll show you what I mean," Joe went on. "The prairie dogs eat some plants and not others. They leave the plants with many seeds. The seeds are food for mice and birds. The mice and birds that come to the town for seeds are food for bobcats and coyotes. So are the young prairie dogs. In this way the prairie dogs—the plant-eaters—provide food for the meat-eaters—the predators.

"Prairie dogs help predators in other ways, too. Cows and deer come to prairie dog towns. They like to graze where prairie dogs have cropped the grass short. The cows drop manure. The manure attracts insects. The insects are food for birds and mice and snakes and toads. So there are always many kinds of animals around a prairie dog town. That makes good hunting for predators. The black-footed ferret lives its whole life in prairie dog towns. It couldn't live without prairie dogs. So, though prairie dogs don't seem useful to us, they are important to other animals."

Exploring the town and watching from a blind, or hiding place, Paul saw many of the things that Joe had told him about. He saw deer and cattle come to graze on the town. He saw hawks circling. He caught small snakes and toads and held them a moment to look at them; then he let them go. He watched rabbits hopping and nibbling the short grass. Several times he saw coyotes, and at night he heard a bobcat yowl. The prairie dogs knew which animals were dangerous to them. When a hawk or coyote came, they ran for their holes. They paid little attention to cows or deer or rabbits.

Joe gave Paul the job of digging up a prairie dog hole so that he could examine the nest. It was a hard job. The hole went down a few feet, then turned and went along under the earth. At last Paul reached the nest, a round room packed with weeds and grass. The tunnel went on and on, farther than Paul could dig. Joe thought that somewhere it met other tunnels so that a prairie dog had many ways to escape an enemy that chased it underground.

One day Joe and Paul took a day off and went into town for some food. It was a long trip. They didn't get back to camp until nearly sundown. Just as they crossed the river, they heard the crack of a gun. Paul

saw a puff of dust where a bullet hit in the center of the dog town.

Joe and Paul jumped out of the truck. Two boys rose from the weeds where they had been lying hidden. Nearby were their motor scooters. It was Mike Taylor and his friend Jim Hughes, sons of the local ranchers. Joe went to the boys; and Paul ran out to see what they had hit.

Lying in the dust he found a brown, furry, dead lump. He reached to pick it up and drew back at the sight of blood. A few yards away lay another dead prairie dog; over there another

lay. A sick, awful feeling came over him. He ran to where Joe was talking to the boys.

"I'm sorry," Mike was saying. "We just shot a couple of dogs. We didn't think that would mess up the study or whatever it is."

"Well, it certainly does," Joe said. "I've been watching those prairie dogs day after day. Each one is important." He looked furious.

Mike seemed truly sorry. But Jim looked sullen. He fingered his gun. "Some big deal!" he said. "All this stuff about a couple of lousy prairie dogs. They're nothing but vermin! The more we get

rid of the better. That's what my dad says. So what's the use of studying them? Big deal! Studying lousy prairie dogs!"

"I guess you're one of the people I can't explain it to," Joe said. Angrily he turned away.

Paul stood speechless. He hated the boys. He hated the guns that gave them the power of life and death. Then he saw something move a short distance away. A small prairie dog was crawling slowly over the dusty ground. Paul ran over to it and let out a shout. "You've shot Sam," he cried. "Did you have to do that!" He picked up Sam, mindless

of the blood and of Sam's teeth. But Sam didn't bite. He lay still, but warm, in Paul's arms. Paul carried him over to Joe.

"It's Sam," he said helplessly.

"What do you mean, 'Sam'?" Mike asked, coming up to look.

"It's the first one we marked," Paul said. "He's only a pup and he's practically tame. What did you have to shoot him for?" Paul was surprised by his own feeling of sorrow and fury, surprised that his voice sounded strange. Sweat prickled his neck.

"He's not dead," Joe said. "Let me look at him. Bring him over to the table."

Paul carried the little prairie dog to the table and put him down. Sam squirmed feebly in his grasp and made crying noises. He seemed dazed. "Let's wash off the blood," Joe said.

Paul got water and a sponge. Gently Joe wiped away the blood that matted the hair on Sam's hind quarter. He felt along the leg bones.

"I don't think his leg is broken," Joe said. "It's just a flesh wound."

"Is he going to die?" Paul asked.

"Maybe not," Joe said. "Do you want to try to save him?"

"Sure I do," Paul said.

"Get the first-aid kit," Joe said.

Paul brought it, and Joe took out some antiseptic ointment. "If we can get this to heal without getting infected, I think he'll be all right," he said, "but we'll have to keep him for a few days."

"I'll make a nest for him," Paul said. He dumped a few cans out of a deep cardboard carton. There were some old newspapers in the tent. He got them and began tearing the paper into strips to make bedding.

Mike came over and knelt down beside him. "I'll help you," he said. Paul scowled at him. Still too angry to speak, he turned away without a word. They worked in silence, filling up the carton with strips of paper.

Then Mike tried again. "I didn't know he was a pet," he said. "I'm really sorry about it."

"That's okay," Paul said. "I guess you couldn't help it." He forgave Mike, but he still felt bad. The prairie dogs the boys had shot still lay dead. Paul had forgotten that he had ever thought it would be fun to shoot living animals. Now that he knew the prairie dogs—knew how alive they were—there could be no fun in killing them.

Joe had put a bandage on Sam's leg. "I think it has stopped bleeding," he said. He put Sam in the carton. Sam had opened his eyes, and he scrambled to hide in the heap of paper. Paul put some clean dishtowels on top to make him feel more safely hidden.

"I guess we'll be going," Mike said. "I sure hope Sam gets better." He and Jim Hughes picked up their guns and got on their scooters. They waved good-bye. Paul watched the trails of dust left by their scooters as they raced over the prairie.

In the morning Paul woke early and hurried to Sam's box. The little prairie dog seemed much stronger. When Paul opened the box, he tried to hide in a corner. Paul put a pile of oats in front of him. In a moment, Sam had forgotten his fear and was eating them.

All through the day Paul took care of Sam. He brought him tender green grass and plenty of oats. Sam was less afraid each time the box was opened. He didn't struggle when Paul carefully took off the bandage and put ointment on the wound.

During the next few days Sam became more and more tame. Paul found that Sam liked to kiss his hand in greeting the way he kissed other prairie dogs. Then he would let Paul stroke him. Sam showed that he liked it by rolling on his back. Soon he was so tame that he was nuzzling Paul's hand, asking for more petting. The wound was healing well.

One afternoon Paul heard a motor scooter. He looked up to see Mike, alone, splashing through the creek. Mike rode up to the tent where Paul was sitting.

"How's Sam?" Mike asked.

"Okay," Paul said. "He's going to be okay."

"That's great!" Mike said. He smiled at Paul.

Suddenly Paul realized he was glad the boy had come. It would be great to have a friend his age. "Here," he said, "take a look at Sam. I'll show you how tame he is." He proudly lifted the little prairie dog out of the box and put him in Mike's outstretched hands.

"Where's the other kid?" Paul asked.

"He didn't want to come," Mike said. "He's out shooting."

Paul noticed that Mike had left his gun behind.

Just then Joe came out of the tent. "Hi, there," he said. "What can I do for you?"

"I was wondering," Mike said slowly, "about what it is you're finding out about prairie dogs. What are you studying anyway?"

Joe looked at him as though he was trying to decide something. "Do you really want to know?" he asked.

Mike nodded.

"Stick around," Joe said. "Sit in the blind with us for a while, and maybe I can show you."

Mike put Sam back in his box. The three walked over and climbed into the blind. While they waited for the prairie dogs to decide that it was safe to come out, Joe talked about the prairie dog's way of life.

Prairie dogs, he said, like people, had found safety in numbers. A single prairie dog could not live long. With only one hole to hide in, it could not escape the animals that hunt it, for long. But with many holes to run into and with many pairs of eyes watching for danger, most prairie dogs found safety.

At the same time, if too many prairie dogs crowded together too closely, there was danger they would eat all the nearby grass and starve. Therefore they had to stay just the right distance apart.

Joe had wondered how the prairie dogs managed to stay together and at the same time not be too crowded. His study had answered these questions.

"Almost everything they do," Joe said, "is something that helps keep them close to each other." He pointed to two prairie dogs running to each other to kiss. "Kissing," Joe said, "is the way they recognize a friend. And grooming is something they enjoy, so it makes them want to stay close to each other. These two things have a real purpose. They help them survive."

A moment later Joe pointed out two prairie dogs sniffing each other and making little jumps at each other. Suddenly one turned and ran away. The other chased it a short distance.

"That was a fight," Joe said. "No one gets hurt, but it settles the argument. The prairie dog that ran away must have crossed the line into the other one's yard."

"I don't see any line," Mike said.

"It's invisible," Joe said. "But all the prairie dogs know where it is."

Joe explained that each prairie dog belonged to a small group. All the prairie dogs in a group were friends. They shared their holes, groomed each other, and stayed close together. But they had nothing to do with prairie dogs of other groups. Each group stayed in its own area, and if a stranger crossed the line, he was chased out. That kept any part of the town from getting crowded.

"Just like people," Joe said, "a prairie dog is braver when he's in his own home than when he is in somebody else's home. In a prairie dog fight, the prairie dog that has crossed into somebody else's yard is the first to give up and run away. For this reason, the true owner always wins."

"What about the pups?" Mike asked. "If a group had a lot of pups, wouldn't its area get too crowded?"

"When the pups are little," Joe said, "they can go anywhere they please. Even the prairie dogs

of other groups will groom them and nurse them. But, little by little, as they get older, the strange prairie dogs reject them and chase them home. That's how young prairie dogs learn about the invisible lines that mark off each area. When the pups get big and the group feels crowded, some of the older prairie dogs move out into new land. I think they move because the pups are such pests. They want to be groomed all the time. The older ones never refuse them. They just go away to get some peace."

"Gosh," Mike said as they left the blind, "I never knew so much went on in a dog town. I thought they just sat there and ate grass."

When he left at sunset, Paul felt as though he had found a new friend and that perhaps the prairie dogs had also.

In the book PRAIRIE DOG SUMMER, *Faith McNulty goes on to tell how Paul and Mike worked together to keep the prairie dog town from being destroyed and how, before the summer was over, they managed to photograph the rarest animal in America.*

AUTHOR

Faith McNulty feels that some of her best friends are animals. When she was growing up, it was common for her family to have such wild and domestic animals as a baby robin, a baby woodchuck, and a litter of kittens in the house. She is often sad at the way animals are treated by many people. "I felt, and still believe, that animals have a right to exist, just as people do," she says.

Ms. McNulty learned that many ranchers regularly poison prairie dogs, mainly because of the amount of grass they eat. She found out that the little black-footed ferret that also lives in prairie dog towns is in danger of becoming extinct. She wrote a magazine article about this situation, hoping to make people aware of the danger to the animals. It then occurred to her that young readers also might be interested in ferrets and prairie dogs, so she wrote *Prairie Dog Summer*.

In addition to an award-winning book, *The Whooping Crane*, and several books for young readers, Ms. McNulty has written articles and fiction for magazines. She has worked as a newspaper reporter and editor in New York City, where she was born.

Faith McNulty and her husband, Richard Martin, live in Rhode Island.

USING CONTEXT TO GET
WORD MEANINGS

Sometimes in your reading you come to a word for which you know one or more meanings, but none of those meanings makes sense in what you are reading.

You have seen and heard the word *bay* before, and you know what it means in this sentence:

The boat sailed across the **bay.**

But do you know what *bay* means in the next sentence?

Andrea felt sure that the **bay** would win the blue ribbon.

The meaning for *bay* that fits the first sentence does not make any sense in that sentence, does it? By reading the next paragraph, in which this sentence appears, you can learn more about *bay*.

Andrea felt sure that the bay would win the blue ribbon. She thought that its reddish-brown coat and black tail made it the most beautiful animal in the horse show.

Do you know now what *bay* means in those sentences? Of course! A bay is a horse. The other sentence lets you know this by telling you that it has a reddish-brown coat and a black tail, that it is an animal, and that it is in a horse show. You were able to figure out the meaning of *bay* by thinking what would make sense with the rest of what is being said.

The boat sailed across the **bay.**

Andrea felt sure that the **bay** would win the blue ribbon.

Figuring out the meaning of a word by using what is being said by the other words around it is called **using the context to get the meaning of a word.** Sometimes things that are said before the word will help. Sometimes you can get help from what is said after the word. Often, help you need comes both before and after the word.

Sometimes in your reading you will come to a word which you have never seen or heard before, and for which you have no meaning at all. For example, read the following group of sentences carefully.

When Jack was telling the class about the book he had read, he talked on and on. After he had finished, his teacher said, "Your report was too long, Jack. If you had made it **concise,** there would have been time for others to tell about books they have read."

You have probably never seen or heard the word printed in heavy black print before. But by **using the context** you could teach yourself the meaning that *concise* has in that group of sentences. The context tells you that the teacher thought Jack's report was too long and that if he had made it *concise*, there would have been time for other reports. The word *concise* must mean short, or brief.

When you meet a printed word whose meaning you don't know, use the context to help figure out a meaning that makes sense in what you are reading. The parts of the context that can help you may be single words, short groups of words, or sentences. The helpful parts may come before or after or both before and after the word.

Discussion

Help your class answer these questions:
1. What is meant by using the context to get the meaning of a word?
2. Why do you sometimes need to figure out the meaning of a word for which you already know one or more meanings?
3. What may the helpful parts of the context be? Where might you find them?

On your own

As you read the paragraph that follows, use the context to help you figure out the meaning of any word in heavy black print that you do not already know.

Today the list of winners in the art contest was **posted** on the door of the classroom. Hanging there, it caused a great **stir.** The excited pupils were anxious to find out who the winners were. That is why they all **clustered** around the door trying to read the names. When the pupils returned to their seats, it was **obvious** who the winners were. Shining eyes and broad smiles gave their faces an **elated** look.

Checking your work

If you are asked to do so, tell what one of the words in heavy black print means. Then tell which parts of the context helped you decide what that meaning is.

The Great Penobscot Raid

by Kay Hill

In the old stories told by the Wabanaki Indian tribes of North America's eastern woodlands, the Great Chief Glooscap is a god of huge size and magic powers. In this tale he changes himself into something very tiny in order to help a Wabanaki woman of the Penobscot tribe outwit the Mohawk Indians who are holding her captive.

The Penobscot captive walked back to the Mohawk palisade with an armload of firewood, and as she passed the shocks of corn, she noticed something lying on the ground. The white and purple pattern stood out sharply against the yellow of bleached grass, and she bent to look at it more closely. Her heart gave a tremendous leap. It was a belt of spruce-root fibers she had woven for her husband, Pulwaugh, long ago when both were happy in their home in the Penobscot country. She recognized both the dye and the pattern.

What was it doing here in the Mohawk land, far from their Penobscot village where Pulwaugh had been struck down? Did this mean that he was alive after all, somewhere close at hand? Had he left the belt in the path to warn her of his presence? It must be! Should she pick it up? No. The Mohawks lounging at the gate might notice. Menaagan walked on, and entered the palisade of wooden stakes.

What did Pulwaugh want her to do? Was he alone or with a war party? Was she to wait in the long house for him to come for her? Surely not. The long house would be crowded with Mohawk families. Then did he want her to come to that place where the belt was after the camp was asleep? Much more likely! It would not be easy to creep away without being seen, but she would try. How they would get away from Mohawk territory, she could not imagine. She must leave that to Pulwaugh.

Menaagan passed through the gate, not hurrying, trying to appear the usual silent and unhappy prisoner. She must wait through the long day and not allow the enemy to suspect that her heart was dancing with hope.

The women of the various families in the long house where she lived seemed to notice nothing, and she managed to do her work as usual. At last the sun slipped down behind the trees, and Menaagan seated herself in the doorway of the house with some mending. As the blue of the evening deepened to black, the people came in and prepared for bed. Soon

they would all be asleep. Fortunately, it was not the custom of the Mohawks to set guards at night, for they had no fear of being surprised in their own strong village. Menaagan would be able to creep away quietly as soon as the moon——

What was that! A sudden uproar at the gate set the dogs barking.

Menaagan's heart sank like a stone. Six Mohawk warriors entered the palisade with a pair of prisoners—Pulwaugh and Nokum, her brother. She sat very still as they passed, and Pulwaugh's eyes stared past her, showing no recognition. She knew therefore that she must pretend not to know him. When the Mohawk chief summoned her, she went with a calm, indifferent face.

"Woman, these men speak a Wabanaki dialect," the chief said. "You, a Penobscot, may understand them. Ask what they are doing here and if they are alone."

Menaagan put the question quietly, and Pulwaugh answered with a taunting smile.

"Four moons past, the Mohawks paid our tribe a visit. We have grown lonely for our friends and have come to return the compliment."

The Mohawks moved uneasily when they heard the translation, for this was the roundabout Indian way of saying the Wabanaki men had come with a war party to seek revenge. Menaagan was told to ask how many braves were in the party and how far off they were encamped, but this the prisoners refused to answer.

"Very well," said the Mohawk chief, "you have from the setting of the sun to its rising." And he ordered the captives tied to stakes in the center of the palisade.

Menaagan was obliged to follow the others back to the long house without so much as a glance at her husband and brother. Her heart was sore, for their fate was now certain. Their scouts failing to return by morning, the Penobscot war party would assume the enemy was warned, and they would not risk an attack. There might not even be a war party! Pulwaugh and her brother might have come alone. The more she thought about it, the more she was sure this was so.

She resumed her place by the door and sewed with trembling fingers. Anything that might be done must be done by her alone. Should she try to set them free? If she succeeded, it would be only a brief respite. They would be overtaken and brought back. Yet something must be attempted before it was too late! Time was passing. Menaagan tried to come to a decision.

A mosquito buzzed loudly in her right ear and she brushed it away. It came again on her other side and buzzed louder than ever, and suddenly she found herself listening with strained attention. It was a voice speaking in her own tongue!

"Menaagan, my daughter," were the words she heard, "do as I tell you. They may yet be saved." It was the voice of the Great Chief Glooscap! "Collect all the moccasins and hide them. Tie strings across all the doorways. Then go and cut the prisoners' bonds. Tell them to go outside and stand at the gate, making a great noise. At the last moment, go and pour water on all the fires. You understand?" Menaagan nodded breathlessly, and the mosquito circled and disappeared with a whine into the night.

Menaagan rose with fast-beating heart. It was quiet now except for the light crackle of the campfire and the cry of a nightbird. The people slept. Moving like a shadow, the Penobscot woman crept about gathering up the Mohawks' moccasins. When she had them all, she hid them under a pile of skins. Then she stole about tying strings of rawhide across all the doorways. For good measure, she scattered sharp stones on the ground. A woman stirred in her sleep, murmuring, and Menaagan stood like a rock. A brave turned over with a grunt. Then all was still again.

Menaagan ran to the prisoners and whispered to them what they must do, at the same time cutting the cords that

bound them. Arming themselves with sticks from the pile of firewood, Pulwaugh and Nokum slipped out through the gate and waited for the signal. Menaagan was back in the long house now, lifting the heavy bark vessels and pouring water on the fires. The flames scattered and went out with a hiss of steam, and the woman fled into the darkness.

The Mohawks awoke with muttered cries and felt in vain for their moccasins. The steamy air confused them and they crashed into each other in the dark. Then from outside came the frightening sound of Penobscot war cries. The two young men were each making as much noise as ten, whooping and beating their clubs against the palisade. Now the dogs began to add their barking to the rumpus and the children to cry. It sounded to the Mohawks as though they were being attacked by an entire army.

Feeling in the dark for weapons, they rushed out of the long house only to trip over the strings and fall headlong. Picking themselves up, they danced as the sharp stones cut

their feet, and they struck blindly at shapes in the steamy darkness, thinking they struck at the enemy. In their excitement, they confused friend with foe, and soon nearly half the Mohawk braves were stretched on the ground, every one struck down by a friend. Those who were left started for the gate, but the Penobscots were waiting, their eyes accustomed to the gloom, their clubs ready. As each Mohawk emerged through the narrow gateway, the sky seemed to fall on him. One after another, the Mohawks were dispatched in this way until only the three Penobscots stood on their own feet.

"Quickly now—to the river," whispered Pulwaugh, and taking Menaagan's hand, he led her to the shore where Nokum drew the canoe out of hiding and launched it. Swiftly in the darkness they crossed the stream. Then the two men bore it to the next stream, Menaagan carrying paddles and blankets, and so on, until they reached their own country seven days later.

"But didn't the Mohawks come after you?" asked their friends at home in amazement.

"No," said they, and only Glooscap knew why.

It was some hours before all the Mohawks had picked themselves up from the ground and recovered from ringing headaches, but when they had, they congratulated themselves on their narrow escape. "What a terrible battle," they said. "The enemy must have numbered thousands to attack us like that in our own village! We beat them off, of course, but it was fortunate we were not all killed!" And for years they talked of the Great Penobscot Raid, never knowing that the raiding army had consisted of two men and one brave woman.

And so—*kespeadooksit*—the story ends.

AUTHOR

Kay Hill became interested in the tales of Glooscap at the age of seven, when she spent a summer in the town of Wolfboro, Nova Scotia. The elderly women with whom she stayed felt that they could care for her best by keeping her in the house all summer. She spent much of the time leaning out of the window, making up stories about the headland she could see in the distance. Someone told her that the headland was called Blomidon and was the home of a mythical Indian giant called Glooscap, but nobody could tell her more than that. "Then," she says, "people knew little about the Indians and their grand literature of poetry and humor, passed down almost entirely by word of mouth."

Thirty years later, when Kay Hill was a writer, she was asked to adapt for children's television the folktales of Glooscap. "People were at last beginning to be interested in the Indians and their culture," she said, "so at last I learned about Glooscap and actually met and talked with the people of Blomidon."

These tales were later put together in book form: *Glooscap and His Magic* and *More Glooscap Stories,* from which this story was taken. One long tale is a complete book, *Badger the Mischief Maker.*

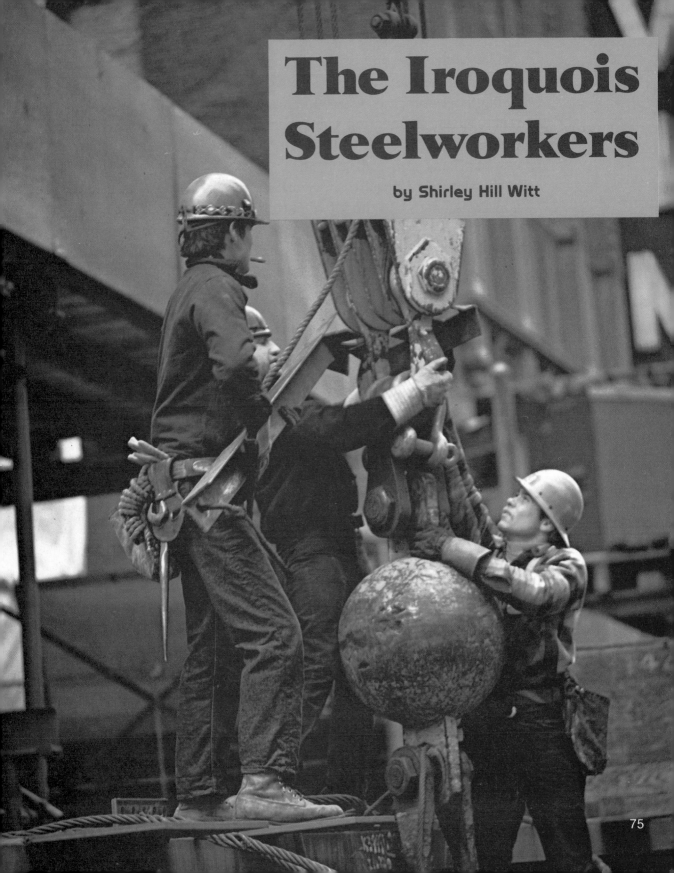

The Iroquois Steelworkers

by Shirley Hill Witt

The Mohawks, one of the six tribes of the Iroquois nation, were the first Indians to be steelworkers. It all began in 1886. A big steel company was building a bridge over the St. Lawrence River, connecting Canada with the United States. The bridge was being built near the Mohawk Reserve called Caughnawaga (kahg´nuh-wah´guh), near Montreal. Some of the Mohawk men were hired to do work on the ground. Some of the non-Indian men had the job of putting up the big steel beams for the bridge out over the water. It was a very dangerous job. Very few men dared to do such a dangerous job perched high up in the windy sky over a roaring river far, far below.

Every so often, one of the non-Indian men far out on the beams would sense that there was someone near him. He would turn around and find a Mohawk standing there, looking over his shoulder. The Mohawks would run up and down and over and across the beams as though on dry land. They wore no safety belts, and they did not hang onto things as they went. They had no fear of the heights, no fear of walking on the narrow beams.

The old Iroquois men say that there are two reasons for this. The first reason is that, in the olden times, the boys were tested to see if they were ready to be men. On a very windy day, the boys would be told to climb the tallest pine tree they could find. If a boy climbed to the very thin top and could stand the wind blowing him back and forth all day, then he came back down a man. All the boys had to do this, had to pass this test. The old men say that is one of the reasons the men have no fear of heights.

The other reason they tell about is really not a matter of being brave. They say it is a matter of how the Iroquois people walk. They say that Iroquois people walk with one foot in front of the other, in a straight line. The footprints of non-Indian people show one foot out on this side and the other foot out on that side. Their path looks like two paths, not one, so they say. When an Iroquois man walks across a narrow beam, he walks in

a way that is natural for him. When a non-Indian man walks across a narrow beam, he must put one foot directly in front of the other as the Iroquois do. This is not his natural way and so his body is off balance. That is the difference, the old men say. That is the other reason the Indians do not have fear on the high steel.

Those first Mohawk men taught other men of their nation.

And then they taught men from the other Iroquois nations as well.

The Iroquois steelworkers have helped to build many famous things in the years since 1886. They worked on the George Washington Bridge, Rockefeller Center, the Golden Gate Bridge, and many other buildings and bridges. It is said that when the Empire State Building was being built, all the non-Indian men quit when the top tower was due to be built. So the Iroquois men finished it alone, not afraid.

Now the Iroquois workers in high steel are asked to go all over the United States and Canada to do this dangerous work. And sometimes they go overseas, as well, to places like Venezuela and Saudi Arabia.

So, in a way, the Iroquois men are still the brave warriors they used to be. Their courage is as strong now as it ever was.

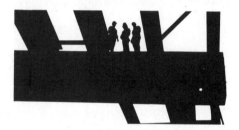

AUTHOR

Shirley Hill Witt was born in Whittier, California. Like the steelworkers she describes in this article, she is a Mohawk, but her book *The Tuscarora*, from which this article was taken, is mainly about another of the Iroquois nations. In studying the Tuscarora, she learned much that is important about all Iroquois and calls it "an awesome heritage."

As a young woman, Dr. Witt was one of the founders of a national Indian youth group, and she has been named to a number of civil-rights commissions. She received her B.A. and M.A. degrees in anthropology from the University of Michigan and her Ph.D. degree from the University of New Mexico. Dr. Witt has written and edited a number of works in the field of anthropology. She now teaches at Colorado College and is the mother of two children.

You may not be a great sculptor, but that doesn't mean that you can't carve figurines, head-and-shoulder portraits, and any other small objects.

Oh, but you haven't any marble! Well, don't let that bother you. To carve in marble is hard work and takes a great deal of time. Soap, just white hand soap, is much easier and quicker to work with and less expensive. You will be surprised at the statues you'll be able to produce from it with a little effort and imagination. And you will be learning an old, old art.

To start your own sculpture, get a cake of white hand soap, a small knife, and an orange stick or nail file. Since this is your first experience with soap carving, it would be better to start with something simple, such as a fish.

FUN WITH SOAP SCULPTURE

by Pauline Rothrauff

First, draw a picture of whatever you want to make. Next, scrape all the lettering from your soap so that it is smooth and even. Now place the drawing on the soap and trace around it with a soft, fairly sharp pencil that will press through onto the soap, or trace your drawing over carbon paper. Some soap carvers transfer their designs by making pinpricks through it into the soap and then following the pattern made by the pinpricks.

After you have the design marked off on the soap, start cutting away the soap outside the outline of the object. Then round it out and carve the details. Don't hurry your carving. You will want to use an orange stick or nail file to carve grooves and lines. Very often a small penknife will work better for fine, intricate cutting.

When you have finished, you can smooth your sculpture by rubbing it with your fingertips or lightly washing it with your hands.

When your sculpture is dry, it can be painted with watercolors or poster paints. Or if you prefer to keep its marble-like finish, coat it with clear nail polish.

SKILL LESSON

USING AN INDEX

How do you find the information that a book has on a given topic or a question you want answered? Do you open the book just anywhere and keep turning pages to the left or right until you come to the information you want? There is no need for you to use that slow way of finding what you are looking for. Instead, you can use the index that is at the back of most books you use in studying.

Look at the part of the index of a book on the next page. The words printed in heavy black print and farthest to the left in each column are called **main topics.** They name people and things that the book tells about, and they are arranged in the order of the letters in the alphabet.

When you use the index of a book to help you find the information the book gives on some topic or question, you must decide what word to look for among the main topics. We call that word a **key word.** Always try to choose a key word that names what your topic or question talks about.

Sometimes the key word to use for a question is in that question. What word would you use as a key word for each of these questions?

1. What are the different uses of helicopters?
2. What did the first automobiles look like?

Sometimes there may be in a question more than one word which you should use as a key word. For example, take the question *How does climate affect travel?* If you used only the

word *climate* as a key word, you might miss some of the information the book gives. That is why you may also need to use the word *travel* as a key word.

What two words would you use as key words for each of the following questions?

3. Is coal mined in Illinois?
4. How is radio used in fighting crime?
5. Why is cement used in building bridges?

Sometimes a word you need to use as a key word is not in the question. For example, take the question *In what states are the most peaches and apples grown?* If the index did not list the words *peaches* and *apples* among its main topics, would you decide that the book gave no information you needed? You should not do that. You might get the help you need by using the word *fruits* as a key word.

Suppose that an index you are using does not have among its main topics either of the italicized words in each of the following sentences. What other word that is not in the question would you try to use as a key word?

6. For what purposes are *tin* and *copper* used?

7. Are both *wheat* and *corn* grown in the same places?

Look again at the part of an index used in this lesson and find the main topic **Airplanes.** After it you can see five groups of words. They are *first, how controlled in the air, how supported in the air, how they came to be, uses of.* Each of these groups of words is called a **subtopic.** The subtopics show what the book tells about the main topic **Airplanes.** In some indexes, the subtopics are arranged in the order of the letters of the alphabet. In others, they are arranged in the order in which they are talked about in the book.

After each subtopic are one or more numbers. Each of them is the number of a page on which information is given about that subtopic. A dash between two numbers, such as 63—72, means that information on the subtopic begins somewhere on page 63 and ends somewhere on page 72. In some indexes the letter *m, p, d,* or *t* is used after a page number to tell you that on the page is a map, a picture, a diagram, or a table. For example, after the main topic **Airplanes,** you will find: first, 8, 9*p.* This means that on page 9 there is a picture of the first airplane.

What subtopic in the part of an index you looked at would you use to find information on each of these questions?

1. How are cargoes loaded on ships?
2. In what ways were the first bicycles different from those we use today?

It is easy to choose the right subtopic to use for the first question, because one or more important words in the question are also in the subtopic. It is not so easy to choose the right subtopic for the second question, because none of the important words in the question are in the subtopic. You need to look at all the subtopics that come after the main topic **Bicycles** and

try to decide which is the best one to try. Probably the subtopic *how they came to be* is the one to use.

Find the main topic **Coke** in the part of an index. No subtopics come after that topic, but you will find there the words
"*See* Fuel." Those words mean that by using the main topic
Fuel you may be able to find the information you want about
coke.

Find the main topic **Donkeys** in the part of an index. After
the subtopics you can see the words "*See also* **Burros**." Those
words mean that by looking under the main topic **Burros** you
can find where to look for other information about donkeys.

Discussion

Help your class answer these questions:
1. How can using an index help you find information on a
   topic or question?
2. How are the main topics in an index arranged? In what ways
   may the subtopics be arranged?

3. What is the key word for each of questions 1 and 2 near the beginning of this lesson?
4. Why will you sometimes need to use more than one word as a key word for a question? What words should be used as key words for questions 3, 4, and 5?
5. When would you need to use a key word that is not in the question? What word should probably be used as a key word for each of questions 6 and 7?
6. Why may it sometimes be harder to choose the right sub-topic than it is at other times?
7. What does the dash between two page numbers tell you? What does the word *See* tell you? What do the words *See also* tell you? What do the letters *m, p, d,* and *t* in an index tell you?

On your own

On what pages listed in the part of an index on page 82 would you expect to find information on each of the following questions? Write and number your answers on a sheet of paper.

1. What are some of the main canals in the United States?
2. What heavy loads do people in Africa carry?
3. Were more automobiles made in the United States in 1964 than in 1960?
4. In what countries in Europe are bicycles commonly used?
5. Where were the first airplane flights made?
6. What improvements have been made in railway cars?
7. What are the main airports in Chicago?
8. What were the first balloon flights over large bodies of water?

Checking your work

If you are asked to do so, read aloud the answers you wrote for some of the questions. If you made a mistake in any answer, find out why it is a mistake.

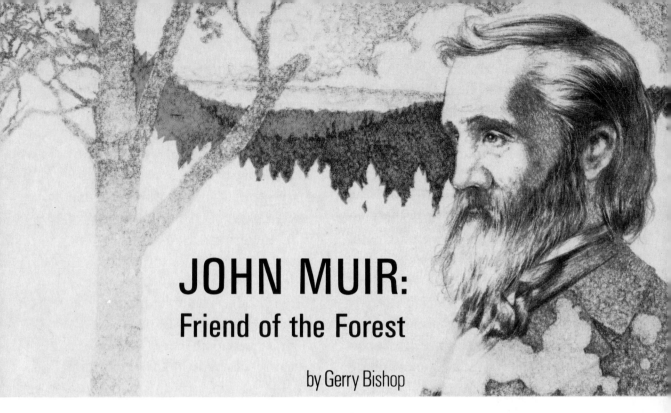

JOHN MUIR:
Friend of the Forest

by Gerry Bishop

John Muir was born in Scotland in 1838 and came with his family to a farm in Wisconsin when he was eleven. As a student of natural science, he hiked over much of North America. He was thirty when he first explored the Sierra country of California.

The wild creatures hardly noticed as a strange-looking man with quick, sparkling eyes slipped through the forest. He moved as quietly as a deer, his keen senses alert to every sound and smell. When he stood still, he looked almost like a tree—old clothes like wrinkly bark, strong trunk-legs, long branch-arms, shaggy hair that sprouted from his head like leaves, and a bushy beard.

With nothing but a bit of hard bread and a notebook tied to his belt, John Muir would roam for days, studying in the forest school. The great old trees, the animals, and even the cold winds and rain were his teachers. His favorite classroom was the Sierra Nevada Mountains of California.

Here lived such close friends as that fluff of noisy energy, the Douglas squirrel. John called this little animal "a hot spark of life, making every tree tingle with its prickly toes."

Another good friend was the

water ouzel. He loved to watch this robin-sized bird dive into the swift mountain streams for its insect dinner, then perform its crazy dipping dance on a nearby rock. In rain storms, other birds would huddle together, fluffing their feathers. But this ball of sunshine chirped away to celebrate the beautiful falling water.

John even loved the rocks. He looked closely at their glittering crystals, and they seemed alive. The plants' roots that fastened themselves to the rocks made acids that slowly dissolved the rocks. Soon the rich minerals would become parts of growing leaves, trunks, and flowers.

He always felt part of the forest world. He saw the many animals and plants living together and providing for each other's needs. He wished he could stay there as one of them. The sweet, rich smells, soft, mysterious sounds, and shadowy movements and colors soaked into his body. This world charged him with energy and health.

His strength carried him up mountains that never before had been climbed. Here he studied the remains of the great glaciers. Thousands of years ago they had crunched their way down the mountains to carve deep canyons and broad valleys.

John also had great feeling for the people who had to work their lives away in the crowded, noisy, dirty cities. One day he returned to San Francisco with a bunch of wildflowers he had picked. The people crowded around him to touch and smell the blossoms. "Everybody needs beauty as well as bread," he thought.

His notebook soon became a treasure chest filled with golden stories of the wild forests and mountains. Many people had never seen a rabbit burst from the bushes, never walked barefoot on a bed of soft green moss. He hoped his stories would take people to the mountains. To him, the people were like caged birds. He wanted to set them free.

Every trip into the woods taught him a new secret. He would watch the Douglas squirrel busily preparing for the long, snowy mountain winter. The sky would look as though it were raining pine cones when the little acrobat jumped from one springy branch to another, chewing off every cone he could reach. Then he would scramble down and

quickly bury each cone. During the next winter the little animal would dig down through many feet of snow for a feast from his well-hidden dinner. Any cones he forgot might sprout into sequoia saplings that years later would feed the squirrel's grandchildren.

Of course, not all in nature is peaceful. One warm afternoon as he walked home through the falling autumn leaves, he heard a sharp squeal and hurried toward the sound. At the bottom of a slope lay the warm body of a jack rabbit. The only signs of struggle were some missing fur and some blood on its neck. Its death had been very quick. He wondered whose dinner he had interrupted. As if to answer his question, the proud cry of a Cooper's hawk filled the air. John called back to the hungry hunter, "I wish you a good feast!" He understood the ways of nature well and knew that the death of one animal simply meant life for another.

One day, as John lay watching a covey of timid mountain quail pecking at seeds and insects, he suddenly jumped to his feet, sniffing. A flash of orange caught his eye. *Fire!* He raced down the hill. Through thick white smoke he saw a group of men setting fires with torches as they walked through a grove of trees and bushes. In the distance John heard the bleating of sheep. Then he understood: Acres of plants, the homes of countless animals, were being burned so a flock of sheep could have a clear path up the mountain.

John decided the sheepherders were not people to argue with, so he hid and sadly watched. When the fire finally died out, the sheep crashed through the smoking ruins and swarmed up to a beautiful mountain meadow. There the thick carpet of tender leaves and flowers were quickly chewed away to bare rock. The flock moved on.

A few days later, still sad and angry, John wandered into one of his favorite forests. Here to comfort him were the giant sequoias. The biggest of these trees had started growing thousands of years ago. By the time Columbus landed in America—500 years before—these trees already stood as tall as skyscrapers. John noticed the black scars that told of fires the trees had survived. He thought of the centuries of mountain storms and the plagues of insects that had not been able to kill the beautiful giant sequoias.

Suddenly a loud "boom!" shook the forest. Some loggers were sawing down the old giants and then blasting them with dynamite. The small pieces were just the right size to feed their sawmill. Trees that had fought natural enemies for two thousand years were now being turned into shingles and fences that would last less than a human lifetime.

John understood that people needed sheep for food and clothing, and lumber for houses. He also understood that the sheepherders and loggers had a right to make a living. The land would easily feed, clothe, and house people if managed properly. But John feared that the sheepherders and the loggers, in order to get rich quickly, would destroy the land rather than use it wisely. His stories had taught many people to love the forests. Now he knew he would have to call on these people to help save the forests.

John's pleas spread across the country. People flooded Congress with letters. Even President Harrison heard him. At last the areas being destroyed became Yosemite National Park and Sequoia National Park. The sheep and sawmills were kept out.

But John Muir was not satisfied. Most forests were still not protected. A growing population was demanding more sheep and lumber. Millions of firs and pines, whose roots held valuable soil in place, were being cut down. Once, rain had dripped from their branches and had gently soaked into the soil. Now rain was washing the soil down the mountainsides. Water that had kept the valleys green was now crashing to the sea in flash floods. The farmers' wells began drying up. The valleys would soon become deserts.

To save the remaining trees, John organized his friends into the Sierra Club. They told the people what was happening. Many sheepherders and loggers were careful in their use of the land. Only a few greedy people were making great clearings in the forests to feed too many sheep. They never planted trees to replace those they cut down.

John's new book, *The Mountains of California*, also told about the destruction. Finally, President Harrison, and later President Cleveland, asked that millions more acres of forest be put under Government care.

This was too much for those who gained great profits from their use of the trees and meadows. They threatened Congress, "If you don't give us back the forest, we'll use all our money and power to get you voted out of office!"

Congress was almost ready to give in. John fought back. The cries of John and his friends finally won out. The Government promised to protect the trees.

Then the new President, Theodore Roosevelt, visited John at Yosemite Falls. Roosevelt, a lover of the outdoors, knew that if he was to help save forests, he would have to learn all he could about them. John Muir was the teacher he wanted.

Around lonely campfires John and the President talked. Ecology was just becoming a science, but John had known togetherness with nature since he was a child. He explained that only a healthy earth can provide for us and that we must guard, not destroy, its delicate cycles and balances.

Deeply impressed, President Roosevelt created 150 national forests, five national parks, and 23 national monuments in the next few years. Perhaps the most beautiful of these monuments was an uncut stand of redwoods, sheltered in a foggy valley north of San Francisco on the California coast. It was named Muir Woods.

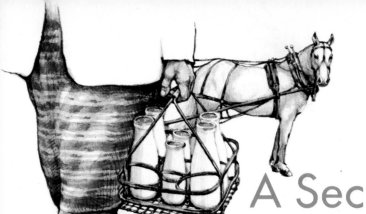

Pierre and his horse
shared a special secret which
no one else knew.

A Secret for Two

by Quentin Reynolds

Montreal (mahn-tree-awl′) is a very large city, but, like all large cities, it has some very small streets. Streets, for instance, like Prince Edward Street, which is only four blocks long. No one knew Prince Edward Street as well as did Pierre (pee-yair′) Dupin, for Pierre had delivered milk to the families on the street for thirty years now.

During the past fifteen years, the horse that drew the milk wagon used by Pierre was a large white horse named Joseph. In Montreal, especially in that part of Montreal which is very French, the animals, like children, are often given the names of saints. When the big white horse first came to the Provincale Milk Company, he didn't have a name.

They told Pierre that he could use the white horse henceforth. Pierre stroked the softness of the horse's neck, he stroked the sheen of its splendid belly, and he looked into the eyes of the horse.

"This is a kind horse, a gentle and a faithful horse," Pierre said, "and I can see a beautiful spirit shining out of the eyes of the horse. I will name him after good St. Joseph, who was also kind and gentle and faithful, with a beautiful spirit."

Within a year Joseph knew the milk route as well as Pierre. Pierre used to boast that he didn't need reins. He never touched them. Each morning Pierre arrived at the stables of the Provincale Milk Company at five o'clock. The wagon would be loaded, and Joseph hitched to it. Pierre would call,

"Bon jour, viel ami" (Good day, old friend), as he climbed into his seat. Joseph would turn his head, and the other drivers would smile and say that the horse would smile at Pierre.

Then Jacques (zhahk), supervising, would say, "All right, Pierre, go on," and Pierre would call softly to Joseph, *"Avance, mon ami,"* and this splendid combination would stalk proudly down the street.

The wagon, without any direction from Pierre, would roll three blocks down St. Catherine Street, then turn right two blocks along Roslyn Avenue, then left, for that was Prince Edward Street. The horse would stop at the first house, allow Pierre perhaps thirty seconds to get down from his seat and put a bottle of milk at the front door, and then go on, skipping two houses and stopping at the third. So it went, down the length of the street.

Then Joseph, still without any direction from Pierre, would turn around and come back along the other side.

Pierre would boast at the stable of Joseph's skill. "I never touch the reins. He knows just where to stop. Why, a blind man could handle my route with Joseph pulling the wagon."

So it went on for years — always the same. Pierre and Joseph both grew old together, but gradually, not suddenly. Pierre's huge walrus mustache was pure white now, and Joseph didn't lift his knees so high or raise his head quite as much. Jacques, seeing them at the stables, never noticed that they were both getting old until Pierre appeared one day carrying a heavy walking stick.

"Hey, Pierre," Jacques laughed. "Maybe you got the gout, hey?"

"Mais oui, Jacques," Pierre said, uncertainly. "One grows old. One's legs get tired."

"You should teach the horse to carry the milk to the front door for you," Jacques told him. "He does everything else."

Pierre knew every one of the forty families he served on Prince Edward Street. The cooks knew that he could neither read nor write, so instead of following the usual custom of leaving a note in an empty bottle if an additional quart of milk was needed, they would sing out when they heard the rumble of his wagon wheels over the cobbled street, "Bring an extra quart this morning, Pierre."

Pierre had a remarkable memory. When he arrived at the stable, he would always remember to tell Jacques, "The Paquins took an extra quart of milk this morning. The Lemoines bought a pint of cream."

Jacques would note these things in a little book he always carried. Most of the drivers had to make out the weekly bills and collect the money, but Jacques, liking Pierre, had always excused him from this task. All Pierre had to do was to arrive at five in the morning, walk to his wagon, which was always in the same spot at the curb, and deliver his milk. He returned some two hours later, got stiffly from his seat, called a cheery "*au'voir*" to Jacques, and then limped slowly down the street.

One morning, the president of the Provincale Milk Company came to inspect the early morning deliveries. Jacques pointed Pierre out to him and said, "Watch how he talks to that horse. See how the horse listens and how he turns his head toward Pierre? See the look in that horse's eyes? You know, I think those two share a secret. I have often noticed it. It is as though they both sometimes chuckle at us as they go off on their route. Pierre is a good man, Monsieur President, but he gets old. Would it be too bold of me to suggest that he be retired and perhaps given a small pension?" he added.

"But of course," the president laughed. "I know his record. He has been on this route now for thirty years, and never once has there been a complaint. Tell him it is time he rested. His salary will go on just the same."

But Pierre refused to retire. He was panic-stricken at the thought of not driving Joseph every day. "We are two old men," he said to Jacques. "Let us wear out together. When Joseph is ready to retire, then I, too, will quit."

Jacques, who was a kind man, understood. There was something about Pierre and Joseph that made a man smile tenderly. It was as though each drew some hidden strength from the other. When Pierre was sitting in his seat, and when Joseph was hitched to the wagon, neither seemed old. But when they finished their work, then Pierre would limp down the street slowly, seeming very old indeed, and the horse's head would droop and he would walk very wearily to his stall.

Then one morning Jacques had dreadful news for Pierre when he arrived. It was a cold morning and still pitch dark.

"Pierre, your horse Joseph did not wake this morning," Jacques said. "He was very old. He was twenty-five, and that is like seventy-five for a man."

"Yes," Pierre said, slowly. "Yes. I am seventy-five. And I cannot see Joseph again."

"Of course you can," Jacques soothed. "He is over in his stall, looking very peaceful."

Pierre took one step forward, then turned. "No . . . no . . . you don't understand, Jacques."

Jacques clapped him on the shoulder. "We'll find another horse just as good as Joseph. Why, in a month you'll teach him to know your route as well as Joseph did. We'll . . ."

The look in Pierre's eyes stopped him. For years Pierre had worn a heavy cap, the peak of which came low over his eyes, keeping the bitter morning wind out of them. Now Jacques looked into Pierre's eyes and he saw something that startled him. He saw a dead, lifeless look in them. The eyes were mirroring the grief that was in Pierre's heart and his soul. It was as though his heart and soul had died.

"Take today off, Pierre," Jacques said, but already Pierre was hobbling down the street. Had one been near, one would have seen tears streaming down his cheeks and have heard half-smothered sobs. Pierre walked to the corner and stepped into the street. There was a warning yell from the driver of a huge truck that was coming fast, and there was a scream of brakes, but Pierre apparently heard neither.

Five minutes later an ambulance driver said, "He's dead. Was killed instantly."

Jacques and several of the milk wagon drivers had arrived, and they looked down at the still figure.

"I couldn't help it," the driver of the truck protested. "He walked right into my truck. He never saw it, I guess. Why, he walked into it as though he were blind."

The ambulance doctor bent down. "Blind? Of course, the man was blind. This man has been blind for five years." He turned to Jacques. "You say he worked for you? Didn't you know he was blind?"

"No . . . no . . ." Jacques said softly. "None of us knew. Only one knew, a friend of his named Joseph. . . . It was a secret, I think, just between those two."

AUTHOR

Quentin Reynolds had a very interesting career. He started out as a sports writer on a newspaper. Then he was sent to Europe as a reporter for a news service. During World War II, he served as a news correspondent on battle fronts and also helped make two wartime movies in France and England. After the war, he wrote books and articles for adults and children until his death in 1965. He also appeared on television many times.

Among the topics he chose to write about in books for children are the Wright Brothers, the F.B.I., and Custer's Last Stand. Even though he wrote "A Secret for Two" in 1936 when milk was still delivered in horse-drawn wagons, he has instilled a special feeling for Pierre Dupin and his horse Joseph that is timeless.

the GRASSHOPPER

by David McCord

Down
a
deep
well
a
grasshopper
fell.

By kicking about
He thought to get out.
  He might have known better,
  For that got him wetter.
To kick round and round
Is the way to get drowned,
  And drowning is what
  I should tell you he got.

But
the
well
had
a
rope
that
dangled
some
hope.

And sure as molasses
On one of his passes
   He found the rope handy
   And up he went, *and he*

it
up
and
it
up
and
it
up
and
it
up
went

And hopped away proper
As any grasshopper.

from

Jennifer, Hecate, Macbeth, William McKinley, and Me, Elizabeth

by Elaine Konigsburg

Witches and Onion Sandwiches

Jennifer said she was a witch disguised as a perfectly normal fifth grader. Perhaps she was, as she certainly called Elizabeth by her right name the first time they met, and she knew exactly how many chocolate-chip cookies Elizabeth had in her bag. She knew, too, that Elizabeth had just moved to town and was an only child. Being shy and lonely, Elizabeth jumped at the chance to be Jennifer's apprentice and to learn witchcraft. Of course, as an apprentice, she had to eat special foods. One week, for example, she had to eat one raw onion each day. Another special thing about witchcraft is that it is a very private affair, so the girls had to pretend they hardly knew each other. But it helped Elizabeth to know that Jennifer felt the same way she did about mushy school plays and gushy drama teachers and about that mean Cynthia whom all the adults thought was so perfect.

The minute we got back from Thanksgiving weekend, the whole school started getting ready for Christmas and the Christmas play —especially our grade. This year the fifth grade was to put on the play. The play is always presented twice, once for the whole school and once for the Parent and Teachers Association meeting at night. There are three fifth grade classes in William McKinley Elementary School, that's my school. Three fifth grades add up to about sixty kids. All the other classes of William McKinley Elementary School were to sing carols and recite poems.

That first Monday afternoon after Thanksgiving all the fifth graders met in the auditorium. Each classroom teacher had read the play in the morning. Mrs. Stuyvestant would direct the play, Mrs. Stuyvestant would choose the cast for the play, Mrs. Stuyvestant had written the play. The play was long. It had to be long so that all sixty kids could get a chance to act. Our school was democratic about Christmas. Here's the play:

101

There is a king who lives once upon a time (of course). He has a beautiful daughter (of course). He loves his beautiful daughter very much (of course). She is very unhappy. No one knows why she is very unhappy. The king wants to make her happy, so he asks her what can he give her for Christmas. She doesn't know (of course). The king goes to Santa's workshop, and he asks Santa what can he give his beautiful, unhappy daughter for Christmas. Santa's workshop is full of merry elves who all love the princess like crazy. They are all hammering

and sawing and carrying on. Santa holds up all these dolls and things, but the king doesn't think they will make the princess smile.

He shakes his head and walks away. Then the king goes to the queen's chamber, and he asks the queen what can he give their beautiful, unhappy daughter for Christmas. The queen's chamber is full of beautiful ladies-in-waiting who all love the princess like crazy. They are all singing and

dancing and carrying on. The queen holds up all these clothes and things, but the king doesn't think they will make the princess smile. He shakes his head and walks away. Then the king goes to the kitchen, and he asks the chef what can he give his beautiful, unhappy daughter for Christmas. The kitchen is full of cook's helpers who all love the princess like crazy. They are all stirring big pots and being jolly and carrying on. The chef holds up all these cakes and cookies and things, but the king doesn't think they will make the princess smile.

He shakes his head and walks away. He walks to his throne room. He sits down to think. He thinks and thinks. He thinks he has a real problem. Soon an old scrubwoman comes in. She looks so happy scrubbing that the king thinks she has an answer to unhappiness. He asks her what can he give his beautiful, unhappy daughter for Christmas. She tells

him that he should give the beautiful, unhappy princess a puppy because to be happy you have to love and take care of someone as well as be loved and be taken care of. She tells him that that is one of the lessons of Christmas. The king thinks this is a great idea. He gets his beautiful, unhappy princess a puppy (of course). She smiles happily (of course), and the play is over (at last).

Guess who was the beautiful princess? Cynthia (of course). Guess who was the little puppy? The smallest kid in the class—me (of course). Jennifer was a lady-in-waiting. I couldn't tell whether she enjoyed being a lady or not. She kept her eyes up the whole time Mrs. Stuyvestant was choosing the cast. No one knew that Jennifer and I had made a pact sealed in blood. No one knew that we were witch and apprentice or that we even knew each other. Witchcraft is a private affair—very private. It's secret.

Remember that my apprentice food that week was one raw onion per day. It was no problem because I love onion sandwiches. I loved onion sandwiches even before I was a witch's apprentice . . . when I was an ordinary, fussy eater. Here is my recipe for onion sandwiches: toast the bread, butter it, slice the onions, salt them, place them on the buttered slice of toast and cover with an unbuttered slice, cut off the crusts (of course), and eat. Delicious. On Sunday I had announced to my mother that I would be having an onion sandwich for lunch every day the next week.

"*Every day?*" my mother asked.

"Yes, *every* day," I answered.

"Hot dogs last week, onions this week. There must be some special reason," she said.

"There is," I said. My voice

trailed because I was stalling for time to think of a reason.

"Tell me," my mother said. I could tell her patience was small because her voice was very slow and very patient. My father was home. That was the way she talked when she was angry if my father was home.

I thought fast. "I am conducting an experiment. I think I can keep from catching a cold for a whole year if I eat one onion a day for a whole week before winter officially begins."

"Well," my mother said, "you'll surely keep from catching cold for the week, if not for the whole year. No one will be able to get close enough to give you any germs." Her voice was still slow and low.

"Please, may I try it?" I asked.

"Thank goodness you don't know about asafetida," she said.

"What's asafetida?" I asked.

"I'll never tell," she answered.

I believe that if you like onions, you should love onions. Nice people love onions. If you love onions, you should find the odor of onions on someone's breath very pleasant.

Our first full rehearsal for the Christmas play was on Friday

afternoon. It was a long rehearsal. All the teachers except Mrs. Stuyvestant took coffee breaks. Everyone had to be prompted. Everyone stood in the wrong places. Mrs. Stuyvestant would bounce up on the stage and move the people around. She made chalk marks on the stage where they were to stand. By the end of the first rehearsal, the floor looked like our classroom blackboard just after Miss Hazen explained long division by the New Math. Mrs. Stuyvestant was the tallest woman I have ever seen. Everyone called her Mrs. Sky-high-vestant.

My part was toward the end of the play. The king brings me (the puppy) to Cynthia (the princess). I didn't have any lines to memorize. My role meant putting on an old doggie costume and crawling around on all fours and making bow-wow sounds. When the king gives me (the puppy) to Cynthia (the princess), Mrs. Stuyvestant said that I was to stand up on my hind legs and put my hands (paws) on Cynthia's lap, look up at her face, stick out my tongue, and pant. "Pant with excitement," Mrs. Stuyvestant said. "Frolic around," Mrs. Stuyvestant said. I was afraid that Mrs.

Stuyvestant would ask me to wag my tail. Cynthia (the princess) was to snuggle her head up to mine and smile. Then everyone from Santa's workshop, from the Queen's chamber, and from the royal kitchen was to come back onstage and sing and dance and carry on.

Even though this was not a dress rehearsal for anyone else, I had to be in costume to get used to walking on all fours. Mrs. Stuyvestant said that, too. The puppy costume was made of some fuzzy black orlon stuff that was thick, heavy, and hot. Inside, it smelled like a small glue factory. We rehearsed the elves and the ladies-in-waiting and the cooks. Long before I had to walk onstage, I was so hot inside the costume

that I was sure I was going to commit spontaneous combustion. But I had heard that the show must go on. Mrs. Stuyvestant said that. The only thing I did, the only thing I could do, was to unzip the head part of my costume and fling it back like a hood. I got some relief. Since this was only a rehearsal and no one else was in costume, I figured that it didn't make any difference.

Cynthia had been onstage almost the whole rehearsal. The king keeps visiting her during the play to see if she is smiling yet. She smiled the whole time she was onstage. She was supposed to be unhappy, but she was grinning. She wasn't laughing, just grinning like the Mona Lisa. Mrs. Stuyvestant would say, "Be unhappy." Cynthia would frown, but soon the grin would creep back over her face. She was grinning when the king brought me in.

The king announced, "Princess, it is Christmas now, and it was Christmas then . . . when you last smiled. Here is our gift. We give you this puppy with our love for you to love." Then the king took me (the puppy) up to the princess. I put my hands (paws) on her lap.

I stuck out my tongue. I panted. Cynthia, who had been grinning when she was not supposed to, was now supposed to smile very large. Large enough for the audience in the back rows to see, Mrs. Stuyvestant said. Cynthia took a deep breath and began to snuggle her head up to mine. Instead of sighing and smiling, she stopped the sigh and the smile and puffed out her cheeks like the old North Wind and clamped her hands over her nose and mouth and ran from the stage. Mrs. Stuyvestant ran after her. I don't know what they discussed offstage, but Mrs. Stuyvestant came back to me and sniffed me and asked me to kindly take the puppy costume home and have my mother kindly launder it, and she asked me to kindly not eat raw onions before rehearsal. Since this was Friday, the end of my onion week, I kindly agreed.

Jennifer was offstage. As I walked away, I saw a Mona Lisa smile on *her* face. She winked. No one saw that but me.

We had rehearsals every gym period, every music period, and every art period. They didn't call it "rehearsal" during art period because we stayed in the art room and painted the sets and made cardboard crowns (covered with aluminum foil, glued, and sprinkled with glitter dust). For the kitchen scene, we made a stove out of big cardboard cartons that we painted black. It looked nice from the back rows where the audience sat. It looked nicest from the very last row. Mrs. Stuyvestant asked each of us to bring in a cookie sheet or a pan or a kettle or a stirring spoon. We were to be sure to put our names on what we brought in so that we could get it back when the play was over. I brought in two cupcake pans and put one letter of my name on the inside of each

cupcake hole. It looked like this:

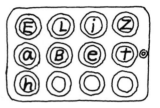

I hoped that the whole audience, even the very last row, would see. Mrs. Stuyvestant asked me to kindly wash it off and kindly Scotch tape my name on the bottom—very small. She said, "In the theater one does not get top billing just because one can write one's name very large. One gets top billing because one has earned stardom." One always knew when Mrs. Stuyvestant was scolding because she always called you *one* instead of your name.

Cynthia brought in her mother's electric mixer. She knew that she was the only kid in the whole U.S. of A. whose mother would let her carry the family's electric mixer to school. Mrs. Stuyvestant told her that it was very generous of her mother to lend it, and it was very generous of her to have carried it all the way from home. (I knew that Cynthia's mother had driven her to school that day, but

Cynthia didn't mention it. Another example of the way Cynthia was—two-faced.) But Mrs. Stuyvestant didn't consider the mixer picturesque enough. In other words, in the days when there were kings and princesses, there just weren't any electric mixers. Cynthia didn't even have sense enough to be insulted. She sighed sadly and told Mrs. Stuyvestant that she would manage to get the mixer home, somehow, even though it was heavy.

Jennifer caused a small sensation. She brought in a huge, black, three-legged pot. It would hold about twenty quarts of water. A little kid could swim in it almost. Jennifer didn't have to write her name on that pot to identify it. No one else had ever seen anything like it except in a museum. I happened to know that it was the pot we were going to cook our flying ointment in.

Mrs. Stuyvestant was overjoyed. She put her hands on her waist (with her elbows pointing out and

her toes pointing out, too, she looked like a long, tall, five-pointed star) and exclaimed, "Oh, Jenny, how *won*-derful! It's *too* cute! A *three*-legged kettle!"

If you ever want to make Jennifer angry, call her what Mrs. Stuyvestant did. Call her Jenny instead of Jennifer, her rightful name.

Jennifer looked up, way up at Mrs. Sky-high-vestant, and said, "That makes one, two, three, doesn't it?"

Mrs. Stuyvestant looked down, way down at Jennifer, and said, "What do you mean, Jennifer?"

Jennifer answered, "*Won*-derful, *too* cute, *three*-legged. That's one, two, three." Jennifer didn't smile.

Mrs. Stuyvestant said, "I had no idea you were so clever." She smiled. I could tell that Jennifer wished that Mrs. Stuyvestant had not smiled. She wanted her to notice how angry she was at being called Jenny instead of Jennifer.

Everyone was a little surprised at how clever Jennifer was. She almost never spoke in class or during rehearsals. She never spoke to me; she would just slip me a note every now and then. I was worried that everyone would find out how clever Jennifer was. It feels wonderful to have a secret. Sometimes I thought I wanted our secret to be discovered accidentally, but I didn't want to share Jennifer with the entire fifth grade. It was lucky the kids of William McKinley Elementary School weren't ready to make the discovery. They were no longer paying any attention. Mrs. Stuyvestant walked all around the pot, pleased and smiling. She smiled over at Jennifer and asked, "By the way, Jenny, how did you get it here?" She was still feeling cozy toward Jennifer.

Jennifer pretended that she didn't hear the question. She was making herself very busy shaking a can of spray paint, and that little ball inside the can was rattling away. Mrs. Stuyvestant said, "Jenny. Oh, Jenny!" No answer from you-know-who. "Jenny. Oh, Jenny!" No answer from you-know-who again. Finally Mrs. Stuyvestant started walking toward Jennifer and said, "Jenny. Oh, Jennifer!" The minute she said *Jennifer*, you-know-who looked up.

"Yes?" asked Jennifer.

"I was wondering," Mrs. Stuyvestant said, "how you got that heavy kettle to school."

"Brought it in my wagon," answered Jennifer.

"Then your wagon is parked at school?" asked Mrs. Stuyvestant.

"Yes," answered Jennifer.

"Do you think that you can lend it to Cynthia to help her get her mixer home?"

Jennifer asked, "You want me to put the mixer in my wagon?"

Mrs. Stuyvestant said, almost sarcastically, "That's what I had in mind."

Jennifer replied, "I'll be happy to."

Mrs. Stuyvestant said, "Thank you." She smiled pleasantly at Jennifer and began to turn around.

Before she was completely turned around, Jennifer said, "Do you think I should tie my wagon to the bumper?"

Mrs. Stuyvestant spun around. "The bumper? Bumper? The bumper of what?"

Jennifer answered, "The bumper of their car."

Mrs. Stuyvestant was too puzzled to get angry. She merely asked, "Why do that?"

Jennifer answered, "Because Cynthia brought the mixer here in their car, so I guessed that that was the way she would get it home, too." Somehow, Jennifer managed to look innocent.

Mrs. Stuyvestant looked at Jennifer. Mrs. Stuyvestant looked at Cynthia. Of course, Jennifer's conversation had been just one shade on the safe side of fresh. But Cynthia's conversation had been just one shade on the safe side of lying. Mrs. Stuyvestant looked from Jennifer to Cynthia and then back again. She threw her arms in the air, turned around,

and walked out of the room. Cynthia glared at Jennifer. Jennifer kept shaking the spray paint and kept looking up at the ceiling.

"Oh, Jennifer," I thought to myself, "how strong you are. Nerves of steel and the heart of a witch!"

No one noticed when Jennifer passed me a note later in the period. I was painting hinges on one of the oven doors. The note had only one word on it. It said:

I knew what Jennifer meant, and I put my head inside the oven and laughed and laughed.

ABOUT THE AUTHOR

The first two books Elaine Konigsburg wrote were published in 1967. One of them, *From the Mixed-up Files of Mrs. Basil E. Frankweiler*, won the Newbery Medal as the best children's book of that year. Chosen as a runner-up for the Medal was her other book, *Jennifer, Hecate, Macbeth, William McKinley, and Me, Elizabeth,* from which the story you have just read was taken. Such an unusual honor would make a veteran author proud, and yet Mrs. Konigsburg had been a writer for only about two years. But Mrs. Konigsburg is an unusual person. Before finishing her college and graduate-school studies as a chemist, she was at different times a bookkeeper, manager of a laundry, playground instructor, waitress, library worker, and laboratory researcher. She also taught science in Florida after her marriage to Dr. David Konigsburg. Later she studied painting and became an artist.

Then, for several years, two sons and a daughter kept her busy at home. Not until all three children were old enough to go to school did she have time for writing. The youngsters gave her helpful suggestions when she read to them what she had written each day, and they were the models she used in illustrating her stories. Little League baseball is the subject of *About the B'Nai Bagels*, which she wrote when her family was excited about baseball.

Other books by Mrs. Konigsburg include *George, Altogether One at a Time, A Proud Taste for Scarlet and Miniver*, and *The Dragon in the Ghetto Caper*. She won the Lewis Carroll Shelf Award in 1968 and the William Allen White Children's Book Award in 1970, both of which are awarded to outstanding authors of books for children.

BOOKS TO ENJOY

GRANDMA DIDN'T WAVE BACK *by Rose Blue*

Since Debbie's mother is busy with her law practice and Grandma seems to need constant care, a nursing home for Grandma is the answer. This understanding story reveals for young people the special problems of the old.

THE ART OF THE NORTHWEST COAST INDIANS
by Shirley Glubok

Many fine photographs show the arts and crafts of the Indian groups that live along the Pacific Coast of the United States and Canada — decorated totems, canoes, masks, and other items.

ALVIN'S SWAP SHOP *by Clifford B. Hicks*

Here is another hilarious adventure in the popular series about Alvin Fernald, the "Magnificent Brain."

STAND IN THE WIND *by Jean Little*

A Canadian girl is longing to go to summer camp, but she has to give it up and spend a whole endless week alone with her sister and two American girls they do not even know.

OUTSIDE *by André Norton*

In this exciting science-fiction story set in the far future, a girl in a sealed-off city tries to find out what is outside.

LITTLE DOGS OF THE PRAIRIE *by Jack Denton Scott*

Generously illustrated with photographs, this book describes in great detail the life of prairie dogs and the many dangers they face.

SOMEBODY ELSE'S CHILD *by Roberta Silman*

Peter, who is adopted, is deeply hurt when his best friend, the school bus driver, says he does not believe in adoption.

Magnets

Magnets

STORIES

PLAY

ARTICLES

THE TUNNEL

by Virginia Hamilton

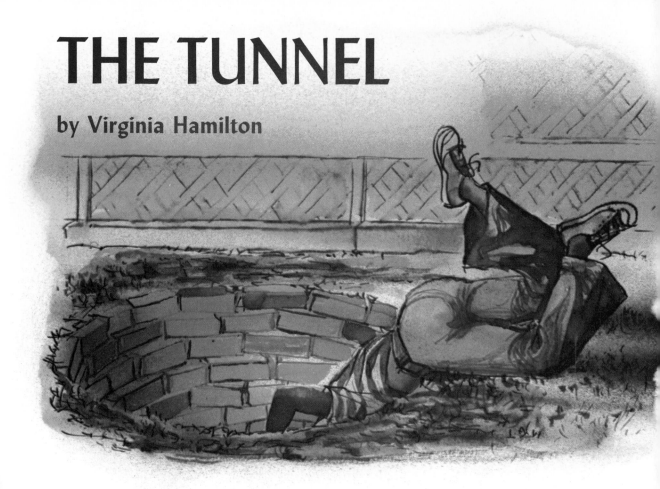

Thomas Small, with his parents and young twin brothers, has just moved from North Carolina to a college town in Ohio where his father will be teaching history. Mr. Small has rented a huge, old mansion that was once a station on the Underground Railroad. This strange house, said to be haunted, stands high and alone on a rock ledge from which flow mineral springs.

Thomas can't wait to explore the house, for the floor plan shows exciting hidden rooms and secret passages. While examining the carvings on the front door, he finds a tiny button with a stream of cold air coming from around it. He pushes the button. At once the front steps move aside, revealing a deep hole. Lying flat on his stomach, Thomas leans over to look into the hole, loses his grip, and falls head first into darkness.

118

There was gray light filtering down from the opening of the steps to where Thomas lay, and he could see that he was at the edge of a steep stairway cut out of rock. The stairs were wet; he could hear water dripping down on them from somewhere.

"Move slowly. Think fast," Thomas whispered. "Keep in mind what's behind and look closely at what's in front."

Thomas always carried a pencil-thin flashlight, which he sometimes used for reading in the car. He sat up suddenly and pulled out the flashlight. It wasn't broken from the fall, and he flicked it on. He sat in a kind of circle enclosed by brick walls. In some places, the brick had crumbled into powder, which was slowly filling up the circle of sod.

"That will take a long time," thought Thomas. He looked up at the underside of the veranda steps.

Thomas got to his feet and made his way down the rock stairway into darkness. At the foot of the stairs was a path with walls of dirt and rock on either side of it. The walls were so close, Thomas could touch them by extending his arms a few inches. Above his head was a low ceiling carved out of rock. Such cramped space made him uneasy. The foundation of the house had to be somewhere above the natural rock. The idea of the whole three-story house pressing down on him caused him to stop a moment on the path. Since he had fallen, he hadn't had time to be afraid. He wasn't now, but he did begin to worry a little about where the path led. He thought of ghosts, and yet he did not seriously believe in them. "No," he told himself, "not with the flashlight. Not when I can turn back . . . when I can run.

"And besides," he thought, "I'm strong. I can take care of myself."

Thomas continued along the path, flickering his tiny beam of light this way and that. Pools of water stood in some places. He felt a coldness, like the stream of air that came from around the button on the oak doorframe. His shoes were soon

soaked. His socks grew cold and wet, and he thought about taking them off. He could hear water running a long way off. He stopped again to listen, but he couldn't tell from what direction the sound came.

"It's just one of the springs," he said. His voice bounced off the walls strangely.

Better not speak. There could be tunnels leading off this one. You can't tell what might hear you in a place like this.

Thomas was scaring himself. He decided not to think again about other tunnels or ghosts. He did think for the first time of how he would get out of this tunnel. He had fallen five feet, and he wasn't sure he would be able to climb back up the crumbling brick walls. Still, the path he walked had to lead somewhere. There had to be another way out.

Thomas felt his feet begin to climb; the path was slanting up. He walked slowly on the slippery rock; then suddenly the path was very wide. The walls were four feet away on either side, and there were long stone slabs against each wall.

Thomas sat down on one of the slabs. It was wet, but he didn't even notice.

"Why these slabs?" he asked himself. "For the slaves, hiding and running?"

He opened and closed a moist hand around the flashlight. The light beam could not keep back the dark. Thomas had a lonely feeling, the kind of feeling running slaves must have had.

And they dared not use light, he thought. How long did they have to hide down here? How could they stand it?

Thomas got up and went on. He placed one foot carefully in front of the other on the path, which had narrowed again. He heard the faint sound of movement somewhere. Maybe it was a voice he heard; he couldn't be sure. He swirled the light around over the damp walls, and fumbled it. The flashlight slid out of his hand. For a long moment, he caught and held it between his knees before finally dropping it. He bent quickly to pick it up, but he stepped down on it. Then he accidentally kicked it with his heel, and it went rattling somewhere over the path. It hit the wall, but it had gone out before then. Now all was very dark.

"It's not far," Thomas said. "All I have to do is feel around."

He felt around with his hands over smooth, moist rock; his hands grew cold. He felt water, and it was icy, slimy. His hands trembled; they ached, feeling in the dark, but he could not find the flashlight.

"I couldn't have kicked it far, because I wasn't moving." His voice bounced in a whisper off the walls. He tried crawling backward, hoping to hit the flashlight with his heels.

"It's got to be here. . . . Papa?" Thomas stood, turning toward the way he had come, the way he had been crawling backward. He didn't at all like walking in the pitch blackness of the tunnel.

"I'll go on back," he said. "I'll just walk back as quick as I can. There'll be light coming from the veranda steps. I'll climb up that wall, and then I'll be out of this. I'll get Papa and we'll do it together."

He went quickly now, with his hands extended to keep himself from hitting the close walls. But then something happened that caused him to stop in his tracks. He stood still, with his whole body tense and alert, the way he could be when he sensed a storm before there was any sign of it in the air or sky.

Thomas had the queerest notion that he was not alone. In front of him, between him and the steps of the veranda, something waited.

"Papa?" he said. He heard something.

The sound went, "Ahhh, ahhh, ahhh." It was not moaning, nor crying. It wasn't laughter, but something forlorn and lost and old.

Thomas backed away. "No," he said. "Oh please!"

"Ahhh, ahhh," something said. It was closer to him now. Thomas could hear no footsteps on the path. He could see nothing in the darkness.

He opened his mouth to yell, but his voice wouldn't come. Fear rose in him; he was cold, freezing, as though he had rolled in snow.

"Papa!" he managed to say. His voice was a whisper. "Papa, come get me. . . . Papa!"

"Ahhh." Whatever it was, was quite close now. Thomas still backed away from it; then he turned around, away from the direction of the veranda. He started running up the path, with his arms outstretched in front of him. He ran and ran, his eyes wide in the darkness. At any moment, the thing would grab him and smother his face. At any time, it would paralyze him with cold. It would take him away. It would tie him in one of the tunnels, and no one would ever find him.

"Don't let it touch me! Don't let it catch me!"

Thomas ran smack into a wall. His arms and hands hit first, then his head and chest. The impact jarred him from head to foot. He thought his wrists were broken, but ever so slowly, painful feeling flowed back into his hands. The ache moved dully up to the sockets of his shoulders. He opened and closed his hands. They hurt so much that his eyes began to tear, but he didn't seem to have broken anything.

Thomas felt frantically along the wall. The wall was wood. He knew the feel of it right away. It was heavy wood, perhaps oak. Thomas pounded on it, hurting himself more, causing his head to spin. He kept on because he knew he was about to be taken from behind by something ghostly and cold.

"Help me! It's going to get me!" he called. "Help me!"

Thomas heard a high, clear scream on the other side of the wall. Next came the sound of feet scurrying, and then the wall slid silently up.

"Thomas Small!" his mother said. "What in heaven's name do you think you are doing inside that wall!"

"I see you've found yourself a secret passage," said Mr. Small. "I hadn't thought you'd find that button by the front door so soon."

Mr. Small, with Billy and Buster, was seated at the kitchen table. They were finishing supper. Mr. Small smiled at Thomas, while the twins stared at him with solemn eyes.

Mrs. Small stood directly in front of Thomas, and then she stepped aside so that he could take a few steps into the kitchen. Thomas glanced behind him at the tunnel, a gaping space carved out of the comfortable kitchen. He saw nothing at all on the path.

He sat down beside his father. There was the good smell of food hanging in the air. The twins seemed full and content.

"You knew about that tunnel, Papa?" Thomas said. He felt discouraged, as though he'd been tricked.

"If anyone came unexpectedly to the front door," said Mr. Small, "the slaves could hide in the tunnel until whoever it was had gone. Or, if and when the callers began a search, the slaves could escape through the kitchen or by way of the veranda steps."

"It's not any fun," Thomas thought. "Not if he already knows about it."

"Thomas, you frightened me!" Mrs. Small said. She had recovered enough to take her eyes from the tunnel and sit down beside Thomas at the table.

"Goodness, yelling like that all of a sudden," she said, "I didn't know what it was." She jumped up, remembering Thomas hadn't eaten, and quickly fixed his plate. Then she seated herself as before.

"Yes, why were you calling for help, Thomas?" asked Mr. Small. "You really made your mama scream."

Thomas bent down to take off his shoes and socks. A pool of water stood dark and brackish on the linoleum. "There was something there," he said. "There was something on that path. It was coming after me as sure as I'm sitting here."

"You shouldn't make up stories like that," his mother said, "not even as a joke."

"There was something there." His voice quivered slightly, and the sound of that was enough to tell Mr. Small that Thomas wasn't joking.

"Then what was it?" asked Mr. Small. He watched Thomas closely.

"I don't know," Thomas said. "I didn't see anything."

His father smiled. "It was probably no more than your fear of the dark and strange surroundings getting the best of you."

"I heard something, though," Thomas said. "It went 'ahhh, ahhh' at me, and it came closer and closer."

Mrs. Small sucked in her breath. She looked all around the kitchen, at the gaping hole and quickly away from it. The room was large, with a single lamp of varicolored glass hanging from the ceiling on a heavy, black chain. Her shadow, along with Thomas's, loomed long and thin on a far wall.

"Thomas, don't make up things!" his father said sternly.

"I'm not, Papa!" There was a lump in Thomas's throat. He gripped the table and swallowed a few times. He had to find just the right words if ever his father was to believe him.

His hands rose in the air. They began to shape the air, to carve it, as though it were a pretty piece of pine. "It was like no other voice," he began. "It wasn't a high voice or a low voice, or even a person's voice. It didn't have anything bad in it or anything. I was just in its way, that's all. It had to get by me, and it would have done anything to get around me along that path."

"I forbid you to go into that tunnel again!" whispered Mrs.

Small. She was afraid now, and even Mr. Small stared at Thomas.

Mr. Small seemed to be thinking beyond what Thomas had told them. "You say you saw nothing?" he asked.

"I thought I heard somebody moving around," Thomas said, "but that could have been you all in here."

They all fell silent for a moment. Then Mr. Small asked, "And you're sure you heard nothing more than that sighing?"

"That's all," Thomas said. "It just kept coming at me, getting closer."

Mr. Small got up and stood at the tunnel opening. He went into the long hall after a few seconds and came back with a flashlight. "I'll go with you," Thomas said.

"I'd rather you stayed here. I'll only be a minute," said his father.

Mr. Small was gone less than a minute. Thomas and his mother waited, staring into the tunnel opening, flooded with the light from the kitchen. A few feet beyond the opening, the kitchen light ended in a wall of blackness. They could see the light from Mr. Small's flashlight darting here and there along the ceiling of the tunnel until the path descended.

Mr. Small returned by way of the veranda steps. His white shirt was soiled from scaling the brick wall. As he came into the kitchen, muddying the floor as Thomas had, he was thoughtful, but not at all afraid.

He walked over to a high cabinet on the opposite wall from the tunnel. Beneath it, a small panel in the wall slid open at his touch. The panel had been invisible to the eye, but now revealed what seemed to be a jumble of miniature machinery. Mr. Small released a lever. The tunnel door slid silently down, and the patterned wallpaper of the kitchen showed no trace of what lay hidden behind it. Lastly, Mr. Small removed a mechanism of some kind from the panel.

"Did you see anything?" Thomas asked him. "Did you find my flashlight?"

"I didn't see anything," Mr. Small said, "and I didn't hear any sighing."

"Well, that's a relief," said Mrs. Small. "Goodness, if you'd found somebody. . . . I'm sure my nerves would just give way."

"Your flashlight must have fallen into a crack," said Mr. Small. "I couldn't find it. Oh, yes, I removed the control from the panel. Without it, a giant couldn't raise that tunnel door."

"But you said there wasn't anything in the tunnel," said Thomas.

"That's so, but I don't want you wandering around in there," his father said. "The walls and ceiling are dirt and rock. There hasn't been a cave-in that I know of in a century, yet I think it best we don't take chances. I also removed the gears that control the front steps."

Although Thomas's father told him that fear of the dark and strange surroundings was probably what got the best of him in the tunnel, Thomas isn't afraid to go on exploring the old house and trying to unlock its secrets. The book THE HOUSE OF DIES DREAR *tells of the other chilling adventures Thomas has as the Smalls discover that the house does hold real danger for them.*

AUTHOR

Virginia Hamilton was born in Yellow Springs, Ohio, a town which once was a station on the Underground Railroad. Her mother was the daughter of a fugitive slave, and her grandfather Perry was one of the thousands of slaves who fled from the South. Ms. Hamilton remembers that there was no incident in black history that her father, a Creole, did not know and tell about. She says, "I grew up with the knowledge of slavery, and the past creeps into my writing."

Ms. Hamilton believes that children need to know more about black history and traditions, and her books presenting such themes have won high praise. *Zeely, The House of Dies Drear, The Time-Ago Tales of Jahdu,* and *W. E. B. DuBois: A Biography* were all chosen as Notable Children's Books by the American Library Association. *The Planet of Junior Brown* was a Newbery Honor Book and also a candidate for the National Book Award.

Ms. Hamilton studied at Antioch College and Ohio State University. From an early age she wanted to write. She started writing short stories for adults but soon switched to children's books. "I want to be able to tell children, 'This is what I wanted to say,' so that they can reply, 'That is what I wanted to know.' Then we've communicated."

Virginia Hamilton lives in Ohio with her husband, Arnold Adoff, and their two children.

DRUMS

by Larry Kettelkamp

Many hollow materials give pleasant sounds when they are struck. A section of bamboo or the rotted trunk of a fallen tree are natural hollow objects, and some of the earliest drums were made from such materials.

A section of bamboo, open at the top and closed at the bottom by one of the joints that grow inside it, will produce a hollow sound with a definite pitch if the bottom is struck sharply on the ground. The pitch depends on the length of the tube—the shorter the section of tube, the higher the pitch.

This bamboo section, called a stamping tube, was one of the earliest drums. Today, stamping tubes are still played on some of the Pacific islands. A group of women or girls sit in a semicircle on the ground. The players hold a tube in each hand by a handle carved at the top. Many tubes of different sizes are used to produce an organlike sound.

Another early drum was made of part of a tree trunk hollowed out through a long narrow slit in its side. The ends of the trunk were solid, and the only opening was the long slit.

At first, these slit drums were quite large, but gradually they were made smaller until some could be carried around easily. Today, a small double-slit drum, called a wood block, is used in both Latin-American dance bands and in orchestras. It is struck sharply with a stick near the edge of either slit.

True drums, which have been used by people in every part of the world, are made of animal skins stretched tightly over hollow containers to strengthen their sound. Some drums are deep, some shallow; some have skins stretched over both ends of vase- or bowl-shaped containers.

The kettledrum, snare drum, and bass drum of today were first used for military music before they became an important part of the orchestra. The snare drum and bass drum are still the core of the military band, in which they sound the beat of marching feet even when no other instruments are playing.

Stamping tube

Photograph by Hillel Burger. Courtesy of Peabody Museum, Harvard University.

130

Modern pedal timpani

Kettledrums, also called timpani, are of great importance to the modern orchestra. They are made of calfskin stretched over large copper bowls. These calfskin drumheads are struck with felt- or wool-covered sticks.

Timpani can be tuned to clear and definite pitches, and they can be played softer or louder than any other instrument in the orchestra. At first, two drums were usually used, one tuned to the basic note of a piece and the other to the fifth tone of the scale in which the piece was written.

Over the years, a tuning mechanism has been developed that makes it possible to change the pitch of the timpani quickly. Hand screws and a foot pedal are used to tighten or loosen the head, or the skin that is stretched across the top of the drum.

The timpanist must have a fine sense of pitch in order to retune the drums during the course of a piece. An accurate sense of rhythm is also needed because the timpani often provide a foundation for the rest of the orchestra. A great deal of skill is required for the solo passages now written for the timpani in music for an orchestra.

Today one drum can sound five notes of a scale and the half steps in between. A drum with a head twenty-eight inches in diameter and another with a twenty-five-inch head can be used together to play a range of over one octave, which is quite remarkable for two drums.

CROSS SECTION OF TIMPANI

Tightening the hand screws lowers the hoop to which the head is fastened, stretching the head to an even starting tension.

When the foot pedal is pushed forward, connecting rods pull the head tighter, raising the pitch. When the pedal is tipped back, the head loosens, lowering the pitch.

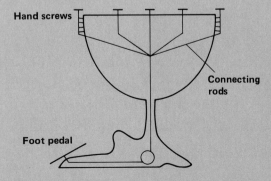

Hand screws

Connecting rods

Foot pedal

Snare drum

Bongo drums

Congo drums

In contrast to the timpani, the snare drum is double-headed and is played with two hickory sticks. The top head is called the batter head. The lower is called the snare head, because several strings of gut or wound metal, called snares, are stretched across it. When these touch the head, they vibrate against it as the upper head is struck. This gives a crisp, pitchless sound.

The drum can also be played without the snare effect. Then it sounds a more definite pitch, though it is not as clear as that of the kettledrum. The snare drum is also used as a jazz instrument. Here it is often played with wire brushes so that the accents it makes are softer.

The bass drum, which is also double-headed, is much larger than the snare drum. It is struck with a felt or lamb's-wool beater held in the hand. The sound is low and muffled, but the drum can be played quite loudly. In jazz bands, the bass drum is played with a foot pedal, leaving the hands free to play the snare drum or some other percussion instrument.

Several drums are used especially for the rhythms of Latin-American dance music. The largest is the congo drum. This drum, whose length is much greater than its width, is covered at only one end and tapers so that it is slightly smaller at the open end. It is played only with the hands. Bongo drums are smaller and not as deep. Often a player uses a pair of different sizes, the smaller one having a higher pitch. They are usually held between the knees and are struck with the hands, much like the larger congo drum.

There are other drums, large and small, around the world. Drums provide a foundation of rhythm for the music of other instruments. They might be called the heartbeat of music.

JOKES

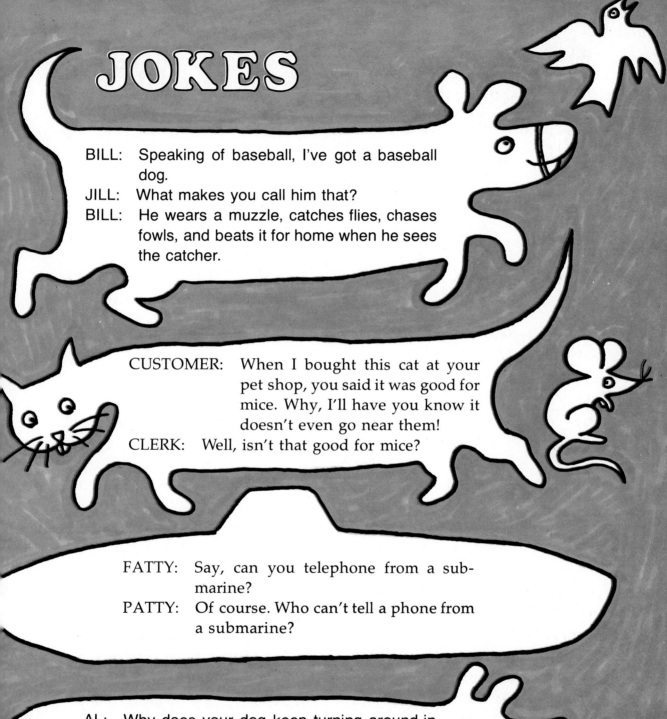

BILL: Speaking of baseball, I've got a baseball dog.

JILL: What makes you call him that?

BILL: He wears a muzzle, catches flies, chases fowls, and beats it for home when he sees the catcher.

CUSTOMER: When I bought this cat at your pet shop, you said it was good for mice. Why, I'll have you know it doesn't even go near them!

CLERK: Well, isn't that good for mice?

FATTY: Say, can you telephone from a submarine?

PATTY: Of course. Who can't tell a phone from a submarine?

AL: Why does your dog keep turning around in circles?

SAL: He's a watchdog and he's winding himself up.

Lucy's father, Will Snow, was very much against the idea of giving women the right to vote, and he disliked the women called suffragists who in 1904 were working for that cause. Lucy and her mother, however, were interested in the idea, and they secretly attended a suffragist rally. Much to their surprise, the speaker of the evening turned out to be Mr. Snow's sister, Letitia, who was visiting them. But Aunt Letitia never finished her speech, for men and boys armed with rotten eggs drove her from the platform. Mr. Snow was angry when he learned that his sister was a suffragist. He was even angrier when Lucy stood up for her and for women's rights. In fact, he punished Lucy for arguing with him about it.

Now Lucy, her mother, and Lucy's friend Tom are attending a rally for President Theodore Roosevelt. The state senator will be the speaker, and Lucy's young brother, Sam, is going to be introduced to him as a reward for having fought some of the anti-Roosevelt boys.

Lucy Speaks Out

by Elizabeth Hall

"I think we can work our way a little closer," said Tom. He pulled Mother and Lucy along behind him as he threaded his way through the crowd. The space around the bandstand was packed, but Tom managed to dart between shoulders and hips.

"How's this?" he asked.

They stood on a slight rise in the ground, ten feet from the front. Lucy could see over the heads to the bandstand, where empty chairs awaited the Senator and his party.

"That's much better, Tom," said Mother. "It would be too bad if all I saw of the Senator was his tall silk hat."

Only a week ago, Lucy had

stood here beside Mother and heard the words that had made her both miserable and proud— words that had driven her into a quarrel with Father. Tonight, as she stood between Tom and Mother, she smiled bitterly as she listened to the excited men and women and children. When Aunt Letitia had spoken, they came armed with jeers and rotten eggs. For Senator Throckmorton the whole town turned out, from the Mayor to the fire brigade. Tonight the crowd honored democracy—last week they had denied it.

As the Senator mounted the steps, Lucy clapped politely; then her hands froze at the sight that met her eyes. There, his foot on the top step, just three paces behind the Senator, was the familiar cap, the carrot curls, and the snub nose of her brother. Somehow Sam had become a member of the official party.

"Say, Lucy," said Tom, "isn't that . . ."

"It most certainly is," said Lucy. "The little ruffian's black eye has put him on the platform."

"That's not fair, Lucy," said Mother. She leaned across Tom to speak, and darkness could not hide the concern in her voice. "He worked hard all day for President Roosevelt."

"The Senator's really a great guy," said Tom. "He told Father that he would be delighted to meet Sam." He laughed out loud. "Said the Party needed men who were willing to do battle."

Lucy edged away. For a moment Tom was just another male. She was glad they had not been able to find Father. His pride in Sam would have been too much to bear.

The last note of the trombones wailed through the park. Judge Clark began to speak, comparing the Senator with Abraham Lincoln and other great people of our fair land. As his words poured out, his voice grew louder. "And we can be sure," he shouted, "that tonight's speech will see none of the disturbance that marked last week's disgraceful display in this very same park."

"It's plain to see how the Judge feels about you suffragists," said Tom, "but some of us still love you."

It was an effort for Lucy to bite back the words that suddenly rose to her lips. It would be easy to speak sharply, and it would make her feel better. But even as her mouth formed the words, she realized that she had no business being angry with Tom.

The Senator's mellow tones rolled across the park. He had earned his reputation as an orator fairly, and—against her will—Lucy found herself nodding in agreement. He made it seem as if the United States would reach new heights of glory under a second term with Theodore Roosevelt, that every family would have an automobile, a telephone, and electricity, that everlasting peace would spread across the world. And he made it plain that if Parker and Davis were elected, the Republic would perish. Every sentence was interrupted by applause, and once Lucy discovered herself clapping her hands.

But in the blink of an eye, it all changed. The Senator began to speak of the women's crusade. At the word *suffragette*, Lucy stiffened. The word was *suffragist*; only people like Father, who felt that votes by women were unnatural or silly, allowed the other term to cross their lips. Surely Senator Throckmorton would rise above prejudice and silly arguments.

The Senator's next words could have been written by Father. "The ladies will always vote just as their husbands do. What woman would support Parker once her husband points out the great benefits of Theodore Roosevelt's leadership? To give the ladies the vote would double the cost of elections. And we must keep taxes down. I tell you, my friends," he said with a chuckle, "it is only economical to restrict the vote to males." Laughter swept across the crowd, and Lucy became angered.

"That's no reason," she muttered to herself. When Tom stared at her, she realized that she had spoken out loud.

One by one, the Senator gave the usual arguments against suffrage that she had heard repeated by Father and Sam and all the males of Smithville. And one by one, Lucy found herself answering them—out loud. After each of the Senator's claims, people around her turned to Lucy, waiting for the replies that rose to her lips. But most of the crowd greeted Senator Throckmorton's statements with applause; as

Lucy's anger deepened, her voice grew louder.

"Consider the fair flower of American womanhood," urged the Senator. "Such delicate blooms have no wish to soil themselves with the vote."

"That's not true!" cried Lucy. "Have you asked us?" With each beautifully shaped syllable that poured from the Senator's mouth, her anger mounted.

"Agitation for the ballot comes," he said, "from a small group of unnatural women who

would overturn society and destroy the sanctity of the home. Politics will ruin the lovely ladies who set the standards of behavior of our community, and woman suffrage will surely lead to an undesirable society."

That was the final straw. An undesirable society indeed. "You're not only a liar," Lucy shouted; "you are an evil man!" She must show the crowd what terrible falsehoods the Senator was spreading.

Against her will, she found her feet moving. Tom grabbed her arm, but she angrily shook off his hand. Mother gasped, "Lucy, what are you doing?" but she paid no attention. She shoved and pushed her way through the crowd, squirming between the closely packed bodies.

"That's not true. That's not true. You've got to listen!" she shouted.

Not a hand was laid upon Lucy as she struggled toward the speaker. Men and women drew back, their eyes wide with astonishment. The entire crowd was motionless, as if a wizard had waved his wand across the park.

She thought of Aunt Letitia— whose words had brought a hail

of eggs—and hesitated, but only for a second. Let them do what they liked, she must make them see the truth. On she went, each step taking her closer to the stage.

From the platform the Senator's words swept across the park, but fewer people heard each sentence. Lucy's struggles were now the center of all eyes.

She reached the stage and climbed the steps. She crossed the wooden floor to the Senator's side. He stared at her as if she were a visitor from Mars. His mouth was open, yet he did not utter a sound. Sam stood up and stretched an arm toward his sister, but he was unable to walk over to her.

Lucy looked out at the crowd, and row after row of pale, up-turned faces looked back at her. She shook with righteous anger, but even as she began to speak, in a tiny corner of her mind a voice repeated in horror, "Lucy Snow, what are you doing?"

"It's a lie," she called out in a small voice, but clearly. "Every word the Senator has said about women is a lie."

By now Sam had regained the use of his feet. He rushed across the platform and grabbed her. His eyes were as wide as dinner plates as he gasped, "Sit down!"

Without pausing or looking around, she shook him off with a sweep of her arm. Thrown off balance, he staggered back and landed heavily on his bottom. He sat like a statue, watching his sister with horror.

"Women are slaves in this society," continued Lucy. "The mothers of your children are chained to the kitchen. Have you no justice? It is . . ."

The words vanished and she could not finish the sentence. Until now the crowd below her had been a blur, but as her excitement passed, faces came into

focus. And the first one she saw was Tom. His face was twisted and he was motioning desperately for her to stop.

Lucy's silence broke the spell. Up the stairs ran the chief of police. Behind him other policemen and several men from the Senator's train shoved their way to the stage. Quickly they surrounded Lucy and rushed her down the steps. They formed a wedge around her with their bodies and pushed straight through the crowd like a locomotive with its throttle open.

When they reached the edge of the crowd, the policemen slowed down. They walked over to the black van that waited across the street behind its two patient horses. One of the officers opened the rear door.

Lucy spoke her first words since the police had reached her. She swallowed hard and said, in hushed tones, "You're not going to put me in there, are you?"

"It's the usual way we transport prisoners to jail, Miss," said one policeman. His voice was gentle, but the words were a knife that cut deep.

She had been arrested like a common criminal.

The inside of the van was dark. The only light came through the small barred opening at one end, and all Lucy could see was the back of the driver's neck.

She braced herself as the van swayed around the corner.

Soon the driver reined in the horses, and the motion of the van stopped. There was a screech of metal as someone drew back the iron bolt. The door swung open, and a voice called, "Come out, Miss."

Lucy got to her feet and edged toward the opening. As she put her foot on the first step, a hand steadied her. She walked toward the police station between two officers, each with a firm grip on one of her arms. Their grasp was no tighter than Tom's had been, but their touch seemed cruel and harsh.

Lucy looked around the shabby station. An officer sat beside a glowing potbellied stove. When he saw Lucy, his eyes widened. "What's the charge?"

"Creating a public disturbance," said one of the officers. The hard words seemed to slap against the wall.

To hear her defense of truth described in the cold language of the law sent a chill down Lucy's spine. When Bill Masters had ridden his horse through the town, firing a gun into the air as fast as he could put bullets into it, Father had called it a "public disturbance." It wasn't the same at all.

The policeman sighed and walked over to the desk. He drew a large book to him and dipped a pen in the inkwell.

"Name?" he asked.

"Lucy . . . Lucy Snow, sir," she said, her voice quavering.

"Where do you live?"

"236 Elm Street."

"Oh, you're Will Snow's daughter." The pen scratched busily. "Never expected to see you in here, young lady."

As he wrote down the details of her crime, she wondered when they would thrust her into a cold, bare cell, when the judge would rap his gavel and sentence her to prison.

The policeman scratched his head and frowned. "I don't know what I'm going to do with you." he said.

There was a long silence, broken only by the pounding of her heart. Then one of the officers leaned over and whispered in the ear of the man behind the desk. They talked together quietly, and Lucy could not catch their words. She wondered what they were plotting. Would they send her directly to prison?

"Just sit there by the stove, Miss," the policeman said at last. "We'll figure out something when the chief comes back."

On legs that trembled, Lucy walked over to the chair and sat stiffly on the edge of the seat, hardly daring to breathe. Perhaps if she made no noise, the policeman would forget that she was there.

She looked straight ahead, at a board covered with "wanted" posters. The hard eyes that stared back at her no longer belonged to people who lived in a distant world. Lucy Snow was now one of them.

What would happen when she finally got out of jail—a convicted criminal? She saw herself disowned by her family and friends. She wondered if Tom would ever speak to her again. Perhaps he would cross to the other side of the street as she passed. She would hear Father say, "I had a daughter once, but we don't speak of her anymore."

The slamming of a door pulled

her back to the dingy room. Striding toward her was Aunt Letitia, a determined look on her face. Behind her was Jonathan Harrison, Aunt Letitia's fiancé. Without a word to the policeman, her aunt drew up a chair and sat beside her.

"Are you all right, Lucy?" she asked. "We saw them take you away, and we got here as fast as we could. Your father is coming along. There was such a crowd around the cart that he couldn't get the horses moving."

"I . . . I suppose they're going to send me to jail," Lucy said. "I'm charged with creating a public disturbance."

"I don't think you have to worry about jail," said Aunt Letitia. She patted her hand. "Not during an election campaign." She smiled. "They're always afraid of bad publicity just before the vote is taken."

"Keep your chin up," said Mr. Harrison. A warm smile creased his face. "You mustn't lose heart. Letitia is counting on you to help organize the women of New York. We're going to open a special office for woman suffrage."

Before Lucy could answer, the station door burst open and Father rushed in. He strode to the desk and demanded to see the police chief.

"Sorry, Will," said the officer, "he's down at the park."

"You are holding my daughter," said Father, out of breath, "and I demand her release."

"She's right over there," said the officer. He pointed at Lucy. "But I can't release her yet. She's charged with creating a public disturbance."

For the first time Father realized that Lucy was in the room. He took one step toward her, then—as his glance fell upon Aunt Letitia—he stopped. He stared at her. Then, with a curt "I suppose you put her up to this," he turned his back on his sister and put his hand on Lucy's shoulder.

"Are you all right?" he stammered. "Have they harmed you in any way?"

"No one hurt me, Father," she said. "But I'm so glad to see you."

"We'll have you out of here in no time," he said. He looked down at her, and his face became stern. "What a fool thing to do," he said. "I thought my daughter had a little horse sense."

Before she could reply, the door burst open, and Senator Throckmorton hurried into the room, followed by three men from the train.

"I understand you're holding that girl who jumped up on the stage," said the Senator. His voice had lost the mellowness that charmed crowds; it was harsh and edgy.

Lucy shrank back in her chair. He might ask them to keep her in jail until after the election next month. She was sure that the police would do whatever the distinguished visitor asked.

Like the dawning of the sun, a smile broke across Father's face, and he stepped toward the desk.

"It's a good thing you've come, Senator!" he said.

The Senator brushed aside his greeting and pounded on the desk. "I want that girl released immediately," he shouted. "I refuse to press any charges."

"Yes, sir," said the policeman, now alert. He picked up the pen and began to write. "If you refuse to press charges," he said, "we can't hold her any longer." He looked at Father and Lucy. "Guess you can take her home, Will," he said. "Just keep her off public platforms."

The Senator shook Father's hand. "Mr. Snow," he said, the sharp edge gone from his voice, "you certainly are raising a flock of politicians." He smiled at Lucy. "But this young suffragist is a little embarrassing."

"We're going to have a talk when we get home," said Father.

"Next time you give a speech, young lady," said the Senator, "be sure you've been invited."

He bowed over Lucy's hand. "It's the best way to stay out of jail."

Lucy gave a tiny, stiff smile but said nothing. She was sorry she had been arrested, but she doubted that suffragists would ever be invited to speak in Smithville.

As they all walked away, Aunt Letitia grinned and said to Father, "There's nothing more I can do here."

Father stared at her.

"Goodbye, Aunt Letitia," said Lucy. "Thank you for helping to rescue me. And goodbye . . . Uncle Jonathan. Thank you for helping."

Senator Throckmorton and his committee followed Aunt Letitia and Uncle Jonathan out the door. As he left, the Senator glanced back over his shoulder.

"Why didn't one of you tell me this town was such a nest of suffragettes?" he asked his committee. The edge was back in his voice. "I'd never have given that fool speech."

The moment the horses pulled into the yard, Lucy slid down and ran into the house. She hoped to slip up the stairs and into her room without meeting anyone, but as she hurried, Mother came out of the parlor.

"Lucy!" she said and held out her arms.

Safe inside Mother's warm embrace, Lucy felt the tears gather. In another second she would be sobbing aloud.

The slamming of the kitchen door twisted in her stomach. The tears froze; dry eyed, she turned to face Father.

"I think we'd better have a talk," he said. There was no warmth in his voice.

Lucy and Mother followed him into the parlor. No fire had burned that day and the room was cold. But the shiver that came over Lucy had nothing to do with the temperature.

Father stood in the center of the flowered carpet, his feet planted wide apart, his hands clasped behind his back. "My father would have given me a good whipping for what you did tonight," he said.

Lucy's glance darted about the room. She forced herself to look squarely at Father. Inside she was trembling, and it took all her strength to keep from dropping her eyes to the floor.

He sighed. "I suppose you're

too big to be whipped," he said. "But you've disgraced the Snow name."

"I'm sorry, Father," said Lucy. "I didn't intend to." Her voice was so faint that he had to lean forward to catch her words.

"Didn't intend," said Father. "That's the whole trouble, you never intend. You act without thinking of the consequences." He warmed to his lecture. "You made a public spectacle of yourself and shamed your mother and me."

"The charges were dropped," she whispered.

"So they were." He chewed on his mustache. "But the Senator could have pressed charges," he said, "and then where would you be? Behind bars, that's where."

"He said things that weren't true," she said. Her voice grew stronger. "He lied."

"And that gave you the right to act like a crazy person?" asked Father. "That was his rally. The Party paid for the lights and the fireworks and the barbecue and the parade. You had no business on that stage."

Lucy sorted desperately through her mind for something that would excuse her. Then a fragment from a civics lesson turned up, and she grasped it. "I was exercising my freedom of speech," she said.

"By denying the Senator his freedom?" said her father. "By insulting a United States Senator? That doesn't make good sense."

He paced back and forth in the narrow space between the sofa and the big chair. Lucy waited for his next words. She feared the worst was yet to come. Father had not yet decided what to do with her.

Suddenly he whirled on her, and his voice was crosser than before. "It was bad enough when you passed out leaflets," he shouted. "That at least was orderly. But I will not stand for this kind of—of—of violent disruption." He shook his finger in her face. "As long as you're under my roof . . ."

During the argument Mother had stepped to his side. She laid her hand on his arm, and he stopped in mid-sentence. He dropped his finger and began again, this time in a softer voice.

"I want you to promise me," he said, "that you will keep all your activities within the bounds of the law." Again he chewed on his mustache.

Lucy relaxed. This would be easier than she expected. "I promise," she said. "I didn't mean to break the law tonight, Father. I was on that stage before I knew what I was doing."

Father raised an eyebrow. "Perhaps," he said. "But just to make sure that you're not carried away again, I want you to come straight home after school for the next three weeks. By that time, the election will be over."

Her shoulders slumped. "Yes, Father," she said in a tiny voice.

She turned and walked slowly out of the parlor and up the stairs. Sam's door opened and he tiptoed out on his bare feet, his nightshirt flapping around his legs.

"Did they put you behind bars?" he asked. "Did they take your fingerprints?"

"No," said Lucy. "Your friend the Senator made them let me go." She tried to push past Sam but he followed her.

"I never saw Father so mad," he said. "I hope he never gets that mad at me."

She paused, her hand on the doorknob. "I have to come straight home after school and stay in the house for the next three weeks," she said. "That's what you wanted to find out, isn't it?"

Sam whistled. "Three weeks!" he said. "That's past Halloween. I'd rather have a whipping any day than miss Halloween."

"Halloween is for children," said Lucy in her proudest voice.

Sam trudged back to his room and slammed the door. Before Lucy went into her room, there was a loud knocking downstairs. She waited in the hall, listening as Father went to answer it.

There stood Tom's father, and before he could step over the threshold, he asked about Lucy.

"She's home and she's safe," said Father. "Thank you for getting the Senator to the station so fast."

"It must have been a terrible experience for her," said Mr. Bryan. "Maybe it cured her of politics."

"Not my daughter," said Father. He chuckled. "That girl has spunk. If women ever do get the vote, she'll be the Governor of New York."

Lucy went into her room in a daze. The pride in Father's voice could not be hidden. Suddenly the gulf between them seemed only half as wide.

AUTHOR

Elizabeth Hall was born and grew up in Bakersfield, California. While she attended college there, she was editor of the college newspaper and learned about writing copy and meeting newspaper deadlines.

She interrupted her education at Bakersfield College to get married. Later, she completed college through a correspondence course at Fresno State College and became the public librarian in Shaftner, California. Through conducting story hours and introducing children to her favorite books, she became interested in children's literature and soon began writing for young readers. *Phoebe Snow* was the first book she wrote about Lucy Snow. The story "Lucy Speaks Out" is from her book *Stand Up, Lucy.*

Elizabeth Hall still lives in California, three miles from the coast. She is managing editor of the magazine *Psychology Today,* but she is writing for young people as well.

The Clockmaker and the Timekeeper
by Isabelle Chang

There was once a clockmaker who had a shop in the center of the village. Every day a man stopped by and looked in the window, before hurrying on his way. After a year, the clockmaker hailed the man one day and asked him why he always hesitated by the window, but never entered the shop.

The man replied, "I am the timekeeper for the town, and I have to ring the church bells at exactly twelve o'clock noon. To be accurate, I always check with your clock first."

"Ah," said the clockmaker, "but I always set my clock after I hear the chimes of the church bells."

DAMON AND PYTHIAS
A PLAY BY FAN KISSEN

CAST

DAMON	KING	SECOND ROBBER
PYTHIAS	MOTHER	FIRST VOICE
SOLDIER	FIRST ROBBER	SECOND VOICE

THIRD VOICE   NARRATOR

NARRATOR: Long, long ago there lived on the island of Sicily two young men named Damon and Pythias. They were known far and wide for the strong friendship each had for the other. Their names have come down to our own times to mean true friendship. You may hear it said of two persons:

FIRST VOICE: Those two? Why, they're like Damon and Pythias!

NARRATOR: The King of that country was a cruel tyrant. He made cruel laws, and he showed no mercy toward anyone who broke his laws. Now, you might very well wonder:

SECOND VOICE: Why didn't the people rebel?

NARRATOR: Well, the people didn't dare rebel, because they feared the King's great and powerful army. No one dared say a word against the King or his laws—except Damon and Pythias. One day a soldier overheard Pythias speaking against a new law the King had proclaimed.

SOLDIER: Ho, there! Who are you, that dares to speak so about our King?

PYTHIAS (*Unafraid*): I am called Pythias.

SOLDIER: Don't you know it is a crime to speak against the King or his laws? You are under arrest! Come and tell this opinion of yours to the King!

NARRATOR: When Pythias was brought before the King, he showed no fear. He stood straight and quiet before the throne.

KING (*Hard, cruel*): So, Pythias! They tell me you do not approve of the laws I make.

PYTHIAS: I am not alone, your Majesty, in thinking your laws are cruel. But you rule the people with such an iron hand that they dare not complain.

KING (*Angry*): But *you* have the daring to complain *for* them! Have they appointed you their champion?

PYTHIAS: No, your Majesty. I speak for myself alone. I have no wish to make trouble for anyone. But I am not afraid to tell you that the people are suffering under your rule. They want to have a voice in making the laws for themselves. You do not allow them to speak up for themselves.

KING: In other words, you are calling me a tyrant! Well, you shall learn for yourself how a tyrant treats a rebel! Soldier! Throw this man into prison!

SOLDIER: At once, your Majesty! Don't try to resist, Pythias!

PYTHIAS: I know better than to try to resist a soldier of the King! And for how long am I to remain in prison, your Majesty, merely for speaking out for the people?

KING *(Cruel):* Not for very long, Pythias. Two weeks from today, at noon, you shall be put to death in the public square, as an example to anyone else who may dare to question my laws or acts. Off to prison with him, soldier!

NARRATOR: When Damon heard that his friend Pythias had been thrown into prison and learned about the severe punishment that was to follow, he was heartbroken. He rushed to the prison and persuaded the guard to let him speak to his friend.

DAMON: Oh, Pythias! How terrible to find you here! I wish I could do something to save you!

PYTHIAS: Nothing can save me, Damon, my dear friend. I am prepared to die. But there is one thought that troubles me greatly.

DAMON: What is it? I will do anything to help you.

PYTHIAS: I'm worried about what will happen to my mother and my sister when I'm gone.

DAMON: I'll take care of them, Pythias, as if they were my own mother and sister.

PYTHIAS: Thank you, Damon. I have money to leave them. But there are other things I must arrange. If only I could go to see them before I die! But they live two days' journey from here, you know.

DAMON: I'll go to the King and beg him to give you your freedom for a few days. You'll give your word to return at the end of that time. Everyone in Sicily knows you for a man who has never broken his word.

PYTHIAS: Do you believe for one moment that the King would let me leave this prison, no matter how good my word may have been all my life?

DAMON: I'll tell him that *I* shall take your place in this prison cell. I'll tell him that if you do not return by the appointed day, he may kill *me,* in your place!

PYTHIAS: No, no, Damon! You must not do such a foolish thing! I cannot—I *will* not—let you do this! Damon! Damon! Don't go! *(To himself)* Damon, my friend! You may find yourself in a cell beside me!

NARRATOR: Damon hurried to the King to request this special favor for his friend.

DAMON: Your Majesty! I beg of you! Let Pythias go home for a few days to bid farewell to his mother and sister. He gives his word that he will return at your appointed time. Everyone knows that his word can be trusted.

KING: In ordinary business affairs—perhaps. But he is now a man under sentence of death. To free him even for a few days would strain his honesty—*any* man's honesty—too far. Pythias would never return here! I consider him a traitor, but I'm certain he's no fool.

DAMON: Your Majesty! I will take his place in prison until he comes back. If he does not return, then you may take *my* life in his place.

KING *(Astonished):* What did you say, Damon?

DAMON: I'm so certain of Pythias that I am offering to die in his place if he fails to return on time.

KING: I can't believe you mean it!

DAMON: I do mean it, your Majesty.

KING: You make me very curious, Damon, so curious that I'm willing to put you and Pythias to the test. This exchange of prisoners will be made. But Pythias must be back two weeks from today, at noon.

DAMON: Thank you, your Majesty!

KING: The order with my official seal shall go by your own hand, Damon. But I warn you, if your friend does not return on time, you shall surely die in his place! I shall show no mercy!

NARRATOR: Pythias did not like the King's bargain with Damon. He did not like to leave his friend in prison, with the chance that he might lose his life if something went wrong. But at last Damon persuaded him to leave, and Pythias set out for his home. More than a week went by. The day set for the death sentence drew near. Pythias did not return. Everyone in the city knew of the condition on which the King had permitted Pythias to go home. Everywhere people met, the talk was sure to turn to the two friends.

FIRST VOICE: Do you suppose Pythias will come back?

SECOND VOICE: Why should he stick his head under the King's axe, once he's escaped?

THIRD VOICE: Still, would an honorable man like Pythias let such a good friend die for him?

FIRST VOICE: There's no telling what a man will do when it's a question of his own life against another's.

SECOND VOICE: But if Pythias doesn't come back before the time is up, he will be killing his friend.

THIRD VOICE: Well, there's still a few days' time. I, for one, am certain that Pythias *will* return in time.

SECOND VOICE: And *I* am just as certain that he will *not*. Friendship is friendship, but a man's own life is something stronger, *I* say!

NARRATOR: Two days before the time was up, the King himself visited Damon in his prison cell.

KING (*Mocking*): You see now, Damon, that you were a fool to make this bargain. Your friend has tricked you! He will not come back here to be killed! He has deserted you!

DAMON (*Calm and firm*): I have faith in my friend. I know he will return.

KING (*Mocking*): We shall see!

NARRATOR: Meanwhile, when Pythias reached the home of his family, he arranged his business affairs so that his mother and sister would be able to live comfortably for the rest of their years. Then he said a last farewell to them before starting back to the city.

MOTHER *(In tears):* Pythias, it will take you only two days to get back. Stay another day, I beg you!

PYTHIAS: I dare not stay longer, Mother. Remember, Damon is locked up in my prison cell while I'm gone. Please don't make it harder for me! Farewell! Don't weep for me. My death may help to bring better days for all our people.

NARRATOR: So Pythias began his return journey in plenty of time. But bad luck struck him on the very first day. At twilight, as he walked along a lonely stretch of woodland, a rough voice called:

FIRST ROBBER: Not so fast there, young man! Stop!

PYTHIAS *(Startled):* Oh! What is it? What do you want?

SECOND ROBBER: Your money bags.

PYTHIAS: My money bags? I have only this small bag of coins. I shall need them, perhaps, before I die.

FIRST ROBBER: What do you mean, before you die? We don't mean to kill you, only to take your money.

PYTHIAS: I'll give you my money, only don't delay me any longer. I am to die by the King's order three days from now. If I don't return to prison on time, my friend must die in my place.

FIRST ROBBER: A likely story! What man would be fool enough to go back to prison, ready to die?

SECOND ROBBER: And what man would be fool enough to die *for* you?

FIRST ROBBER: We'll take your money, all right. And we'll tie you up while we get away.

PYTHIAS *(Begging):* No! No! I must get back to free my friend! I must go back!

NARRATOR: But the two robbers took Pythias's money, tied him to a tree, and went off as fast as they could. Pythias struggled to free himself. He cried out for help as loud as he could, for a long time. But no one traveled through that lonesome woodland after dark. The sun had been up for many hours before he finally managed to free himself from the ropes that tied him to the tree. He lay on the ground, hardly able to breathe. After a while Pythias got to his feet. Weak and dizzy from hunger and thirst and his struggle to free himself, he set off again. Day and night he traveled without stopping, desperately trying to reach the city in time to save Damon's life. On the last day, half an hour before noon, Damon's hands were tied behind his back and he was taken into the public square. The people muttered angrily as Damon was led in by the jailer. Then the King entered and seated himself on a high platform.

SOLDIER (Loud): Long live the King!

FIRST VOICE (Softly): The longer he lives, the more miserable our lives will be!

KING (Loud, mocking): Well, Damon, your lifetime is nearly up. Where is your good friend Pythias now?

DAMON: I have faith in my friend. If he has not returned, I'm certain it is through no fault of his own.

KING (Mocking): The sun is almost overhead. The shadow is almost at the noon mark. And still your friend has not returned to give you back your life!

DAMON (Quiet): I am ready, and happy, to die in his place.

KING (Harsh): And you shall, Damon! Jailer, lead the prisoner to the —

FIRST VOICE (Shouting): Look! It's Pythias!

SECOND VOICE: Pythias has come back!

PYTHIAS *(Breathless):* Let me through! Damon!

DAMON: Pythias!

PYTHIAS: Thank the gods I'm not too late!

DAMON: I would have died for you gladly, my friend.

CROWD VOICES *(Loud, demanding):* Set them free! Set them both free!

KING *(Loud):* People of the city! Never in all my life have I seen such faith and friendship, such loyalty between men. There are many among you who call me harsh and cruel. But I cannot kill *any* man who proves such strong and true friendship for another. Damon and Pythias, I set you both free. *(Roar of approval from crowd)* I am King. I command a great army. I have stores of gold and precious jewels. But I would give all my money and my power for one friend like Damon or Pythias! *(Roar of approval from crowd)*

MUMMY SLEPT LATE AND DADDY FIXED BREAKFAST

Daddy fixed breakfast.
He made us each a waffle.
It looked like gravel pudding.
It tasted something awful.

"Ha, ha," he said, "I'll try again.
This time I'll get it right."
But what I got was in between
Bituminous and anthracite.

"A little too well done? Oh well,
I'll have to start all over."
That time what landed on my plate
Looked like a manhole cover.

I tried to cut it with a fork:
The fork gave off a spark.
I tried a knife and twisted it
Into a question mark.

I tried it with a hack-saw.
I tried it with a torch.
It didn't even make a dent.
It didn't even scorch.

The next time Dad gets breakfast
When Mummy's sleeping late,
I think I'll skip the waffles.
I'd sooner eat the plate!

John Ciardi

SKILL LESSON

DECIDING ON PARAGRAPH TOPICS

The paragraph that follows talks about the clothing which Eskimos wore years ago. Notice that each sentence in the paragraph tells something about that Eskimo clothing.

Clothing made of fur kept Eskimos warm in temperatures that were sometimes as low as sixty degrees below zero. Men, women, and children, all dressed alike in trousers, boots, mittens, and hooded coats called parkas. In coldest weather, Eskimos wore two complete sets of clothing, the inner set with the fur inside and the outer set with the fur outside. Most of the clothing was made from light but warm skins of caribou, a kind of reindeer, although tough walrus hide and sealskin were often used for boots. Eskimo women cut the skins and shaped the garments, sewing the pieces together with thread made from animal tendons.

A good paragraph, like the one above, talks about only one thing. That one thing is called *the topic of the paragraph.* Every sentence in the paragraph tells or asks something about that one topic.

If you are not sure what the topic of a paragraph is, read each sentence of the paragraph again and then try to figure out what one thing all the sentences are talking about. Usually that will show you what the topic of the paragraph is. The following statements tell what the five sentences in the paragraph on

Eskimo clothing talk about. Notice that each sentence listed contains the words *clothing Eskimos wore.*

Sentence one tells about the warmth of *clothing Eskimos wore.*

Sentence two lists the articles of *clothing Eskimos wore.*

Sentence three tells the amount of *clothing Eskimos wore.*

Sentence four tells the materials used for *clothing Eskimos wore.*

Sentence five tells about the making of *clothing Eskimos wore.*

Being able to tell what the topic of a paragraph is will often help you to understand what you are studying, and paragraph topics are good points to use in making notes. Sometimes your first reading of the paragraph will tell you quickly what the topic is. But if you are not sure what the topic is, make a list like the one made for the paragraph about the clothing Eskimos wore. Put into your list statements that tell what the sentences of the paragraph are talking about. If there is one topic that you can use in every statement, as the topic *clothing Eskimos wore* is used, that is the topic of the paragraph.

Now and then in your studies you may come across a paragraph in which all the sentences do not tell something about the same topic. Usually in such a paragraph, most of the sentences talk about only one topic, but the other sentences talk about one or more other topics.

An Eskimo igloo is one topic that the following paragraph tells about. As you read the paragraph, think what each sentence is talking about. Does every sentence in the paragraph tell about *an Eskimo igloo?*

An igloo provided temporary shelter for an Eskimo family while on a hunting trip or traveling in winter. In summer, most Eskimos lived in tents. An Eskimo igloo was a round snowhouse which could be built in only about an hour. It was made from fairly large blocks of wind-packed snow that had been cut with a long knife. The dome-shaped hut was formed by fitting the blocks together in circular rows that became smaller toward the top. The entrance to the igloo was a long tunnel dug out under the snow or built of snow blocks. Inside the igloo was a single room that was ten feet or more from wall to wall. In New England, where there are often heavy snowfalls in winter, children have always enjoyed building playhouses out of snow.

Here is a list that shows what is told by each sentence in the paragraph you have just read:

Sentence one tells the purpose of *an Eskimo igloo.*

Sentence two tells that in summer Eskimos lived in *tents.*

Sentence three tells how long it took to build *an Eskimo igloo.*

Sentence four tells the materials used in making *an Eskimo igloo.*

Sentence five tells how *an Eskimo igloo* was built.

Sentence six tells about the entrance of *an Eskimo igloo.*

Sentence seven tells about the inside of *an Eskimo igloo.*

Sentence eight tells about *children's playhouses* built from snow in New England.

You can see that the first sentence and sentences three through seven tell something about *an Eskimo igloo.* But what do the other two sentences tell about? Sentence two tells about *tents,* and sentence eight tells about *children's playhouses.*

You can understand that if a paragraph talks about several topics, none of those topics can be *the* topic of the paragraph. But usually such a paragraph contains one topic which most of the sentences talk about. We can call that topic the *main* topic *in* the paragraph. The main topic in the paragraph on the opposite page is *an Eskimo igloo.*

When a paragraph talks about more than one topic, try to figure out what the *main* topic in the paragraph is. This will help you to understand what you are reading.

Now read Paragraph A that follows. Think what each sentence in the paragraph is talking about and decide what the *main* topic in the paragraph is. If you need to, make a list of statements that tell what each sentence in the paragraph is talking about.

Paragraph A:

Years ago most of the food Eskimos ate came from the sea, but land animals like the caribou and polar bear were also eaten. The flesh of seals, walruses, fishes, and whales provided most of the Eskimo's meat. Some meat was boiled, but often it was served raw and frozen because fuel was scarce. Most Eskimos had powerful jaws and strong teeth, the result of chewing raw, tough meat and eating foods that contained little sugar. Heads of small fish were sometimes swallowed whole. Since no fruits or vegetables grew in the frozen land, such parts of the animal as the liver, heart, and stomach were eaten because they provided necessary vitamins and minerals. A special treat was Eskimo "ice cream" which was not ice cream at all but caribou fat shaved fine and mixed with oil to form a cream.

Which of the following is the main topic in Paragraph A?

   1. Why Eskimos ate raw meat
   2. Eskimos' skill in hunting
   3. The food of Eskimos
   4. Why Eskimos had strong teeth

Discussion

Help your class decide on answers to these questions:
1. What is meant by the topic of a paragraph? If you need to figure out the topic of a paragraph, how can you do it?
2. What is meant by the main topic in a paragraph? How can you decide what the main topic of a paragraph is?
3. What is the main topic in Paragraph A? Why is each of the three other topics listed not the main topic in that paragraph?

On your own

In which of the following two paragraphs do all the sentences talk about only one topic? What is the topic of that paragraph? What is the main topic in the other paragraph?

Paragraph B:

Eskimo dogs are a very useful animal in the Arctic regions. They are very strong and can withstand the extremely cold weather of the Arctic. These beautiful animals are used by many Eskimo families for pulling sleds and for hunting. Because of their great strength and endurance, they can pull heavy loads for many miles without tiring. The sleds that they pull are made of wood and bone fastened together with rawhide. The Eskimo dogs are particularly useful in hunting seals. They help the Eskimo hunters find the seals by locating air holes in the ice through which the seals breathe. Eskimos do most of their hunting on the ice, but sometimes they hunt from boats.

Paragraph C:

The one-person boat which some Eskimos use to hunt in open waters is called a kayak. A kayak is usually less than two feet wide but might be twenty feet long. The frame of the kayak, like that of a dog sled, is made of pieces of wood tied together with strips of walrus hide. Except for a round cockpit near the center of the deck top, the entire frame of the boat is covered with wet seal or walrus skin which shrinks as it dries and thus stretches tightly over the frame. The floor of the cockpit is the place where the Eskimo paddler sits. A kayak is a light but seaworthy boat which one person can easily paddle and control.

Checking your work

If you are asked to do so, tell which paragraph talks about only one topic and what that topic is. Tell also what the main topic in the other paragraph is. If a topic you decided on was incorrect, find out why it was incorrect.

Cerebral palsy kept John Sumner, a twelve-year-old Australian, from being all he wanted to be. From his worried mother he had always heard too many "no's" and too many warnings that kept him from doing the things other young people did. But except for those spells he kept having, those times when he shook and couldn't make his muscles do what he wanted them to do, he was perfectly normal. So today, having been allowed for the first time to stay home alone while his mother drove into the city, he decided to climb the huge gum tree in his yard, the one with the first branch fifteen feet above the ground. Although he managed to drag a ladder over to the tree, he couldn't prop it high enough against the trunk to reach the branch. At the height of his frustration, he imagined that the gum tree had become a tower and that trapped up there was Mamie, his golden-haired classmate, begging to be rescued. Even this daydream failed to give him the power he needed to raise the ladder higher, and he gave up, exhausted.

HI-YA, BIRD

by Ivan Southall

That was the way his world went. The other world where kids did as they pleased was about a million miles away.

He cried inside himself for a few minutes, then wandered across to the ladder and sat on the bottom rung. It wasn't a comfortable seat, and something moved him to try a somersault, but he made an absolute mess of it as usual and rolled onto his side. The mail carrier's whistle blew somewhere, an empty, lonely sound. He cried a bit more and ended up on his back looking at the sky. The sky was miles away; the top of the gum tree was miles away. A hawk wheeled in the emptiness between. It was lonely up there, too, but different.

"Hi-ya, bird. Hi-ya, cloud. Hi-ya, Mr. Sun."

Saying it made him cry again and he hated crying, even when no one else was around.

A voice came to him from a long way off, one of those *imagined* voices. It sounded a bit cross. "I didn't put myself up in this tower, you know. You did, John Sumner, with your stupid make-believe. You can't expect me to jump. I'll break my neck. You've got to come up to carry me down."

It was Mamie still waiting to be rescued, but John wasn't interested any more. "I can't climb that high," he said. "I can't get the ladder up."

"I bet Harry Hitchman would get the ladder up."

"Harry Hitchman gives me a pain."

"Save me, Harry. John Sumner can't get me down."

"You shut up, Mamie van Senden. It's not fair bringing Harry into it."

"I won't shut up. Save me, *Harreee!*"

"Harry can't hear you. He's gone away to do things of his own. I suppose you're going to go away, too, aren't you, Mamie van Senden?"

She went away.

Nothing was left but the sky and the gum tree and the ladder.

"Why don't you go away, too?" he snarled at the ladder.

But the ladder was real and didn't have to go away.

"I'm going to do my model. It's got 227 pieces. When it's finished, it'll be a yacht for putting on the shelf. Then I'll paint it white and take it to school and all the kids'll say it's terrific. But they'll know it's only 227 pieces out of a box."

He rolled over sideways, over and over downhill into the geraniums at the fence. "I hate geraniums. They stink." But he put up with the smell because he couldn't be bothered moving. He didn't care about anything. What was the use of caring? The answer to everything was either "Don't" or "Can't." There was only one John Clement Sumner, and he was the one who shook and jerked and smudged his pages.

He squinted across the grass to the foot of the ladder, then up the ladder. The top was only about five feet from the bough, but might as well have been fifteen feet or fifty. He might as well have left it under the house and saved himself a lot of agony, because he still had to get it back in place just as though it had never been touched.

Perhaps if he asked Percy and Harry, they'd help. They couldn't even *think* he was weak if it took three of them to get it back, but Harry would say, "I'll do it." Then Harry would pick it up by himself and do it. Then they'd say, "But what did you take it out for?" They wouldn't know that before he had asked for help, he had dragged it all the way to the tree and back to the house again. "Aw, I don't know," he'd say, "just for fun, I suppose."

But it wasn't for fun. It was deadly serious. It was for something terrific that hadn't happened—like everything else that never happened and never would.

"I'm going to do my project. I'll cut some pictures out of *Women's Weekly* with my plastic scissors."

The ladder began to sneer at him. He wanted to rush it and give it a good kick or push hard from the side so that it would fall with a crash. Several times the urge came like a command, but his body wouldn't move; it wanted only to lie on the ground.

"I wish you'd go away, you bloomin' old ladder."

But the ladder leaned against the tree like a tough character in a film. The ladder spat a squirt of tobacco juice. "I'm stayin' right where I am, see. Are you makin' somethin' of it?"

"Oh, go away. You're only a ladder."

"I'm goin' no place, kid. I'm stickin' right where I am. No one pushes me around."

John edged off a yard or two from the geraniums; the smell of the leaves crushed by his own body was too strong.

"I wish I'd gone with Mom."

He sat up and clasped his legs, rocking miserably backwards and forwards. For a moment he remembered something of a long time ago: a curious and uneasy memory of perhaps a three-year-old sitting up in his cot, clasping his knees, rocking. For a moment there weren't any years between: He *was* little again; then the moment was gone.

"No," he cried.

He felt hot and prickly and cruelly ashamed. His face twitched, his hands jerked, and on impulse he scrambled to his feet and rushed at the ladder. He grabbed it viciously near the bottom and wrenched it from the grass. The top rung shot up the trunk of the tree as though propelled and struck the bough.

It hit with a crack almost like a whip and jarred all the way to the ground; but it stayed there and did not fall down.

Something happened to John. A storm passed through him. There was a battlefield, and he was in the middle of it flaying at heads in armor with a flat sword. There were screams and shouts and sour smells. It was savage.

Then there was absolutely nothing.

After a time he saw the ladder against the tree, butted up to the bough. It was a road to the sky and the road was open.

He was puzzled. He had not done it himself; of that he was sure. He *could* not have done it. Lifted that great ladder?

Numbed, he moved aside and sat back from it on the grass with legs crossed, not sure of himself, not sure of anything.

Oddly, the ladder did not break up rung by rung, did not

melt like wax, did not disappear in a puff of smoke. It would not have surprised him if it had. But it was not a ladder that he had invented; it was not imagined; nor was the miracle a feat of strength performed in a dazzling dream.

He had been so certain that this extraordinary event could not occur; but there stood the ladder ready for his use, as though it had never stood anywhere else. His heartbeat was becoming a thud in his head and a breath-catching pulse in his throat. He was becoming frightened, and something inside him seemed to be falling endlessly. The longer he stared, the more frantic his fall became, the faster his fears tumbled one over the other like dozens of people falling head over heels into an ever-deepening hole.

Then he looked up again to the long, slender curves of branches way up high like thin arms, to the topmost twigs like hands, to the last leaves groping like blind fingers for the sky, and there was a giddiness in him and a sickening wave of alarm. There was a cliff, and he was on crutches at the edge of it.

He scarcely realized it any longer, but he continued to shuffle away in nervous fits and starts. All the things he should be doing were nagging at him, were noises that could not properly be heard: his model and its 227 pieces, his project and its pictures of cheeses, a library book half-read and worth finishing. Thousands of things he had to do; he could think of only three. But they were urgent, they were immediate, and nothing else was of any importance at all.

The noises became louder and louder, completely demanding, and he had to run to them, had to race across the lawn towards the house because that was where they were; the project, the model, the library book were all in the house shouting for attention behind doors and walls.

Then he stopped as though caught suddenly in his flight by a pair of strong arms, but nothing touched him; ahead of him was something that he saw. It was a girl.

171

She said, "Are you a nut or something?"

It was Mamie in blue jeans and yellow sweater, with golden hair like a bright helmet. She was eating an apple and drooped a bulging shopping bag to the ground by one handle. It was not the Mamie of the tower, but the real Mamie who lived seven houses away on the right-hand side of Dawson Street, going up.

John stammered at her, but it was a sound that meant nothing to him or to Mamie either.

She took a bite from the apple. "Isn't your mother home?"

He shook his head.

"She'll shoot you when she comes home. You're awful dirty."

He was so breathless, so distressed, so ashamed. He was dust and grass and sweat and dirt from head to foot. He wouldn't have cared if he had dropped dead. He tried to speak, but couldn't, and realized that his hand was beating his thigh. It was a painful effort of will to stop it.

"I've been shopping," Mamie said. "Mom told me not to dawdle. But I did. She's going to be cross. Do you want a bite?"

He shook his head.

"I've eaten *two*." She rolled her eyes. "Mom'll scream. What are you doing?"

He tried to explain, but couldn't; tried to say that he was playing big-game hunting and was fleeing because his rifle had jammed, but it was a meaningless gabble.

Mamie began to look uncomfortable, began to wish she hadn't come.

"I'd better be going," she said. "Mom'll scream."

"Don't go," he blurted out.

Mamie looked at her feet (she was just a bit frightened) and gathered up the stray handle of her shopping bag. "Got to," she said.

She skipped a little as she went, but not because she was happy. Mamie really wanted to run, and when she was around the side of the house, out of sight of John, she made no secret of it to herself and scuttled down the drive as fast as she could go. When she hit the road, she looked back, but John wasn't behind her, and she thanked her stars for that.

John still stood where his scramble to the house had halted. He was furious, mad with himself, mad with Mamie, mad with the world. He wanted to break things, wanted to swear, wanted to jump up and down and stamp his feet. Never, never had he shaken with a fury like this. He was so ashamed; he was so burnt up with all the frustrations and prohibitions and failures and *Don't do this*'s and *Can't do that*'s of a whole lifetime that he was almost beside himself.

"You lousy, rotten ladder," he screamed and started jerking about in circles and snatching at clods of dirt from the garden and hurling them at the tree.

"It's not fair, it's not fair. Other kids climb. Other kids don't make fools of themselves in front of their girls. You rotten old tree."

He rushed it and hit it with his fists. He kicked the tree. He swore at it. He grabbed at the ladder, and not comprehending his actions, he all but ran up the rungs, stumbling, clawing, fumbling, until he was at least ten feet from the ground. There he stopped, suddenly shocked.

Everything went cold and became a mist.

So suddenly it happened; cold inside; cold outside; no fury left; no violence; not even any words.

The mist cleared, and his legs somewhere below were trembling like reeds, and his hands up above were clenched white around the side rails.

John was stretched on the ladder, frozen in the act of a stride.

He panted rapidly through his teeth, and all the world was a gigantic ache, a terrible pain, and a continuing fright.

The sweat on his hands was like grease, and his fingers were slipping down those varnished rails a fraction of an inch at a time, in tiny jerks. Each jerk was a spasm of fear that he felt in his heart as though something there had ripped.

He tried to go up but couldn't. He pleaded with himself, commanded his body to climb, but nothing responded. His body could have been another person a mile away for all the attention it paid. It was like calling to his mother in the middle of the night when she was asleep and all the doors had slammed shut.

He bore down on his legs, he pushed, he heaved, but nothing was there, no strength and no feeling; he could have been dead down there in his legs for all the use they were. He clung on, held on, pleaded, prayed.

Nothing answered him; nothing from the inside; nothing from the outside. It was Mamie who had driven him up here, but even she was gone. Only the ground was down there—way, way down there. It was hard, that ground. It hadn't rained for a month. The thick roots of the gum tree broke the surface, and they were there, too, like rods of iron, like rails. It wasn't soft grass or deep grass. It was dry grass, shaved to the surface by Dad's lawn mower. There was nothing down there to fall on—only things to break on—and that ghastly slipping away through his fingers went on and on, each jolt another drop of life gone.

There were not even splinters to bite into the flesh of his hands. The ladder was so smooth, rubbed smooth with sandpaper and varnished. That was Dad all over. Even his ladder was perfect. If he hadn't sanded it, hadn't varnished it, hadn't washed it clean after every use, *it wouldn't have slipped through his fingers.*

There were weary voices inside him, arguing. One was

stern (though tired) and the other desperate. One sounded something like Mom; the other sounded like part of himself.

"I didn't mean to climb the rotten thing in the first place. Never, ever. It was only pretending. All the time I wasn't going to do it. All the time it was only *pretending*."

"It wasn't pretending."

"It was, it was, it was. Like everything else, it was only pretending."

"Getting the ladder down from the rack—was that pretending? Getting it up to the tree—was that pretending?"

"Of course it was. I'm not silly. I'm not crazy. I know I can't climb."

"Kicking the ladder. Punching it. Swearing at it. Running away from it. Were they all pretending?"

"I don't know, I don't know."

"You got up here, didn't you? You climbed here. You could not have got here any other way. All the time you knew it was going to happen, but you knew that when you got here, you'd fall."

A whimper broke out that he had striven to hold back and with the whimper came the shakes—shakes that he could feel even in the ladder. It shook under him, throbbed under him, and nothing was left in his hands, nothing at all. They stayed there, still slipping, still sliding, but numb.

He would lie down there, perhaps broken, perhaps dead, and no one would know. People coming to the back door wouldn't see him; Mom coming home wouldn't see him because the ladder was hidden from the house. Mamie had faced the tree but had never guessed that the ladder was there.

Mom would call, "John. Where are you, darling?" And she would become more frantic; she would dash here and dash there crying out—and then after a while she would find him. "Oh, John. I knew all the time I should never have left you. All these years I have kept you safe. In one day you kill yourself."

Even now if he yelled (if there was breath enough), would anyone hear? Would they take notice? Would they come? Would they understand if they found him not on the ground but still hanging onto the ladder? Would they understand why he had done it, or would they say in scathing grown-up tones, "Silly child, get down from there"?

"I can't."

"If you can get up, you can get down."

"I can't."

"Come on down at once, John Sumner."

"It's no use. I can't go up and I can't get down and I can't even fall."

He flowed like fluid into the crevices of the ladder and hung there by the crook of an arm, by a knee bent through the rungs, and by his chin. He became hooked by the chin, his head went back, and he strained against something solid—himself—his own body fighting and crying to prevent its strangulation. There were no shakes, not now, only a war to the death against a rung of wood and his own weight.

He was not going to fall, not going to die on the ground; he was going to choke on the ladder, and they would find him there strung up like a chicken. The flag would be at half-mast and kids at school would say, "Did you hear about that stupid John Sumner? Couldn't even climb a ladder."

He screamed with anger deep inside, and not a sound came out, but his body of jelly turned into muscles and sinews and bones. His hands and arms moved; his legs moved; he fought off the pressure at his throat and raised himself up. He raised himself up three excruciating steps and with clawing fingers touched the bough.

He wanted to let go, to hit the ground in a heap, simply to know that it was over, but his fingernails were clawing bark, and he could see this thing happening, as though he stood a short distance off and something started cheering like thousands of people.

"That's the boy, John. Stick at it, John. You'll show 'em, John. Keep going, John. Don't stop now, John."

"I can't. I can't."

"You'll do it, John. It's a long way down but a short way up."

"It's *impossible.*"

"Fight for it, John."

He fought to hold the moment and keep the mood, and thousands cheered. He clawed and snatched and swung and madly scrambled and suddenly was crying. He was weeping as he had never wept in his life.

Only women and girls wept for joy—that was what people said—but it was not true. Boys wept like that, too.

He was sitting on the bough.

He couldn't see for tears, couldn't think, couldn't reason, couldn't look ahead or look back, but he knew what he had done.

"Hi-ya, bird. Hi-ya, cloud. Hi-ya, Mr. Sun. Here I am."

John went on to climb to the very top of the tree, and by doing so, he changed the whole course of his life. You can read the rest of the story in LET THE BALLOON GO *by Ivan Southall.*

AUTHOR

Ivan Southall is one of Australia's most distinguished children's book authors, and his books have received praise internationally as well. Australia, where he was born and lives, is the setting of his stories partly because when he was young none of the books for children were about Australia, and few were about children who seemed to be like him. However, he does not write only for Australian children; his books are published in many countries and many languages.

About John Clement Sumner in *Let the Balloon Go*, Ivan Southall has said, "John is my favorite hero, overcoming every obstacle, fighting like mad to be right. In a way, it's the story of everyone's life."

Mr. Southall's books for older readers *Hills End* and *Ash Road* have been on the American Library Association Notable Books list, and another, *Josh*, won the 1971 Carnegie Medal.

The Sneaky Water-Stealer

by William D. Hayes

Strange things happened in the Old West, especially in the town of Simpsonville—if the stories told about the place are to be believed. Simpsonville people always said that anyone who drank from the Hassayampa River was stretching the truth, for the Hassayampa was dry.

The Hassayampa wasn't the only river in the West that didn't have any water in it. Not by a long shot. And there came a time when the wells and water holes were going dry, too.

Folks in Simpsonville more or less expected Bart Winslow to come up with a way to solve the problem. Now, Bart didn't have any more idea what to do about the water shortage than the next fellow. But everybody knew Bart was the man who single-handedly wiped out the Jimson gang, which was known as the scourge of the West. So, naturally, folks considered Bart an expert on everything, including the water problem.

The bone-dry water shortage began to cause a lot of mighty hard feelings. The cattlemen said the sheepmen were stealing it all. Things got tense and more tense until nerves were strung tight as a fiddle string.

Now, the biggest cattleman in the territory was Matt Carney.

One day Carney rode into town shouting a lot of insulting things about sheepmen. Folks could hear him yelling clear from the Wells Fargo office at one end of town to the livery stable at the other. Carney stood right in the middle of Main Street, ankle-deep in dust, and yelled, "All sheepmen are low-down, thieving water-stealers. And none of them better ever cross my path. And that goes especially for Brod Reed."

Carney emphasized the point by patting his gun holster.

Now, everybody knew that Brod Reed was the biggest sheepman in the territory.

Some of the boys rode out to Reed's place and just happened to mention what Carney had said.

Not long after that, Reed stood in the same spot on Main Street where Carney had stood. "All cattlemen are yellow-bellied, sniveling water-stealers," Reed yelled. "I'd go hunt them all down right now—except that I just plain can't tell them from the cattle. And that goes especially for Matt Carney."

Some of the boys rode out to Carney's spread and advised him of what Reed had said.

Before long, the social arrangements were made, and Carney and Reed agreed to shoot it out on Main Street the following day at noon.

"Tomorrow noon!" Bart Winslow said when he heard about it out at the B-Bar-X. "That doesn't give me much time. But if somebody doesn't do something to stop that gun duel, we could have the biggest range war the West has ever seen."

"Look, Bart," Will Kingman said, "Carney and Reed are shooting mad. Nobody can stop that gun duel now. Not even you."

"I can try," Bart said. "There's something mighty peculiar about all that water disappearing. Maybe neither the cattlemen nor the sheepmen are to blame."

So, while folks in town prepared for the social event that was to take place the next day at noon, Bart took off from the

ranch. He rode out past Razorback Ridge. He studied the mountains and the sky, and he studied the rain clouds over Old Four Peaks.

All that night Bart rode over the hills watching those rain clouds.

Along about sunup the sky over Old Four Peaks split itself wide open with thunder and lightning. The clouds poured down their rain.

A few drops fell around Bart. But most of that rain funneled itself down toward just one place. Bart picked out a landmark that was right in the middle of where that rain was funneling. The landmark was a tall tamarisk tree.

Bart made his way to the tamarisk. There wasn't a drop of water in sight. He stomped his feet. Dust curled up from the dry, hot ground.

"Something must have soaked that rain right out of the air," Bart said to himself.

He looked at the rocks and the ground, and he looked up and down that tamarisk. But there wasn't a sign of where all that rain had gone.

The early morning sun bore down hot. Bart mopped the sweat from his face with a bandana. He went around and sat down on the shady side of the tree. That is, it *should* have been the shady side. As Bart took a sip of water from his canteen, he realized something.

There wasn't any shade.

Where the shade ought to be, there wasn't anything but sunshine.

Bart set his canteen down. He stared up at the branches. "Amazing!" he said to himself. "All that rain disappearing! A tree without any shade! I wonder if . . ."

A rustling sound made Bart freeze. He didn't move, except to look in the direction of the rustling sound.

And what to his amazement did he see but a root of that big tamarisk tree poking up right out of the ground and waving from side to side.

The root waved around in the air a few seconds. Then it leveled out and stretched along close to the ground. It came snaking right toward Bart's canteen.

When it reached the canteen, the root raised up and hovered there. It moved from side to side. Then it twisted itself right around the lid.

Bart could hardly believe his eyes.

That root unscrewed the lid and set it carefully on the ground. The root poked itself down inside and slurped every drop of water out of that canteen. Then it picked up the lid and screwed it back on.

The root slithered away, slow and sneaky, as if it knew it was being watched.

When it was back where it came from, it wiggled around and settled itself down into the ground. And there it stayed, all still and innocent-like.

Bart searched around to find some shade. Then he remembered. There wasn't any shade.

"Why, a tree like that," he said out loud, "a tree that drinks the rain before it gets to the ground and uses up all its own shade and steals the water right out of a man's canteen—a tree like that could almost . . ."

Bart jumped up. He looked at his railroad dollar watch that he got from a mail-order house in Kansas City.

There wasn't any time to lose.

Back in Simpsonville the folks were gathering along Main Street for the big social event—the shoot-out between Matt Carney and Brod Reed. The loose board in front of the Elite Hotel had kept up a steady clatter since sunup.

Everybody was all decked out in good picnic clothes, and there was a brass band, such as Simpsonville had to offer. All in all, it was turning into a right gala occasion.

Along toward noon the festivities quieted down. The loose board was still. The ring of the blacksmith's hammer stopped. The horses stopped whinnying. A kind of hushed silence settled over Simpsonville.

Matt Carney stood at one end of Main Street at the Wells Fargo Office.

Brod Reed stood at the other end of the street at the livery stable.

The big bank clock struck noon.

Carney and Reed started walking toward each other.

The only sound was the jangle of spurs as each step closed the distance between them.

They walked in a slow, measured rhythm, like counting the seconds till one or the other would die.

The place was so quiet you could almost hear a shadow on the wall.

"Stop!" somebody yelled.

Carney and Reed crouched.

"Stop!"

It was Bart Winslow.

Bart ran into the street. He jumped between Carney and Reed.

"Bart!" Carney yelled. "You trying to get your head shot off?"

"Beat it, Bart!" Reed yelled. "This is a private matter."

"Listen, everybody!" Bart shouted. "The water! I found out what's happening to all the water. And it isn't the cattlemen, or the sheepmen either, that are stealing it."

Well, at first folks were mighty sore at Bart for breaking up their social event. They grumbled as they came down off the sidewalk into the street. But they stopped grumbling when Bart told them about the rain funneling down toward that big tamarisk and how it used up all its own shade and how that root stole the water right out of his canteen.

There probably wasn't another man around who could have got away with breaking up that event. But everybody knew that Bart was the man who single-handedly wiped out the Jimson gang, which was known as the scourge of the West.

Bart took Carney and Reed and Mayor Hawkins and Judge Harper and a lot of other folks out for a close look at the wells and water holes. The roots of that one tamarisk had reached out for miles. Every one of those dry wells and water holes had a tamarisk root growing in it.

Finally Bart said to Carney and Reed, "Boys, I think it's time for you two to shake hands."

Carney and Reed looked down at the ground and scrubbed their toes in the dust. They grinned and shook hands.

It wasn't any easy job to get rid of that big tamarisk tree that was stealing the rain and most of the water for miles around. But Bart and a bunch of folks finally sawed clean through the trunk. That tree was so tall and fell so far and hit so hard, it split the ground wide open and sprung out some new springs of water that nobody knew about up to that time.

AUHTOR

William D. Hayes was born in Texas and grew up in Arizona in the desert and mountain country near the town of Mesa. A number of his books have as their setting the Southwest that he knows so well.

At an early age, he showed a talent for drawing, and at fourteen he decided to become a famous cartoonist. He and a friend filled the high-school newspaper with as many cartoons as they could.

Mr. Hayes graduated from the Journalism School at the University of Missouri and later attended the Art Students League in New York. His first professional writing experience was on a weekly newspaper, but he began his work in children's books as an illustrator. He has illustrated many books written by others and several of his own. He draws two weekly cartoon strips.

This story is from his book *How the True Facts Started in Simpsonville and Other Tales of the West*. Another of his recent books is *Hold That Computer!*

He lives in New York with his wife, Kathryn Hitte, who has written many books for children.

SONG OF AN UNLUCKY MAN

Chaff is in my eye,
A crocodile has me by the leg,
A goat is in the garden,
A porcupine is cooking in the pot,
Meal is drying on the pounding rock,
The King has summoned me to court,
And I must go to the funeral of my mother-in-law:
In short, I am busy.

unknown African poet

SKILL LESSON

USING AN ENCYCLOPEDIA

When you need to find information, you will often use special books called **reference books.** Reference books such as encylopedias, dictionaries, almanacs, and atlases contain information on many topics. The information in these books is organized so that you can find it quickly.

One of the most useful reference books for your purposes is likely to be an **encyclopedia.** It contains hundreds of articles which give information about famous people, about places, about things, about events, and about ideas. There you can find answers to such questions as: Why do volcanoes erupt? How were the first pyramids built? What causes tornadoes? Who invented baseball?

Because an encyclopedia contains so much information on so many different topics, it is usually made into a set of books. Each book in the set is called a volume.

The topics in an encyclopedia are arranged in alphabetical order. You will find on the spine (the narrow back edge) of each volume a guide letter or letters indicating the topics covered in that volume. In the picture at the top of the next page, notice the guide letter or letters and the number on each volume.

The guide letter or letters on each volume tell you the beginning letters of all the main topics listed in that volume. In the encyclopedia shown on the opposite page, so many topics start with *c* and *s* that there are two volumes for each of those

letters. The number on each volume helps you to place the volumes in order quickly, or to talk about a volume by its number.

In order to find information that an encyclopedia gives, you must first choose a key word to look for, just as you do when using an index. Suppose you need to answer this question: What is a star? You would use as your key word *star*. Since volumes 17 and 18 both contain topics beginning with the letter *s,* you will have to use the second letter in *star*. Because *st* comes between *so* and *sz* in alphabetical order, you would choose volume 18.

Often you will use more than one key word to find information on a topic. Suppose you need to answer the question: What is the difference between a planet and an asteroid? If you use only the word *planet* as a key word, you may not find all the information the encyclopedia gives. That is why you may also need to use the word *asteroid* as a key word. Thus, you should choose both volume **P** and volume **A** to find the answer to the question.

Topics having more than one word are usually alphabetized by the first word. You would find *North America* in the **N** volume and *Los Angeles* in the **L** volume. To find information about a person, you should use the person's last name as your key word. When you have selected the correct volume, you can find your key word quickly by using the guide words printed in heavy black type at the tops of most of the pages just as you use the guide words in a dictionary. What are the guide words on the encyclopedia pages shown in the first illustration on the opposite page?

Sometimes the title of an article, appearing in large type as the heading on a page, serves as the guide word. If there is a picture at the top of both facing pages, as in the illustration at the bottom of the opposite page, guide words are often omitted. If so, use as your guide words the first main topic on the left-hand page and the last main topic on the right-hand page. What words would you use as guide words for the pages shown in that bottom illustration?

When you have located the article you are looking for, you may find that it is a long one. Most long articles in an encyclopedia are divided into sections. Each section has a heading in heavy black type that tells what information that section contains. To find the information you are looking for, skim over these section headings until you find the one that seems to point to the information you want. In the bottom illustration on the opposite page, notice in the article on the BAT the headings *The Bodies of Bats* and *How Bats Navigate*. If you were trying to find information about how bats can find their way in the dark, in which section would you most likely find it?

As you read through an article in the encyclopedia, you may find the words *See* or *See also* followed by the name of another topic or topics. These cross-references name topics under which you can find more information on the subject of the article. Notice in the bottom illustration on the opposite page the cross-references at the end of the article on the BAT.

Sometimes you will find *only* a cross-reference after a topic you look up. For example, find the topic BATFISH in the bottom illustration on the opposite page. Notice that only the cross-reference *See SEA BAT* follows that topic. This means that all the information the encyclopedia gives about the BAT-FISH can be found in the article about the SEA BAT.

Mobiles sway gracefully in the wind, casting shadows on the walls or the floor.

MOBILE, *MOH beel,* is a contemporary type of sculpture. It is distinctive from other types of sculpture in that it achieves expression or meaning through movement. Traditional sculpture achieves its expression through the arrangement of solid forms. Mobiles are usually frail constructions of many rod-like projections loosely joined together. They are delicately balanced so they can swing freely in an infinite variety of moving arcs. The rods may end in *finials* (ending shapes) that recall the erosion effects of wind or water, or imaginative flight forms in space. Sculptors use many colors, textures, and materials for mobiles.

Most mobiles are suspended from above, so they can move freely overhead. Some are pivoted on a base. They are planned to present artistic interest not only in their actual shape, but also in the moving shadows they cast on walls and floor. Mobiles usually move as the result of natural currents of air, or the vibration of the earth. A few are designed for mechanical power.

A mobile's movement is of greater aesthetic value than its actual shape. The constantly swinging projections form arcs that cut shapes or volumes out of space. These volumes have no weight or substance, but they do remain fixed in our memory. The real design of a mobile is in this variety of space shapes, and in their abstract relationships with one another. Artists of many times and many places have created things that depend on movement for some part of their expression. But an American sculptor, Alexander Calder, was the first to create the true mobile, in which movement is the basic aesthetic purpose. Calder is regarded as the foremost creator of mobiles.

Wide acceptance of this new art form is obviously based on two significant facts. First, our art concepts have quite naturally grown to include the beauty of the machine in motion. Second, our minds have been freed to think and feel in terms of volumes of space that our eyes cannot see. BERNARD FRAZIER

See also CALDER, ALEXANDER; SCULPTURE (Form and Treatment; picture: Red Petals).

MOBILE, *moh BEEL,* Ala. (pop. 202,779; met. area 363,389; alt. 15 ft.), is the only seaport of Alabama, and one of the largest ports in the United States. Several streets of the city and its suburbs form the 35-mile Azalea Trail, featuring thousands of flowering azalea plants every spring.

Location, Size, and Description. Mobile is the second largest city in Alabama. It lies on the Mobile River at its entrance to Mobile Bay, 31 miles north of the Gulf of

MAKING MOBILES

Adapted from *How to Make Mobiles* by John Lynch © 1953 by Studio Publication, Inc.

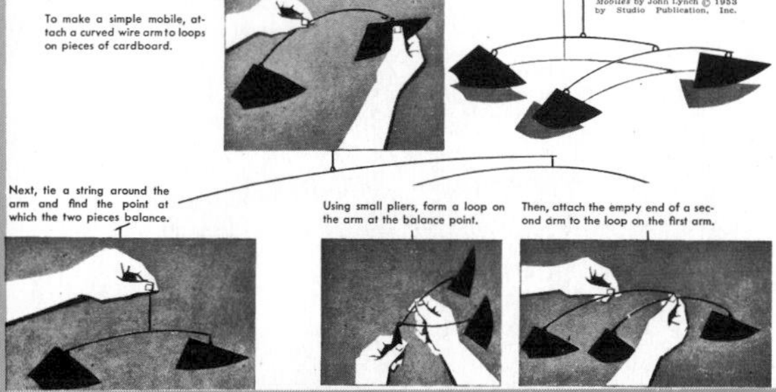

To make a simple mobile, attach a curved wire arm to loops on pieces of cardboard.

Next, tie a string around the arm and find the point at which the two pieces balance.

Using small pliers, form a loop on the arm at the balance point.

Then, attach the empty end of a second arm to the loop on the first arm.

Thigpen, Mobile Chamber of Commerce

Fort Gaines, on Dauphin Island at the entrance to Mobile Bay, protected Mobile from the Union Navy during the Civil War.

Mexico. For location, see ALABAMA (political map).

Huge moss-draped oak trees towering over historic Government Street form the entrance to the city from the west. Large trees and handsome homes line the residential streets. In the downtown district, small parks with giant shade trees provide relief from the office buildings. Beautiful suburbs such as Chateauguay, Delwood, and Spring Hill surround the city. Mobile is the home of Spring Hill College.

Industry and Commerce. Mobile is an important industrial and transportation center. Brookley Air Force Base, with more than 13,000 civilian employees, is Mobile's largest single employer. Paper and wood pulp used for paper is Mobile's largest single industry. Wood pulp is also the basic raw material for a large rayon fiber plant. Other important products include aluminum, lumber, rayon, roofing, cement, naval stores, chemicals, clothing, fertilizer, paint, and petroleum products. Shipbuilding and repair, and shipping itself, are other important industries. The Alabama State Docks can accommodate 30 ocean-going vessels at one time. The Port of Mobile handles over 17 million tons of cargo a year. Commercial fishermen in the area do a lively business in fish and oysters.

The city is served by four railroads and four bus lines. Four major airlines use Mobile's busy Bates Field. Bankhead Tunnel, the first underwater tunnel in the South, handles traffic under the Mobile River.

History. Founded originally in 1702 as Fort Louis de la Mobile, Mobile is one of the oldest cities in the United States. The settlers moved to the present site in 1711 because of flood waters. Mobile is often called *The City of Six Flags.* It has been ruled by the French, British, and Spanish, and has also flown the flags of the Republic of Alabama, the Confederate States, and the United States. The United States captured Mobile from the Spanish in 1813. Mobile was the last Southern stronghold to surrender to the Union forces at the end of the Civil War. Mobile received a city charter in 1819, and adopted commission government in 1910. It is the seat of Mobile County. CHARLES G. SUMMERSELL

For the monthly weather in Mobile, see ALABAMA (Climate). See also ALABAMA (pictures); IBERVILLE, SIEUR D'.

MOBILE BAY, BATTLE OF. See CIVIL WAR (Mobile Bay).

MOBILE COLLEGE. See UNIVERSITIES AND COLLEGES (table).

MOBILE HOME. See TRAILER.

MOBILE RIVER is a short stream in southwestern Alabama. It offers transportation for cotton and other farm products of its valley. The Mobile was named for the Mobile, or Maubila, Indians who once lived along its banks. The Mobile River is formed where the Alabama and Tombigbee rivers meet in Clarke County. The Mobile flows southward for 38 miles before it empties into the Gulf of Mexico through Mobile Bay. For location, see ALABAMA (physical map). The port of Mobile lies at the mouth of the river. WALLACE E. AKIN

MÖBIUS, AUGUST FERDINAND. See MATHEMATICS (A Strange Twist).

MOBUTU, *mo BOO too,* **JOSEPH DÉSIRÉ** (1930-), seized control of the government in Congo (Kinshasa) in 1960 and again in 1965. In 1965, he declared himself president for five years.

Mobutu was born in a small village in what was then the colony called the Belgian Congo. He studied in Belgium and served in the colonial army. Trouble broke out among Congolese groups when the colony gained independence in 1960, and it threatened to destroy the nation. Mobutu headed a military government that restored order. He ruled for five months. Mobutu seized power again when new trouble broke out in 1965.

MOBY DICK. See MELVILLE, HERMAN.

MOCCASIN, *MAHK uh sin.* The American Indians called their slipperlike footwear *moccasins.* They made moccasins of animal skin and often decorated them with beads, and sometimes porcupine quills. Moccasins are soft, closely fitted, and have no heels. They may be ankle-length or extend to the hip. Hair is left on the skin of winter moccasins to serve as a lining. See also INDIAN, AMERICAN (color picture). LYNN FARNOL

MOCCASIN FLOWER. See LADY'S-SLIPPER.

MOCCASIN SNAKE. See WATER MOCCASIN.

MOCHA. See COFFEE (Kinds).

MOCK ORANGE, sometimes called *syringa,* is a bush covered with clusters of small, single or double, white or creamy flowers. The flowers of some kinds of mock orange have purple spots at the base of their petals. In most plants, the flowers are fragrant, but some are odorless. Some types of mock orange have leaves with toothed edges. The bush generally does not grow very high, although some species do reach 20 feet.

Gardeners in the United States and Mexico grow many different kinds of mock orange. A few kinds also grow in Asia and Europe. Almost all types of this hardy plant bloom in June. Breeders have produced many beautiful hybrids of mock orange. One of these hybrids, *Philadelphus virginalis,* is among the best and most fragrant of the mock oranges. Many mock orange plants escape from gardens and grow wild. The syringa is the state flower of Idaho (see IDAHO [color picture]).

Scientific Classification. Mock oranges belong to the saxifrage family, *Saxifragaceae.* They make up the genus *Philadelphus.* J. J. LEVISON

MOCK-UP. See AIRPLANE MODEL.

MOCKINGBIRD is an American bird famous for its ability to imitate the sounds of other birds. One naturalist reported a mockingbird in South Carolina

Harold E. Edgerton

The Little Brown Bat, *above,* uses the skin attached to its tail as flying equipment. To stop or turn, it bends its tail downward as a brake, much as an airplane does. The thin skin of the fruit bat's wings, *below,* is stretched like the silk of an opened parasol upon the long, slim bones of its forearms and fingers.

BAT is a small furry animal that flies. Its wings are thin skin that stretches from the arm-like front limb along the side of the body to the leg. Long bones allow the wings to stretch even farther. The bat's small body looks somewhat like a mouse's body. *Flittermouse* is an old-fashioned name for this animal.

Like mice, dogs, cats, and elephants, bats are *mammals.* That is, they feed their babies milk that is made in the body of the mother. But bats are the only mammals that can fly.

The world contains several hundred *species* (kinds) of bats. They are most common in warm climates, and the biggest bats live there. But there are about 40 species of bats in the United States. Four small kinds are even found in Alaska and northern Canada. Some of the northern bats fly south when winter begins. Others sleep through the winter in the hollow trees, caves, and buildings where they make their homes.

Most kinds of bats are useful to mankind. They eat vast numbers of harmful insects. Sometimes hundreds of thousands of insect-eating bats live together in caves or empty dwellings. The bat manure, or "bat guano," which collects on the floors of such places, is a valuable fertilizer for plants. Since prehistoric times, large populations of bats have lived for many years in caves. In some of these caves, the bat guano has formed layers many feet thick.

A few kinds of tropical bats are harmful. Among them are the large fruit-eating bats, or *flying foxes,* and the *vampire bats.* Flying foxes may gather in orchards and destroy fruit crops. Vampire bats live on the blood of other animals and human beings. The bite of a vampire bat and the bites of other kinds of bats may transmit rabies. But most bats do not harm human beings. Many people dread bats and have strange beliefs about them. This is probably because most bats fly at night and are not seen very often at close range.

The Bodies of Bats. Most bats are small. The little brown bat, which is common in the United States, has a body less than four inches long. It can spread its wings to a distance of 14 inches. One of the largest bats, the flying fox, lives in southeastern Asia. This bat's body is one foot long, and its wingspread may measure about five feet.

The heads of bats have many extraordinary shapes. Some of them look like the heads of tiny bulldogs, or like bears with long, pointed teeth. Other kinds, such as the *horse-headed bat* and the *long-tongued bat* of the tropics, have long snouts. Many have growths on their noses that look like horseshoes, leaves, or flowers. These growths carry *sensory* (feeling) nerve endings.

How Bats Navigate. Some insect-eating bats that feed on the wing have a keen sense of hearing that guides them in the dark. They produce twittering sounds so high-pitched that human beings cannot hear their full range. These sound waves strike objects in the path of flight and send back echoes to the bats' ears. The echoes tell the bats how they must turn in the air to avoid colliding with objects or with one another. By using their ears, bats can fly skillfully at night or in the utter darkness of caves. Experimenters, stringing threads across a room, have found that bats can find their way even with their eyes covered. But bats become nearly helpless in the dark if their ears or mouths are covered.

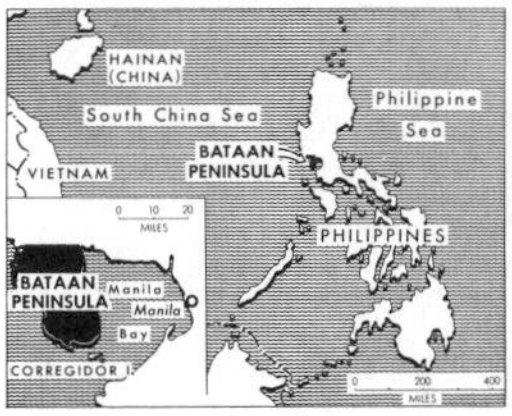

United Press Int.

Bataan Peninsula shelters Manila Bay from the South China Sea. Olongapo, *above,* lies on the northwestern part of the peninsula. In World War II, outnumbered U.S. and Filipino troops fought gallantly on the peninsula before surrendering to Japanese forces.

While they are flying, some bats catch large insects in their mouths. Some kinds of bats use their tail membranes to catch flying insects. Others use their wings to do the same job. During the day, bats sleep hanging from the ceilings of their homes by their hind feet. They usually hang upside down, with their wings draped around their bodies like cloaks. Bats are clumsy on the ground, because their wings get in their way and their knees bend backward. But in the air, few birds can fly as expertly as bats.

Scientific Classification. The bat belongs to the order of mammals called *Chiroptera,* meaning *hand-winged.* The most common bats in the United States are the red bat and the little brown bat. They belong to the family *Vespertilionidae.* The red bat is genus *Lasiurus,* species *L. borealis.* The brown bat is *Myotis lucifugus.* FRANK B. GOLLEY

See also ANIMAL (color picture: Animals of the Deserts); FLYING FOX; VAMPIRE BAT; GUANO.

BATA, *BAH tah* (pop. 27,024; alt. 7 ft.), is the capital of Río Muni, a province of Equatorial Guinea. Bata is a seaport on the Gulf of Guinea. For location, see EQUATORIAL GUINEA (map).

BATAAN DEATH MARCH. See WORLD WAR II (Burma and the Philippines).

BATAAN PENINSULA juts into Manila Bay from the southwestern coast of Luzon, largest of the Philippine Islands. On Bataan Peninsula, United States and Filipino troops held out for more than three months against much larger Japanese forces during World War II. Early in January, 1942, General Douglas MacArthur managed to withdraw his scattered troops into this hilly country. Once established on the peninsula, U.S. and Filipino forces found themselves hemmed in by the Japanese and cut off from any help.

For 98 days, this band of defenders beat back Japanese attacks. When an estimated 200,000 Japanese broke through their lines, the Americans and Filipinos withdrew to the very tip of the peninsula. MacArthur was ordered to report to Australia, and Lieutenant General Jonathan M. Wainwright took command of U.S. and Filipino forces in the Philippines. Major General Edward P. King, Jr. took command of U.S. and Filipino forces on Bataan Peninsula. On April 9, 1942, General King surrendered to the Japanese. The Japanese took about 75,000 Americans and Filipinos prisoner. Some men escaped to the fortress of Corregidor in Manila Bay, where they fought until May 6, 1942.

In February, 1945, troops under the command of MacArthur returned to Bataan. They landed on southern Bataan, captured points on Corregidor, and opened Manila Bay. Japanese forces surrendered, and surviving Americans and Filipinos were freed. In 1954, President Ramón R. Magsaysay of the Philippine Republic issued an order making the battlefield areas of Bataan and Corregidor national shrines. RUSSELL H. FIFIELD

BATAVIA. See DJAKARTA.

BATES, KATHARINE LEE (1859-1929), an American poet and educator, wrote the words of the hymn, "America the Beautiful." She wrote short stories and books of travel, as well as poetry. Her hymn may be found in her *Selected Poems* (1930). *Fairy Gold* (1916) is a book of verse for children. Miss Bates was born in Falmouth, Mass. She graduated from Wellesley College and taught there from 1885 to 1925. PETER VIERECK

See also AMERICA THE BEAUTIFUL.

BATES COLLEGE. See UNIVERSITIES AND COLLEGES (table).

BATFISH. See SEA BAT.

BATH (pop. 85,870; alt. 405 ft.), is a health resort in England. It lies on the River Avon near Bristol in southwestern England (see GREAT BRITAIN [map]). The city is built on hills, and is famous for the Georgian architectural style of its houses. Some persons believe Bath's warm springs and mineral waters have health-giving qualities. The Romans founded Bath and used the springs. Baths the Romans built still stand. Bath became a resort for English high society in the 1700's. The *Wife of Bath* is a famous character in Geoffrey Chaucer's *Canterbury Tales.* JOHN W. WEBB

BATH, Me. (pop. 10,717; alt. 5 ft.), has been a shipbuilding center since the days of wooden ships. Today, it produces guided-missile destroyers for the U.S. Navy. Bath lies about 12 miles from the Atlantic Coast (see MAINE [political map]). The town is named for Bath, England. Founded in 1781, it was incorporated as a city in 1847. Bath has a council-manager form of government. ROBERT M. YORK

BATH, KNIGHTS OF THE. See KNIGHTS OF THE BATH.

From *The World Book Encyclopedia.* © 1970 Field Enterprises Educational Corporation.

Discussion

Help your class answer these questions:

1. Why are reference books good sources to use when you need to find information?
2. How do guide letters, key words, and guide words help you in locating information in an encyclopedia?
3. How do section headings help you to find quickly in an article the information that you want?
4. What do cross-references tell you?

On your own

Answer the following questions on a sheet of paper. Write the number and letter of each part of a question first (1a, 1b, and so on) and then your answer to it.

1. What key word or key words would you use to find information to answer each of these questions?
   a. How is a boomerang made?
   b. What does the Painted Desert look like?
   c. How does the moon affect the tides?
2. What is the number of the volume of the encyclopedia pictured on page 189 in which you would look for information to answer each of the following questions?
   a. For what kind of paintings was Bradley Walker Tomlin best known?
   b. When was San Diego first settled?
   c. Why is Yellowstone National Park an interesting place to visit?
3. In a long article about the planet Mars in an encyclopedia, the following section headings appear: Size, Movement and Distance, Moons of Mars, Life on Mars, and The Canals of Mars. In which section would you look to find information to help you answer each of the following questions?
   a. How far is Mars from the sun?
   b. Is there any plant life on Mars?
   c. Is Mars larger than our own planet Earth?
   d. Is there any positive evidence that there are canals on Mars?
   e. About how long would it take a space ship to travel from Earth to Mars?

Checking your work

If you are asked to do so, read aloud one or more of your answers. Then tell why you answered each question as you did. Listen while other boys and girls read their answers, and compare your answers with theirs. If you made a mistake, find out why it was a mistake.

IVIAHOCA

by Pura Belpré

Iviahoca, whose name in the Indian language meant "Behold the mountain that reigns," was the wife of an Indian chief, a brave *cacique*. Her husband was loved and respected by all. When she bore him a son and named the boy Ocoro, the news filled the tribe with joy and the *cacique* with pride.

The *bohique*—the doctor and high priest, historian and preserver of the heroic past—ordered the ritual *Areitos* in honor of the event. That day the village was thronged with *caciques* from far and near. They wore their multicolored feather headdresses. Never had dances been more spirited nor games played with greater skill. Ocoro's parents were pleased and proud of their people's expression of love.

But the joy of the Indians was soon changed to sorrow. Those were days of strife and frequent invasions. The Indians had to protect their island home not only against their old enemies, the Caribs, but against the new invaders from far across the sea—the Spanish Conquistadors. Ocoro was still

From *Once in Puerto Rico* by Pura Belpré. Copyright © 1973 by Pura Belpré. Used by permission of the publisher, Frederick Warne & Co., Inc.

a baby when his father was mortally wounded in a battle. As the wife of the *cacique*, Iviahoca knew that her duty was to be buried with him. But as she prepared for the ceremonies, the tribe was so stricken with grief that they appealed to the *bohique* to have mercy on Iviahoca. His heart was touched by their sorrow, and he spared her life so that she might rear Ocoro to fill his father's place.

True to the meaning of her name, Iviahoca retired to the mountains to rear her son. She was happy and proud of her tribe. She realized the great privilege she had been granted, the great responsibility and trust that were laid upon her. She wanted her son to grow as sturdy as the trees and as sensitive as the flowers. And so Ocoro grew.

His mother taught him the names of the trees and plants and their uses, and she showed him the mountain trails and caves. In the clear sparkling nights, while he learned about the sky and the stars, she told him the story of the past and explained his duty for the future. Ocoro grew wise, strong, and as free as the mountain air.

At last Iviahoca came down from the mountain and left her son with the old *bohique*, who could teach him the arts of fighting and playing games and, above all, songs and dances of the Areito, the great ceremony of his tribe.

When Ocoro was wise in all these things, he was assigned to the service of a famous chief, Mabodamoca. The Chief was so impressed by the boy's strength that he compared Ocoro to the *acaná*, the strongest and finest of all the trees on the mountain. Ocoro won a place of honor in all warlike and ceremonial activities, and the Chief kept him constantly by his side.

Ocoro was by his side when Mabodamoca launched an attack on Diego de Salazar, the brave Spanish captain. The Spanish soldiers were few, but they were fierce fighters, and the thunder of their guns was terrible. Ocoro fought like a wild lion while his companions fell like flies about him. He was beside his chief when Mabodamoca fell, slain by a shot from one of the Spanish guns. Ocoro would have chosen to share his leader's fate, but instead he was captured by the Spaniards and carried off to their camp.

Up in the mountain, Iviahoca heard the news of the battle and came down to inquire about the fate of her son. She searched the battlefield until she was certain that her son was not among the dead and wounded. Then she went boldly to the Spanish camp and demanded to see him, but her request was denied.

Then she told the Spaniards she had come to offer her life for her son. With a shrug of his shoulders, one of the soldiers brought forth Ocoro. Iviahoca clung to her son while he tried to comfort her. She held him with the strength of a young woman, and when the soldiers dragged him away, Iviahoca refused to leave the camp. She crouched by the tent of the Spanish captain and spent the night in sorrow.

At dawn Don Diego de Salazar sat down to write a letter to Ponce de León, the leader of the Spanish invaders. The letter told of the bitter fighting and the need for reinforcement. Don Diego knew that the *caciques* of the island had united for a great attack. He knew of their anger, their longing to win back the land they had lost to the Spaniards. He could not expose his small army to another—and far greater—battle with the Indians.

The letter must be sent at once, but who could be trusted to carry it? As he pressed his seal upon the folded paper, he heard some sounds outside his tent. A soldier told him it was an old Indian woman. She had come looking for her son who was held a prisoner, and she had refused to leave without him.

"Let her come in," ordered Don Diego de Salazar, "and send me her son."

Mother and son were soon reunited. Iviahoca sensed the

kindness of the Spanish captain, and she said to him, "Señor Salazar, I know you must have a mother. Because of her, you can understand my suffering. My son is young and loves his liberty. He should live to enjoy it. I am old. If he were kept in captivity, my last remaining days would be agony. But if I knew he was free, I could pass those days in peace, whatever tasks and trials might come to me. Take my life and my services for his liberty."

Astonished at her offer, the Captain handed her the letter and said, "Woman, if you manage to take this letter to Don Ponce de León, who camps at the bend of the Aymaco River, your son will be set free, as you desire. As soon as I have proof that you have fulfilled your part, I will fulfill mine."

Immediately Iviahoca sprang from the tent and plunged into the thicket beyond the camp. In spite of her age, she ran as swiftly as a deer.

But she did not see that she was being followed. Three soldiers, envious of her mission, wanted to steal the letter and deliver it themselves. With them went Becerrillo, the great dog trained for war, who drew a soldier's salary for every battle won. On and on they ran, dashing through the underbrush and brambles, but no matter how fast they went, Iviahoca ran faster. Unable to catch up with her, they decided to set Becerrillo on her trail.

On went the dog, his black eyes sparkling, his liver-colored hide showing red against the green of the forest. He was famous for trailing Indians. He ran with head low and mouth open, his black nose sniffing the Indian scent. The soldiers followed at a distance, not daring to cross his path. Suddenly Becerrillo gave a yelp and tore through a thicket. It was a yelp of triumph.

Iviahoca heard him and stopped. She saw the dog come plunging through the thicket with his teeth bared. She thought he was a *hupía*, a devil in the shape of a dog, feared by all Indians, and she fell on her knees. "Señor Dog," she cried, "do not harm me! I am on my way to deliver a letter from the

Europeans to their Chief. Do not harm me, Señor Dog!"

The three soldiers could not believe what they saw. There stood the fierce Becerrillo, quietly listening as though he understood what the woman said. Then, to their amazement, the dog moved aside and let her pass.

Iviahoca darted away faster than ever, and soon she was out of sight. Becerrillo turned back the way he had come. The soldiers tried to set him on the trail again, but the dog refused to obey. In disgust they followed him home to the camp.

By sundown of the same day, Iviahoca returned to Don Diego with a letter in her hand. The three soldiers were among the first to see her and could only stare in stunned surprise. Don Diego tore open the letter and read it and then relayed its message to all his men. His words were drowned by their cheering. They were no longer alone; Juan Ponce de León was bringing his entire company to help them!

In their excitement, the three soldiers who had followed Iviahoca pressed forward to tell their captain what had happened. Captain Salazar turned to Iviahoca and asked her if she had met any difficulties in delivering his message.

"Just once," she said, "when a *hupía* crossed my path. But after I had pleaded with him, the *hupía* turned back and let me go."

Even as she spoke, the sound of trumpets filled the camp. The first of the reinforcements had arrived! Captain Salazar stepped forward to meet his commander, Don Juan Ponce de León. After exchanging greetings and news, the captain invited Ponce de León to see a hundred Indian captives, taken prisoner in the last battle. As the two Conquistadors viewed the silent prisoners, the sight of Ocoro reminded Captain Salazar of his promise to Iviahoca. He told the story to Ponce de León, and both men decided to free Ocoro at once.

A group of soldiers brought mother and son to face the Spanish captains. Captain Salazar explained that Ocoro was to be free, but Iviahoca must remain as hostage.

Ocoro shook his head when he heard this. "Captain," he said, "I am grateful for your generosity to me, but I cannot accept it. I cannot leave my mother enslaved. I prefer to be killed, or made a slave myself, rather than to gain my freedom at such a price."

Both captains were deeply moved by his speech. They exchanged glances, and without the need of words they came to an agreement. Ponce de Leon gave a sharp command.

"Release Ocoro from his bonds!"

When this was done, the great captain spoke to Ocoro and Iviahoca in a voice the soldiers never forgot. "Both of you have shown in words and deeds the nobility of your souls. We are assured of your gratitude. We are giving both of you your freedom. Go and may heaven protect you."

Her eyes dimmed by tears, Iviahoca kissed the hands of the Spanish captains. Ocoro, more reserved but just as thankful, bent his head to them. Then Iviahoca whispered something to her son; they turned together, crossed the clearing, and began to run toward the mountain.

The Spaniards never saw them again, but they never forgot them. When all the island was conquered, and Spaniards and Indians were no longer at war, the names of Iviahoca and Ocoro were still remembered. The Spaniards kept their memory alive whenever parents told their children the story of Iviahoca, whose name in the Indian language means "Behold the mountain that reigns."

AUTHOR

Pura Belpré was born and educated in Puerto Rico. After she moved to New York City, she worked in the New York Public Library and attended library school. A tale she prepared for a storytelling course became her first book, *Perez and Martina*. She has written other books for young readers, as well as such collections of folk stories as *The Tiger and the Rabbit, Dance of the Animals,* and the book from which this story was taken, *Once in Puerto Rico*. Pura Belpré has presented puppet shows based on legends from her native land as another way of helping all children to become acquainted with the culture and background of Puerto Rico. She also continues to tell stories aloud to groups of children.

Her late husband, Clarence Cameron White, was a violinist and composer.

Mary Cassatt:
Child in a Straw Hat

by Marian King

Mary Cassatt, a famous American artist, painted this picture, "Child in a Straw Hat," in about 1886. Probably the artist was then living in the French countryside. This appealing French country child wears a quaint high-necked pinafore over a white short-sleeved dress. Her large, yellow straw hat with its broad crown trimmed with black and white ribbons

sits at a jaunty angle on her straggly, blond hair. Her dark-brown eyes look very sad, almost tearful. Her pouting mouth makes her seem all the more unhappy.

Why do you think she is unhappy? Is it because she doesn't like having her picture painted? Or do you think she is afraid to raise her arms to straighten the big hat that the artist has placed on her head?

Mary Cassatt was born in 1845 in Allegheny City, Pennsylvania, which is now a part of Pittsburgh. She was one of five children—two girls and three boys. Her mother, a well-educated person, shared her learning with her family.

When Mary Cassatt was seven years old, she went with her parents, sister, and brothers to Europe. In schools in France and Germany, the children learned both languages. After a seven-year stay in Europe, the Cassatt family came back to the United States. They settled in Philadelphia, where the children went to school. Mary Cassatt spent much of her spare time drawing. She knew even then that she wanted to be an artist.

When she finished school, Mary Cassatt attended her first art classes at the Pennsylvania Academy of the Fine Arts in Philadelphia. She soon realized, however, that drawing sketches of plaster casts of ancient statues was not what she wanted. It was not until she was twenty-three years old that her father finally agreed that she should go to Europe to study art.

After studying and copying the old masters in the galleries of Italy, Spain, Belgium, and Holland, Mary Cassatt settled in Paris in 1874. During the following three years, her paintings were included in exhibits at the Paris Salon. In 1877, at the suggestion of her family but against her own will, she entered an artist's studio, where she studied for only a short time. Mary Cassatt wanted to work on her own and develop her own way of painting.

About this time, Edgar Degas (day-gah′), a noted French artist whom Mary Cassatt had never met, was impressed by her talent. He asked her to exhibit with the impressionists, a group of artists who had found a new way of expressing in paintings the things they saw. She was the only American invited to exhibit with this group, and she accepted with joy.

It was not until her own first exhibition in Paris, when she was forty-seven years old, that Mary Cassatt's name as an artist became fully established.

Mary Cassatt worked on and on through the years, painting, drawing, and etching. She did pictures of young women, of mothers with delightful babies, and children of all ages. No matter what her subject, Mary Cassatt's works of art have brought much pleasure to many people. During her lifetime, she was given many honors and awards.

In her later years, Mary Cassatt spent much time helping Americans who came to Europe to add to their collections of art. It is due to her wonderful judgment that many fine paintings of the impressionists and old masters have come to the United States.

As she grew older, her eyesight began to fail more and more until finally she was blind. On June 14, 1926, at the age of eighty-one, Mary Cassatt died at her country home in France.

Although she lived in France for forty-six years of her life and made only three return visits to the United States, Mary Cassatt was an American at heart. She vowed, "I am an American . . . frankly an American." And she truly was.

Since Mary Cassatt's death, exhibitions of her work have been held in the United States. Among the delightful, beautifully painted works of art by Mary Cassatt is this much-loved painting of a little girl in a big straw hat.

A detail from CHILD IN A STRAW HAT, *Mary Cassatt, Collection of Mr. and Mrs. Paul Mellon.*

Delicatessen

Gosh! Look at all the food!
The show window is crammed;
And inside—
Shelves, counter and showcases
                are jammed
With all kinds of food.

There's sausage and goat cheese,
Sauerkraut and pig's feet;
Things with funny names
That must be good to eat.
Braunschweiger, limburger,
                pickled beets,
Pumpernickel, liverwurst and
                all kinds of sweets.
Corn beef, ravioli, Chinese chow mein,
Kielbasa, noodles, head-cheese plain;

Bread-and-butter pickles,
                whole-grain bread,
French-fried potatoes and catsup red.
Wienerwurst, herring,
                dill pickles and rye;
Blintzes and bagels—
                don't pass them by.
Get your money out
            from the pockets in your pants,
And don't forget
            the chocolate-covered ants!

Foods with funny names
            must be good to eat;
Delicatessen
            is the place for a treat!

Lois Lenski

THOMAS JEFFERSON:
Dollars, Dimes, and Cents

by S. Carl Hirsch

The summer night had turned hot. Thomas Jefferson tested the wind and wondered if there was enough stir in the air to carry the ship out of Boston Harbor and onto the high seas, It was July 4, 1784. Jefferson was bound for France as United States minister. The American Revolution was only a few years behind him.

In the lantern light, beaver skins in bundles of ten were being passed hand to hand by the men loading the ship.

"Eight tens. Nine tens. A hundred." The captain counted aloud as the last of the cargo moved steadily toward the hold.

For days, weeks, Jefferson had been absorbed with the way people count and reckon. In some primitive time early people had invented a system of numbers. Their ever-ready computers were their ten fingers or toes. This was the simplest kind of arithmetic— counting fingers, then repeating the process. Jefferson recalled that this was the same method he had learned as a child in a Virginia school. "Count to ten, then start over again."

In ancient times, many groups of people used the fingers of only one hand, counting by fives. A few counted by twenties, apparently using the fingers of both hands and the toes of both feet as well. But somehow the system based on ten numbers survived the longest. The decimal system, with a number base of ten, was the most common of all counting schemes.

It was this thought that became

most important in Jefferson's mind when the government of the United States called on him to think of a system for money and for weights and measures to be used by the newborn nation.

The moneys being used then in America were a jangling tangle of confusion. Most people could not make head nor tail out of it all. Spanish and English, French and Portuguese coins passed from hand to hand, and few Americans had any notion of their fixed worth. In addition, the individual colonies had made their own coins in a confusing range of sizes, shapes, and values.

Jefferson was wisely chosen to lead the United States out of the mess. The Virginian was a man who loved order and had a talent for finding it.

Within a few months, while doing many other major duties, Jefferson put together a new plan for United States coinage. Jefferson's money system was to become a model for all the world. It was as easily understood as it was useful.

To begin with, the commonly used counting system was based on the number ten. Then why not tie all other systems to the same

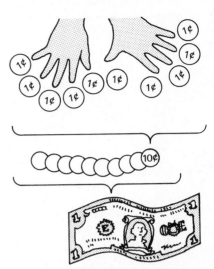

base of ten? No other system lent itself to such easy reckoning. Jefferson wanted a system so easy to use that not even a child would be likely to make a mistake.

Take, for example, that remarkable little decimal point. One could multiply or divide by ten, a hundred, or a thousand simply by moving the decimal point. As for adding and subtracting, the decimal system was by far the fastest and easiest.

The dollar was to be the new standard of United States money. There would be a simple decimal ratio between the dollar and all larger and smaller pieces of money. When Jefferson left for Europe, he knew that he had completed a good plan. The nation agreed and adopted his system of dollars, dimes, and cents.

A Cat Called Good Fortune

from

The Cat Who Went to Heaven

by Elizabeth Coatsworth

Once upon a time, far away in Japan, a poor young artist sat alone in his little house, waiting for his dinner. His housekeeper had gone to market, and he sat sighing to think of all the things he wished she would bring home. He expected her to hurry in at any minute, bowing and opening her little basket to show him how wisely she had spent their few pennies. He heard her step, and jumped up. He was very hungry!

But the housekeeper lingered by the door, and the basket stayed shut.

"Come," he cried, "what is in that basket?"

The housekeeper trembled, and held the basket tight in two hands. "It has seemed to me, sir," she said, "that we are very lonely here." Her wrinkled face looked humble and obstinate.

"Lonely!" said the artist. "I should think so! How can we have guests when we have nothing to offer them? It is so long since I have tasted rice cakes that I forget what they taste like!" And he sighed again, for he loved rice cakes, and dumplings, and little cakes filled with sweet bean jelly. He loved tea served in fine china cups, in company with some friend, seated on flat cushions, talking perhaps about a spray of peach blossoms standing like a little princess in an alcove. But weeks and weeks had gone by since anyone had bought even the smallest picture. The poor artist was glad enough to have rice and a coarse fish now and then. If he did not sell another picture soon, he would not have even that. His eyes went back to the basket. Perhaps the old woman had managed to pick up a turnip or two, or even a peach, too ripe to haggle long over.

"Sir," said the housekeeper, seeing the direction of his look, "it has often seemed to me that I was kept awake by rats."

At that the artist laughed out loud.

"Rats?" he repeated. "Rats? My dear old woman, no rats come to such a poor house as this where not the smallest crumb falls to the mats."

Then he looked at the housekeeper and a dreadful suspicion filled his mind.

"You have brought us home nothing to eat!" he said.

"True, master," said the old woman sorrowfully.

"You have brought us home a cat!" said the artist.

"My master knows everything!" answered the housekeeper, bowing low.

Then the artist jumped to his feet, and strode up and down the room, and pulled his hair, and it seemed to him that he would die of hunger and anger.

"A cat? A cat?" he cried. "Have you gone mad? Here we are starving, and you must bring home a goblin, a goblin to share the little we have, and perhaps to suck our blood at night!

Yes! It will be fine to wake up in the dark and feel teeth at our throats and look into eyes as big as lanterns! But perhaps you are right! Perhaps we are so miserable it would be a good thing to have us die at once and be carried over the ridge-poles in the jaws of a devil!''

"But master, master, there are many good cats, too!'' cried the poor old woman. "Have you forgotten the little boy who drew all the pictures of cats on the screens of the deserted temple and then went to sleep in a closet and heard such a racket in the middle of the night? And in the morning when he awoke again, he found the giant rat lying dead, master— the rat who had come to kill him! Who destroyed the rat, sir, tell me that? It was his own cats; there they sat on the screen as he had drawn them, but there was blood on their claws! And he became a great artist like yourself. Surely, there are many good cats, master.''

Then the old woman began to cry. The artist stopped and looked at her as the tears fell from her bright black eyes and ran down the wrinkles in her cheeks. Why should he be angry? He had gone hungry before.

"Well, well," he said, "sometimes it is good fortune to have even a devil in the household. It keeps other devils away. Now I suppose this cat of yours will wish to eat. Perhaps it may arrange for us to have some food in the house. Who knows? We can't be worse off than we are."

The housekeeper bowed very low in gratitude.

"There is not a kinder heart in the whole town than my master's," she said, and prepared to carry the covered basket into the kitchen.

But the artist stopped her. Like all artists he was curious.

"Let us see the creature," he said, pretending he scarcely cared whether he saw it or not.

So the old woman put down the basket and opened the lid. Nothing happened for a moment. Then a round, pretty, white head came slowly above the bamboo, and two big yellow eyes looked about the room, and a little white paw appeared on the rim. Suddenly, without moving the basket at all, a little white cat jumped out on the mats and stood there as a person might stand who scarcely knew if she were welcome. Now that the cat was out of the basket, the artist saw that she had yellow and black spots on her sides, a little tail like a rabbit's, and that she did everything daintily.

"Oh, a three-colored cat," said the artist. "Why didn't you say so from the beginning? Three-colored cats are very lucky, I understand."

As soon as the little cat heard him speak so kindly, she walked over to him and bowed down her head as though she were saluting him, while the old woman clapped her hands for joy. The artist forgot that he was hungry. He had seen nothing so lovely as their cat for a long time.

"She will have to have a name," he declared, sitting down

again on the old matting while the cat stood sedately before him. "Let me see: She is like new snow dotted with gold pieces and lacquer; she is like a white flower on which butter-flies of two kinds have alighted; she is like——"

But here he stopped. For a sound like a teakettle crooning on the fire was filling his little room.

"How contented!" sighed the artist. "This is better than rice." Then he said to the housekeeper, "We have been lonely, I see now."

"May I humbly suggest," said the housekeeper, "that we call this cat Good Fortune?"

Somehow the name reminded the artist of all his troubles.

"Anything will do," he said, getting up and tightening his belt over his empty stomach, "but take her to the kitchen now, out of the way." No sooner were the words out of his mouth than the little cat rose and walked away, softly and meekly.

The next morning the artist found the cat curled up in a ball on his cushion.

"Ah! the softest place, I see!" said he. Good Fortune im-mediately rose, and moving away, began to wash herself with the greatest thoroughness and dexterity. When the house-keeper came back from market and cooked the small meal, Good Fortune did not go near the stove, though her eyes wandered toward it now and then and her thistledown whis-kers quivered slightly with hunger. She happened to be pres-ent when the old woman brought in a low table and set it before her master. Next came a bowl of fish soup—goodness knows how the housekeeper must have wheedled to get that fish!—but Good Fortune made a point of keeping her eyes in the other direction.

"One would say," said the artist, pleased by her behavior, "that she understood it is not polite to stare at people while they eat. She has been very properly brought up. From whom did you buy her?"

"I bought her from a fisherman in the market," said the old

woman. "She is the eldest daughter of his chief cat. You know a junk never puts out to sea without a cat to frighten away the water devils."

"Pooh!" said the artist. "A cat doesn't frighten devils. They are kin. The sea demons spare a ship out of courtesy to the cat, not from fear of her."

The old woman did not contradict. She knew her place better than that. Good Fortune continued to sit with her face to the wall.

The artist took another sip or two of soup. Then he said to the housekeeper, "Please be kind enough to bring a bowl for Good Fortune when you bring my rice. She must be hungry."

When the bowl came, he called her politely. Having been properly invited, Good Fortune stopped looking at the other side of the room, and came to sit beside her master. She took care not to eat hurriedly and soil her white, round chin. Although she must have been very hungry, she would eat only half her rice. It was as though she kept the rest for the next day, wishing to be no more of a burden than she could help.

So the days went. Each morning the artist knelt quietly on a mat and painted beautiful little pictures that no one bought: some of warriors with two swords; some of lovely ladies doing up their long curtains of hair; some of the demons of the wind blowing out their cheeks; and some little laughable ones of rabbits running in the moonlight or fat badgers beating on their stomachs like drums. While he worked, the old woman went to market with a few of their remaining pennies. She spent the rest of her time in cooking, washing, scrubbing, and darning to keep their threadbare clothes together. Good Fortune, having found that she was unable to help either of them, sat quietly in the sun, ate as little as she could, and often spent hours with lowered head before the image of the Buddha on its low shelf.

"She is praying to the Enlightened One," said the housekeeper in admiration.

"She is catching flies," said the artist. "You would believe anything wonderful of your spotted cat." Perhaps he was a little ashamed to remember how seldom he prayed now when his heart felt so heavy.

But one day he was forced to admit that Good Fortune was not like other cats. He was sitting in his special room watching sparrows fly in and out of the hydrangea bushes outside, when he saw Good Fortune leap from a shadow and catch a bird. In a second the brown wings, the black-capped head, the legs like briers, the frightened eyes were between her paws. The artist would have clapped his hands and tried to scare her away, but before he had time to make the least move, he saw Good Fortune hesitate and then slowly, slowly, lift first one white paw and then another from the sparrow. Unhurt, in a loud whir of wings, the bird flew away.

"What mercy!" cried the artist, and the tears came into his eyes. Well he knew his cat must be hungry, and well he knew what hunger felt like. "I am ashamed when I think that I called such a cat a goblin," he thought. "Why, she is more virtuous than a priest."

It was just then, at that very moment, that the old house-keeper appeared, trying hard to hide her excitement.

"Master!" she said as soon as she could find words. "Master! The head priest from the temple himself is here in the next room and wishes to see you. What, oh what, do you think His Honor has come here for?"

"The priest from the temple wishes to see me?" repeated the artist, scarcely able to believe his ears, for the priest was a very important person, not one likely to spend his time in visiting poor artists whom nobody thought much of. When the housekeeper had nodded her head until it nearly fell off, the artist felt as excited as she did. But he forced himself to be calm.

"Run! run!" he exclaimed. "Buy tea and cakes," and he pressed into the old woman's hands the last thing of value he owned, the vase which stood in the alcove of his room and always held a branch or spray of flowers. But even if his room must be bare after this, the artist did not hesitate: No guest

could be turned away without proper entertainment. He was
ashamed to think that he had kept the priest waiting for even
a minute and had not seen him coming and welcomed him at
the door. He scarcely felt Good Fortune rub encouragingly
against his ankles as he hurried off.

In the next room the priest sat, lost in meditation. The artist bowed low before him, drawing in his breath politely,
and then waited to be noticed. It seemed to him a century before the priest lifted his head and the far-off look went out of
his eyes. Then the artist bowed again and said that his house
was honored forever by so holy a presence.

The priest wasted no time in coming to the point.

"We desire," said he, "a painting of the death of our Lord
Buddha for the temple. There was some discussion as to the
artist, so we put slips of paper, each marked with a name, before the central image in the great hall, and in the morning all
the slips had blown away but yours. So we knew Buddha's
will in the matter. Hearing something of your circumstances,

I have brought a first payment with me so that you may relieve your mind of worry while at your work. Only a clear pool has beautiful reflections. If the work is successful, as we hope, your fortune is made, for what the temple approves becomes the fashion in the town.'' With that the priest drew a heavy purse from his belt.

The artist never remembered how he thanked the priest, or served him the ceremonial tea, or bowed him to his narrow gate. Here at last was a chance for fame and fortune. He felt that this might be all a dream. Why had the Buddha chosen him? He had been too sad to pray often and the housekeeper too busy—could it be that Buddha would listen to the prayers of a little spotted cat? He was afraid that he would wake up and find that the whole thing was an apparition and that the purse was filled with withered leaves. Perhaps he never would have come to himself if he had not been roused by a very curious noise.

It was a double kind of noise. It was not exactly like any noise that the artist had ever heard. The artist, who was always curious, went into the kitchen to see what could be making the sound, and there, sure enough, were the housekeeper and Good Fortune, and one was crying for joy and one was purring for joy, and it would have been hard to have said which was making more noise. At that the artist had to laugh out loud, but it was not his old sad sort of laugh; this was like a boy's—and he took them both into his arms. Then there were three sounds of joy in the poor old kitchen.

The story you have just read is the first chapter in the book THE CAT WHO WENT TO HEAVEN. *The book goes on to tell how Good Fortune brought about a bold change in her master's plan as he worked on the great painting for the temple—a change which made a miracle happen.*

ABOUT THE AUTHOR

Elizabeth Coatsworth was born in Buffalo, New York. One of the best-known children's authors, she began creating stories as a child. When she was too young to write, her mother would write them down for her.

She graduated from Vassar College, received an M.A. degree from Columbia University, and studied for a year at Radcliffe College. Soon her short stories, articles, and poetry began to appear in many magazines. She has written nearly eighty books, including a Newbery Award winner, *The Cat Who Went to Heaven*, from which this story was taken. In 1968, she was a runner-up for the Hans Christian Andersen Medal, which is given to outstanding authors chosen from all over the world.

Miss Coatsworth feels that every book should, in some way, sharpen the reader's appetite for living. "So many elements go into writing a book that it is difficult to unravel the strands," she says. "In the case of *The Cat Who Went to Heaven*, I can trace a life-long interest in legends . . . joined to a year in the Orient, a large family of Maine cats, and a period of leisure in a small house between the bare hills of California and the sea."

Her greatest interest, besides writing, has always been travel. Since the age of five, she has traveled widely in Asia, Europe, and North America, including Mexico, Guatemala, and many parts of the United States and Canada. Some of her recent books reflect her interest in different parts of the world: *The Princess and the Lion* is set in ancient Africa; *Jon, the Unlucky* is set in Greenland; Canada is the setting of *Jock's Island.*

Miss Coatsworth spent many of her adult years living and traveling in New England, and she now lives on an old farm overlooking a lake in Maine.

BOOKS TO ENJOY

J. D. *by Mari Evans*

J. D. is the hero of four lively stories set in the black neighborhood of a small Midwestern city.

WILL YOU SIGN HERE, JOHN HANCOCK? *by Jean Fritz*

This is a comical and interesting biography of the first signer of the Declaration of Independence.

EMERGENCY! 10-33 ON CHANNEL 11 *by Hilary Milton*

Jane's ability to call for help for her family on the CB radio leads to a frantic search-and-rescue effort.

RACING ON THE WIND *by Edward and Ruth Radlauer*

There are many ways of taking part in wind-powered sports — as a glide-kite flier, a balloonist, a water-ski-kite flier, or an ice boater, among others.

DORRIE'S BOOK *by Marilyn Sachs*

Dorrie's delightful life as an only child is shattered when her mother has triplets.

MAGGIE MARMELSTEIN FOR PRESIDENT

by Marjorie Weinman Sharmat

She really wants to be Thad's campaign manager in the classroom elections, but when he turns her down, Maggie herself decides to run. A sequel to *Getting Something on Maggie Marmelstein.*

A BICYCLE FROM BRIDGETOWN *by Dawn C. Thomas*

A boy who lives on the Caribbean island of Barbados unexpectedly has a problem when he finds his dream come true — owning a real racing bicycle.

Spirals

Spirals

STORIES

ARTICLE

POEMS

JUST FOR FUN

SKILL LESSONS

A Horse for Reg

by *Anne Huston and Jane Yolen*

Reg, who lived in New York City, was spending the summer on Jim and Dee Bradshaw's farm. He had hoped that they would have a horse he could take care of, but unfortunately their only horse had died. Reg wasn't too happy on the farm and after a while wondered if he would be able to finish out the summer. Then something happened that caused Reg to change his mind. A truck that was carrying several horses to a farm, where they were to be killed for horsemeat, ran off the road into a ditch. The horses escaped, but soon all except one were recaptured. Reg discovered the one escapee up in the hills near the Bradshaws' farm. Reg befriended the poor animal and hid him in an old deserted cabin. Every night he would secretly slip away from the farm to be with his horse, Roachy.

For the next few days, Reg kept his self-imposed schedule. He got up early and helped on the farm whenever he could. Sometimes he worked in the fields with Jim and Frank. When he did, he was always careful not to say or do anything that might make either one suspicious.

More often, however, Reg stayed around the farmhouse with Dee. He found her more comfortable to work with, for she never questioned anything he did. And he could always manage to hide a few things to take to Roachy at night.

He wrote three postcards home, too, careful to say what a good time he was having. He asked Dee how to spell a few words and gave the cards to Jim to mail. Then they both could read what he had written. He felt like a secret agent fooling the enemy.

Reg didn't like to admit it, but he was getting pretty tired. Still, he kept going. All the Bradshaws were behaving as he hoped they would. No one suspected he was making midnight journeys up the mountain, he felt sure.

And no one seemed to be missing any of the things he was borrowing for Roachy. They were all pleased that he was adjusting to farm life so well.

But Reg was not completely happy with his midnight visits. It wasn't just that he had to lie and sneak in order to be with his horse; that was only part of it. Mainly, Reg was unhappy because he never got to see Roachy in the daylight. It wasn't enough just to feel the horse's sides in the dark and guess if he were filling out. It wasn't enough just to touch the horse's soft muzzle in the blackness. Reg wanted, more than anything, to be with Roachy during the day.

Besides, he thought, a horse shouldn't be cooped up all day. Jim's cows aren't. It's not healthy. Roachy should be out in the sun, like humans. He shouldn't only be a night horse—a nightmare! Reg giggled at the last thought, though Roachy was really a male.

But, try as he might, he couldn't figure out a solution.

It was Dee who found the answer. Toward the end of the

week, Reg was in the kitchen with her, canning cherries. Dee called him the best helper she had ever had. "Though I must admit," she had added, "I never had a helper before."

They both laughed at that.

Reg was sitting at the table with a big bowl of cherries in front of him. His job was to pit them, and it was a simple task. All he had to do was stick a fork in the cherry and pull out the hard little seed. But his eyes kept closing, and he had to jerk himself awake constantly.

"Reg? Reg, did you hear me?"

Reg quickly jerked awake again. "What? Did you say something?"

Dee laughed. "Why, you are a sleepyhead. I said it to you four times. I'm ready for more cherries. You really must be tired."

"No, I'm all right. Honest, I am." Reg sat up straighter and forced his eyes wide open.

Dee came to the table and sat down beside him. "Reg, Jim and I have noticed how hard you have been working this week. We think it's wonderful. But we've also noticed that you've begun to look very, very tired. That's not so good. We don't want you to work so hard that you fall over from exhaustion. You're really a city boy, not used to the hard physical labor on a farm."

"I'm all right. Honest," Reg repeated. He sensed something coming and he couldn't tell what it was.

"Maybe so, but we thought you might like a change, a little recreation. A little more fun." She paused. "Frank is taking this afternoon off and riding his bike over to the Warshams'. They live down the road, and they're twins, a boy and a girl—maybe Frank has told you about them already. Well, I have an old bike you could ride, and you could go along with Frank. It's a girl's bike, but

had ever spent. It was cool and peaceful, and a light wind rustled the trees that surrounded the clearing. First, Reg made a branch broom and cleaned out the cabin. It was smelly, messy work, but he kept singing, "It's for Roachy. Old horse Roachy," and the work went quickly.

Then he started talking to the horse—sweet-talking—and getting the horse really used to him. At last, he led Roachy from the cabin and took out the cow brush.

"It's time you got cleaned up, old horse," he said. He brushed and brushed until this time the old horse's coat really did shine. "Boy! You sure don't look like the scarecrow horse I saw that first day," Reg said. "You're beautiful now. Really beautiful . . . in a funny sort of way," he added honestly.

Roachy almost looked like a different horse. His lip still hung down in a pout, but the sharp angles of his body were mostly gone. In their place were the beginnings of nice, round curves.

"Just round enough to ride," Reg said. Then he added softly, "Will you let me get on your back? I just want to sit there a little while. It'll be your first time with me, and my first time ever on a horse. Please, Roachy?"

He stood looking at the broad brown back. Then he stretched his arms up and put his hands on Roachy's withers. The horse didn't move away; he only bent his neck to eat the grass that grew in the clearing. Reg tried to boost himself up. He jumped several times. Once, he got his chest across the horse's back, but he couldn't hang on long enough to swing his legs over. Roachy turned his head and watched the proceedings with interest. He nibbled at Reg's pants, looking for some more sugar.

Reg slid to the ground, discouraged. "At least you stood still for me," he said to Roachy, "even if I couldn't get on."

Reg then looked all around for something to stand on, but there wasn't even a tree stump. Then he had an idea. He led Roachy back to the cabin and placed him alongside the wall, under the window.

"Don't move," he said to the horse, and ran inside. He then

scrambled up onto the window sill. Clinging to the window with one hand, he put his leg out and over the horse. Then he pushed off with his other foot and landed squarely on Roachy's back.

Reg held his breath anxiously. Would Roachy try to buck him off?

The horse only turned his head and nibbled at Reg's leg again.

"You *are* my pal," Reg said joyfully. "You want me to be here." He leaned over and stroked Roachy's neck. Then he straightened up. He felt like an Indian brave; he felt like a soldier; like a knight. No, he felt like a king, a king on his faithful charger.

Reg became aware of Roachy's warmth underneath him. He tightened his grip with his legs and felt the horse's sides swell with breath.

Suddenly the old horse threw his head up as if he had heard a call. He swiveled his ears forward and whinnied loudly, for he had caught the feeling, too.

"Let's take a walk," Reg said proudly as he touched his heels to Roachy's sides. "Let's take a walk around our kingdom!"

AUTHOR

The two authors who wrote *Trust a City Kid,* the book from which the story you just read was taken, are Anne Huston and Jane Yolen.

Miss Huston was born in Lyndhurst, Ohio. After graduation from an Ohio college, she moved to New York to become an actress. Since that time, she has appeared on television, in movies, and in the theater. Another of her activities was organizing a company of actors to perform children's plays in the New York City area. Besides *Trust a City Kid,* Miss Huston has written another book called *The Cat Across the Way.*

Jane Yolen, whose married name is Jane Stemple, enjoys skiing, camping, dancing, and folk-singing. She and her husband spent eight months camping in Europe and in the Middle East. Before returning to the United States, Mr. and Mrs. Stemple worked in Israel on a kibbutz — a kind of farm.

Mrs. Stemple was born in New York City, but she was raised in Westport, Connecticut. Besides writing books for boys and girls, she also writes musical plays for children's theater.

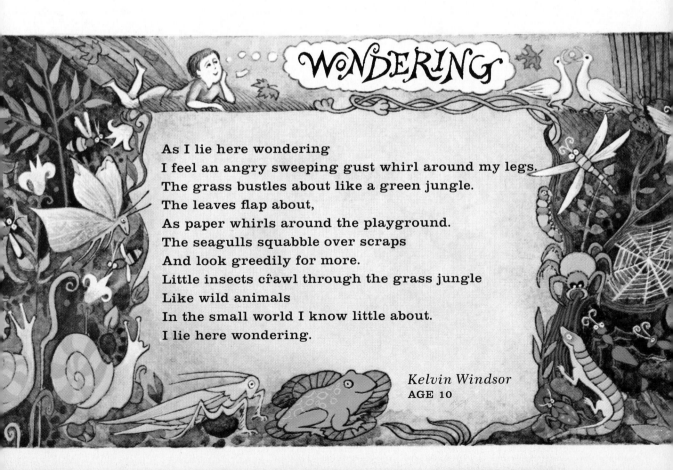

WONDERING

As I lie here wondering
I feel an angry sweeping gust whirl around my legs.
The grass bustles about like a green jungle.
The leaves flap about,
As paper whirls around the playground.
The seagulls squabble over scraps
And look greedily for more.
Little insects crawl through the grass jungle
Like wild animals
In the small world I know little about.
I lie here wondering.

Kelvin Windsor
AGE 10

The King of the Frogs

This fable from Humphrey Harman's book TALES TOLD NEAR A CROCODILE *tells how the frogs learned a lesson — the hard way.*

Have you ever been beside a lake in Africa at night and listened to the frogs? You haven't? Then you cannot imagine what the noise is like. And it's not just one kind of noise; it's several. Over there, for instance, are a thousand creaking doors that have never had their hinges oiled, and someone opens and shuts them—and keeps on doing just that. Over *there* are a thousand fat men snoring, and no one wakes them up. Then there are a thousand carpenters sawing planks, and all the saws need a touch of grease, and a thousand little bells are being struck, and a thousand corks are being pulled out of bottles.

Noise! You can hardly hear yourself think.

Then you go a little closer until you can just see the edge of the water and perhaps a reed or two, and there is silence. Just the splash of a frog jumping into the water late because he was asleep and didn't hear you coming. Then nothing, and you can hear the whole world breathe. There's a story about this.

Long ago the frogs did as they pleased, and the result was dreadful. Not one of them would listen to what another said, and they all shouted at once. Children wouldn't obey their parents, and husbands and wives wouldn't listen to one another, which is, indeed, something hardly to be understood. It was all noisy and untidy beyond bearing, and nothing ever got done.

At last a wise, wise old frog called everyone to a meeting. Since he had a very fine voice and went on shouting for long enough, he managed to get them all there at once, for, to tell you the truth, they were pretty sick of living the way they did.

"Frogs!" said the old frog, puffing himself up. "We cannot go on like this. It's no sort of life for anyone and, anyway, when you see how all the other creatures live, it makes one ashamed of being a frog. There is only one thing to do. We must get a king. When people have kings, there is peace and order and everyone does as he is told."

"Agreed!" they all shouted, and they stayed long enough to commission the old frog to see what he could do about getting them one, before everybody fell to quarreling and pushing and splashing. The meeting—as usual—broke up in disorder.

Then the wise, wise old frog went to see the great god Mmumi (you will say the two m's correctly if you hum a little before you begin the word). Mmumi happened to be in charge of that part of the world.

Mmumi is a very slow god and usually gives people more than they bargain for. He agreed drowsily that the frogs needed a king and promised to do something about it. Then he went to sleep again.

So the frogs went on as usual, which was badly, until one day Mmumi woke up, remembered his promise, took a great green mossy boulder which had the rough shape of a gigantic frog, and threw it into the water.

splash

"There you are!" he shouted (it sounded like thunder). "There's your king. His name's Gogo and, like me, he doesn't want to be disturbed. Respect him and be satisfied."

The whole lake was shaken by Gogo's fall. The waves washed through the reeds and tore up the shore, and in the middle of a great cloud of mud Gogo settled on the bottom, and the fat green waterweeds curled round and over him. He looked shocking.

The frogs were terrified and fled under stones and into dark corners and holes under the bank. Their long white legs streaked behind them as they swam. Parents found their children, and husbands found their wives, and then they settled down to explaining what had happened.

"This is our king," they said, "and a fine, terrible one he seems, and from the splash he made, not the sort to fool about with. Now all will be well and this scandalous behavior will stop." And so it did, for a while.

But although Gogo had made such a wonderful first impression, as time passed, they noticed that he never moved. He just sat quietly in the mud and stared in the same direction. Presently they began to get used to him, until finally some young, bold, bad frogs ventured to swim close to him, and then one of them touched his nose.

And still Gogo said and did nothing.

"Bah! He's not a king!" they shouted. "He's not even a frog. He's just an old stone and couldn't hurt anyone." And they swam round him until they were dizzy, and jumped all over his back, and went away and spoke rudely about him to their elders.

At first none of the elders believed them. They had told their children Gogo was a king, and a king he had to be, but soon it was impossible to deny that the children were right, and then . . . Well, the noise began again, and things were as they had always been, only worse. Terrible!

The wise, wise old frog sighed and set out to see Mmumi again, who was not at all pleased at being woken again.

"All right!" he shouted in a rage. "*All right!* You aren't satisfied with the king I've given you. Is that the way it is? Very well, you shall have another, and I hope you like him."

And the very next night he gave them Mamba the Croco-dile.

Gogo had come to his people with a splash that shook the lake, but Mamba slid into the water with only a whisper and left but one small ring spreading gently to show that he had come. Then he swam, silent as a shadow, lithe and long and secret, his jaws grinning like a trap. Gogo had never visited the people he had been given to rule, but Mamba visited them often and suddenly. And whenever he met a subject, the great jaws gaped and closed, and often it was the last of that frog.

The frogs developed great respect for their new king and lived quietly, looking over the backs of their heads as frogs can. Now and again at night they break out, but they keep their ears open, and if you go near the lake, they shut up.

They think that it's Mamba coming to put a little order into them, and they keep quiet.

A FLYING TACKLE

by Rafe Gibbs

"No, I'm sorry . . . . My sister can't talk to you even if it *is* very important. No, it wouldn't be a good idea to hold the line. Maria takes very long showers. She . . ."

"Angelita, who's that on the phone?"

"It's Mr. Roston of the mine at Coralio. He says there's an emergency. But you said you just *had* to get some rest tonight. You . . ."

"Angelita! Tell Mr. Roston to hold on."

Angelita was just old enough— twelve—to think she should take care of her sister, Maria, who thus far in her twenty-three years had done very well taking care of herself—and of Angelita. MARIA CARRERA, her business card read, PRESIDENT, WIDE WEST CHARTER AIR SERVICE, EL PASO, TEXAS. It wasn't a very big air service, but it was all Maria's.

Now, wearing a bathrobe and drying her hair with a towel, Maria hurried into the living room of the apartment. She flicked the towel at Angelita and picked up the phone.

Charlie Roston was in charge

of reopening the old Solitas Gold Mine. Angelita couldn't help but overhear his excited voice:

"Look, Maria, I'm calling on a matter of life or death. We were blasting, and Pete Drummond got hit in the head with flying rock! Now he doesn't know what he's doing or saying. We've got to get him to the hospital at El Paso in a hurry. That's why I called you. Only your two pilots have ever landed on our canyon airstrip. It's so short it's tricky even in the daytime, and this landing and takeoff at night . . . I'll set out burning oil drums, but . . ."

"Jerry's on an overnight to Los Angeles to pick up supplies," broke in Maria. "But Ed's at Marfa. He could fly from there."

"Great! Great! If Ed can get him to the hospital, Pete Drummond will be one grateful mining engineer. He . . ."

"Wait a minute! Did you say mining engineer?"

"Yes. He's a mining engineer."

"Charlie, you just said two magic words. All that I am and all that I have I owe to another mining engineer. I've been wanting to pay off the debt for a long time. I'll pick up this Pete Drummond myself."

"But Maria, you've never made a landing here!"

"I'll be there, Charlie. This is something I *have* to do."

Ten minutes later, Maria was hurrying out of the apartment building—with Angelita right behind her.

"Angelita, you're not coming."

"But it's necessary."

"Necessary?"

"Well, you said the injured man is Pete Drummond. Don't you know who he is?"

"Never heard of him before."

"Shame on you, Maria. He made all-American tackle at Michigan Tech."

"So?"

"So he's six feet four and weighs two hundred and fifty pounds. Somebody will have to be looking after him in the plane, and for taking off on that short airstrip, you'll want that somebody to weigh as little as possible."

Maria never ceased to be amazed by her little sister. Angelita knew a lot about airplanes and much more about sports. Not only was she well on her way to becoming a tennis star, but watching sports on television had made her a walking encyclopedia on football, basketball, and baseball.

"All right, Angelita, you win," Maria said with a sigh.

And she was going to be very glad that Angelita did win.

A half-hour later the Carrera sisters were airborne. Their plane was an old but sturdy single-prop craft that had been stripped of seats so that it could be used for hauling light cargo. It could be landed in places too tight for heavier cargo planes. And there were many such places in this part of Texas.

Now the girls were flying over ruggedly beautiful Big Bend National Park. There was still a touch of purple light in the sky, and below they could see the park's high mountains, deep canyons, sprawling deserts—and, moving through a patch of prickly pear, a herd of pronghorn antelope.

Maria and Angelita loved every inch of this giant land. It was like their home country in Mexico where they had found that other mining engineer . . . beside his crashed plane. . . .

It was hot that day nine years earlier. Maria and little Angelita were astride their burro, Terco (Spanish for *Stubborn*), watching a herd of goats grazing in a

canyon south of the little village of Placido.

"Look," said Angelita suddenly, pointing to the sky. "A big bird."

"That's not a bird," Maria told her. "It's an airplane. But I think something's wrong. Listen to the sound. The motor's growling like an angry dog."

As they watched and listened, the motor stopped, started again, and once more sputtered into silence. Then the plane began to go down rapidly and disappeared from sight. In the distance a great cloud of dust arose.

"Let's find the airplane! Someone may be hurt!" cried Maria. Angelita held her sister around the waist, expecting a fast ride.

But there was no fast ride. Terco lived up to his name, and it took twenty minutes to get to the scene. One wing of the plane was a mass of twisted metal. Beside it, on the ground, a slim man with graying hair was lying motionless. Maria jumped from Terco's back, lifted off Angelita, and hurried to the still figure.

"He's breathing!" Maria cried. "But his arm is badly cut—there, below his elbow! Maybe I can stop the bleeding with a pressure bandage."

As little Angelita watched with great interest, Maria tore the shirt sleeve from the injured arm. Then, ripping off the other sleeve, she folded it into a thick pad.

"Angelita, hand me the belt from your dress!"

Angelita looked puzzled but handed over the soft belt. With it Maria tied the pad tightly over the cut and then sat back with a sigh. "There," she said, "I hope that does it. I don't see any other wounds."

"Look!" cried Angelita, "He moved, and now he's opening his eyes!"

Maria bent over the man, who was now trying to sit up. As calmly as she could, she told him, "You've been thrown from your plane. Don't try to get up unless you're pretty sure you didn't break any bones."

The man looked American, but he understood the Spanish that Maria was speaking, because he did as he was told. And then he too spoke in Spanish. "I don't feel any broken bones," he said, "but I don't think I *can* get up yet. I feel so weak."

"You've lost much blood, sir. That's a very bad cut you have on your arm. I have put a pressure bandage on it the way they showed us in school. It has stopped the bleeding."

"You learned well in school, but I'm glad you weren't in school today."

"It's a holiday. I like holidays, but I like school, too. Someday, if I can find a gold mine and get lots of money, I may study at a university."

"Well, I'm a mining engineer, and I may be able to help you find that gold mine. But what I need to do right now is find a doctor. I'm beginning to feel a bit stronger."

"There's one in Placido, near here. If you're able to climb onto Terco, my sister and I will take you there."

So Maria and Angelita, pulling an unwilling Terco along as fast as they could, managed to get their grateful patient to the Placido doctor.

Two months later, Maria was very much surprised when she received a letter from a man named Carlos L. Delgado, president of the Lone Star State Bank in El Paso. It said in part:

Mr. Robert G. Mitchell, the well-known mining engineer, is very grateful to you and your sister for saving his life, and he wants to thank you in a special way. A bachelor, he has no children, so he wants to educate you two as he would have educated children of his own.

We have learned that your parents are no longer living and that you are now staying in Placido with grandparents. However, an uncle and aunt in El Paso would be pleased to have you live with them. Wherever you choose to be, a trust fund for each of you, set up by Mr. Mitchell, will pay for all your expenses through college. . . .

That wonderful letter brought the Carrera sisters to El Paso, the mountain-rimmed city on the Texas side of the Rio Grande— and to a new way of life. For Angelita, not yet in school, the change was easy. For Maria, it was abrupt and hard.

Language was Maria's main problem, for she had to learn a new one. At first, because she was shy and because she couldn't speak English, she made friends only with others of Mexican descent. She soon realized that she wasn't learning English by speaking Spanish so much. She began to look for new friends among those who spoke only English, and that didn't please her old friends. Then Maria went to great lengths to explain why she was doing what she was doing, and soon everybody wanted to help her with her English. Maria was on her way. She became a member of the high school Pep Club. At first, she wasn't always certain what she was cheering about at football games, but she thought that being there was great fun anyway. She graduated with honors and went on to study business administration at the University of Texas in Aus-

tin. Not wanting to leave Angelita in El Paso, she took her with her to share an apartment.

Midway through the university, Maria added flying lessons to her studies. She had her mind made up. When she graduated, she would go into the aviation business, but first she had to learn to fly. She didn't want to ask banker Delgado whether her trust fund could be used to pay for flying lessons, so she took a job at the university library to pay for them.

Throughout the years, the girls never saw Mr. Mitchell. Once in a while he sent them a letter from

some distant and fascinating land. He had promised that he would try to attend Maria's graduation, but just a week before the big day Maria opened her morning newspaper to a headline that brought a rush of tears to her eyes:

ROBERT MITCHELL, NOTED MINING ENGINEER, DIES OF TROPICAL DISEASE IN SOUTH PACIFIC

Mr. Delgado attended the graduation exercises with Angelita, and when he congratulated Maria, he spoke of Mr. Mitchell. "He wanted this to be such a happy day for you," Mr. Delgado said, handing Maria an envelope, "and it would have been for him, too. . . . But he left something for you."

Maria didn't open the envelope until she and Angelita got home. Inside were two pieces of paper. One was a note to Mr. Delgado, written on hotel stationery:

I know that you have wisely invested the trust funds for Maria and Angelita and that the funds have grown with the years. As you know, I said that what is left in her fund should be given each of the girls upon her graduation from college. I plan to be at Maria's graduation, so will you please have a check ready for me to give to her?

P.S. In case I shouldn't make it, will you kindly do the honors for me?

The other piece of paper in the envelope was a check for $24,567. It was with this money, and with a loan from Mr. Delgado's bank, that Maria had started the Wide West Charter Air Service.

Such were the thoughts that both Maria and Angelita were thinking as they flew toward the Solitas Gold Mine to pick up another injured mining engineer. Yes, this was one flight Maria had to make herself. With luck, she could at last repay the debt.

When she saw the lights marking the tiny airstrip at the mine, Maria's heart sank. They weren't much—twelve burning oil drums and the headlights of five trucks. But Maria didn't hesitate. As if she had aimed a dart at a target and hit the bull's eye, she set the plane down at the very beginning of the strip and braked to a stop with yards to spare.

Charlie Roston had a crew ready with a stretcher bearing Pete Drummond. Four men strained to get him into the plane.

"We've bandaged his head and given him a knockout shot. He should sleep like a baby all the way to El Paso," said Roston.

"Don't worry. I'll stay right at his side," said Angelita.

Roston smiled. "Thank you—both of you—for coming. And good luck!"

"We'll need a whole pocketful of luck," thought Maria as she revved the engine and started her takeoff with the 250 added pounds of Pete Drummond stretched out on the floor behind her. The airstrip looked short—terribly short—as the plane moved through the makeshift rows of lights.

"Speed . . . We need speed!" Maria said to herself, and the engine responded. Just before the plane began to lift, there was a slight bump and a popping sound.

"We're away! We made it!" cried Angelita.

"Not quite," Maria called back to her. "I think the right-hand tire just blew."

"That's bad!"

"I'll call the El Paso tower and ask for standby emergency equipment and foam on the runway."

Angelita thought a moment.

"Maria!"

"Yes."

"If there's trouble, I'm glad we'll be together."

"Angelita, you're O.K."

Tension hung heavy in the plane, but the sisters had no more conversation until they were nearing El Paso. Then Pete Drummond began to moan and cry out. Maria couldn't hear him well enough above the roar of the engine to understand what he was saying. She called to Angelita, "Try to soothe him. He probably thinks he's still trapped in the mine."

"He doesn't think he's in any mine! He's delirious—he thinks he's in the locker room at Michigan Tech during his last big game

with Aurora University. He injured his leg in that game and never played again. I know. I saw the game on television."

"Well, talk to him. Try to distract him. Just don't let him get up."

But there was no distracting Pete. "I've got to get back into the game," he cried. "Aurora's going through right tackle like a knife through butter. We'll never hold on to our lead if I don't. Where's the doc?"

"Uh, he'll be there when we land," Angelita began. Then, realizing she must humor Pete in his fantasy, she continued, "I mean, it won't be long now. And Michigan Tech has the ball again. Hey! Larry Kowiski just caught a forty-yard pass!"

"Yeah . . . good old Larry . . . great play! But Burt Stevens . . . he's fumbled. . . . It's Aurora's ball. I've got to get out there!"

Pete raised himself up onto one elbow, and Angelita pressed her hand against his shoulder.

"Coach Helber says you're to lie still."

"I know—I know. The coach is saving me for next week's game. Oh, no! Aurora scored. If they kick the point, the score'll be

tied. Wahoo! They didn't make it! But fourteen to thirteen is too close. I've got to get back in."

Pete pushed himself up to a sitting position.

"Now, Pete, don't you worry," said Angelita soothingly. "Michigan Tech is going to win."

Then she remembered! At that point in the game an Aurora sophomore had picked up a Michigan Tech fumble and run eighty-two yards to score and defeat Michigan Tech.

Pete remembered the run at the same time. He struggled to his feet and staggered toward the door.

"Stop him! Stop him!" screamed Maria from the cockpit.

Angelita dove—a flying tackle—and hung on. Pete reached for the door handle, missed it, and toppled to the floor. He lay very still.

"I didn't mean to hit him *that* hard," cried Angelita.

"Check his breathing," called Maria.

"His breathing's fine."

"Then relax, but keep a close eye on him."

There was no relaxing, however, for either Maria or Angelita— not with the thought of landing in a crippled plane. Angelita tried singing and was on her fifth song when she stopped abruptly.

"Maria, how long will it be before we reach El Paso?"

"We're over El Paso—flying in a pattern to use up gas. The less gas, the less danger of fire when we land, you know."

"Well, Pete's starting to come to. He may try to get out again, and he's so big to tackle."

Maria made her decision.

"I'll call the tower and ask for clearance to come in now."

Within minutes, Maria was making her landing approach.

"Angelita, there are a couple of blankets in back. Put one under Pete's head. Fluff it up like a pillow. Then you lie down on the floor, too, and put the other blanket under your head."

A ground crew with two fire trucks and two ambulances stood ready at the foamed runway. They watched, mostly in silence.

"She'll make it," said a fire fighter. "She's good."

The plane moved down . . . down. . . .

"This is it! She's touching!"

The left wheel hit the runway, bounced once, and began to roll.

"Attagirl! Keep on that good tire as long as you can."

But now the plane settled on both wheels . . . started to twist . . . to turn. . . .

Maria fought to keep her craft on the runway. Rubber strips from the blown tire began to fly off. Sparks shot from the right wheel. The plane lurched sideways, tipped alarmingly, and then slid on the foam to a quivering stop.

Maria turned to Angelita.

"Are you and Pete all right?"

"I know I am, and I think he is, too," replied Angelita. "He's beginning to talk again about getting back into the Aurora game."

"My debt to mining engineers is now paid," Maria said quietly to herself.

As the girls stepped out of the plane, they were greeted by the cheering ground crew.

"Good show, Maria! You were great—just great."

"Thank you, everybody," said Maria.

Angelita squeezed her sister's hand. "I think you were great, too," she said.

"Thanks, Angelita, but I didn't do it all. The flying tackle played an important part, and I intend to let everyone know it."

Five days later, when Pete Drummond was able to see some

visitors, Maria and Angelita visited him in the hospital.

"I'm glad you came," he said, smiling up at them from the bed. "I've been wanting to say, 'Thank you,' to you both. That reminds me—I received a telegram today from Coach Red Helber at Michigan Tech. Here, Angelita, read it to your sister."

Angelita read:

GLAD YOU SURVIVED. STILL EXPECTING YOU TO LEAD HOMECOMING PARADE. INVITE CARRERA SISTERS TO GAME FOR US. WILL AWARD THEM TECH TEAM BLANKETS. ANGELITA VOTED HONORARY MEMBER OF THE TEAM.

AUTHOR

Rafe Gibbs decided to be a writer when he was eleven years old. At thirteen, he wrote and sold his first short story for thirty-five dollars. He wrote his stories while sitting between boxes of canned goods in the storeroom of his father's grocery store in Yakima, Washington.

Mr. Gibbs studied writing at the University of Idaho. While in college, he had many articles published in magazines. He paid for much of his college education with the money that he earned by writing.

After graduating with honors, Mr. Gibbs worked for five years for a newspaper in Milwaukee, Wisconsin. During World War II, he rose to the rank of colonel in the United States Air Force. From 1946 to 1970, he was Director of Information and also taught a course in magazine writing at the University of Idaho. In 1970, he helped start Florida International University in Miami, Florida, where he was Dean of University Relations for three years. Recently, he worked with the Idaho Historical Society, writing a history of the state.

The Race with Two Winners
by Sherwood Harris

On the Fourth of July, 1969, the big airport at San Diego, California, was filled with excitement. Out on the field, ninety-two light planes were warming up. Their wings shone from polishing. The buzz of their finely tuned engines filled the air. A few minutes after nine o'clock in the morning, a single-engined Cessna with a big number 1 on its tail taxied up to a woman holding a flag at the end of the runway. The flag dropped and number 1 zoomed down the runway and into the air.

The twenty-third annual All-Women's Transcontinental Air Race had just begun. From here on, it would be full speed ahead across the United States to Washington, D.C.

A few planes back was Joan Steinberger of California in the TAR 10 position (Transcontinental Air Race starting position number 10). The takeoff positions were won by lot, and Mrs. Steinberger was delighted to get off to an early start in her single-engined Piper Cherokee. Much farther back, Doris Bailey of California was in TAR 66 position in a Cessna 172. Behind her, in the TAR 68 spot with a twin-engined Piper Comanche, was Mara Culp, also a Californian. Of these three women, one would be the surprise winner of the race, and the other two would be part of high drama along the way.

The first leg of the race stretched to the northeast toward Las Vegas, Nevada. The pilots climbed as they left the coast of California and headed for the bleak, bare mountains of the San Bernardino Range. The winner of the race would be the pilot who hit the highest average ground speed from coast to coast in relation to her type of plane. In past races, the difference between first and second place was often just a few minutes.

The total distance was 2,515 miles, and this was no race for amateurs. Along the route the fliers would have to cope with every kind of land and every type of summer weather to be found in the United States. The rules did not make it any easier. Instrument flying (flying by mechanical controls instead of by what the pilot can see outside the plane) and night flying were not permitted. Strict safety rules told pilots what the planes should include. The power and equipment of each plane was limited so that the contest would be fair.

Every woman in the race had to have at least a private pilot's license plus an instrument or an instructor's rating. Though no American airline hired a woman pilot until 1972, there were hundreds of qualified women with thousands of hours of flying experience throughout the country. Joan Steinberger, for instance, often flew emergency medical supplies to hospitals in California. Doris Bailey was a flight instructor, and Mara Culp was a charter pilot.

Most of the fliers decided to spend a night at St. Joseph, Missouri, one of the official stopover points. Joan Steinberger was one

of these. On the morning of Monday, July 7, she got out to the airport early and prepared her plane for a full day at top speed. But when she checked the weather, she wondered if she would get in a full day's flying after all. Already thunderstorms were reported building up over a wide area on either side of the route to the next checkpoint at Mt. Vernon, Illinois.

"I might as well push on through and see how far I can get," she thought to herself as she filed her flight plan.

The pilots leaving St. Joseph that morning began to meet the first thunderstorms after they crossed the Mississippi River near St. Louis. At first the storms were scattered, and all that was needed to avoid them was a slight detour now and then. But as Joan Steinberger neared the field at Mt. Vernon, the sky was dark, almost black near the ground. The dense clouds at the edge of the storm had a solid, rolling look that Mrs. Steinberger knew meant high winds and rough air

far beyond the strength of her little plane.

As Joan Steinberger flew toward the field from the northwest, she called the Mt. Vernon tower. The news was bad.

"TAR ten, this is Mt. Vernon tower. The field is below minimums. Visibility one and one-half miles in heavy rain. Hold south of the field and await further instruction."

By law, the air must be clear enough for the pilot to be able to see at least three miles, and the clouds must be no lower than one thousand feet before a plane can land at any airport unless the plane is guided by instruments. Because the use of those instruments was forbidden by the rules of the race, Mrs. Steinberger had no choice but to stay clear of the field until the visibility was good enough for her to land.

At the field itself, air-traffic controller Charles Thomas was having a difficult day. His "tower" was a small truck with radio equipment in the back. The Mt. Vernon airport was a small one

and did not have the usual equipment. So Thomas had been sent over from a large airport at nearby Evansville, Indiana, with his truck and radio to help the pilots on their way. As he stood by the truck, the wind-whipped rain lashed at him, and the lightning crackled in his radio earphone. But that was not the worst thing. He knew that every minute he delayed the new arrivals would reduce their chances of winning. There was nothing he could do, though. As long as the heavy rain continued to reduce the visibility, no plane could legally land.

Joan Steinberger followed the tower's instructions and turned south. Soon she passed over a wide highway that gave her a good landmark to circle while she waited.

Mrs. Steinberger was not the only one in the air around Mt. Vernon, however. As she circled south of the field, she heard one of her competitors call in.

"Mt. Vernon tower, this is TAR sixty-six. Can you give me a radio bearing to the field?"

"That was odd," Mrs. Steinberger thought. "She must be having some kind of trouble if she needs directions to the field."

"TAR sixty-six, this is Mt. Vernon tower. Unable to give you a bearing. We don't have the right equipment."

The same question came again.

"Mt. Vernon tower, this is TAR sixty-six. Can you give me a steer? Over."

The tower repeated its message, but again TAR 66 asked for directions to the field. For some reason, TAR 66 was unable to hear anything the tower was saying. "This could be serious," Mrs. Steinberger thought as she listened in on her radio. She scanned the dark, storm-whipped clouds that boiled around the Mt. Vernon airport, but there was no sign of the other plane.

The storm and the land below had sprung a trap on Doris Bailey in TAR 66. Normally, the course between St. Joseph, Missouri, and Mt. Vernon would have been a straight line. But Mrs. Bailey had discovered severe storms lying directly across that course. She had turned aside to try to get around the fast-moving storms, but they had closed in behind her. She was forced to wander farther and farther from her course to remain clear of the clouds.

As Mrs. Bailey dodged the clouds, she searched the ground for landmarks that would help her find her position on her map and work her way back to the airport. But in southern Illinois and nearby Indiana, everything looks very much the same, even on a clear day. This is beautiful, flat, farm country, and for miles in any direction, a person in an airplane can see few things that stand out as landmarks. Nearly all the country roads run in straight lines from north to south and east to west, the towns are all about the same size and shape, and the little winding rivers all look alike. With the sky darkened by the storm, it was all but impossible to pick out points on the land below.

With each passing minute, the needle of Mrs. Bailey's gas gauge moved slowly toward the empty mark. Airport or no airport, she would soon be down. Again she called for help.

This time Mrs. Steinberger answered. "TAR sixty-six, this is TAR ten. Can you read me?"

"Roger, TAR ten."

"The tower can hear you, but they can't give you a steer. No equipment. Try to tell me where you are, and I'll relay the message for you."

"I'm in the clear above a highway and a railroad. I can see a tower of some sort."

Mrs. Steinberger repeated the message to the traffic controller at Mt. Vernon. On the ground, Charles Thomas tried to picture the countryside. He had flown over the area many times, but he could not quite visualize the landmarks that Mrs. Bailey had described.

"Tell her to keep circling and call in anything else she sees," Charles Thomas radioed to Mrs. Steinberger.

A few minutes later, Mrs. Bailey described a river and mentioned that she saw smoke from some sort of factory or power plant. When Joan Steinberger told this to Thomas, he could picture the scene.

"Tell her she's over the Wabash River now," Thomas called to Mrs. Steinberger. "She can probably contact the Evansville tower." Thomas told her on what radio channel to call Evansville, and she relayed the information to Mrs. Bailey. Mrs. Steinberger tuned in Evansville herself and listened to find out if she could be of further help, even though every extra minute in the air would reduce her chances of winning the race. After a while, she heard TAR 66 speak on the radio with the Evansville tower and get landing instructions. When Mrs. Steinberger was sure Mrs. Bailey was safely on the ground, she threaded her way through the thunderstorms back to Mt. Vernon, found the field was clear, and landed.

The incident took only twenty minutes, and Joan Steinberger, Doris Bailey, and Charles Thomas made it sound almost routine. But routine it definitely was not. Mrs. Bailey's plane ran out of gas as she touched down at Evansville. And by spending so much time in the air to help her, Mrs. Steinberger had lost all chances of winning.

When the race was over and all the flying times had been figured, Mara Culp, TAR 68, was announced the winner. She made the 2,515-mile trip in eleven hours and fifty-seven minutes—an average of 210 miles per hour. It was her very first try at this race, and a great personal victory for her. A native of Latvia, she had come to the United States and learned to fly. Now she had won the toughest and most professional women's air event in the world.

Joan Steinberger and Doris Bailey could not finish the race because more bad weather kept them from completing it by the deadline. But in the hearts of pilots everywhere, men and women alike, the flier who gave up the race to help another in trouble was a winner too.

The Women Were Digging Clams

The women were digging clams.

At low tide the village women
Were out with the digging sticks
For cockles and clams.

Daughter-of-a-Chief
Saw the enemy coming,
Saw their canoes driving to shore.

She threw down her stick.
She looked at the enemy coming,
She sang her magic song:

Sisters-of-the-Sun, the clouds,
Sucked daylight into their blackness.

She sang:

Thunderbird came to the door of his lodge,
Raised his blanket,
Lightning flashed,
Sheared the sky and the water.

She sang:

North Wind emptied hail from his bag,
Filled the canoes with hailstones,
Sank them.

Daughter-of-a-Chief with her magic song
Saved the women.

a Kwakiutl poem

USING A CARD CATALOG

It had rained all day Sunday, but Kay didn't mind a bit. She had spent the afternoon reading *Mishmash,* which a friend had let her borrow. Kay hadn't laughed so much at a story in months, and she was sorry when she finally came to the end of it. She wondered whether the author had written other books about adventures of the big friendly dog called Mishmash. How could she find out?

That same afternoon, Tony had watched a science-fiction movie on television. In one exciting part, there had been a fierce battle between two enormous dinosaurs. Those strange-looking creatures had interested Tony, and he wanted to learn more about them. He felt sure that there must be many books telling about dinosaurs, but where should he look for them?

When you have questions like those raised by Kay and Tony, you can usually find the answers to them easily by using the card catalog in your school or public library. Knowing how to use the card catalog makes it possible for you to discover quickly what books are to be found in that library.

Almost every library has a card catalog, and all card catalogs provide the same kinds of information even though they may differ somewhat in size and appearance. Let us suppose that the card catalog in your library looks like the one pictured on the opposite page. Notice that there are twelve drawers and that each drawer has one or more letters on it. Cards inside the drawers are arranged in alphabetical order. The letters on each drawer show you what cards are in it, just as the letters on an encyclopedia indicate what topics are included in each volume. The card catalog can be used as a kind of index, an alphabetical list of all the books the library owns.

For every book in the library, two different cards are filed in the card catalog—an author card and a title card. For many of the books there is a third card—the subject card. The three cards filed for one book in the catalog in your library might look like those shown on page 265.

On the author card, the name of the author is most important, so it appears on the top line, with the last name listed first. Below it, other information is given about the book, such as its title, the location and name of the publisher, year of publication, number of pages, whether or not it is illustrated, and perhaps a sentence or two explaining what the book is about. An author card is filed alphabetically by the author's last name. If the library owns six different books written by one person, there will be six cards giving his or her name as author, one for each book. Kay, who enjoyed the book *Mishmash* by Molly Cone, could find out if her library has other books about the dog by looking at author cards filed under **Cone, Molly.**

On a title card, the title of the book appears on the top line. The information that follows it, as you can see from the illustration, is the same as on the author card. A title card is filed alphabetically by the first word in the title, unless that word is *A, An* or *The,* in which case the second word in the title is used for filing. To find the card for *A Bear Called Paddington,* for example, you would check under **B** for **Bear.** When you know nothing about a book except its title, you can get more information by reading the title card in the catalog.

The top line of a subject card tells the subject of the book, or what the book is about. From the first line of the bottom card on the opposite page, for example, you learn that the subject of the book is dinosaurs. Information below the top line is the same as that on the author card. Tony, who was interested in dinosaurs, could find the titles of books that have been written about them by looking at the different subject cards filed under **DINOSAURS.** If you are trying to locate information about subjects like satellites, hurricanes, or monkeys, use those words as key words and check the subject cards listed under them in order to learn what books your library has on those subjects. Or if you would like to read an adventure story about clipper-ship days or a detective story, you can locate what you want by looking through the subject cards filed under **SEA STORIES** or under **MYSTERY AND DETECTIVE STORIES.** When a subject has more than one word in it, the subject card is filed

Craig, M. Jean
    Dinosaurs and more dinosaurs, by M. Jean Craig. Pictures by George Solonevich. New York, Four Winds Press, 1968.
    96 p.   illus.

    A colorfully illustrated account of the monsters who roamed the earth millions of years ago. Explains what different dinosaurs looked like, where and how they lived, and why they died out.

AUTHOR
CARD

Dinosaurs and more dinosaurs
Craig, M. Jean
    Dinosaurs and more dinosaurs, by M. Jean Craig. Pictures by George Solonevich. New York, Four Winds Press, 1968.
    96. p.   illus.

    A colorfully illustrated account of the monsters who roamed the earth millions of years ago. Explains what different dinosaurs looked like, where and how they lived, and why they died out.

TITLE
CARD

DINOSAURS

Craig, M. Jean
    Dinosaurs and more dinosaurs, by M. Jean Craig. Pictures by George Solonevich. New York, Four Winds Press, 1968.
    96 p.   illus.

    A colorfully illustrated account of the monsters who roamed the earth millions of years ago. Explains what different dinosaurs looked like, where and how they lived, and why they died out.

SUBJECT
CARD

alphabetically by the first word. **SCIENCE FICTION** is under **S,** for example, and **GHOST STORIES** under **G.**

For subjects like **ANIMALS, COWBOYS, FOOTBALL,** or **FISHING,** there may be a great many subject cards. You will see that some of the books listed give facts about the subject while other books are made-up stories about the subject. Under **FOOTBALL,** for instance, you will find books that explain the rules of the game, the equipment needed, and how to play and coach the game. In other books authors tell stories that they have thought up themselves about football players and games. You can decide which of the books you want by reading the information that the various cards give.

Discussion

Help your class answer these questions:

1. How are cards arranged in a card catalog? In what way is a card catalog like an index?
2. What three kinds of cards are in a card catalog? What different information is on the first line of each? What information appears on all three cards shown on page 265?
3. How is each of the three cards filed alphabetically?
4. Give an example of when you might need to use each of the three cards.

On your own

On a sheet of paper, copy the number and letter of each of the following questions and then write your answer.

1. Which kind of card would you look for in the card catalog in order to answer these questions?
   a. What books have been written about snakes?
   b. Who wrote *Charlotte's Web?*
   c. What books by Herbert S. Zim does the library have?
   d. Has a woman written a book about Mark Twain?
2. In the illustration on page 263, what letter or letters are on the drawer in which you would expect to find the answer to each of these questions?
   a. Who is the author of *Viking Adventure?*
   b. How many Revolutionary War books are in the library?
   c. What are some books Carolyn Haywood has written?
   d. What makes a stamp collection valuable?
   e. Who wrote *The Noonday Friends?*
   f. What books by Beverly Cleary are in the library?

Checking your work

Read some of your answers aloud if you are asked to do so. Check your paper as others read their answers. If you made a mistake, be sure to find out why it was a mistake.

After living in New York City for most of his childhood, Federico Ramirez returned with his family to the small village of La Parguera, Puerto Rico. Although he was homesick and lonely at first, he soon made friends and began to have fun.

In the book by Peter Buckley called I AM FROM PUERTO RICO, from which this story was taken, the author writes about Federico's life in Puerto Rico as though Federico himself is telling the story.

Federico Discovers the Sea

by Peter Buckley

On Sunday, my mother wanted to go to church in Lajas. Lajas is a town only ten minutes away, and everybody there would fit into a couple of blocks in New York City. But next to La Parguera it looks good. In Lajas they've got stores and one movie and doctors and a marketplace and garages and pinball machines. There's even a travel agency, where people buy their plane tickets to New York, and just behind the church on the main square, you can pick up a *público-taxi* to take you to San Juan.

When we came to the church, I looked at the *público-taxi,* and I looked at the travel agency, and I wondered when I would ever have a chance to use either one.

My father drove home quickly from church because he'd planned to take us all on a picnic. "Would you like to bring your friend Neri to the beach?" he asked me on the way home.

"Sure," I answered. "When are we going?"

"As soon as you change your clothes and we get the food packed into the car."

Neri wanted to come along, and he wanted to bring his mask and his flippers and his spear gun because, he said, there was a small reef just off the beach where we were going.

The car was very crowded on the way to the beach, and it became even more crowded when we picked up a large friend of my father's on the way.

Manuel, my little brother, counted everybody in the car, and he decided to count two for the friend, but only one-half for himself, for Abi, and for Mira and Ramón. The friend and Neri knew the way to the beach. My father had never been there. He'd only heard about it. It took about half an hour to get there, and the last part of the trip was on a very narrow, bumpy dirt road that twisted through a big sugar-cane field. The road was so narrow that when we met another car coming the other way, we had to back up till we could pull off into the field a little bit and let the other car go by.

It was really pretty. The beach where we stopped was the prettiest place I'd ever seen. There were a few houses down toward one end. But the rest of the big beach was just white sand and tall coconut trees.

The beach was like a piece of watermelon after you've eaten all the meat, a long green-edged curve. We walked to one end of the curve, and then we came to another curved beach. There wasn't anybody anywhere except just us. I couldn't help thinking of the last time we all went to a beach last year on Long Island, of all the people—too many people—of all the trash cans and trash, of the people yelling, and of the dirty water.

My mother is good at making picnics. She always brings along enough food—even too much—but that's better than not enough, and she soon had it spread out. We all were hungry, so we ate right away.

After lunch I played dominoes with my father. Neri watched us, and after a while he said, "Hey, why don't we go find some coconut trees to take home?"

"What's the matter? Are you crazy?" I said. "These trees are a hundred feet high."

"You'll see what I mean," Neri said. "Come on."

He led me back from the beach toward a clump of trees that grew wild just between the coconut orchard and the sugar-cane field.

"Look," said Neri. He pointed to what looked like a very, very small coconut-tree branch less than one foot long, sticking out of the ground. He dug his fingers into the soft earth. In less than a minute he'd scooped up a coconut, and sticking out of one end of the coconut was the small branch I'd seen sticking out of the ground.

"You see now?" Neri said. "You see how all these trees began?"

"Wow! You mean out of a coconut a tree comes?" I asked.

"Where else?" Neri answered.

I helped Neri scoop up another one, and then I scooped up another two myself.

"You could plant them around the house," Neri said.

"How long before they'll be as high as the trees around here?" I asked.

"I don't know," Neri answered. "But I think a long, long time."

My mother was glad to have the coconut trees to plant. She and my father talked about the best place to plant them. It seemed to me that it wasn't a very good idea to plant them because I just couldn't imagine that anything so small could ever grow into something as big as the trees over our heads.

"Come on, let's play catch," Neri said, picking up a dry coconut from the ground. We ran down the beach tossing the coconut to each other, and we got hot, very hot. In the places on the beach that were not shaded by the palm trees, the sand was too hot to touch with our bare feet, so we stepped into the shallow water just up to our ankles and tossed the coconut back and forth.

We moved out a little deeper until the water reached our bathing suits. The water was just a little cool, and it felt very nice. It was so clean and clear that I could see my toes through the water as if there were no water at all.

Neri decided that it would be more fun to play with two

coconuts, so we got another one, and soon we were tossing them both back and forth to one another at the same time. Sometimes they would bump in midair and go splashing into the water.

Once I made a lunge to catch a coconut, and I slipped and fell into the water until the water was over my head. It really felt good. I lay back and floated for a minute. I heard Neri calling, but I didn't pay any attention. The water held me up as if I'd been lying in my bed at home. Little waves not even an inch high rolled over me, and, looking up through the leaves of the coconut palms, I watched clouds being blown by a wind that came from far at sea. I think I almost went to sleep, because for a few minutes I don't really know what happened.

Then suddenly Neri was splashing next to me. He had on his mask and his flippers, and he held his spear gun in his hand. I stood up with a jump, a little afraid, because that was the first time I'd ever been over my ankles in water that wasn't water in a swimming pool.

"Do you want to swim out with me," Neri asked, "when I go out there to see if I can get a fish?"

"No," I said, standing up and walking onto the beach. "I'll wait for you here."

Neri was gone a long time, and I felt lonely. I read the funnies when Abi and Mira were through reading them. But I didn't want to play dominoes with my father, and I didn't want to catch coconuts with Manuel and Ramón when they asked me to play with them. What I really wanted to do was to be with Neri. I don't know, but I think maybe it was half an hour before he came back, and he came back without a fish.

"I saw a small barracuda, but I didn't want a fish that is mostly teeth and bones," he said.

"Barracuda?" I said. "You mean there are barracuda in the water here?"

"Sure," Neri answered. "Lots of them, all over the place. Little ones. Big ones. Some of them farther out are as big as your father."

"And you went swimming out there?" I asked.

"Yeah, why not?" Neri answered.

"Why not?" I replied. "Because barracuda are dangerous."

"No, they're not. They are not dangerous at all. They don't bite. Sometimes one of them will come up to you and look at you and open and close his mouth, and you won't like that, and sometimes they'll follow you. But nobody ever heard of anybody being bitten by a barracuda around here. If you shot some fish and were dumb enough to hang them from a string around your waist, like some tourists do, then a barracuda might come around to eat some of the dead fish. And if you were in the way, he might get a piece of you too, but that's all."

I walked over to my father and asked him to tell me what he knew about barracuda. He told me exactly the same thing that Neri had. Then he turned to his friend and asked him if he agreed. The friend agreed.

The friend said, "I've fished around here, in the water and out, since I was a little boy. Don't worry, Federico. Barracuda won't bite you, but they'll scare you."

I went back to the beach with Neri and sat at the water's edge. I turned to Neri, who was sitting next to me holding his mask and flippers in his lap, and I knew what I wanted to ask him, but I couldn't quite do it yet.

Then suddenly I said, "Show me how you put on your flippers."

"Here, it's easy. Just stick your feet in here and pull. Now lie down on your back and kick your feet as you always do."

I lay on my back and kicked my legs a little. Suddenly I was shooting through the water. I've got strong legs and with the flippers on, I found that I moved through the water ten times faster than I ever had before. I flipped my way

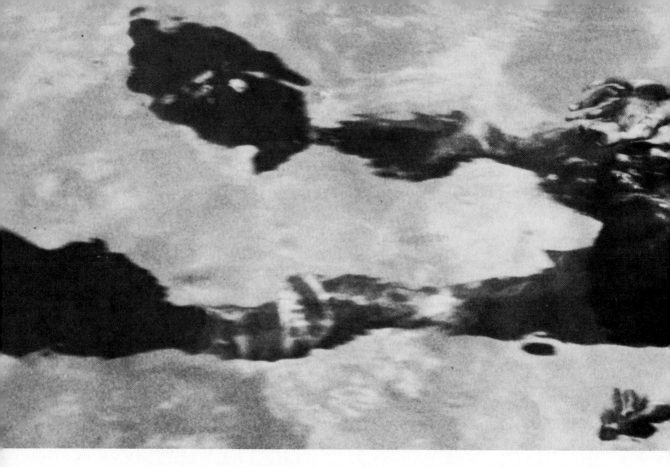

back to Neri. "O.K. They feel good. Show me about the mask and that tube thing."

"That tube thing," Neri said, "is called a snorkel." He showed me how to make the mask fit my head and how to stick the snorkel in my mouth and breathe through it. "Go ahead now and swim along the edge of the beach," he said.

I swam in shallow water, one, two, three feet deep at most, above clear white sand. With my mask on, I looked through the water at the bottom; it seemed as if there was no water at all.

I swam slowly, not using my arms, only kicking a little, trying not to splash with my flippers, because I felt like being quiet like the water through which I was swimming. I slowed down even more to look at two bright silver spots. I stopped. I put my hand out to touch the silver spots that shone in the sun, and suddenly they were gone. I flipped backward

because I was scared. The silver spots had been two little fish, and they looked like two eyes shining out from the sandy bottom. They were the first things I'd ever seen alive in the water. I couldn't believe I was really in the water, that I was seeing things through water, because everything looked as if it were just there, as if there was nothing really between my eyes and what I was looking at.

I swam out from shore a little way and found a grassy ridge. I stopped because I didn't know what might be in the grass. As I watched, the grass bent toward the shore— all together—and then bent away from the shore—all together—as if a wind were blowing it. I wondered how that could be; then I realized that it must be because of the slow, soft, back-and-forth motion of the water coming onto the beach and then going out again.

I had turned to go toward shore when below me I saw a

shape that I knew, or at least I thought I knew it. I could have touched it by just putting my hand out straight below me, but it wasn't till I had swum over it several times that I was sure it was a big conch shell.

I've often seen these shells in front of people's houses or in their gardens as decorations. My mother sometimes makes cold conch-meat salad with chopped onions and oil and vinegar, and it tastes good. She even used to buy conch meat in New York. Suddenly the shell began to move slowly, and I decided that I would capture it.

Now it seems to me a little dumb to think of capturing a shell because I think you only really capture something that's dangerous. But the way I felt, to touch even a conch shell that was moving in the water took a lot of courage.

I reached down, grabbed the back of the shell, and shot up out of the water, holding my prize for everybody to see. I swam back toward the beach. Neri met me at the water's edge. I showed him the shell. He held it. I took off the flippers and the mask; then I took back my shell, and looking inside it, I said, "Where's the animal?"

Neri said, "It must be a dead shell, because there's no animal in it."

I said, "But there is an animal, Neri. I saw it move."

"Not true," Neri said. "Can't be true. Unless a wave made it move, and there aren't any waves today."

"O.K.," I said. "You know more about these things than I do. Maybe I didn't see it move. Maybe it was just a shadow." I walked over to show the shell to my mother. The best way to carry the shell was to curl my fingers around inside the big opening.

Just as I handed the shell to my mother, I screamed, and I screamed so loud that she dropped the shell. Hanging onto the end of one of my fingers was a big crab, and his claw really hurt. I shook my whole arm hard until he dropped off, leaving my finger bleeding.

"Well, I guess you were right. There was something in the shell after all," Neri said. "That happens sometimes. After the conch animal dies, a crab comes along and uses the shell as a house. You're lucky, though. I once picked up a conch when I was just a kid, and I thought it was empty until I felt something slimy and slippery sucking at my fingers. It didn't hurt, but I was scared, and I couldn't shake it off like you shook off the crab."

"What was it?" I asked.

"Oh, nothing but a small octopus," Neri answered. "Now I play with them. But when I was a kid, I sure didn't like having this thing slipping and sucking all over my hand and not being able to get it off either."

For a while we forgot about the sea and all the things in it. We played dominoes, and then we helped pack up the picnic things. When we walked along the beach to go back to the car late in the afternoon, I looked out across the water, and I thought about the water. I had the strange feeling that having gone underneath the surface, I had really discovered something new. It was almost as if I had discovered myself, but I wasn't sure because I was still confused. I was sure of only one thing. I would never again be able to look at the sea without wondering what was in it. Now the sea was no longer an empty place to me.

AUGHTOR

Peter Buckley was born in New York. He grew up in Europe, attending schools there, but he returned to the United States and graduated from Princeton University. Since then, his work has taken him to various parts of the world. Mr. Buckley loves Puerto Rico, and he especially enjoys swimming there, diving with mask, snorkel, and flippers as the boys did in this story.

Federico Ramirez, whose story Mr. Buckley tells, is a real boy who actually did live in New York and Puerto Rico. Mr. Buckley has also written a number of books about children of Europe and Africa.

As I Walk Through the Water

As I walk through the water, a new world appears before me.
A world of colors, red, yellow, green and orange.
This whole world appears before me.
I wish to soar like a bird in the yellow-green sky,
I wish to fly.
I wish to swim, like a tiger-striped fish,
Through blue waters and coral gardens.
I wish to run, like a swift and graceful impala,
Oh, my dreams, oh, my wishes.
Oh, to swim like a fish, in water.
Oh, to run like an impala through woods.
Oh, to fly like a bird through a wonderful sky,
But alas, I am naught but I.

Ruben Marcilla
Sixth Grade

PICTURE PROVERBS

A proverb is an often-used short saying that expresses a well-known truth or fact. For example, "A stitch in time saves nine" is a proverb that you may have heard.

Look at the pictures below. Each one illustrates a common proverb. Try to guess each one, and then check your answers with the ones printed upside down at the bottom of the page.

1. The early bird catches the worm.
2. You can't teach an old dog new tricks.
3. Half a loaf is better than none.
4. A bird in the hand is worth two in the bush.
5. Birds of a feather flock together.
6. Too many cooks spoil the broth.

KEPLIK, THE MATCH MAN

by Myron Levoy

Many years ago, when the elevated trains still rattled and rumbled along Second Avenue in the Lower East Side of New York City, a wonderful thing happened to a lonely old man who lived there.

There once was a little old man who lived in a big old tenement on Second Avenue. His name was Mr. Keplik and he had once been a watchmaker. In the window of his tiny watch-repair shop, Keplik had put up a little sign that read: IF YOUR WATCH WON'T TICK, IT'S TIME FOR KEPLIK. Keplik loved watches and clocks and had loved repairing them. If a clock he was repairing stopped ticking, he would say to himself, "Eh, eh, eh, it's dying." And when it started ticking again, he would say, "I am *gebentsht*. I am blessed. It's alive."

Whenever an elevated train rumbled by overhead, Keplik would have to put down his delicate work, for his workbench and the entire shop would shake and vibrate. But Keplik would

close his eyes and say, "Never mind. There are worse things."

While he worked, Keplik never felt lonely, for there were always customers coming in with clocks and watches and complaints.

"My watch was supposed to be ready last week," a customer would say. "I need my watch! Will you have it ready by tonight, Keplik?"

And Keplik would answer, "Maybe yes, maybe no. It depends on how many el trains pass by during the rush hour." And he would point his finger up toward the el structure above.

But when Keplik grew very old, he had to give up watch repairing, for he could no longer climb up and down the three flights of stairs to his apartment. He became very lonely, for there were no longer any customers to visit him and complain. And his hands felt empty and useless, for there were no longer any gears or pivots or hairsprings or mainsprings to repair. "Terrible," said Keplik to himself. "I'm too young to be old. I will take up a hobby. Perhaps I should build a clock out of walnut shells. Or make a rose garden out of red crepe paper and green silk. Or make a windmill out of wooden matchsticks. I'll see what I have in the house."

There were no walnuts and no crepe paper, but there were lots and lots of burned matchsticks, for, in those days, the gas stoves had to be lit with a match every time you wanted a scrambled egg or a cup of hot cocoa. So Keplik started to build a little windmill out of matches.

Within a month's time, the windmill was finished. Keplik put it on his kitchen table and started to blow like the east wind. The arms turned slowly, then faster, just like a real windmill. "I'm *gebentsht*," said Keplik. "It's alive."

Next, Keplik decided to make a castle, complete with a drawbridge. But the matches were expensive; he would need hundreds and hundreds for a castle. So he put a little sign outside his apartment door, and another in his window: USED MATCHSITCKS BOUGHT HERE. A PENNY FOR FIFTY. IF YOU HAVE A MATCHSTICK, SELL IT TO KEPLIK.

The word spread up and down the block very quickly, and soon there were children at Keplik's door with bags and boxes of used matches. Keplik showed them the windmill on the kitchen table and invited them to blow like the east wind. And Keplik was happy, because he had visitors again and lots of work for his hands.

Day after day, week after week, Keplik glued and fitted the matches together. And finally the castle stood completed, with red and blue flags flying from every turret. The children brought toy soldiers and laid siege to the castle, while Keplik pulled up the drawbridge.

Next, Keplik made a big birdcage out of matches and put a

real canary in it. The bird sang and flew back and forth while the delicate cage swung on its hook. "Ah ha," said Keplik. "The cage is alive. And so is the canary. I am double *gebentsht*."

Then he made little airplanes and jewelry boxes from matchsticks and gave them to the boys and girls who visited him. And the children began calling him "The Match Man."

One day, Keplik decided that it was time for a masterpiece. "I am at my heights as an artist," Keplik said to himself. "No more windmills. No more birdcages. I am going to make the Woolworth Building. Or the Eiffel Tower. Or the Brooklyn Bridge. Eh . . . eh . . . but which?"

And after much thought, he decided that a bridge would be better than a tower or a skyscraper, because if he built a bridge, he wouldn't have to cut a hole in the ceiling. The Brooklyn Bridge would be his masterpiece. It would run across the living room from the kitchen to the bedroom, and the two towers would stand as high as his head. "For this I need matches!" Keplik said aloud. "Matches! I must have matches."

And he posted a new sign: MATCH FOR MATCH, YOU CANNOT MATCH KEPLIK'S PRICE FOR USED MATCHES. ONE CENT FOR FIFTY. HURRY! HURRY! HURRY!

Vincent DeMarco, who lived around the corner, brought fifty matches that very afternoon, and Cathy Dunn and Noreen Callahan brought a hundred matches each the next morning. Day after day, the matches kept coming, and day after day, Keplik the Match Man glued and fixed and bent and pressed the matches into place.

The bridge was so complicated that Keplik had decided to build it in separate sections and then join all the sections afterward. The bridge's support towers, the end spans, and the center span slowly took shape in different parts of the room. The room seemed to grow smaller as the bridge grew larger. "A masterpiece," thought Keplik. "There is no longer room for me to sit in my favorite chair. But I must have more matches! It's time to build the cables!"

Even the long support cables were made from matchsticks, split and glued and twisted together. Keplik would twist the sticks until his fingers grew numb. Then he would go into the kitchen to make a cup of coffee for himself, not so much for the coffee, but for the fact that lighting the stove would provide him with yet another matchstick. And sometimes, as he was drinking his coffee, he would get up and take a quick look at his bridge, because it always looked different when he was away from it for a while. "It's beginning to be alive," he would say.

And then one night, it was time for the great final step. The towers and spans and cables all had to be joined together to make the finished structure. A most difficult job. For everything was supported from the cables above, as in a real bridge, and all the final connections had to be glued and tied almost at the same moment. Nothing must shift or slip for a full half hour, until the glue dried thoroughly.

Keplik worked carefully, his watchmaker's hands steadily gluing and pressing strut after strut, cable after cable. The end spans were in place. The center span was ready. Glue, press, glue, press. Then suddenly, an el train rumbled by outside. The ground trembled, the old tenement shivered as it always did, the windows rattled slightly, and the center span slid from its glued moorings. Then one of the end cables vibrated loose, then another, and the bridge slipped slowly apart into separate spans and towers. "Eh, eh, eh," said Keplik. "It's dying."

Keplik tried again, but another train hurtled past from the other direction. And again the bridge slowly slipped apart. "I am too tired," thought Keplik. "I'll try again tomorrow."

Keplik decided to wait until late the next night, when there would be fewer trains. But again, as the bridge was almost completed, a train roared past, the house shook, and everything slipped apart. Again and again, Keplik tried, using extra supports and tying parts together. But the bridge seemed to enjoy waiting for the next train to shake it apart again.

"Ah me," thought Keplik. "All my life those el trains shook

the watches in my hands, down below in my shop. All my life I said things could be worse.

"But why do the el trains have to follow me three flights up? Why can't they leave me alone in my old age? When I die, will there be an el train over my grave? Will I be shaken and rattled around while I'm trying to take a little well-deserved snooze? And when I reach heaven, will there be an el train there, too, so I can't even play a nice, soothing tune on a harp without all this *tummel*, this noise? It's much too much for me. This is it. The end. The bridge will be a masterpiece in parts. The Brooklyn Bridge after an earthquake."

At that moment, another el train roared by, and Keplik the Match Man called toward the train, "One thing I'll *never* do! I'll never make an el train out of matches! Never! How do you like *that*!"

When the children came the next afternoon to see if the bridge was finished at last, Keplik told them of his troubles with the el trains. "The bridge, my children, is *farpotshket*. You know what that means? A mess!"

The children made all sorts of suggestions: Hold it this way; fix it that way; glue it here; tie it there. But to all of them, Keplik the Match Man shook his head. "Impossible. I've tried that. Nothing works."

Then Vincent DeMarco said, "My father works on an el station uptown. He knows all the motormen, he says. Maybe he can get them to stop the trains."

Keplik laughed. "Ah, such a nice idea. But no one can stop the Second Avenue el."

"I'll bet my father can," said Vincent.

"Bet he can't," said Joey Basuto. And just then, a train sped by: raketa, raketa, raketa, raketa, raketa. "The trains never stop for anything," said Joey.

And the children went home for dinner, disappointed that the bridge made from all their matchsticks was farpoot . . . farbot . . . *whatever* that word was. A mess.

Vincent told his father, but Mr. DeMarco shrugged. "No. Impossible. Impossible," he said. "I'm not important enough."

"But couldn't you *try*?" pleaded Vincent.

"I know *one* motorman. So what good's that, huh? One motorman. All I do is make change in the booth."

"Maybe he'll tell everybody else."

"*Assurdità* (ah-ser-de-tah′). Nonsense. They have more to worry about than Mr. Keplik's bridge. Eat your soup!"

But Mr. DeMarco thought to himself that if he did happen to see his friend, the motorman, maybe, just for a laugh, he'd mention it. . . .

Two days later, Vincent ran upstairs to Keplik's door and knocked. *Tonight* his father had said! Tonight at one A.M.! Keplik couldn't believe his ears. The trains would stop for his bridge? It couldn't be. Someone was playing a joke on Vincent's father.

But that night, Keplik prepared, just in case it was true. Everything was ready: glue, thread, supports, towers, spans, cables.

A train clattered by at five minutes to one. Then silence. Rapidly, rapidly, Keplik worked. Press, glue, press, glue. One cable connected. Two cables. Three. Four. First tower finished. Fifth cable connected. Sixth. Seventh. Eighth. Other tower in place. Now gently, gently. Center span in position. Glue, press, glue, press. Tie threads. Tie more threads. Easy. Easy. Everything balanced. Everything supported. Now please. No trains till it dries.

The minutes ticked by. Keplik was sweating. Still no train. The bridge was holding. The bridge was finished. And then, outside the window, he saw an el train creeping along, slowly, carefully: cla . . . keta . . . cla . . . keta . . . cla . . . keta . . . cla . . . keta . . . Then another, moving slowly from the other direction: cla . . . keta . . . cla . . . keta . . .

And Keplik shouted toward the trains, "Thank you, Mister Motorman! Tomorrow, I am going to start a great new masterpiece! The Second Avenue el from Fourteenth Street to Delancey Street! Thank you for slowing up your trains!"

And first one motorman, then the other, blew his train whistle as the trains moved on, into the night beyond. "Ah, how I am gebentsht," said Keplik to himself. "In America there are kind people everywhere. All my life, the el train has shaken my hands. But tonight, it has shaken my heart."

Keplik worked for the rest of the night on a little project. And the next morning, Keplik hung this sign made from matches outside his window, where every passing el train motorman could see it:

AUTHOR

Myron Levoy says of his childhood, "I grew up in a time of change: The old New York of Keplik was moving rapidly toward World War II and TV and jet travel. When I was very young, vegetables and ice were still sold from horse-drawn wagons, and chickens were still kept in some backyards. A ride on the Second Avenue el, above the pushcarts and crowds, was a trip across the known world. In our apartment building, seven languages were spoken: Russian, Italian, German, Yiddish, Lithuanian, Hungarian, and Polish. Oh, yes, and English, with a half-dozen accents, like the facets of a diamond." All this has found its way into *The Witch of Fourth Street*, the book from which this story was taken.

Myron Levoy is an aerospace engineer as well as a writer. He has worked on nuclear propulsion for aircraft and rockets and on space-vehicle propulsion. He has written stories, plays, poems, an adult novel, and another book for children, *Penny Tunes and Princesses.*

SKILL LESSON

MAKING AND USING AN OUTLINE

PART ONE

What would you do to study an article so well that you remember the important points it gives and understand how those points are related to one another? Would you read that article two or more times? Would you make notes as you read, just one for each paragraph topic? Making and using a good outline that shows the important points in the article is a more helpful thing to do.

To make such an outline, first look to see whether the article has a title. If it does, you can use that title to start making your outline. If the article does not have a title, read the paragraphs quickly to decide what one thing they all talk about. Then use that one thing as the title for your outline.

After you have read the title of the article or have made one for your outline, think of a question which you expect the article to answer about that title. Your question may ask *How, What, When, Where, Which, Who,* or *Why,* and it can be your guide in deciding just which points in the article are the main ones. If an article had the title *Some Fire Hazards in the Home,* what question would you think of?

The next thing to do in making your outline is to read all the paragraphs to get answers to the question you have in mind. Do that now with the article which follows. You may want to use the question *What are those fire hazards?*

Some Fire Hazards in the Home

Different kinds of carelessness are a major fire hazard in the home. One kind is simply the mishandling of small flames. Throwing a burning match into a wastebasket, placing a lighted candle near curtains, or failing to screen a flaming or crackling fire in a fireplace are foolish things to do. Another kind of carelessness is the misusing of liquids that catch fire easily. Pouring kerosene on a smoldering fire in a fireplace is a dangerous act, and using gasoline to clean clothes in the house or the garage may lead to a bad fire.

Accumulated rubbish in the cellar, a closet, or the attic where it can be overheated or struck by sparks or a flame is a fire hazard. This rubbish may be paper such as old newspapers, empty cartons, or unused wrappings. Often it is old cloth, particularly oily rags, discarded clothing, or perhaps worn-out bedding. All such rubbish can be good fuel for a fire.

Another hazard is the use of poor equipment. Some of this equipment is unsafe electrical parts. A worn or broken appliance cord, a damaged outlet, or wires which become overheated when trying to supply enough power for too many appliances should be replaced. Damaged or faulty parts of the central heating system are also poor equipment. A broken coal furnace chimney, with openings left by loose

bricks and crumbling mortar where it passes through the attic, should be repaired. On a gas furnace, poorly operating controls which fail to keep that furnace from becoming overheated should be replaced. Sparks, a small flame, or too much heat that poor equipment may create and send out can cause nearby rubbish to start burning.

What answers did you get to the question *What are those fire hazards*? They should be: (1) different kinds of carelessness, (2) accumulated rubbish, and (3) use of poor equipment. Those three ideas are the *main* points that the article gives about its title. In an outline of the article, they are called **main topics,** and they look like this:

Some Fire Hazards in the Home
I. Different kinds of carelessness
II. Accumulated rubbish
III. Use of poor equipment

You can see that the first word, the last word, and each important word in the title of an outline begins with a capital letter. The right Roman numeral and a period come before each main topic. Where is a capital letter used in each main topic? Is there a period at the end of that topic?

Often, but not always, a part or all of the topic of a paragraph in an article will be a main topic in an outline of that article. The topic of the first paragraph in the article about fire hazards can be stated as *Different kinds of carelessness as a fire hazard.* Is the first main topic in the above outline all, or just part of, that paragraph topic? Is each of the other main topics in the outline a part of the topic of a paragraph in the article?

When you are making an outline, try to find out whether the points you have chosen for main topics are good ones. To do that, see if you can use the *same word or words* in the title with each main topic to make a sensible statement. For example, in checking the main topics in the outline above, you could make these statements: (1) Different kinds of careless-ness are a *fire hazard in the home*, (2) Accumulated rubbish is a *fire hazard in the home*, and (3) Use of poor equipment is a *fire hazard in the home*.

Usually an article you are studying gives points that tell about the main topic in your outline. To find those points for each main topic, think of a question you expect the article to answer about that topic. Then read all or part of the article again to get all the answers it gives. Do these things now with the article on fire hazards to get all the points that tell about the first main topic in the outline. Use the question *What are those kinds of carelessness?*

What answers did you get? They should be: (1) mishandling of small flames, and (2) misusing of liquids that catch fire easily.

To find points that the article gives about the second main topic, use the question *What is that rubbish?*

Your answers should be: (1) paper and (2) old cloth.

Can you now find answers that the article gives about the third main topic? Try using the question *What is this poor equipment?*

Your answers should be: (1) unsafe electrical parts and (2) damaged or faulty parts of the central heating system.

When we put into the outline the points that the article gives about the main topics, we call them **subtopics,** and they look like this:

Some Fire Hazards in the Home
  I. Different kinds of carelessness
    A. Mishandling small flames
    B. Misusing liquids that catch fire easily
 II. Accumulated rubbish
    A. Paper
    B. Old cloth
III. Use of poor equipment
    A. Unsafe electrical parts
    B. Damaged or faulty parts of a central heating system

Notice that the subtopics are indented under the main topics. The indenting shows that the subtopics under a given main topic tell about that particular main topic. The right capital letter and a period come before each subtopic. Where is a capital used in each subtopic? Is there a period at the end?

You can find out whether the points you have chosen to use as subtopics under a certain main topic are good ones. To do this, see if you can use the *same word or words* in that main topic with each subtopic to make a sensible statement. For example, in checking the two subtopics under the first main topic in the outline, you could make these statements: (1) Mishandling small flames is a *kind of carelessness,* and (2) Misusing liquids that catch fire easily is a *kind of carelessness.*

What statements could you make to check all the other subtopics in the outline?

Discussion

Help your class answer these questions:
1. In what ways can making and using an outline help you study an article?
2. Why is it important to have a question in mind when you read an article to choose points to use as main topics in an outline of that article? To choose points to use as subtopics?
3. What do the main topics in a good outline tell about? What do the subtopics tell about? Why are the subtopics indented?
4. How can you find out whether points you have chosen to use as main topics in an outline are good ones? How can you check the points you have chosen to use as subtopics?
5. What statements could be used to check the subtopics under the last two main topics in the outline about fire hazards in the home?
6. Where should capital letters be used in writing the title of an outline? In writing each main topic? In writing each subtopic? What should be placed before each main topic? Before each subtopic?

PART TWO

You already know how to find in an article good points to use as main topics and subtopics in an outline you are making of that article. Now you are ready to go on a little further.

Sometimes an article gives points that tell about one or more subtopics in your outline. To find out what those points are for a certain subtopic, think of a question you expect the article to answer about that subtopic. Then read part or all of the article again to get all the answers it gives to your question.

To get the points that the article on fire hazards in the home gives about the first subtopic in the outline on page 297, use the question *What is the mishandling of small flames?*

What answers did you get? They should be: (1) throwing a burning match into a wastebasket, (2) placing a lighted candle near curtains, and (3) failing to screen a fire in a fireplace.

To get the points that the article gives about the next subtopic in the outline, use the question *What is the misusing of liquids that catch fire easily?*

The answers should be: (1) pouring kerosene on a smoldering fire in a fireplace and (2) using gasoline to clean clothes.

Now try to find by yourself the points that the article on fire hazards gives about all the other subtopics in the outline on page 297. Remember to think of a question about each subtopic to use as a guide in deciding which points are good ones.

When we put into an outline of an article the points which that article gives about the subtopic, those points are called **details.** What are the details in the complete outline of the article on fire hazards shown on the next page?

Some Fire Hazards in the Home

I. **Different kinds of carelessness**
- A. **Mishandling small flames**
  - 1. **Throwing burning match into wastebasket**
  - 2. **Placing lighted candle near curtains**
  - 3. **Failing to screen fire in fireplace**
- B. **Misusing liquids that catch fire easily**
  - 1. **Pouring kerosene on smoldering fire in fireplace**
  - 2. **Using gasoline to clean clothes**

II. **Accumulated rubbish**
- A. **Paper**
  - 1. **Old newspapers**
  - 2. **Empty cartons**
  - 3. **Unused wrappings**
- B. **Old cloth**
  - 1. **Oily rags**
  - 2. **Discarded clothing**
  - 3. **Worn out bedding**

III. **Use of poor equipment**
- A. **Unsafe electrical parts**
  - 1. **Worn or broken appliance cord**
  - 2. **Damaged outlet**
  - 3. **Wires which become overheated**
- B. **Damaged or faulty parts of central heating system**
  - 1. **Broken coal furnace chimney**
  - 2. **Poorly operating controls on gas furnace**

In the outline you just read, notice that each detail is indented under the subtopic to which it belongs. The right Arabic number and a period come before each detail. Where is a capital letter used in writing each detail? Is there a period at the end?

How can you find out whether the points used as details under a certain subtopic in the outline about fire hazards in the home are good ones? Just try to make sensible statements that use the *same word or words* in that subtopic with each detail. Such statements for the first subtopic in the outline could be: (1) Throwing a burning match into a waste basket is *mishandling a small flame*, (2) Placing a lighted candle near curtains is *mishandling a small flame*, and (3) Failing to screen a fire in a fireplace is *mishandling a small flame*.

What statements could you use to check the details under the subtopic *Old cloth?* Under *Unsafe electrical parts?*

After you have made an outline that shows many of the points an article gives, use that outline to test yourself. See if you can use each main topic with its subtopics and the details to make statements that give clear information about that main topic. For example, in testing yourself with the first main topic in the outline about fire hazards, you could make statements like these: (1) One kind of carelessness is the mishandling of a small flame by throwing a burning match into a waste basket, placing a lighted candle near curtains, or failing to screen a fire in a fireplace; and (2) Another kind of carelessness is the misusing of a liquid that catches fire easily, such as pouring kerosene on a smoldering fire in a fireplace, or using gasoline to clean clothes. Making such statements will help you understand and remember the important things the article says.

Discussion

Help your class answer these questions:

1. Why should you have a question in mind when you read an article to get points to use as details in an outline of that article? What should that question ask about?
2. What do the details in an outline tell about?
3. How can you find out whether points you have chosen for details in an outline you are making are good ones?
4. What statements could you use to check the details under the subtopic *Old cloth?* Under *Unsafe electrical parts?*
5. Where should each detail in an outline be written? Why should it be indented? What should come before each detail? Where should a capital letter be used?
6. How can you test yourself with an outline you have made?

On your own

On a clean sheet of paper, make an outline of important points that the following article gives. To help you choose good points to use as main topics, subtopics, and details, you may need to use questions that ask *What, How,* and *For what reasons.* Be sure to leave space between main topics so that you can write subtopics there, and between subtopics for the details you will need to write.

Some Small Fires That Help Us in the Home

Have you ever thought how a fireplace fire helps us? It provides warmth to take the chill off a room on a raw day late in the spring or early in the fall when the furnace is not running. On a very cold day, we sometimes use that warmth to add to the heat from the furnace. The pleasure that a fireplace fire gives may be simply a feeling of coziness, the sight of colored flames, or the sound of wood crackling as it burns.

In some homes gas flames provide heat for keeping the house warm, for cooking, and for heating water. A few small gas flames, called pilot lights, start the burners in gas appliances. Some of these appliances are cooking stoves, water heaters, and incinerators that burn trash.

Candle flames supply light for emergencies, and sometimes they offer us pleasure. The failing of electric power at night and needing to find something in a dark and unfamiliar room are two such emergencies. The soft glow that candle flames cast on a dinner table and the gayness they add to a room on special occasions, such as a birthday or Christmas Eve, are two of the pleasures those small fires offer.

Checking your work

If you are asked to do so, read part of your outline aloud. Find out why any mistake you may have made in choosing a point for a main topic, a subtopic, or a detail is a mistake.

Our Friends—The Bees, Wasps, and Hornets

By
Russ
Kinne

Are you afraid of bees? Most people are. Did you ever notice, when a large insect flies near people, how many will try to duck or shoo it away? If you ask them what kind of insect it is, they will probably say, "A bee." Now, with your sharp eyes, you may have noticed that these "bees" are not all the same size. Furthermore, they come in a good many different color combinations. Are *all* of them really bees?

No, they are not. There are many of these insects, but they all belong to the same family. Scientists have named the family *hymenoptera* (hie′muh-nahp′tuh-ruh).

Since most of the hymenoptera can sting, parents are wise when they tell their children to stay away from them. For the very few persons who are extra sensitive, or even allergic to stings, a single sting can be a very serious matter indeed. In most cases stings are unpleasant, and usually unnecessary. But that doesn't mean you can't look and learn. If you move slowly and gently, chances are you won't have any trouble. But if you hit at these insects, or hurt them, they will sting you. So, *don't do it!*

Around flower gardens, the honeybee is the most common.

A honeybee sucking nectar from a coneflower.

A honeybee stinging. Tiny barbs on the shaft hold the stinger in the victim's skin and cause the stinger to be pulled out of the bee's body. This injures the bee to the extent that it will soon die.

A honeybee leaving a flower carrying a load of pollen on its legs.

Honeybees on a honeycomb looking for cells in which to deposit their load of pollen.

A beekeeper removing honey from a bee hive.

It is about three-quarters of an inch long—the size of a penny—and its color ranges from black to light brown or yellow. You may notice blobs of bright yellow pollen on its hind legs, and as you watch, it may suck a drop of sweet nectar from each flower. It uses pollen as food and makes honey from the nectar. We don't know why, but a hive of bees makes far more honey than it can possibly use. The hive normally makes its home in an old hollow tree. Long ago both bears and people learned about honey. They began to raid the "bee trees" and take the honey stored inside. Bears still do. But people have learned that bees will live quite happily in special wooden boxes in backyards and orchards and let the beekeeper take away the surplus honey every few weeks. This is where the honey that you find in the market comes from.

But this is not the most important thing bees do. The pollen that sticks to the bee's body is carried from one flower to another. This is called cross-pollination. Cross-pollination helps to make healthier plants and bigger and better fruits. Without cross-pollination, some plants cannot produce seeds at all. In commercial apple-growing country, the beekeepers are paid to let their bees loose in the orchards. So you can see how important the little honeybee can be!

Almost everyone in the world knows the big black and yellow bumblebee. It's the largest of our native bees and wasps. It feeds on nectar and pollen, and is a valuable pollinator. It may be that some plants, like the red clover, could not survive without this insect's services.

Do you know where the bumblebee's home

is? The nest is underground. Bumblebees make honey too, but not nearly so much as the honeybees do.

Another large bee is often confused with the bumblebee. This is the black carpenter bee, which drills cavities in soft wood. There are even some nesting in the roof of my house! Once in a while, these bees will drill deeply enough to weaken a piece of wood, but this is rare. I enjoy watching "my" bees, and they are welcome to stay. Carpenter bees have an all-black abdomen, while the bumblebee's abdomen is black and yellow. With a little practice, you can tell them apart quite easily.

You may see a black and yellow insect, about the size of a honeybee, that you will recognize at once—the yellow jacket hornet. If you have met it before, you may know that it has a short temper and will sting immediately if anything disturbs it! If you move slowly and gently, however, it may let you come close enough to watch it. I even let them feed from a drop of honey on the end of my finger—but I wouldn't advise you to try this!

All these insects will let *us* alone if we let *them* alone. But beyond this, they all have their own "personalities," and it helps to be able to recognize them by sight.

Sometimes you may notice a yellow jacket almost three times as big as the common ones. Lots of people think they are yellow jacket "queens," but they are more likely to be European hornets, which have become established in the United States. If you can get a good look, you will see they are really brown and yellow.

A bumblebee on a red clover blossom.

Head-on shot of a bumblebee. Note the large compound eyes and mouth parts.

A carpenter bee.

Yellow jackets in their nest.

A paper wasp on its nest.

Yellow jackets usually build a nest underground. The European hornet sometimes makes its nest from a branch of a tree or under the eaves of a building where it is protected from rain and wind. These nests are very complicated structures that the insects build out of paper. They chew up bits of wood, mix it with saliva, and mold it into shape. When it dries, it is very strong and light in weight.

One of the most common of all wasps, found all around the world, is called the paper wasp. These wasps are almost tame. They usually build a comblike nest under the eaves of a building. It is not hard to find one. These wasps are over an inch long and are usually brown or brown and black. They are very helpful and should not be destroyed. They go quietly about their own affairs, almost never bother people, and eat thousands and thousands of harmful insects. We should be glad to have them around!

There are many other kinds of bees and wasps and hornets, but no one should be scared when they appear. In fact, many of them don't even have stingers! There are also flies and other insects that look a great deal like bees and wasps, and, of course, these can't harm us at all.

Bees, wasps, and hornets are fascinating to study and watch. If we follow the advice of "look but don't touch," we shouldn't get into any trouble.

Henry Reed is spending the summer with an aunt and uncle in Grover's Corner, New Jersey. There isn't much to do in Grover's Corner, which consists of only nine houses. Even if there were, there is only one person to do anything with — Midge Glass. Still Henry manages to find plenty to fill the daily journal he is keeping.

The following entry from Henry's journal is one of the many that appear in the book, *Henry Reed, Inc.*

A Day in the Life of Henry Reed

by Keith Robertson

Not too much has happened since my last entry. Last night I went with the Glasses to the outdoor movies, which I enjoyed a lot. The reason we went to the outdoor movies was that we didn't have any lights in Grover's Corner last night. The reason we didn't have any lights is connected in a way with something Midge and I did.

The Ainsworths, who live down near where the new house is being built, had a wasps' nest in a mulberry tree out near their chicken house. Midge heard about it and went over to look at it several days ago. It was one of those great big gray paper nests that wasps build, and I'd only seen one of them before. Most of the wasps around here just build sort of open cones underneath the eaves of buildings and don't make a paper covering around them. This was one of the biggest wasps' nests I've seen, even bigger than the ones in the Museum of Natural History when I visited there two years ago.

"I'd like to have that," I said.

"Why?" Midge asked. "Is it full of honey?"

I explained that wasps don't store honey like bees do. They kill spiders and flies and store them away instead. Midge doesn't know even the simplest facts about insects and animals.

"Then what do you want it for?" Midge asked.

"I'd like to look at it," I said. "The wasps knew how to make paper before people did. Besides we might be able to sell it."

"Who would want a wasps' nest?" Midge asked.

"A museum," I replied.

She didn't think much of the idea, but I asked Mrs. Ainsworth if she minded if I took the wasps' nest. She said certainly not. In fact, she would gladly pay me a dollar if I would take it away. Midge was a little more in favor of the idea then and agreed to help me.

"We could hang it up near the barn," I said, "and the wasps would eat all the spiders on the second floor."

"Nothing doing," Midge said flatly. "There's not room enough in this firm for the wasps and me, too. Have you ever been stung by a wasp?"

I'd never been stung by a wasp, although I have been stung by bees. Midge said it wasn't the same thing at all. Finally I agreed that we wouldn't try to preserve the wasps, just the nest. We found a five-gallon can that seemed like the perfect container, and we went over to get the nest.

I borrowed Mrs. Ainsworth's ladder and got it up against the tree without any trouble. I was about two-thirds of the way up the ladder with a saw in my hand, planning to saw off the limb where the nest hung, when I got stung. Midge was right. A wasp's sting is nothing like a bee's sting. It really hurts. I decided right then and there that I wasn't going to get the nest until I had the proper equipment.

I asked Uncle Al that night if he knew where I could buy a can of smoke that beekeepers use. Naturally, he wanted to know what I was going to use it for. I told him that I wanted to get rid of some wasps.

"Your mother liked bees and you like wasps," he said, shaking his head. "I suppose you'll be stung less if you have the smoke than if you don't have it. Frankly, my advice is to stay as far away from wasps as possible. I have put off painting the eaves of that garage out there for two years because of those wasps."

He got me the smoke yesterday morning, and I got out my mother's old bee equipment. The net was full of holes, but Aunt Mabel made me a new net out of an old curtain. The net is attached to the hat at the top and comes down over my shoulders. There are two drawstrings to pull it tight around your chest and under the arms. After I got the net on, I put on a jacket and some long gloves. Then I was practically sting-proof.

I tried out my suit first on the wasps' nests under the eaves of Uncle Al's garage. These weren't the kind of wasps that build

the big paper nests, of course, and they weren't very interesting, but my net worked perfectly and I didn't bother using any smoke. I simply climbed up on the stepladder and knocked all the cones down. The wasps buzzed around my head, as mad as could be, but they couldn't get through to sting me.

Next we went over to Mrs. Ainsworth's, and I put up the ladder again. I climbed up to the top, not paying any attention to the wasps. When I got up to the nest, I gave it several shots from my smoke can. I wasn't worried about them stinging me, but I knew that when I started sawing off the limb they would really get mad. Midge was holding the ladder, and she didn't have any net.

Everything went perfectly, which shows that if you plan in advance you can do almost anything without any trouble. I sawed off the outer end of the limb first, then sawed it again between the tree and the nest. That left the nest hanging to the little piece of limb, about a foot long, which I was holding.

I had poked a tiny hole in the lid of the can and had threaded a little piece of wire through this. I climbed down with the nest, hung it to the little wire loop in the lid, and put the lid carefully on the can. Midge had retreated to the corner of the house where she stood watching.

There were quite a few wasps who were out hunting, and I stood there for a few minutes watching them as they came back. They looked pretty silly zooming in, expecting to find a great big nest and instead finding nothing but empty space. I suppose a person would feel the same way if he arrived home to find that a hurricane had blown away his house. I felt a little bit mean, because I certainly played those wasps a dirty trick.

I felt even sorrier for the wasps that were in the nest inside the can. They were prisoners and would starve to death. At least the others could start over again. Midge didn't seem to feel a bit sorry for any of them, though. She said that she hoped all of them got their stingers doubled over trying to sting the tin can.

I picked up the can and we started back toward the barn. As

we passed the new house, we noticed that a bulldozer was digging a hole off to one side of the house.

"Maybe they're going to have a swimming pool," Midge said hopefully. "But I don't know why they didn't start on that first instead of the house. Half the summer's gone."

"I doubt if it's a swimming pool," I said. "It doesn't look big enough."

"Then what is it?"

The bulldozer was digging dirt out of the hole and pushing it into a low spot up near the front of the lot. "Wait until he comes back up here and we'll ask him," I said.

I set the can down beside the road and climbed up the bank to watch the bulldozer. Midge joined me a minute later. The bulldozer came chugging toward us, and Midge waved her hand.

"Is that a swimming pool?" she shouted.

"No such luck," the driver shouted back. "Digging out for the footing for a garage."

He had stopped the bulldozer to answer Midge but now he started again, distributing the dirt around evenly along the front part of the lot. A plumber's truck came tearing down the road and turned in the driveway. The man was driving much faster than he should have been, and I suppose he didn't realize that he had reached the driveway until the last minute. He slammed on his brakes, his tires screeched, and he skidded around the turn into the driveway. I had set the can well out of the way, I thought. It would have been for any ordinary driver, but not for this cowboy. His rear bumper just touched the can, but that was enough to knock it over. It rolled down into the ditch and the lid came off.

"Look out! Wasps!" Midge shouted at the top of her voice, and she took off like a streak for the front of the lot.

I had put my bee hat and net and gloves and can of smoke on top of the can when I'd set it down beside the road. They fell down in the ditch with the can and I couldn't get to them.

I waited a few seconds, but when I saw those wasps coming out of that can like a black cloud, I decided to follow Midge.

"Look out! Those are wasps!" I yelled to the bulldozer driver in case he hadn't heard Midge.

He said later that he hadn't heard either one of us. The first thing he knew about the wasps was that he had been stung on the neck. They zoomed in on him like a bombing squadron and were all around him at once. He started swinging his arms around like mad, and then he noticed that he was headed for the ditch. He gave the wheel a yank and started swinging at the wasps again. By this time they were really after him. Later he counted fifteen wasp stings, so I suppose most of the time he didn't know what was happening. Finally he decided that the only thing to do was to stop the bulldozer and to get out of there. By that time it was too late. Just as he stopped it, it banged against the light pole beside the driveway. The bulldozer wasn't going fast but the ground was soft beside the light pole, and it was just a temporary pole. It didn't break off, but it leaned over at about a forty-five-degree angle. It reached far enough to hit against the main lines at the road and snap one of them.

By this time the wasps had reached the house, and they were still after blood. They chased the mason and the two carpenters out of there and stung all three of them. The man who had caused all the trouble, the plumber, didn't get stung at all.

After a few minutes passed, I found a long stick and I slipped back out by the road. I managed to get my hat and net and put these on. Then I walked down into the ditch, got my gloves, and put the lid back on the can. Most of the wasps had left the nest. It had broken into three or four pieces. I was pretty sore at that plumber for ruining my wasps' nest, but there wasn't much point in complaining. I couldn't ask him to pay for the nest because I didn't know what it was worth. I decided to say nothing. Besides, I thought it might be just as well if that bulldozer operator didn't know where the wasps came from.

I dumped what remained of the nest out in the alfalfa field in back of the lot and put away my bee equipment. I hadn't seen a sign of Midge since the can was knocked in the ditch. As I came out of the barn, she came across the street.

"Where have you been?" I asked.

"I went back to collect that dollar from Mrs. Ainsworth," she said. "I thought maybe I'd better get it before she tried to cook dinner tonight."

"What's that got to do with it?"

"She's got an electric stove," Midge said. "In case you haven't heard, there isn't any power in Grover's Corner."

She was right. Somebody phoned the power company and they promised to be out as soon as they could, but they hadn't appeared yet at dusk. Everybody in Grover's Corner last night ate dinner by candlelight. Of course, some people couldn't even cook dinner at home because they had electric stoves, so they went out to restaurants. Aunt Mabel has a bottle-gas stove so it didn't make much difference at our house. The Glasses have an electric stove, but Mr. Glass grilled a steak outside on the charcoal grill.

Mr. Glass had planned to do some work on a scientific paper that he is writing, but since there weren't any lights he decided to take the family to the outdoor movies and they invited me to go along. The power company worked fast, and by the time we got back from the movies there were lights again.

AUTHOR

Keith Robertson was born in Iowa, and grew up in the Middle West. Following high school, he joined the Navy and spent two years at sea. Later, he graduated from the United States Naval Academy, and during World War II he served aboard destroyers on both the Atlantic and Pacific Oceans.

After the war, Mr. Robertson left the Navy and worked several years for a publisher. During that time he began writing books for young people and has been doing so ever since. Besides *Henry Reed, Inc.,* he has written three other books about Henry Reed: *Henry Reed's Baby Sitting Service, Henry Reed's Journey,* and *Henry Reed's Big Show.*

Mr. Robertson is married and has three children. He says that his children and their young friends supplied him with most of his ideas for the Henry Reed books. But now his children are grown up, and he has to find new sources of ideas for his books.

The Robertsons now live on a small farm in central New Jersey where they have surrounded themselves with farm animals and good books—two things they enjoy very much.

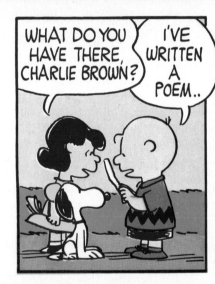

WHAT DO YOU HAVE THERE, CHARLIE BROWN?

I'VE WRITTEN A POEM..

REALLY? READ IT..

ALL RIGHT.. IT ISN'T VERY LONG..

SOME DAYS YOU THINK MAYBE YOU KNOW EVERYTHING... SOME DAYS YOU THINK MAYBE YOU DON'T KNOW ANYTHING... SOME DAYS YOU THINK YOU KNOW A FEW THINGS... SOME DAYS YOU DON'T EVEN KNOW HOW OLD YOU ARE.

© 1959 United Feature Syndicate.

THAT'S THE WORST POEM I'VE EVER HEARD!

4-19

A POEM IS SUPPOSED TO HAVE FEELING! YOUR POEM COULDN'T TOUCH **ANYONE'S** HEART! YOUR POEM COULDN'T MAKE **ANYONE** CRY! YOUR POEM COULDN'T..

Tm. Reg. U. S. Pat Off.—All rights reserved
Copr. 1959 by United Feature Syndicate, Inc.

WAAH!

SOME DAYS YOU THINK MAYBE YOU KNOW EVERYTHING...SOME DAYS YOU THINK MAYBE YOU..

SNIF

GOOD GRIEF!

SCHULZ

317

FROM

CALL IT COURAGE

BY ARMSTRONG SPERRY

It happened many years ago, before the traders and missionaries first came into the South Seas, while the Polynesians were still great in numbers and fierce of heart. But even today, the people of Hikueru sing this story in their chants and tell it over the evening fires. It is the story of Mafatu, the Boy Who Was Afraid.

They worshiped courage, those early Polynesians. The spirit which had urged them across the Pacific in their sailing canoes, before the dawn of recorded history, not knowing where they were going nor caring what their fate might be, still sang its song of danger in their blood. There was only courage. A man who was afraid — what place had he in their midst? And the boy Mafatu — son of Tavana Nui, the Great Chief of Hikueru — always had been afraid. So the people drove him forth, not by violence, but by indifference.

Mafatu went out alone to face the thing he feared the most. And the people of Hikueru still sing his story in their chants and tell it over the evening fires.

It was the sea that Mafatu feared. He had been surrounded by it ever since he was born. The thunder of it filled his ears; the crash of it upon the reef, the mutter of it at sunset, the threat and fury of its storms — on every hand, wherever he turned — the sea.

He could not remember when the fear of it first had taken hold of him. Perhaps it was during the great hurricane which swept Hikueru when he was a child of three. Even now, twelve years later, Mafatu could remember that terrible morning. His mother had taken him out to the barrier reef to search for sea urchins in the reef pools. There were other canoes scattered at wide intervals along the reef. With late afternoon, the other fishermen began to turn back. They shouted warnings to Mafatu's mother. It was the season of hurricane, and the people of Hikueru were nervous and ill at ease, charged, it seemed, with an almost animal awareness of impending storm.

But when at last Mafatu's mother turned back toward shore, a swift current had set in around the shoulder of the reef passage — a meeting of tides that swept like a millrace out into the open sea. It seized the frail craft in its swift race. Despite all the woman's skill, the canoe was carried on the crest of the churning tide, through the reef passage, into the outer ocean.

Mafatu would never forget the sound of his mother's despairing cry. He didn't know then what it meant, but he felt that something was terribly wrong, and he set up a loud wailing. Night closed down upon them, swift as a frigate's wing, darkening the known world. The wind of the open ocean rushed in at them, screaming. Waves lifted and struck at one another, their crests hissing with spray. The poles of the outrigger were torn from their thwarts. The woman sprang forward to seize her child

as the canoe capsized. The little boy gasped when the cold water struck him. He clung to his mother's neck. Moana, the Sea God, was reaching up for them, seeking to draw them down to his dark heart. . . .

Off the tip of Hikueru, the uninhabited islet of Tekoto lay shrouded in darkness. It was scarcely more than a ledge of coral, almost awash. The swift current bore directly down upon the islet.

Dawn found the woman still clinging to the *purau* pole and the little boy with his arms locked about his mother's neck. The grim light revealed sharks circling, circling. . . . Little Mafatu buried his head against his mother's cold neck. He was filled with terror. He even forgot the thirst that burned his throat. But the palms of Tekoto beckoned with their promise of life, and the woman fought on.

When at last they were cast up on the coral, Mafatu's mother crawled ashore with scarcely enough strength left to pull her child beyond reach of the sea's hungry fingers. The little boy was too weak even to cry. At hand lay a cracked coconut. The woman managed to press the cool, sustaining meat to her child's lips before she died.

Sometimes now, in the hush of night, when the moon was full and its light lay in silver bands across the pandanus mats, and all the village was sleeping, Mafatu awoke and sat upright. The sea muttered its eternal threat to the reef. The sea. . . And a terrible trembling seized the boy's limbs, while a cold sweat broke out on his forehead. Mafatu seemed to see again the faces of the fishermen who had found the dead mother and her whimpering child. These pictures still colored his dreams. And so it was that he shuddered when the mighty seas, gathering far out, hurled themselves at the barrier reef of Hikueru, and the whole island quivered under the assault.

Perhaps that was the beginning of it. Mafatu, the boy who had been christened Stout Heart by his proud father, was afraid of the sea. What manner of fisherman would he grow up to be? How would he ever lead the men in battle against warriors of other islands? Mafatu's father heard the whispers, and the man grew silent and grim.

The older people were not unkind to the boy, for they believed that it was all the fault of the *tupapau*, the ghost-spirit which possesses every child at birth. But the girls laughed at him, and the boys failed to include him in their games. And the voice of the reef seemed pitched for his ears alone. It seemed to say, "You cheated me once, Mafatu, but someday, someday I will claim you!"

Mafatu's stepmother knew small sympathy for him, and his stepbrothers treated him with open scorn.

"Listen," they would mock. "Moana, the Sea God, thunders on the reef. He is angry with us all because Mafatu is afraid!"

The boy learned to turn these jibes aside, but his father's silence shamed him. He tried with all his might to overcome his terror of the sea. Sometimes, steeling himself against it, he went with Tavana Nui and his stepbrothers out beyond the reef to fish. Out there, where the glassy swells of the ocean lifted and dropped the small canoe, pictures crowded into the boy's mind, setting his scalp atingle: pictures of himself, a babe, clinging to his mother's back . . . sharks cruising. . . . And so overcome would he be at the remembrance of that time that he would drop his spear overboard, or let the line go slack at the wrong moment and lose the fish.

It was obvious to everyone that Mafatu was useless upon the sea. He would never earn his proper place in the tribe. Stout Heart — how bitter the name must taste upon his father's lips!

So, finally, he was not allowed to fare forth with the fishermen. He brought ill luck. He had to stay at home making spears and nets, twisting coir — the husk of

the coconut—into stout sharkline for other boys to use. He became very skillful at these pursuits, but he hated them. His heart was like a stone in his breast.

A nondescript yellow dog named Uri was Mafatu's inseparable companion—Uri with his thin coat which showed his ribs, and his eyes so puzzled and true. He followed the boy wherever he went. Their only other friend was Kivi, an albatross. The boy had once found the bird on his lonely wanderings. One of Kivi's feet was smaller than the other. Perhaps because it was different from its kind, the older birds were heckling and pestering the fledgling. Something about that small bird trying to fight off its more powerful fellows touched the boy's heart. He picked it up, carried it home, and caught fish for it in the shallows of the lagoon. The bird followed Mafatu and Uri about, limping on its one good leg. At length, when the young albatross learned to fly, it began to find its own food. In the air it achieved perfection, floating serenely against the sky, while Mafatu followed its effortless flight with envious eyes. If only

he, too, could escape to some world far removed from Hikueru!

Now, once more, it was the beginning of the season of storms. Men scanned the skies anxiously, watching for the dreaded signs which might spell the destruction of their world. Soon the great bonitos would be swimming beyond the reef—hundreds, thousands of them—for they came each year at this time with the unfailing regularity of the tides. They were held to be the special property of young boys, since it was by killing them that a youth learned to kill the swordfishes and tiger sharks, progressing from one stage to a higher. Every boy in the village sharpened his spear, tested the shaft, honed his shark knife. Every boy, that is, except Mafatu.

Kana stopped one afternoon to watch Mafatu at work on his nets. Of all the youths of his own age, Kana alone had been friendly. Sometimes he even stayed behind when the others were fishing to help the boy with his work.

"The bonitos have begun to run, Mafatu," Kana said quietly.

"Yes," the other returned, then fell silent. His fingers faltered as they flew among the sennit fibers of the net he was making.

"My father brought back word from the reef today," Kana went on. "Already there are many bonitos out there. Tomorrow we boys will go after them. That's our job. It will be fun, eh?"

Mafatu's knuckles whitened. His ears pounded with the swift fury of the sea. . . .

"That will be fun, won't it?" Kana insisted, watching Mafatu closely. But the boy made no answer. Kana started to speak. He stopped, turned impatiently, and walked away. Mafatu wanted to cry out after him, "Wait, Kana! I'll go! I'll try—" But the words would not come. Kana had gone. Tomorrow he and all the other boys would be taking their canoes out beyond the reef. They would return at sunset, loaded down with bonitos, their faces happy, their shouts filling the dusk. Their fathers would say, "See what a fine fisherman is my son! He will be a Chief one of these days." Only Tavana Nui would be silent. *His* son had not gone.

That night a new moon rose above the edge of the sea, silvering the land with a bloom of magic. Wandering along the outer beach with Uri, Mafatu heard laughing voices and drew hastily into the black shadow of a pandanus. A group of boys were pulling their canoes above high watermark, and laying their plans for the morrow. Their voices were shrill with eagerness.

"Tomorrow at daybreak . . ." one was saying.

"There'll be Timi and Tapu and Viri . . . ."

"*Aué!*" another voice broke in. "It's work for us all. How else will we become fishermen and warriors? How else will we feed our families and keep the tribe alive?"

"True! Hikueru is too poor. There are only the fish from the sea. A man must be fearless to provide food. We will all go— every one of us!"

Mafatu, standing tense in the shadows, heard a scornful laugh. His heart contracted. "Not all of us will go," he heard Kana scoff. "Not Mafatu!"

"Ha! He is afraid."

"He makes good spears," offered Viri generously.

"Ho! That is not man's work. Mafatu is afraid of the sea. *He* will never be a warrior." Kana laughed again, and the scorn of

his voice was like a spear thrust through Mafatu's heart. "*Aiá!*" Kana was saying. "I have tried to be friendly with him. But he is good only for making spears. Mafatu is a coward."

The boys disappeared down the moonlit beach. Their laughter

floated back on the night air. Mafatu stood quite still. Kana had spoken. He had voiced, once for all, the feeling of the tribe. Mafatu — Stout Heart — was a coward. He was the Boy Who Was Afraid.

His hands were damp and cold. His nails dug into his palms. Suddenly a fierce resentment stormed through him. He knew in that instant what he must do. He must prove his courage to himself, and to the others, or he could no longer live in their midst. He must face Moana, the Sea God — face him and conquer him. He must.

The boy stood there taut as a drawn arrow awaiting its release. Off to the south somewhere there were other islands. . . . He drew a deep breath. If he could win his way to a distant island, he could make a place for himself among strangers. And he would never return to Hikueru until he would have proven himself! He would come back with his head high-held in pride, and he would hear his father say, "Here is my son Stout Heart. A brave name for a brave boy. . . ." Standing there with clenched fists, Mafatu knew a smarting on his eyelids and shut his eyes tight, and sank his teeth into his lower lip.

Far off in the *himené* house, the Old Ones were singing. Their voices filled the night with rich sound. They sang of long voyages in open canoes, of hunger and thirst and battle. They sang the deeds of heroes. The hair on the boy's damp forehead stirred. The long-drawn mutter of the reef sounded its note of warning in his ears. At his side, Uri touched his master's hand with a cold nose. Mafatu pulled the dog close.

"We're going away, Uri," he whispered fiercely. "Off to the south, there are other islands. . . ."

The outrigger canoes lay drawn up on the beach like long slim fish. Silent as a shadow, the boy crossed the sand. His heart was hammering in his throat. Into the nearest canoe he flung half a dozen green drinking nuts and his fish spear. He gave his *pareu* a brave hitch. Then he picked up a paddle and called to Uri. The dog leaped into the bow. There was only Kivi. Mafatu would miss his albatross. He scanned the dark sky for sight of the bird, then gave it up, and turned away.

The lagoon was as untroubled as a mirror. Upon its black face, the stars lay tracks of fire. The boy shoved off and climbed into the stern. Noiselessly he propelled the canoe forward, sending it half a length ahead with each thrust of his paddle. As he drew nearer to the barrier reef, the thunder of the surf increased. The old, familiar dread of it struck at his stomach's pit, and made him falter in his paddling.

The voices of the Old Ones were fainter and fainter now.

The reef thunder mounted: a long-drawn, hushed, yet mighty, sound that seemed to have its being not in the air above but in the very sea beneath. Out beyond lurked a terrifying world of water and wind. Out there lay everything most to be feared. The boy's hands tightened on his paddle. Behind him lay safety, security from the sea. What

matter if they jeered? For a second he almost turned back. Then he heard Kana's voice once more saying, "Mafatu is a coward."

The canoe entered the race formed by the ebbing tide. It caught up the small craft in its churn, swept it forward like a chip on a millrace. No turning back now. . .

The boy was aware of a sudden whir and fury in the sky above, a beat of mighty wings. Startled, he glanced upward. There was Kivi, his albatross. Mafatu's heart lifted. The bird circled slowly in the moonlight, its wings edged with silver. It hovered for a moment just over the bow of the canoe, then it rose easily, lightly in its effortless flight. Out through the passage in the reef. Out into the open ocean.

Mafatu gripped the steering paddle and followed.

Days passed on the open sea, where Mafatu and Uri faced the heat of the scorching sun and the dangers of a hurricane. Then one day Mafatu sighted a distant island. Using all his remaining strength, he managed to reach the island. For several days, Mafatu and Uri explored the island and found that it was deserted. He did, however, find enough food and water. Soon he built a small lean-to hut for shelter and a crude raft.

The days passed in a multitude of tasks that kept Mafatu busy from dawn till dark. His lean-to grew into a three-sided house with bamboo walls and a thatch of palm leaves. The fourth wall was open to the breezes of the lagoon. It was a trim little house and he was proud of it. A roll of woven mats lay on the floor; there was a shelf in the wall with three bowls cut from coconut shells; bone fishhooks dangled from a peg; there was a coil of tough sennit, many feet long; an extra *pareu* of tapa waterproofed with gum of the *artu* tree, for wet weather. All day long the wind played through the openings in the bamboo walls, and at night lizards scurried through the hatch with soft rustlings.

One morning, wandering far down the beach, Mafatu came upon a sheltered cove. His heart gave a leap of joy, for there, white-gleaming in the sun, was all that remained of the skeleton of a whale. It might not have meant very much to you or to me, but to Mafatu it meant knives and fishhooks galore, splinters of bone for darts and spears, a shoulder blade for an ax. It was a real treasure trove. The boy leaped up and down in his excitement. "Uri!" he shouted. "We're rich! Come! Help me drag these bones home!"

His hands seemed all thumbs in his eagerness. He tied as many bones as he could manage into two bundles. One bundle he shouldered himself. The other Uri dragged behind him. And

thus they returned to the camp-site, weary, but filled with elation. Even the dog seemed to have some understanding of what this discovery meant. If not, he was at least infected with his master's high spirits. He leaped about like a sportive puppy, yapping until he was hoarse.

Now began the long process of grinding the knife and the ax. Hour after long hour, squatting before a slab of basalt, Mafatu worked and worked, until his hands were raw and blistered and the sweat ran down into his eyes. The knife emerged first, since that was the most imperative. Its blade was ten inches long, its handle a knob of joint.

It was sharp enough to cut the leaves of coconut trees, to slice off the end of a green nut. *Ai*, but it was a splendid knife! All Mafatu's skill went into it. It would be a fine weapon as well, the boy thought grimly, as he ground it down to a sharp point. Some sea robber had been breaking into his bamboo trap, and he was going to find out who the culprit was! Probably that old tiger shark who was always cruising around . . . just as if he owned the lagoon!

Fishing with a line took too long when you were working against time. Mafatu could not afford to have his trap robbed. Twice it had been broken into, the stout bamboos crushed, and the contents eaten. It was the work either of a shark or of an octopus. That was certain. No other fish was strong enough to snap the tough bamboo.

Mafatu's mouth was set in a grim line as he worked on his knife. That old tiger shark—undoubtedly *he* was the thief! Mafatu had come to recognize him, for every day when the boy went out with his trap, the shark, larger than all the others, was circling around, wary and watchful. The other sharks seemed to treat the tiger shark with respect.

Hunger alone drove Mafatu out to the reef to set his trap. He knew that if he was to maintain strength to accomplish all that lay ahead, he must have fish to add to his diet of fruit. But often as he set his trap far out by the barrier reef, the tiger shark would approach, roll over slightly in passing, and the cold gleam of its eye filled Mafatu with dread and anger.

"Wait, you!" the boy threatened darkly, shaking his fist at the *ma'o*. "Wait until I have my knife! You will not be so brave then, Ma'o. You will run away when you see it flash."

But the morning that the knife was finished, Mafatu did not feel so brave as he would have liked. He hoped he would never see the tiger shark again. Paddling out to the distant reef, he glanced down from time to time at the long-bladed knife where it hung about his neck by a cord of sennit. It wasn't, after all, such a formidable weapon. It was only a knife made by a boy from a whale's rib.

Uri sat on the edge of the raft, sniffing at the wind. Mafatu always took his dog along, for Uri howled unmercifully if he were left behind. And Mafatu had come to rely upon the companionship of the little yellow

dog. The boy talked with the animal as if he were another person, consulting with him, arguing, playing when there was time for play. They were very close, these two.

This morning as they approached the spot where the fish trap was anchored, Mafatu saw the polished dorsal of the hated tiger shark circling slowly in the water. It was like a triangle of black basalt, making a little furrow in the water as it passed.

"Aiá, Ma'o!" the boy shouted roughly, trying to bolster his courage. "I have my knife today, see! Coward, who robs traps, catch your own fish!"

The tiger shark approached the raft in leisurely fashion, it rolled over slightly, and its gaping jaws seemed to curve in a yawning grin. Uri ran to the edge of the raft, barking furiously. The hair on the dog's neck stood up in a bristling ridge. The shark, unconcerned, moved away. Then with a whip of its powerful tail, it rushed at the bamboo fish trap and seized it in its jaws. Mafatu was struck dumb. The tiger shark shook the trap as a terrier might shake a rat. The boy watched fascinated, unable to make a

move. He saw the muscles work in the fish's neck as the great tail thrashed the water to fury. The trap splintered into bits, while the fish within escaped only to vanish into the shark's mouth. Mafatu was filled with helpless rage. The hours he had spent making that trap. . . . But all he could do was shout threats at his enemy.

Uri was running from one side of the raft to the other, furious with excitement. A large wave sheeted across the reef. At that second, the dog's shift in weight tipped the raft at a perilous angle. With a helpless yelp, Uri slid off into the water. Mafatu sprang to catch him, but he was too late.

Instantly the shark whipped about. The wave swept the raft away. Uri, swimming frantically, tried to regain it. There was desperation in the brown eyes — the puzzled eyes so faithful and true. Mafatu strained forward. His dog. His companion. . . . The tiger shark was moving in slowly. A mighty rage stormed through the boy. He gripped his knife. Then he was over the side in a clean-curving dive.

Mafatu came up under his enemy. The shark spun about. Its

rough hide scraped the flesh from the boy's shoulder. In that instant Mafatu stabbed deep, deep into the white belly of the shark. There was a terrific impact. Water lashed to foam. Stunned, gasping, the boy fought for life and air.

It seemed that he would never reach the surface. Aué, his lungs would burst! . . . At last his head broke water. Putting his face to the surface, he saw the great shark turn over, fathoms deep. Blood flowed from the wound in its belly. Instantly gray shapes — other big sharks — rushed in, tearing the wounded tiger shark to pieces.

Uri! Where was he? Mafatu saw his dog then. Uri was trying to pull himself up on the raft. Mafatu seized him by the scruff and dragged him up to safety. Then he caught his dog to him and hugged him close, talking to him foolishly. Uri yelped for joy and licked his master's cheek.

It wasn't until Mafatu reached shore that he realized what he had done. He had killed the *ma'o* with his own hand, with naught but a bone knife. He could never have done it for himself. Fear would have robbed his arm of all strength. He had done it for Uri, his dog. And he felt suddenly humble, with gratitude.

Should Mafatu return to his home now? Or should he first find proof to convince his father that he has truly conquered his fear? By reading the rest of Armstrong Sperry's book, CALL IT COURAGE, *you will be able to find out what Mafatu did.*

ABOUT THE AUTHOR

When Armstrong Sperry was a young boy, his great-grandfather, who had followed the sea for many years, liked to fill the ears of the boy with tales of tropic islands, of pearl lagoons, and of sharks and whales.

Many years later, when the boy grew up, he followed his great-grandfather's adventurous trail to some of the remotest parts of the world. He even lived for some months on an island in the South Pacific. That visit gave him much of the background for his book *Call It Courage.* His experiences have found their way into the more than thirty books that Mr. Sperry has written and illustrated for young people.

Some of his books are about places, such as the Arctic, the Antarctic, or the Amazon River. Others are about historical figures, such as John Paul Jones and Christopher Columbus. Some, such as *Storm Canvas,* are stories which combine his interest in the past and distant places with his love of adventure and the sea.

Armstrong Sperry was born in 1897 in New Haven, Connecticut. Before he began his travels around the world, he served in the Navy in World War I. Later, he studied art at the Yale School of Art, the Art Students League in New York, and in France. He felt he could best combine his interests by writing and illustrating children's books.

BOOKS TO ENJOY

THE I HATE MATHEMATICS! BOOK   *by Marilyn Burns*

Here is a lively collection of puzzles, riddles, magic tricks, and brain teasers, all involving math and all fun to do.

THE MARIAH DELANY LENDING LIBRARY DISASTER   *by Sheila Greenwald*

When Mariah finds the New York Public Library closed because of cutbacks, she comes up with an enterprising venture that is more than she bargained for.

SIEGE! THE STORY OF ST. AUGUSTINE IN 1702
by Wilma Pitchford Hays

The pride and strength of the Spanish people in St. Augustine, Florida in 1702 come through in this historical adventure story.

THE MAGIC MEADOW   *by Alexander Key*

A crippled boy and four other hospital patients escape to a fantasy world in the future.

BUT WHAT ABOUT ME?   *by Sandra Love*

In a warm, family story, Lucy's mother's return to work as a newspaper reporter creates all kinds of problems for the sixth grader.

ICEBERGS AND THEIR VOYAGES   *by Gwen M. Schultz*

This interesting description of icebergs and how they form includes a plan to tow icebergs to dry coastal areas as a source of fresh water.

MAGDALENA   *by Louisa R. Shotwell*

Adjusting to new friends and school in Brooklyn and yet respecting her grandmother's traditional Puerto Rican ways causes some problems for Magdalena.

Compass

Compass

STORIES

ARTICLES

POEMS

JUST FOR FUN

SKILL LESSONS

OPEN GATE TO FREEDOM

BY LÁSZLÓ HÁMORI

In the late 1940's, Latsi Kerék's parents had left their native Hungary and gone to Sweden to find work. Little Latsi stayed in Budapest with his grandmother, expecting to join his parents when he was old enough to travel alone. But then the Communists came into power in Hungary. By the mid-1950's, when Latsi was twelve, his country had become a police state, and the authorities no longer allowed people to come and go as they pleased. When his grandmother died, Latsi decided to try to escape and somehow reach his parents in Sweden. He managed to hide in a freight car bound across the heavily-guarded border between Hungary and Austria. However, just short of the border—and freedom—Latsi left the freight car to refill his water bottle, and the train pulled away without him. Tired out and in constant danger of being picked up by the police, Latsi walked on toward the border until help came at last—from Susy, a goose girl, who found him a shelter among cornstalks and who brought him some food.

Once Latsi was alone, his head grew heavier and heavier and his eyes kept closing. In the freight car he hadn't managed to get much sleep, and the long journey on foot had also taken its toll. Stretching himself out on the floor of the shelter, he was sound asleep in a matter of minutes, and he slept well.

He woke to find Susy cautiously pulling his hair.

"Wake up, sleepyhead. It's evening already!" she cried merrily. After Latsi had rubbed the sleep out of his eyes and taken a

long drink of water, Susy said seriously:

"Listen carefully. Tonight you can probably get over the border if you're very careful. One of the farmers here who has a place right near the border was down there this morning gathering his corn. While he and his son were plucking the ears, the horse broke loose. I haven't any idea what got into him. Maybe he got stung by a hornet or something like that. Anyway, he bolted and galloped straight toward the barbed-wire fence. It's possible that he became frightened by the watchmen in the tower, because they were shooting and things were exploding as usual."

"What does that have to do with me?" Latsi asked. "You aren't suggesting that I gallop off in the direction of the barbed wire, are you?"

"No, not exactly. As a matter of fact, you'd never get that far. A two-hundred-yard area on both sides is full of land mines—even before you get up to the barbed wire. And around there, every tree and every bush has been chopped down, so even if you managed to miss the mines, the watchmen could see you, in any case, from their watchtower. A searchlight sweeps across the mine field every few seconds."

"Well, what has this got to do with the horse?" Latsi asked.

"Well, wait. I'm coming to that. The horse landed right in the middle of the mine field, and there he tramped on a mine. It must have been a powerful one, because not only the horse but also the cart exploded into a million pieces. It even tore the fence down for a pretty long way. Don't you understand, you sleepyhead, why I'm telling you all this?"

As yet Latsi didn't understand a single thing, but who in the world would ever let anyone think he was stupid? Therefore he nodded, just as if he had understood the whole idea. Susy went on eagerly:

"You see, I knew all about this before, but I didn't want to say anything about it until I could find out if the border patrol had had time to lay new mines and to fix up the fence. But after I had herded the geese in and eaten my supper . . . hey!" She suddenly interrupted herself. "Did you get something to eat this evening? Of course you didn't!"

Without waiting for a reply, Susy took out what was left of the food. She added to the supply two beautiful red apples, which she produced from her pocket.

"Let me see now. Where was I? . . . Oh, yes. After supper I went over to the neighbor's house. Their daughter goes round with a corporal who is one of the border watchmen. Whenever he has any free time, he sits there in the evening on a bench outside the house with Ilonka. You know how it is when people are in love. I even saw them kissing each other one time."

Angrily, Latsi interrupted to ask her what kissing and hugging had to do with the whole matter.

But Susy only laughed at his peevishness.

"It's plain that all of this has something to do with the matter. There was the corporal sitting beside Ilonka as usual, and I very cleverly managed to find out from him that they hadn't been able to lay any new mines. And they haven't had time to repair the barbed-wire fence either. The corporal said that the incident had been reported to the commanding officer but that the mine experts hadn't arrived as yet. Nothing can be done until a further order is issued. . . . The gates are still wide open, you see. All you have to do is go through."

Finally it dawned on Latsi what the whole thing was all about, and he began to wonder how he would manage to do it.

"There are two difficulties," he said. "First of all, I have to find out where the holes in the barbed wire are, and, secondly, I have to find the spot in the dark."

But Susy knew the answers to everything. She told him to search for the acacia tree growing in a meadow a little way from there. The horse in question had broken loose right under the tree. And the tracks from the wheels of the wagon were still there. If Latsi very, very carefully sneaked through the corn field up to the acacia, nobody would even notice him. But at that point, the pasture land began, and he would have to cross the mine field itself by crawling on his stomach. That was the only way.

Latsi groped around in his pocket until he found what he was looking for — his beloved notebook. The covers were real leather, and on the inside was a pocket with a mirror. It had belonged to Latsi's father, and Latsi had received it from his grandmother on his birthday. He fingered the soft, smooth leather for the last time and handed the book to Susy.

"I can't speak as nicely as you, but I want to give you my little notebook because you've been so wonderful to me."

Leafing through the book as she took it, Susy suddenly discovered the little mirror on the inside of the cover. She looked in it, although she wasn't able to see much in the darkness. But suddenly she thought of something else.

"When you come to the mine field, you've got to keep your face down against the ground. Don't look up. Ilonka's corporal told me one time that they discover refugees because their faces shine in the light of the searchlights."

"Well, that's easily taken care of," Latsi remarked. He spilled a little water from his water bottle onto the ground, broke apart the clumps of earth with his hands, and began to smear his face with the mud. Somewhere he had read that soldiers during the war blackened their hands and faces that way when they attacked at night. And while he was on the subject, he began to think how lucky it was that he had torn his everyday pants on the train. He now had on his dark blue Sunday suit. The dark fabric would never give him away in the light of the searchlights.

When his face was thoroughly smeared, he began to work on his hands. Susy couldn't keep from laughing.

It was time to say good-by. Susy had grown a little uneasy. Maybe her parents had begun to miss her, because she had said, of course, that she was only going over to see the neighbors. The blue-velvet sky of evening lay heavily across the landscape, and Latsi would have to be on his way if he were to reach Austrian soil under the cover of darkness. The summer nights were short, and the shadows of the night were chased away very early by the rays of the morning sun.

After a final handclasp and a promise to write her from Sweden, he heard her quick footsteps running away, back to the farmhouse. Latsi was all alone.

He crept out of the shelter. In the stillness he could hear the song of the crickets; over toward the village a dog barked. Beyond the corn field, rays of light swept along the ground, now and then, back and forth, like a lighthouse along the edge of the sea. But these beams of light were not made to guide one along the way. Soldiers armed with machine guns operated the searchlights from the watchtower.

Cautiously, Latsi sneaked into

the corn field between the tall, straight rows. The half-dried sword-shaped blades rustled with his every movement, and no matter how he walked, he stepped on one now and then that crackled underfoot. In the deep, endless silence, this seemed like thunder in Latsi's ears. At times he stopped and listened, his nerves tense with excitement. Even now, perhaps some armed patrol with a machine gun was following him—to catch him, put him in chains, and throw him into prison. Suddenly he froze, utterly motionless. He had heard something. It took a minute before he realized it was just a rabbit hopping among the stalks of corn.

After what seemed an eternity, Latsi finally sighted the lonely acacia tree. At once he calmed down. Even though Susy had explained to him how he was to find it, he had been afraid he wasn't on the right track and that he might miss it.

But he still had a long way to go. Sweat dripped from his muddy face; his heart thumped with excitement. The summer night was warm, and he had pulled his jacket collar up around his neck so that his white shirt wouldn't show up in the dark. He had almost reached the end of the corn field when the moon suddenly appeared over the horizon. The golden heavenly body rose slowly, lighting up the entire landscape. In Hungary, they say that King David plays his harp at full-moon time, and many times Latsi had looked up and been delighted with its lovely light. *Now* the moon was something else again. It didn't at all remind him of a king out of Biblical times.

He stood under the acacia tree. His legs trembled—not so much from weariness as from tenseness.

Now that he had arrived at the most dangerous point of his journey, he had to support himself against the trunk of the tree in order to summon his courage. Taking a deep breath, he folded down the collar of his jacket and unbuttoned his shirt in order to cool off a bit. As he fumbled with the buttons, he realized that he was soaking wet.

In the soft earth that lay before him, he could see the tracks of the wheels and the horse's hoofs, clearly and distinctly, thanks to the moonlight. They led almost straight up to the place where the mine had exploded. Latsi knew that he had to follow these tracks with no more than a fraction of an inch of difference on either side. The least false step could mean death. As long as he followed the tracks, he could be sure there were no mines along his path. Had there been, they would certainly have exploded. But no more than inches away from the wheel tracks, a mine could be hidden—lying in wait like a poisonous snake in the grass.

And there were dangers other than the mines. The watchtower with its searchlights and the

soldiers with machine guns were also points to keep in mind. The slightest movement in the path of the searchlight would be the cause for their sending a shower of bullets over him.

Once again he pulled up his coat collar, lay on his stomach, and began to slither along between the tracks left by the wheels. Slowly and with infinite care, he moved forward, following the tracks, and every time he raised his head, he could see that he was coming closer and closer to the barbed-wire fence. Suddenly there was no more grassland. Beneath his hands he could feel coarse lumps of earth, and he began to realize that he had reached the mine field it-self. There, all the bushes and trees had been removed, and they had even plowed up the grass. Nothing was left that might shield the escapees. "This is the most dangerous point," he said to him-self. The only thing that mattered was to keep within the bounds of the wheel tracks and to keep pressed as closely to the ground as possible.

He had managed to go forward about thirty yards on the uneven, newly plowed ground when a dazzling searchlight was turned on in the watchtower. The flood of light splintered the darkness. For a moment, Latsi believed they had turned it on because they had discovered him. His first thought was to get up and run as fast as possible. With any luck he might reach the place where the explosion had ruined the fence and escape over onto Austrian soil. And if he were to run terribly fast, perhaps they wouldn't be able to shoot him. He tensed his muscles, but at the last minute he checked his feelings of panic. With his arms at his sides and his legs pressed tightly together, he stretched out flat on the ground. In that position, it would be more difficult for any bullets to hit him. The searchlight had made a quarter turn when it reached the spot where a still figure lay on the ground. Latsi's heart was pounding so hard that he felt his chest would burst; his throat was dry. For a fraction of a second the strong light lingered, and then it continued on its path. But the split second seemed an eternity to Latsi.

By this time the light had made a half-circle turn, and Latsi, who had cautiously peeked upward, could see every thorny barb in the fence. Just as suddenly as the lights had been turned on, they were turned out again, and only a reddish glow, fast fading, remained at the point

from which blinding light had come. Everything was dark and quiet once more, and Latsi began to creep ahead again. Because of the tension, his joints were stiff, but a few yards farther on, it got a little easier, and he made fairly good progress. "Not much faster than a snail, however," he thought sadly. In addition, the passage of time began to bother him. No doubt it was quite late. He had no watch, but he had the feeling that the night was just about at an end. To be sure, the skies were still dark, but the stars had begun to fade; one after the other disappeared at the edge of the horizon. Dawn was coming and with it the dangers increased.

Up to this point the wheel tracks had been almost as straight as an arrow, but suddenly they swung sharply to the left. A couple of yards farther on, his hand touched a coarse, hard piece of wood. Reaching out one hand, he felt all around in front of himself. There were other small pieces of wood, which made him realize that he was near the spot where the mine had blasted the wagon into the air. Pieces of splintered wood were all that remained of it. Lifting his head with utmost caution, Latsi took a good look around. The tracks of the wheels, which had been his guide, ended abruptly, and he was forced to feel his way with his hands and inch his body along. A rash movement, a false touch, and a new mine could explode!

About four yards farther on, he could see a dark spot on the ground. It was where the mine had burst the previous morning, blasting a hole. What if there was another mine on this side or on the other side of the hole?

He didn't have time to worry about that. Moments were precious, and he had to make progress. Once more he felt panic, wanting to rise up and run for all he was worth and forget about everything else. Although he well knew the danger, he began to crawl ahead on all fours. He could not help himself, even though he knew that the watchtower was very close! He reached the hole more quickly than he would have if he had continued to slither along; his hands were touching the edge when the searchlight came on again. Like a flaming sword the beam split the darkness. In other, more peaceful times this would have

been a beautiful sight, but Latsi had no time to enjoy the dramatic wonder. Headfirst, he threw himself into the hole. It was deep enough so that he could curl up and not be seen in the deadly beam of light. As it had before, it returned halfway before it went out again. Darkness once more covered the field, but Latsi had no desire to leave his safe retreat in the hole. All the while he had been inching along, he had been bothered by the heat; he was fairly sure that sweat had washed the mud off his face.

Lying in the hole, his former warmth gave way to a feeling of chilliness. As the dawn approached, a breeze had sprung

up, and it was not strange that he began to feel cold, soaking wet as he was. His whole body shook and his teeth chattered. Shivering, he tried to make himself crawl out of the hole and go ahead, but he couldn't do it. While his will battled his fear, he began, without knowing it, to mumble to himself a football cheer: *"Hoop, hoop, hurrá! Hoop, hoop, hurrá!"*

And it helped. Once more he began to inch along. No longer did his teeth chatter so terribly, and he even dared to raise his head and look around. No more than ten yards away was the open gate to freedom. The explosion had blasted a couple of fence posts almost to pieces, and twisted barbed wire hung over the remains. As rapidly as possible, he made his way toward the opening: There were five, now three yards, now one yard to go—and over there was freedom, life, and Sweden. Cautious though he was, he scratched his hand badly on some barbed wire that lay on the ground. Blood dripped from the gash onto Hungarian soil as Latsi said farewell to his homeland, the beautiful land of Hungary.

This is only the beginning of Latsi's dangerous journey toward freedom and his parents. You can read the rest of his story in the book DANGEROUS JOURNEY *by László Hámori.*

AUTHOR

László Hámori says that people usually are curious about whether this story is true or not. He answers that he has known young people like the characters in the story and that the events might well have happened.

Mr. Hámori was born in Hungary in 1911 and left to live in Sweden in 1949. He says that his journey from Hungary was almost as dangerous as the one described in the book *Dangerous Journey*. However, he was nearly three times as old as Latsi.

László Hámori and his wife have two daughters and a dog. They live in Stockholm, Sweden, where he works as a journalist and writer.

Elizabeth Blackwell, M.D.

by Lynne Vincent Cheney

Elizabeth Blackwell was born in England in 1821. She turned out to be a very determined little girl. No matter how often her aunts tried to help her, she insisted on dressing herself. And that was really hard, since she lived in a time when children wore layers of clothes with many buttons and laces.

She had an unusual father, too. When Elizabeth was little, many people thought it was not important for girls to go to school. But Elizabeth's father knew better. So he had his daughter learn Latin and arithmetic when most girls her age learned only to sing and sew.

When Elizabeth was eleven, her family moved from England to the United States. In America, Elizabeth watched her father fight for the rights of all people—just as he had done in England. He wrote against slavery especially, and the whole family lived by his ideas.

After her father died, Elizabeth and her whole family were so busy earning enough money to live that Elizabeth had little time to think about what she wanted to do with her life. One day she was comforting one of her mother's friends. Even though the woman was very sick, she must have noticed Elizabeth's gentle gray eyes and soothing hands, for she told Elizabeth that she should be a doctor.

Elizabeth was very much surprised. Women just were not doctors in those days. Long ago in ancient Greece and Egypt, there had been women doctors. Women doctors had helped bind up battle wounds in the time of the Crusades. But when Elizabeth was a young woman, respectable ladies did not work outside the house at all, much less think about being doctors.

Elizabeth mentioned the idea to a friend of hers, Harriet Beecher Stowe. She liked to visit with Harriet, whose comfortable house was full of books and babies and whose ideas were as strong as Elizabeth's own. Mrs. Stowe, in fact, would one day write a book called *Uncle Tom's Cabin*, a book famous for having brought many people into the antislavery cause.

Dr. Stowe, Harriet's husband, told Elizabeth that she should give up the idea of medicine. Although being a doctor would be wonderful, for a woman it was simply an impossible undertaking. But Elizabeth was as determined as ever. She became more and more convinced that however hard it might be, she would become a doctor.

It was almost impossible. Philadelphia was the medical center of the United States in those days, and every medical school there refused to admit Elizabeth as a student. Some of the doctors at the schools said that they would admit Elizabeth if she would disguise herself as a man. She refused. It was not only her own education she was interested in; she wanted to clear a path so that all women could have the opportunities men had. If that was to happen, she had to attend medical school as a woman.

Finally, in 1847, Elizabeth was accepted at a small school of medicine in Geneva, New York. At first she caused quite a stir. The ladies in her boarding house would not speak to her when they found out she was studying medicine. Visitors would come to the school to stare at her. Little by little, however, Elizabeth convinced everyone of her seriousness and ability, and in 1849, she became the first woman M.D.—Doctor of Medicine—of modern times.

But her battles were not over. She knew that she could never be a good doctor unless she watched other doctors helping patients. But because she was a woman, no hospital would let her in to observe. She finally went to Paris, France—not to a hospital but to a maternity home. There she knew she could learn by watching the midwives, nurses who had helped hundreds of babies to be born. In fact, the first night she was there, Dr. Blackwell helped the midwives deliver eight babies.

After she finished her training in Paris, Dr. Blackwell went

to England. There she became good friends with Florence Nightingale, another lady who thought that women could make important contributions to medicine. They spent long hours talking, often about how important it was for both well people and sick people to keep clean.

Today almost everybody knows that. But in those days, people didn't know about bacteria and viruses. When a man in Cincinnati, Ohio, installed a bathtub in his house, many doctors became very upset. They thought that taking frequent baths was not healthy. People who went into the hospital with one disease often caught another because bedclothes, table utensils, and medical instruments were not kept sterile. Wounds became infected because they were not kept clean.

When Dr. Blackwell returned to New York in 1851, she saw more examples of how people's living habits harmed their health. She saw poor children in the slums eating spoiled meat after their mothers brushed flies off it. She saw rich women and girls, never exercising, never out in the sun, always squeezing themselves into tight corsets.

Dr. Blackwell began to write and speak about how girls as well as boys should run outdoors and exercise. For the poor she started a free clinic where she treated the sick and taught people how to live in order to be healthy.

Later, she founded the New York Infirmary and Training School, where her ideas about keeping everything clean were used and where other women could learn to be doctors. Because of Dr. Blackwell's work, people began to pay attention to ways of preventing sickness as well as curing it. Other medical schools for women were founded, and those for men began to admit women. Medicine became possible as a career for women.

So Elizabeth Blackwell was a real pioneer—not because she opened up new lands but because she helped open minds long closed by prejudice and ignorance.

AUTHOR

Lynne Vincent Cheney grew up in Wyoming, which was the very first place in the world where women had the right to vote. So, she has always known that girls can grow up to be doctors, lawyers, and presidents or can hold other jobs traditionally held by men. In fact, her own mother was a deputy sheriff.

Dr. Cheney went to grade school and high school in Wyoming, to Colorado College, and to graduate school at Colorado University. She has a Ph.D. degree from the University of Wisconsin. Now, while teaching at a university in Washington, D.C., she writes articles for adults and children.

THE PERSISTENT NUMBER

When something refuses to give up, it is said to be *persistent*.

Here is a persistent number:

142,857

Multiply this number by 2, 3, 4, 5, and 6.

Now do you know why the number is called persistent?

Look at the products: 285,714; 428,571; 571,428; 714,285; 857,142. Each has the same digits as the original numeral and the digits are in the same order, starting with a different digit each time.

355

CITY

In the morning the city
Spreads its wings
Making a song
In stone that sings.

In the evening the city
Goes to bed
Hanging lights
About its head.

Langston Hughes

INDIAN BOY JOINS

Sentinel STAFF

by Evelyn Sibley Lampman

At the end of the nineteenth century, Small Shadow, an Indian boy of the Rogue River tribe, lived with his father, Lew Youngbuck, on a reservation in northwest Oregon. Small Shadow was eleven when his father was sent to prison for a year. Dan'l Foster, the kindly white lawyer who defended Youngbuck, agreed to keep Small Shadow until his father had served his sentence.

Living with Dan'l Foster at Mrs. Hicks's boarding house in the town was a great adventure for Shad, as Small Shadow came to be called. Although some of the town's citizens were unfriendly to the young Indian boy, sharp-spoken but warm-hearted Mrs. Hicks was like a mother to him. Shad earned his keep by running errands and doing chores for her. Then, thanks to Dan'l Foster, Shad suddenly found he had a chance for a real job.

"Shad, how'd you like to have a job?" asked Dan'l Foster one morning. "Earn a little money for yourself?"

Shad had been sifting wood ashes for Mrs. Hicks, who needed them in her preparation of soft soap. He put down the wire sieve and stared up in amazement. No one had ever offered him a chance to earn money before.

"What you doing home this time of day, Dan'l Foster?" Mrs. Hicks had come around the corner of the house, carrying the huge copper kettle she used for soapmaking, but had arrived too late to hear the question.

"I come for Shad," Dan'l told her mildly. "Ralph Evans needs a boy at the *Valley Sentinel*. I figured it might be a chance for Shad to pick up a little spending money."

"Shad works for me mornings as you very well know," she reminded him severely.

"You got first call on his services, all right," agreed Dan'l. "And there's half a dozen boys in town Ralph can get if you really need Shad here. But Abe Flint's oldest boy works on the newspaper regular, and I think it would be nice for Shad to get acquainted with somebody near his own age. It's not right for him to stick with the old folks all the time."

Shad looked back at the ashes. A week ago he would have been delighted to meet some white boys. But the first one he had met insulted him, and a fight resulted. Now Shad wanted to stay as far away from them as possible.

"There's something to that," Mrs. Hicks agreed thoughtfully. "The Flints is good folks, and their young'uns is well spoken. What kind of job?"

"Don't rightly know. But Ralph seems hard put with the *Sentinel* coming out today. That young fellow he had working for him up and lit out this morning. Took the stage to Salem. The Flint boy can help, but Ralph needs somebody to take on the Flint boy's chores. Reckon he can get somebody else, though."

"He'll do no such thing," denied Mrs. Hicks fiercely. "It's high time somebody but me sees what a good, dependable worker Shad is. I can manage with the soap. I always have."

Shad heard her decision with

"Well, what you waiting for?" asked Mrs. Hicks impatiently. "I said you could go."

"Shall I change to my good pants?" He stood up reluctantly. He would have to go. Mrs. Hicks and Dan'l expected it of him.

"Better not," advised Dan'l. "You'll come home black as any inkpot, and Mrs. Hicks may not even let you in the house."

"There'll be plenty of hot water and soap." Mrs. Hicks frowned. "It'll be honest dirt that come from honest work."

As they walked to town, Shad tried to put the uneasy thoughts from his mind. He did his best to act pleased about the job, because that was what Dan'l Foster expected.

The offices of the *Valley Sentinel* were on the first block of Main Street, next to Jackson's Harness Shop and across the street from Cosper's Livery Stable. The front door was flanked by two grimy windows, one displaying a heavy cardboard sign.

Shad tugged at Dan'l's coat. "What does that say?"

"It used to say, 'Job Printing Neatly Done,'" said Dan'l scornfully, opening the door. "But it's got so fly-speckled and dirty, I'm

mixed emotions. He would like to earn some money. Such an opportunity had never come to him before. But he wanted nothing to do with any strange white boy.

not surprised you can't figure it out."

The huge black machine, which stood at the far end of the single room, had not yet been put to work. There was no loud, crashing noise, only a steady clicking, like someone shaking a handful of pebbles in a sack. Coming from the bright sunlight made it difficult to see, for inside they were in a world of semi-gloom. Shad wrinkled his nose at the strange odors: printer's ink, sour paste, and metallic grime. He could identify none of them.

"Morning, Mr. Foster." A boy, a few years older than Shad, stepped forward to greet them. He wore dirty jeans and a long apron that was so speckled with ink spots it was hard to guess the original color. His face, too, was streaked with black, but he was smiling widely.

"Morning," said Dan'l. "You're one of Abe Flint's boys, aren't you? Let's see, you're—"

"I'm Frank. Frank Flint." He had not left off smiling, and his eyes were studying Shad. There was nothing critical in the smile, only friendliness. Shad felt the tight knot in his stomach begin to ease. Perhaps this would not be like his first encounter with a white boy after all. Then he reminded himself that it was too soon to tell. He must move cautiously.

"This is Shad," said Dan'l. "Ralph asked me to bring him over."

"I know," agreed Frank. "Mr. Evans is setting type right now, but he'll be through in a minute."

By now Shad had discovered the source of the clicking sound. The editor of the *Valley Sentinel* was gathering small bits of metal into a long stick. It did not look difficult, but he was concentrating hard and did not look up.

Shad had already met Ralph Evans on his evening excursions downtown. The editor was younger than Dan'l Foster and had thinning black hair carefully parted in the middle. His eyeballs looked too large for their sockets, for they protruded noticeably. He used very large words, many of which Shad had never heard. He wondered why Mr. Evans had offered him this job and decided it was probably because Dan'l had asked him.

When Mr. Evans finished, he placed the column of type carefully on a stone-topped table and then crossed the room to greet them.

"I see you brought him," he observed. "It's a bad day to break in a new printer's devil. Lots to do with the *Sentinel* coming out. Frank will have to help me and supervise your boy at the same time. I don't want him at the cases today, Frank. It's too tricky. Do it yourself, and let him watch."

"Yes, sir," said Frank.

"Blast Ed Wheeler, anyway,"

sputtered Mr. Evans angrily. "He was a good apprentice. But they're all alike. Can't trust them. Get to know a little about the business, and then they take off without a fare-thee-well."

"Didn't give a reason, I suppose?" asked Dan'l curiously.

"A weak one. Claimed he didn't like Mrs. Evans's cooking. He ate with us as part of his salary." He turned to Shad. "We need somebody two days a week: Thursday—when the *Sentinel* goes to press—and Wednesday—when we're getting ready. A couple of days is enough for a printer's devil. We'll see how you work out."

"How about wages, Ralph?" asked Dan'l. "What you figure on paying Shad?"

The editor frowned. "He won't be much use at first. He'll have to be taught everything. Maybe twenty-five cents a day to start."

"That's mighty low, even for a beginner. How about fifty? You won't be boarding him; he'll be eating at home."

"I'll go thirty and not a penny more. And if he's no good, out he goes."

"He'll be good," Dan'l promised. He patted Shad on the shoulder, smiled at Frank, and returned to his office.

"There's not much for us to do while Mr. Evans locks up the type," said Frank. "I can show you around and explain things. Did you bring an apron?"

Shad shook his head. He hadn't known an apron was needed.

"Mr. Wheeler left in such a hurry he forgot his. You can wear that," suggested Frank.

The apron had a bib and covered Shad from his neck to his feet. It was nearly as soiled as the one Frank was wearing, but Shad was glad of the protection. Next week he would put on his reservation clothes. Mrs. Hicks would never approve of ink spots on his new clothes.

Mr. Evans was still busy with his type. He had imposed it on the stone-topped table, locked it in a case, and transferred it to the press. Frank conducted Shad around the room, explaining rapidly as he went. The long central table was for folding papers once they had been printed. That would be one of Shad's jobs. He would also be required to wash the rollers of the press, keep the paste pots filled and the type dampened, carry rolls of paper,

and return the type to the cases that lined one wall.

"But you won't do that today," he concluded. "Mr. Evans wants you to watch me the first time. Mr. Wheeler, the man who left, says printer's devils, like us, aren't always expected to put type back in cases. Lots of times the printer wants to do it himself, to make sure it's right. But Mr. Evans doesn't like to put away type. He hates the job of tidying up."

Shad could well believe it. After the immaculate neatness of Mrs. Hicks's house, the *Valley*

Sentinel was something of a shock. There were papers everywhere, papers in rolls, in stacks of assorted sizes and thicknesses, even small bits scattered here and there. At the far end was a desk, obviously used by the editor, for it was covered with more paper, and there were paste and ink pots and an assortment of quill pens stuck in a drinking glass. There was a trough, filled with water, under one window, and a basin for hand washing beside a grimy roller towel in the corner.

"Everybody quiet now!" Mr. Evans's reedy voice rose threateningly. "I am about to compose. I've made room for another story on the front page, and a follow-up on page two. The public needs to be told of the perfidy of a thankless apprentice who deserted his benefactor on press day."

Frank nodded. He drew Shad away from the type cases and toward the door.

"We'll wait outside," he whispered. "When Mr. Evans is composing a story, he doesn't want anybody around. He'll call us when he's through."

"It's nice of you to help me get started and explain everything," said Shad shyly after the door closed behind them. Maybe Mrs. Hicks was right about the Flints. Frank was not at all like the first white boy he had met. "I've never had a job before."

"This is my first one, too," Frank told him. "My brothers work in Pa's mill, but I wanted to do something on my own."

"Do you like it?"

"Parts of it. I don't like putting away type any more than Mr. Evans does. But after today, you'll be doing that."

"What is type?" Shad hadn't understood those bits of metal Frank had showed him at all, but he hadn't wanted to interrupt the explanation. "What's it for?"

"Why, it's type. You know, letters. Alphabet letters that make up words."

Shad shook his head. He still did not understand.

"You know your alphabet, don't you?" asked Frank, and when Shad shook his head, Frank's dirty face grew long. "Then how can you work on a newspaper?"

"Can't I learn it?" asked Shad anxiously. "Can't you teach me?"

"I don't know," said Frank doubtfully. "It's hard. Haven't you ever been to school?"

Shad shook his head. It hadn't seemed important before, but now he wished he had talked his father into letting him go long enough to learn this thing called an alphabet.

Until last year, the Sisters of the Holy Name had done their best to conduct a boarding school on the reservation. It was situated near the government agency, and when the surrounding land had been assigned to the Indians, the old and feeble had been given the plots closest to the agency. Lew Youngbuck, Shad's father, was an able-bodied man, so his acreage was several miles distant. It was too far for Shad to make the round trip to school daily, and his father wanted him to live at home.

Besides, no one considered the school of real importance compared with the other work that the children could learn to do. Families who enrolled their children often withdrew them after a few weeks. What would it avail a child to learn to read? Reading did not help plow a field or raise a crop. It did not make a better hunter or a fisherman. The stories of their people could not be found in books. They were told and retold by the old men. Learning to read and write was a waste of time, and due to the lack of students, the school had to be closed.

"I'll try hard," pleaded Shad. "Maybe I can learn. Nobody's ever given me a chance at a job before. If you'll help me, I promise to work at it."

Frank hesitated a moment. Then he stood up.

"You wait here," he ordered. "I'm going to sneak back in and get some paper. If I'm careful, Old Man Evans won't even hear me. He's lost to the world when he's composing."

Shad sat down on the edge of the boardwalk, letting his legs dangle down to the dusty road below. There was a hard lump of fear in his stomach, and his hands were damp. Somehow, some way, he had to learn this thing called an alphabet. If he didn't, he couldn't work at the *Sentinel* and earn sixty cents every week. It was a real job, and he knew he would never be offered another. All his hopes depended on this strange white boy, and Shad was afraid that Frank might change his mind about helping him.

Frank returned almost immediately. He brought a stub of indelible pencil and a sheet of foolscap, which he spread on the boardwalk.

"I never taught anybody the alphabet before, and I don't know how to start," he admitted. "I'll just have to write it down, and you can study it."

With Shad peering over his shoulder, he laboriously wrote the twenty-six letters of the alphabet.

"You'll need to learn the little letters, too," he explained. "But we'd better start with these."

"What do they say?" demanded Shad anxiously. "How do you tell them apart?"

"I'll start showing you now, and Mr. Foster will help you later," Frank answered him. "You can't learn the whole alphabet in one day. Nobody can."

"Well, I can," insisted Shad stubbornly.

Frank smiled gently. "It's harder than you think. This is an *A*, and this is *B*, and this is *C*."

Shad repeated the letters, his

eyes devouring the shapes. As they went along, he realized Frank was right. It was hard, but he was sure he could learn. He had to learn. Very few on the reservation could read. What a fine thing it would be to take back at the end of the year, the unraveled mystery of the white man's secret writing.

He had mastered the first five letters by the time Mr. Evans opened the door and shouted that he had finished his story about the untrustworthy apprentice. It was time to start work.

Shortly before noon, Mrs. Hicks appeared at the door, carrying a basket filled with Shad's lunch. She sniffed her disapproval of the cluttered print shop and departed without a word. Her appearance reminded Mr. Evans that he himself was hungry. He would go home to eat, he told them, and they would start the presses immediately on his return.

With a whoop of delight, Frank ran for his own lunch pail, but Shad sat on the floor, spreading out the foolscap beside him.

"What's the name of the next letter?" he asked. "It looks a lot like *E*."

"Eat, eat," urged Frank. "There's time for that later."

"No." Shad frowned, and his fingers traced and retraced the letters on the paper.

"I won't tell you anything else until I've finished eating," declared Frank. "It was a silly thing to try to do, anyway. I'm not a schoolmaster."

"Oh, no," said Shad quickly. "It was good. You are kind to help me. Not many would be so kind."

Frank was embarrassed, but he was pleased, too. As soon as they had finished eating, he was willing to continue the lesson. By the time Mr. Evans returned, Shad was working on *G*.

When the old press was finally started up, Shad was too occupied to be bothered by the noise. It was clattery and awesome in the way it engulfed a plain sheet of white paper and covered it with black alphabet letters.

Shad carried stacks of the printed sheets to the long center table, where they would be folded for delivery. Each time, he stared as he put them down, his eyes searching for the *A*'s and *B*'s and other letters he had memorized. He wondered when they would begin to say words to him.

It took Frank and Mr. Evans two hours to run off the two hundred copies required for the subscription list. Once, during the process, the press stopped entirely, and its owner, wrench in hand, dropped to his knees and disappeared briefly under the press bed. Soon he had it running again.

"Made good time." He sounded pleased as he announced the completion of the run. "I hope Ed Wheeler, wherever he lands, picks up a copy of the *Sentinel* and sees that we got along very well without him. You and Shad better fold papers before you wash the roller and put away type, Frank. Subscribers will start dropping in for their copies pretty soon. I'm going out for some air, but I'll be back."

Folding papers was easy, Shad decided, if you didn't mind a few paper cuts and getting your hands dirty. There were only four pages, which meant that each sheet was folded in the middle and once across. The stack before each boy grew taller by the minute.

"Hey, here's a story about you," cried Frank suddenly. "It's on the second page."

"About me? You mean my name's in the paper?" Shad could hardly believe it. He left his side of the table and came to stare down at Frank's pointing finger.

"'Indian Boy Joins *Sentinel* Staff.'" Frank read it aloud. " 'With this issue, Shad Youngbuck, a member of the Rogue River Indians, officially joins the staff of the *Valley Sentinel* as printer's devil. He replaces Frank Flint, who has been promoted to the position of apprentice, formerly held by Edward Wheeler, whose perfidious act of treachery has already been reported on page one. Ye Editor fully realizes that employing a member of the Indian people will cause comment and criticism from certain bigoted and prejudiced citizens of this valley. After due consideration, this scribe has decided that members of the Indian tribes from our nearby reservation should be given a chance to make what they can of themselves; ergo, the hiring of young Shad as printer's devil.

He is the ward of Daniel Foster, Esquire, if any reader cares to lock horns with him!' "

"Does it really say all that?" asked Shad in an awed voice. His fingers traced the fresh ink, smearing it slightly. "Where does it say my name?"

"Here." Frank showed him. "And here's mine."

"What's going on?" Ralph Evans voice sounded shrilly in their ears. He had come up behind them while Frank was reading. As they turned, they could see the lines of dismay on his face.

"I was just reading your story to Shad," explained Frank. "We'll finish folding the papers right away, Mr. Evans."

"You were reading it *to* him. That means he can't read it for himself. Dan'l never mentioned that when he talked to me." He shook his head despairingly. "It was a good idea. A fine idea. And I wrote a beautiful story. No one will dare criticize, not with that last line about Dan'l. But we can't have a printer's devil who doesn't know how to read. He can't put away type."

"I'm learning, Mr. Evans," Shad told him. "By next week I'll know the whole alphabet."

"He's down to G now," added Frank. "And I just started teaching him this morning. I'll put away the type until Shad's ready. I don't mind."

"You have learned almost a third of the alphabet in one day? And done your work, too?" Mr. Evans's eyes seemed to protrude even farther from his head. "Show me."

Proudly, carefully, Shad pointed out the letters he recognized on the paper. As he watched and listened, Ralph Evans's mouth gaped wider and wider with surprise.

"I can hardly believe it," he declared. "There's many a person in this valley who has to sign his name with an X, and you learned this much in one day."

"Then he can stay?" Frank voiced the question Shad was afraid to ask.

"Stay? Of course he'll stay. And the story of his learning the alphabet for the privilege of working on the *Sentinel* will be on page one next week!" declared Mr. Evans. "But the type is up to you until he's ready, Frank."

Frank nodded, grinning.

Shad looked at him gratefully. He had been wrong. Not all white boys were bad. Maybe the good and bad were equally divided, as in his own people.

When his father came back from prison, Shad had to choose between staying with the new white friends he had made or going back with his father to the reservation. If you read the book THE YEAR OF SMALL SHADOW, *you can find out what Shad decided to do.*

AUTHOR

When Evelyn Sibley Lampman was a child, she and her parents read aloud or her father told stories during the long winter evenings. She never grew tired of hearing about the pioneers who had settled the little Willamette Valley town in Oregon where she grew up. She tells about many of them and about some of the Indians from the nearby reservation in *The Year of Small Shadow*.

Mrs. Lampman has been writing books for boys and girls since 1948 and has published nearly forty in all, several of them about Indians. Among her latest books are *Cayuse Courage* and *Go Up the Road*.

She lives in the country in a house that overlooks Mount Hood, a perpetually snow-capped peak in the Cascade Range.

All-of-a-Kind Family Downtown is one of a series of books about the adventures of a poor but happy and loving Jewish family living on the East Side of New York City in the early 1900's. Of the six children in the family—five sisters and a baby brother—thirteen-year-old Ella was the oldest. This story from the book tells what happened when Ella counted on being given a special part in the Hebrew school play to be presented on Purim, a Jewish holiday.

Purim Jester
by Sidney Taylor

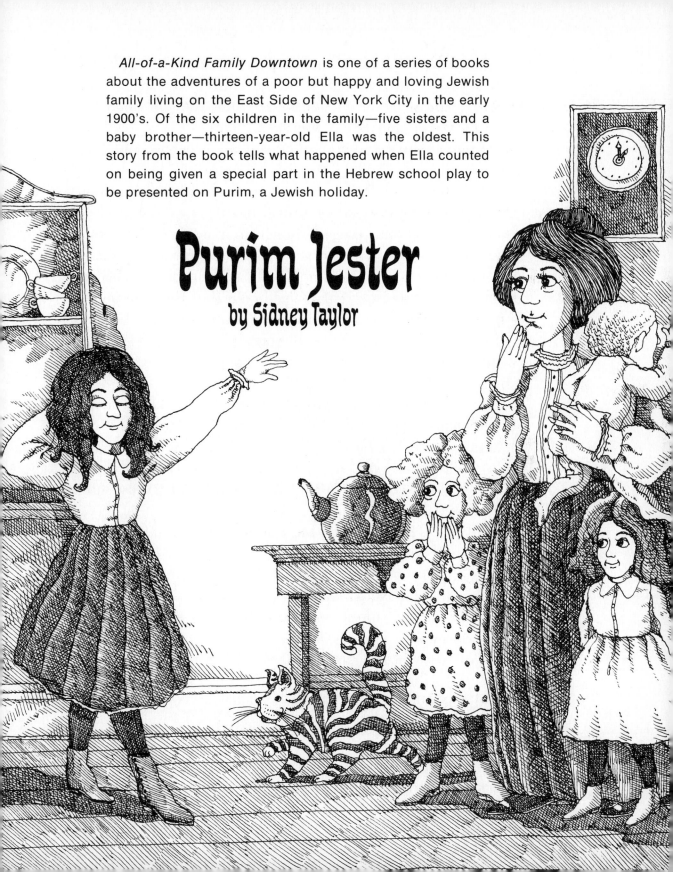

Ella scowled at the kitchen clock. Why did its poky old hands have to drag along so slowly? Didn't they realize how anxious she was to get to Hebrew school? She cried out, "Won't it ever get to be two o'clock?"

"Maybe if you stop watching the clock so much, it might go faster," Mama replied.

"Oh, Mama, just think if I got the part of Queen Esther! Imagine playing the part of a real queen!"

Immediately she began imagining—a dazzling white gown, a golden crown studded with jewels on my head, and my long black hair floating freely around my shoulders. Proudly she lifted her small head. With all the grandeur of a queen, she advanced in slow procession across the kitchen.

Mama watched her with a mixture of pride and amusement. "Better not count your chickens before they're hatched," she advised.

"Oh, Mama, it's such a wonderful part! And I know I could do it! Mama, I just have to get that part! If I don't, I'll die!"

Mama shook her head reprovingly. "Ella, such talk!"

"I wish I were old enough to act in the Hebrew school plays," Sarah said wistfully. "Why don't you try out for a part, Henny?"

"Not me!" Henny cried. "Mr. Rosen expects you to rehearse every single day!"

"It's almost two o'clock, Ella," observed Mama.

"At last!" Ella exclaimed. She snatched up her hat and coat, her sisters' shouts of encouragement trailing after her.

"Good luck!"

"Hope you get the part!"

"All the male parts have been given out," Mr. Rosen said. "Now let's get to the females. Let's see—for the role of Queen Esther . . ."

Ella could feel the increased tension in the auditorium— the swift intake of breath—the shifting about in the seats.

She looked around at the many eager faces, her heart fluttering between doubt and hope.

"Dora, you first, please." Mr. Rosen motioned.

Ella listened intently as Dora read. Nothing to fear from her, she told herself. Dora could never play the part of a queen.

Sophie, Bertha, Lily—one after the other attempted the role. None of those girls is particularly inspiring, Ella concluded.

The lines rolled off the contestants' tongues. Ella had to battle with herself to keep from acting out the queen right there in her seat. Please, please, Mr. Rosen, me next! Let me try!

But the plea went unheeded.

"Rachel!"

A tall, dark-haired girl came forward.

Rachel really looks the part, Ella had to admit as she watched her move gracefully onto the stage. Anxiously she listened. Rachel reads well, Ella thought jealously. But her innate honesty would not permit any clouding over of her judgment.

Still, she would not let her hopes wither. I'm sure I could do as well. Perhaps even a bit better. Mr. Rosen could at least give me a chance to try before he makes up his mind. She jumped up. "Mr. Rosen, please," she cried out, "couldn't I try too?"

Mr. Rosen regarded her thoughtfully. "But, Ella, there's another part that I've been saving especially for you. You're exactly what we need. You're so little and cute, and you sing so well—the jester!"

"Oh, no, Mr. Rosen," Ella pleaded, "I want to try out for Queen Esther."

"That's not for you, Ella." Mr. Rosen was emphatic. "The jester—now there's a part that's just made for you!"

Ella felt as if her insides were suddenly scooped out. She could see it was no use arguing with Mr. Rosen. His mind was made up, and nothing she could say was going to change it. It was the jester or nothing. She could not possibly bear being nothing. A sob caught in her throat. She fought it, even managing to bring a wan smile to her lips.

The feet that had skipped down the stairs so gaily just a few hours before now could be heard dragging upwards.

"I guess that's Ella!" Henny yelled, flinging open the door. She shooed her sisters back. "Make room for the queen!" she announced.

"I'm not," Ella murmured. There were tears in her brown eyes.

A blanket of gloom settled over the kitchen. Gertie gave voice to what they were all thinking. "Ella's not in the play," she wailed.

"Oh, I'm in the play, all right," Ella assured them.

"So that's fine!" Mama said relieved. "That's fine!"

"Only someone else will be Queen Esther." Her voice grew mocking. "Me, I'm too little—too cute for a queen; that's what Mr. Rosen says. Besides, he needs me for a singing part.

It's just perfect for me. Oh yes—perfect all right—the jester!''

"The jester!" all repeated in surprise.

"What's a jester?" Gertie asked.

"A jester is someone everybody laughs at," Ella explained bitterly.

"But in olden times, a jester was very important to a king," Sarah cried. "Whenever the king was tired or troubled, he could always depend on the jester to cheer him up. I think that's a wonderful part!"

"Of course, it is," declared Henny. "I'd a million times rather play a part that will make people laugh. You'll have loads of fun. And anyway, what could you do as a queen? Just walk around with your nose stuck up in the air."

"And a jester always wears such a gorgeous costume, with all different colors, and little bells tied on," Charlotte said.

"And he tells jokes and riddles. And sings and dances," Sarah added enthusiastically.

Mama nodded her approval. "Yes, Ella, I agree with Mr. Rosen. You will be very good in that kind of part."

"Jester Ella—Jester Ella!" Gertie chanted, making it sound like a little song.

Ella looked around at her family. How wonderful they all were! She had dreaded coming home, ashamed to admit that she had failed to get the part. Now all the sore spots of her hurt pride were being smoothed over, melting away in the warmth of the family's enthusiasm. She opened her arms wide and gathered in as many of her sisters as she could. Her heart was bursting with love and gladness. "You'll see!" she cried. "I'll be the best jester Mr. Rosen, or anyone else, has ever seen!"

For Ella, the days took wings. She could talk of nothing but the Purim play and Mr. Rosen. There was the time she came bursting into the house with flushed face and shining eyes. "Mama," she gushed, "Mr. Rosen is just marvelous! The best director the Hebrew school ever had! Of course he's very particular, but you don't mind because he's so patient. Do you know what he did today? He spent a whole half hour just teaching me how to turn my wrist so that when I point my finger, it should look graceful."

At last it was Purim. Throughout the day, the girls romped in their homemade masquerade costumes. From door to door they went, bringing Purim plates full of good things to eat. In exchange they were given other goodies and most often a few pennies.

But the high point of this Purim holiday came when, in the evening, the family found seats in the auditorium of the Hebrew school.

"We have to save a seat for Miss Carey," Henny said.

"For Miss Carey, the settlement-house nurse?" Mama asked. "How did she ever find out about the Purim play?"

Henny grinned. "I told her. And when she heard that Ella was going to sing in it, she said she'd love to come. So, I invited her."

Mama turned to Papa. "Isn't it nice that she takes such an interest in our girls!"

"Oh, Miss Carey's interested in everybody," Henny replied, with a shrug of her shoulders.

"Look, Ma," Henny pointed, "there she is now! Yoo-hoo! Miss Carey! Right over here! We saved you a seat!"

"Henny, shush!" Mama cautioned. She beckoned smilingly to Miss Carey.

"Well, now, isn't this thoughtful of you," Miss Carey said, settling herself comfortably in her seat. "I was afraid I wouldn't make it in time. I was busy teaching a new mother how to take care of her baby. That's always a pleasant job, but it took longer than I expected." She looked around with interest.

"Miss Carey," Gertie spoke up, "the whole family's here 'cepting the baby. I'm glad I'm not the baby and have to stay home with a neighbor to take care of me."

Miss Carey smiled at her. "I don't think the baby minds."

Suddenly there was an outcry from Gertie. "Oh! Oh!" She jumped up and began hopping up and down on one leg.

"What's gotten into you?" asked Mama.

"I got pins and needles in my foot!"

"Your foot went to sleep," Miss Carey explained. "It'll wake up in a minute."

"You shouldn't sit on it," said Charlotte.

"But then I can't see."

Papa folded his coat into a neat bundle and put it on Gertie's seat. "Try it now," he said, settling her on the coat.

Gertie looked around triumphantly. "Now I'm taller than anybody. I can see everything."

"Ssh," whispered Sarah, "it's starting!"

The lights dimmed. The audience grew still, as a piano struck up a rollicking tune. Slowly the curtain went up. There in the center of the stage stood the jester arrayed in a splendid red, yellow, and green costume.

"That's Ella!" Gertie squealed in delight.

The jester bowed, and a cluster of tiny bells on her peaked cap jingled merrily. With a wink to the audience, she began to skip around the stage, twirling a stick adorned with gaily colored streamers.

A loud chord! She danced forward and began to sing.

As she ended her song, she pranced around with such grace and spirit that the audience was captivated. A shower of applause followed her as she strutted offstage.

"Is that all?" Gertie asked, disappointed.

"Of course not!" whispered Charlotte. "That's only the introduction. Now the real play begins."

All through the next hour, the audience laughed and wept and worried along with the characters. But the most enchanting moments were those when Ella was on the stage. She leaped and twirled and turned somersaults. She mocked at the villain, mimicking his voice and gestures. She amused the king with her songs and witticisms. One could hear favorable comments buzzing all over the auditorium.

"That little jester!"

"She's some actress!"

The final triumph was Ella's, too, for she sang the song that ended the play. Her beautiful, strong voice rang through the hall, clear as a bell. "Such a little girl with such a big voice!" someone said aloud. The audience clapped and clapped till their hands ached. The curtain kept squeaking up and down as the players kept bowing and smiling and bowing again.

"Whose child is that little jester, I wonder?" a voice spoke up from somewhere behind the family.

Papa's face shone. He stood up and turned toward the questioner. All the pride in his chest burst forth in an exultant shout. "That's my daughter! My daughter!"

"Papa! Please!" Mama tugged at his sleeve, her face red as a beet.

"It's all right." Miss Carey smiled at Mama. "He has every reason to be proud."

AUTHOR

Sydney Taylor was born on the East Side of New York City and lived there through her childhood. She was always interested in dance and the theater, and after she married, she was a member of the Lenox Hill Players and of Martha Graham's dance company. She began writing plays for children when she was a teacher of dramatics in a summer camp.

Ms. Taylor began writing books for children by telling stories about her life as a child to her daughter. At first, when she wrote them down, she did it only for the sake of putting the stories on paper. Without telling her what he was doing, her husband sent the stories to a contest for juvenile literature. She won the contest, which led to the publication of her book, *All-of-a-Kind Family*, the first in her series about the family.

You can make up your own secret code by scrambling the letters of the alphabet in different ways. One simple way is to reverse the order of the letters in the alphabet like this:

Z Y X W V U T S R Q P O N M L K J I H G F E D C B A

Of course, in order to be able to write or read messages in an alphabet code, you will need to have a code key which tells you what letter in the regular alphabet each code letter in the coded message stands for. Here is a code key for the reverse-alphabet code. Notice that above each code letter is the letter in the regular alphabet for which it stands.

Regular Alphabet:

A B C D E F G H I J K L M N O P Q R S T U V W X Y Z

Code Alphabet:

Z Y X W V U T S R Q P O N M L K J I H G F E D C B A

How would you write the words **SECRET MESSAGE** in this code? The code key shows you that in writing the word **SECRET,** you would substitute the **H** for **S, V** for **E, X** for **C,** and so on. The words **SECRET MESSAGE** would be written **HVXIVG NVHHZTV.** Use the code key to read this message:

BLF PMLD SLD GL IVZW GSRH XLWV.

A more complicated alphabet code is one in which the alphabet is divided into two parts: **A** to **M** and **N** to **Z.** The order of letters in each half is then reversed. Here is the complete key for this code:

Regular Alphabet:

A B C D E F G H I J K L M — N O P Q R S T U V W X Y Z

Code Alphabet:

M L K J I H G F E D C B A — Z Y X W V U T S R Q P O N

Use the key to help you read this message:

AMCI SX MZ MBXFMLIT KYJI YH OYSV YQZ.

LI USVI TY QVETI M CIO HYV ET.

After you've done what the message says, you'll be able to write your own secret messages.

READING TABLES

Have you ever looked at a timetable to see when you could get a bus from one place to another? Or have you ever checked the box score in a newspaper to find out how your favorite major-league baseball player performed in the game the day before? Bus schedules and baseball-game summaries are tables, and if you have used them, you know that the way facts are arranged in a table makes it possible for you to get the answer to a question quickly.

Many different kinds of information can be presented most effectively and understood most easily when they are given in the form of a table. A series of sentences containing a number of city names and departure and arrival times of dozens of buses would be extremely confusing. This same information seems clear and uncomplicated, however, when it is set up in columns and rows. Reading a table is not the same as reading a story, of course, but it is a skill that you can acquire quickly and one that will save you time and effort.

The table on the opposite page is a simple one, but note how much information it gives you. From the caption, as the title of a table is called, you can usually tell at once whether the table will be useful or of interest to you. For example, if you needed to know what the largest continent is, you could expect to get the answer from a table which has the caption: **Size and Population of the Continents.**

The headings above the columns in a table are also helpful to you because they tell just what kind of information is in each column. In most tables, solid lines are used to set off the headings and to separate columns. Sometimes the rows of items are also separated by solid lines.

Table 1. Size and Population of the Continents

Name	Area in Square Miles	Population
Asia	16,988,000	2,267,000,000
Africa	11,506,000	391,000,000
North America	9,390,000	337,000,000
South America	6,795,000	208,000,000
Antarctica	5,500,000	—
Europe	3,745,000	664,000,000
Australia	2,975,000	13,000,000

From the table above, you can learn immediately the total number of continents, their names, how large each one is, and how many people live there. If you wanted to know the population of Europe, you would first look down the column with the heading **Name** until you came to *Europe*. Then you would look along that row to the right until you found the figure 664,000,000 in the column headed **Population.**

In the same way, you could compare the size or population of two continents. That is, to learn whether North America or South America is larger, you would find the name of each continent in the first column and, after it, the figure in the same row in the column headed **Area.** Comparing the two figures would tell you which is the larger continent.

In the first two columns of the table above, you can see that the continents appear in decreasing order of size. In other words, the largest continent is listed at the top and the smallest at the bottom. This arrangement cannot be carried out in the third column, however, because the size of a continent does not necessarily determine its population. Look, for instance, at the population figures for Europe and Antarctica. Europe is listed sixth in the first column because it is the next to smallest continent, but it has the second largest population. Antarctica, on the other hand, which is fifth in size and larger than Europe, has no permanent inhabitants at all. If you were interested in comparing the population, but not the size, of the seven continents, you could easily put the third-column figures into numerical order in your mind or on paper. When reading a table like this one, it is important to pay attention to the order in which items are listed in the various columns.

In using a table, you will not always start with the first column. If you wanted to know the name of the smallest continent, for instance, you would begin by looking down the column headed **Area.** Seeing that each figure in that column is smaller than the one above it, you would know that the smallest must be at the bottom and would then look to the left in that row to find the name of the continent.

Did you notice that the figures in the table on page 383 are rounded off to the nearest thousand or to the nearest million? It would be impossible to give totals for area or population that are exact to the last square mile or person, and the approximate figures are accurate enough for most purposes.

When there are several tables in a book or an article, they are usually numbered so that they can be referred to without difficulty. Because the table on the preceding page is the first one in this lesson, it is numbered **Table 1.** The second table in the lesson, on the next page, is **Table 2.**

Notice how much the caption of Table 2 tells you. From it you learn that the table gives the names of scientists and inventors only and that it lists only black Americans. And the word **Some** lets you know that, because of limited space, not every outstanding person in this category has been included.

Notice, too, that from the headings of Table 2 you know what four kinds of facts are given in the four columns. If you wanted

Table 2.
Some Outstanding Black American Scientists and Inventors

Name	Born	Died	Important Contributions
Banneker, Benjamin	1731	1806	Author and surveyor. Helped map out Washington, D.C.
Carver, George Washington	1864	1943	Researcher. Derived over 300 products from peanut and soybean.
Drew, Dr. Charles R.	1904	1950	Researcher. Perfected modern blood-bank system.
Julian, Dr. Percy	1898	—	Chemist. Created drugs used to treat arthritis and glaucoma.
Lawless, Dr. Theodore K.	1892	1971	An internationally known skin specialist.
Matzeliger, Jan	1852	1889	Inventor of lasting machine that revolutionized shoe industry.
McCoy, Elijah	1844	1928	Inventor of devices used to lubricate machinery in motion.
Morgan, Garrett A.	1877	1963	Inventor of gas mask and automatic traffic light.
Williams, Dr. Daniel Hale	1856	1931	Surgeon famous for pioneering in open-heart surgery.
Woods, Granville T.	1856	1910	Inventor of air brake on trains and of electrical equipment.

to see how far back in time the table goes, you would read down the second column for the earliest date. By looking for dashes in the third column, you could discover which of these individuals are still living. In a table like this, you might be most interested in finding out who has been included and what contribution each person has made. In that case, you would probably read only the first and last columns. Suppose, however, that you had heard of Garrett A. Morgan and wanted to know when he lived and what made him famous. You would look for his name in the alphabetical list in the first column and then read the information given in that same row in the other three columns.

If there are many columns in a table and the rows of items are quite close together, it is often difficult to keep your eye on one particular row as you read from left to right. This is especially true of a table like the following one, where there are ten columns containing nothing but figures. Working with such a table is easy, however, when you lay a ruler, a pencil, or even a piece of paper under the row you are looking at, or when you use your finger as a kind of pointer and move it across the row or down the column of figures you are reading.

Table 3 below shows the mileage by airplane between ten large cities. Notice that in this type of table the cities listed alphabetically in the first column also appear alphabetically as headings of the other ten columns. In a mileage table, you must use one city name from the first column and one city name from the headings in order to get the information you want.

Table 3.
Mileage by Air Between Some Major Cities in the United States

City	Boston	Chicago	Cleveland	Detroit	Houston	Los Angeles	New York	Phila.	St. Louis	Wash. D.C.
Boston	—	851	551	613	1,605	2,596	188	271	1,038	393
Chicago	851	—	308	238	940	1,745	713	666	262	597
Cleveland	551	308	—	90	1,114	2,049	405	360	492	306
Detroit	613	238	90	—	1,105	1,983	482	443	455	396
Houston	1,605	940	1,114	1,105	—	1,374	1,420	1,341	679	1,220
Los Angeles	2,596	1,745	2,049	1,983	1,374	—	2,451	2,394	1,589	2,300
New York	188	713	405	482	1,420	2,451	—	83	875	205
Philadelphia	271	666	360	443	1,341	2,394	83	—	811	123
St. Louis	1,038	262	492	455	679	1,589	875	811	—	712
Washington, D.C.	393	597	306	396	1,220	2,300	205	123	712	—

Try finding the distance between Detroit and New York in the following way. First, run the index finger of your left hand down column 1 until you locate *Detroit*, and run the index finger of your right hand across the column headings until you locate **New York.** Then move your left hand along the row in which *Detroit* in column 1 appears, and move your right hand down the column which has **New York** as its heading. Your two fingers should meet at the figure 482, which is the mileage between those two cities.

It doesn't matter which of the two cities you work from in the first column as long as you locate the second city in the headings. To prove this, find the distance between Detroit and New York again, but this time locate *New York* in the first column and **Detroit** in the headings. What figure do you arrive at? It should be 482, the same figure as before. This won't surprise you, because you know that you would travel exactly the same distance whether you went from New York to Detroit or from Detroit to New York.

Discussion

Help your class answer these questions:
1. Why are tables numbered? How are they numbered?
2. What does the caption of a table tell you?
3. How are column headings in a table helpful to you?
4. According to Table 1, Antarctica has the smallest population—none. Which continent has the second smallest population?
5. From Table 1, is North America or South America the larger continent?
6. What contribution made by Dr. Daniel Hale Williams did you learn about in Table 2?
7. From the dates given in Table 2, who was born earlier, Granville T. Woods or George Washington Carver?
8. Using the figures in Table 3, what is the distance by air between St. Louis and Los Angeles?
9. From Table 3, which city is farther from Houston by air, Washington, D.C., or Detroit?

On your own

On a sheet of paper, copy the number and letter of each question that follows and then write your answer to it.

1. According to Table 1:
   a. What is the area of Africa?
   b. Which continent has only a slightly smaller population than Africa?
   c. How does Australia compare in size with the other six continents?
   d. How many continents have a smaller population than South America? Which continents are they?

2. According to Table 2:
   a. What made Dr. Daniel Hale Williams outstanding?
   b. Of the individuals who are listed, one is still living. What is his name?
   c. Which of the men listed was born in the most recent year? What year was it?
   d. What was the name of the person who invented a lasting machine that revolutionized the shoe industry?

3. According to Table 3:
   a. How far is it by air from Boston to Cleveland?
   b. What is the air mileage between Washington, D.C., and Los Angeles?
   c. Which city is closer to Detroit by air, Chicago or Philadelphia?
   d. Which plane trip is longer, from Houston to Cleveland or from St. Louis to Boston?

Checking your work

If you are asked to do so, read one or more of your answers aloud, and explain why you answered as you did. As the other members of the class read their answers, check what you wrote on your paper. Be sure to find out why any mistake you made was a mistake.

Tiktaliktak was trapped on a rocky island off the coast of Alaska. The ice he had crossed to get to the island had broken into many pieces, and Tiktaliktak had no boat. There was no food on the island, and, slowly but surely, the young Eskimo boy was dying of hunger.

AN ESKIMO BOY'S COURAGE

by James Houston

It was warmer now. True spring was coming to the land. But it helped him not at all, for there was nothing living on the island, nor would there be until the birds came to nest again, and that would be too late for him.

On top of the hill once more, Tiktaliktak scanned the sea and saw nothing but water and glaring ice. A distant voice seemed to say, "This island is your grave." He stood up slowly and looked around. There were many great flat rocks, and Tiktaliktak decided they would be his final resting place. Two of the largest ones lay near each other, offering him a sheltered bed, and with his failing strength, he dragged two more large stones to make the ends, at head and foot. Another large one placed on top covered the lower half. The stones now formed a rough coffin.

He searched until he found a large flat piece to cover his head. Half laughing and half crying, he climbed into his stony grave. After one last look at the wide blue sky and the sea around him, he lay down with his harpoon, knife, and bow arranged neatly by his side. He hoped that his relatives would someday find his bones and know him by his weapons and know what had happened to him.

Tiktaliktak did not know how long he slept. When he awoke, he was numb with cold. Slowly, a new idea started to form in his mind. "I will not die, I will not die, I will not die." With a great effort, he pushed away the stone that formed the top half of the coffin. Painfully, he arose and staggered out of that self-made grave.

Holding himself as straight as he could with the aid of his harpoon, Tiktaliktak staggered down the side of the hill to the beach. He lay there to rest and again fell asleep. This time he dreamed of many strange things: skin boats rising up from their moorings, haunches of fat year-old caribou, rich dark walrus meat, young ducks with delicious yellow fat, juicy seals, and the warm eggs of a snow owl.

He could not tell if he was asleep or awake, but again and again the head of a seal appeared. It seemed so real in the dream that he took up his harpoon and cast it blindly before him. He felt a great jerk that fully awakened him, and, behold, he had a true seal firmly harpooned. He lay back with his feet against a rock and held onto the harpoon line until the seal's spirit left him.

With his last strength, Tiktaliktak drew the seal out of the water and across the edge of the ice until he had all this richness in his hands. He knew that the seal had been sent to him by the sea spirit and that this gift would give him back his life.

After some food and sleep, and more food and sleep again, he soon felt well. Using his bow, he whirled an arrow swiftly into a hollow scrap of driftwood and dried shavings until they grew hot, smoked, and burst into flames. The seal fat burned nicely in a hollow stone in his snowhouse, making it warm and bright. The spring sun helped to restore his health and strength, and Tiktaliktak remembered once more that he was young.

He kept the meat of the seal in the igloo and prepared the fat for use in the stone lamp. The sealskin he turned inside out without splitting it open and scraped it with a flattened bone in the special way that he had seen his mother teach his sister.

One day, he found the tracks of a white fox that had come to the island. After that, the fox came to visit his dwelling every day. It always came along the same way, and that was its mistake. Tiktaliktak built a falling-stone trap across its path, baited with a scrap of seal meat.

The next morning, the fox was in the trap, and after skinning it, Tiktaliktak drew from the tail long strong sinews that make the finest thread. That evening he ate the fox meat and placed the fine white skin above his oil lamp to dry. Tiktaliktak also made a good needle by sharpening a thin splinter of bone on a rock, and with this, he mended his clothes.

After his work was done, he stepped out through the entrance of the small igloo to look at the great night sky. It was filled with stars beyond counting that formed patterns familiar to all his people, who used them for guidance when traveling.

Off to the north, great green and yellow lights soared up, slowly faded, then soared again in their magic way. Tiktaliktak's people knew that these were caused by the night spirits playing the kicking game in the sky. In the way his father had taught him, he whistled and pushed his hands up to the sky, marveling as the lights ebbed and flowed with his movements as though he controlled them.

Life on the island was better now, but still Tiktaliktak longed to return home to his own people.

Half of another moon passed, and now the spring sun hung just below the horizon each night and would not let the sky grow dark. Two seals appeared in the open waters of the bay in front of the snowhouse, and by good fortune, Tiktaliktak managed to harpoon first one and then the other. This gave him an abundance of food and of oil to heat his igloo. He again carefully drew the meat out of the seals, without cutting them open in the usual method, and scraped and dried the skins.

Tiktaliktak sat before his small house thinking and making plans. An idea for building a kind of boat without any tools or driftwood for frame had finally come to him.

He began to prepare one of the three sealskins. First, he tied the skin tightly and carefully where the back flippers had been so that no water could enter. Then where the seal's neck had been, he bound in a piece of bone, hollow through the middle. When he had finished, he put his mouth to the hole and, with many strong breaths, blew the skin up so that it looked again like a fat seal. Next, he fitted a small piece of driftwood in the bone to act as a plug and hold in the air.

The sun was warm on his back as he worked with his floats on that bright spring morning. His stomach was full, his clothes were mended, and he began to make a song in-side himself, hoping that someday he might return to his people on the mainland. The song had magic in it. It spoke of fear and wonder and of life and hope. The words came well. There was joy in Tiktaliktak and yet a warning of danger, too.

He looked up from his work as a huge shadow loomed over him. Tiktaliktak threw himself sideways, rolling toward his harpoon, which he caught hold of as he sprang to his feet. Before him, between his small house and the sea, stood a huge white bear. The bear's mouth was half open, and its blue-black tongue lolled between its strong teeth. Its little eyes were watching him warily as it decided how best to kill him.

Fear stirred the hair on the back of Tiktaliktak's neck and reached down into his stomach. His harpoon was small for a beast such as this one, and although he had often heard of encounters with bears, Tiktaliktak had never met one face to face.

Remembering the wise words of his father, Tiktaliktak carefully studied every movement of the bear. He tried to think like a bear to understand what the great beast would

do next. He slowly knelt down and felt with the chisel end of the harpoon for a crack between two rocks. Finding this, he wedged it in firmly and leveled the pointed end at the bear's throat. He had not long to wait for the attack.

The bear lunged forward, and the harpoon pierced the white fur and went deep into its throat. Tiktaliktak held the harpoon as long as he could, then rolled away, but not before he felt the bear's great claws rake the side of his face. He scrambled to his feet and ran uphill.

The huge beast tried to follow, but the harpoon caught and caught again in the rocks, forcing the point more deeply inward. The harpoon found its life, and with a great sigh, the bear's spirit rushed out and it was dead.

Tiktaliktak managed to fashion a simple boat from the inflated sealskins. But the trip across the cold Arctic water in his tiny boat would be filled with danger. You can share his adventures by reading the rest of Tiktaliktak's story in James Houston's book TIKTA'- LIKTAK: AN ESKIMO LEGEND.

AUTHOR

When James Houston was a young boy, he was fascinated by the tales of Indians and Eskimos told to him by his father, who had traveled widely in the west and north of Canada. When the war was ended and Mr. Houston had completed his art studies in Europe, he journeyed into the Canadian Eastern Arctic and remained there with the Eskimos for twelve years. During this time on Baffin Island, Mr. Houston often heard the story of Tiktaliktak and met his grandchildren. The famous Eskimo legend interested him so much that he felt sure it would be of interest to others. *TIKTA'LIKTAK* and *THE WHITE ARCHER* have both won the Canadian Library Association medal as the best book of the year for children in Canada. Mr. Houston has written eight children's books, including *EAGLE MASK, AKAVAK, WOLF RUN,* and *SONGS OF THE DREAM PEOPLE.*

A RACCOON TO REMEMBER

by Harriett E. Weaver

Harriett Weaver was a ranger in one of California's largest state parks, Big Basin Redwoods State Park, deep in the Santa Cruz (san-tuh krooz′) Mountains, south of San Francisco. One day a camper left an orphaned baby raccoon at her cabin. The tiny animal was hungry and frightened. He had to be given a bottle, and he had to be loved. The little raccoon was soon named Frosty. Ms. Weaver was happy to take care of him until he was old enough to be set free, but the job turned out to be far from easy.

During the summer, the state park rangers were on call around the clock. Like the others, I went to work soon after seven in the morning and often didn't turn in until past midnight. But if things broke right, I almost always could get a little rest after lunch.

Somehow, I was going to have to make sure that Frosty got his bottle and was burped every two hours or so; that he had time to play out-of-doors; that he lived as happy a life as possible. It was a big order in view of my duties in this huge state park.

I had to work at Headquarters part of the day; take out nature walks; be at the Museum a few hours; go through camp and picnic areas to welcome visitors; plan and lead the evening campfires, where hundreds of people gathered from seven o'clock until ten or so; and be around Park Center afterwards for as long as seemed best. If we had no accidents, fires, lost campers, or other troubles, that generally was my day. Caring for little Frosty's needs had to be fitted into these duties from dawn until the wee small hours. Don't ask me how all of this got done, but it did. With the help of several ranger neighbors and a camper or two, Frosty did get his bottle and a burping on time for the next three weeks. With such good care as this, his weak, little body filled out. And something else: his raccoon wits sharpened to a needle-fine point.

Frosty and I were working out a fine way of life together. He had turned his days and nights around to fit in with my work. Raccoons are night animals, but they also use the day-time whenever they feel like it. In turn, I gave every free minute to him—not only because I liked to, but also because I felt I ought to. You might say he was park property. He had been born in the park; therefore he belonged to the public. As growing numbers of campers learned about him, he began to have more public than he needed or was good for him.

One afternoon, when the cabin was almost bursting with Boy Scouts, I thought of something that might make our lives easier.

Since the park was already full, that evening's campfire was going to be the largest of the season. Hundreds of people would be there. Then why not make use of this chance to introduce Frosty and all of his public to each other all at once? Maybe, after that, the two of us could have more time to ourselves. I walked over to Headquarters to talk it over with the chief ranger.

"Sure," he said, laughing, "go ahead and try it. But I'm glad you're doing it and not me."

I knew what he meant, all right. Most campers were afraid of any wild animal. If Frosty should fall in love with this audience, the way he usually did with people, and make a dash for some of them, there wouldn't be nearly enough trees for everyone to climb.

"I know the idea may not work out well," I said. "But I'd sure like all our visitors to see what charmers some of our forest friends are. Talking about them is one thing, but having one there for them to see would be a lot better. And the people would enjoy Big Basin much more if only they could see who's around to visit them in the night. Those who have little fears would lose them, once Frosty turned on his charm."

Before the campfire I took Frosty on my lap for a heart-to-heart talk. Scratching him under the chin so he'd look up and pay close attention, I said, "Little one, listen to me. Listen

carefully to every word I say." And I told him that there were
people camping in this redwood park of ours who neither
understood nor loved wild animals. I explained further that
if we could help them know how interesting and friendly
raccoons were, then the young campers would no longer be
afraid after their Coleman lanterns were out; neither would
grown-up campers awaken and turn their flashlight beams
this way and that every time a twig snapped. "We want them
to rest, to enjoy all of their stay here, and to enjoy our raccoons," I reminded him.

Frosty seemed to be listening. His black, shiny eyes
searched my face as I spoke, although his soft hands never
stopped feeling around over mine, fingering my ring, and
playing with the bottoms of my cuffs. I didn't know whether
he was really paying attention. You can't tell about raccoons.
They're much too smart to let you in on what they are
thinking.

The campfire that night was a fine, booming thing. Some

of the slabs of wood burning in it were as much as a husky ranger could carry. Tongues of flame leaped high and danced a ballet of color against the big trunks of the redwoods. All the log seats were filled; people were standing as far as you could see, both at the back and along the sides of the bowl. Families laughed and chatted together; some of them on the outer rows crowded together under blankets, for Big Basin's summer evenings are chilly.

At first I spoke of raccoons in general, then of Big Basin's raccoons, who liked and trusted their human friends enough to visit their camps and hint for treats. Then I told them that in a moment they would see one of our park raccoons, a little orphan we were raising. I asked them to be very quiet when he appeared, so he wouldn't get excited.

"He dearly loves people," I said, "but he's never been near so many, nor has he ever seen a campfire." I felt like adding, "And if he suddenly dashes out to you and climbs up one of your legs, just relax." But I didn't. Instead, I nodded to the ranger offstage to let Frosty out of his carrying cage.

Through the doorway my little raccoon saw me and with a high trill of pleasure rushed out. As one person, the whole audience in the big outdoor bowl half-rose off the log seats and gasped with delight.

I don't know just what they expected of a baby raccoon—what he would look like or what he would do—but it was easy to see that their hearts melted. Then, remembering to help by remaining quiet, they settled slowly back onto the seats and watched excitedly.

Had it not been for the popping and crackling of the fire, you surely could have heard a leaf fall. As I walked around on the stage, Frosty bobbed along behind, a happy smile lighting his face. After a few minutes I picked him up, stepped to the mike, and went on with my talk.

"This is Frosty," I told them. "He's a raccoon baby—or kit—about two months old. He was orphaned here at Big

Basin, and it's my job to see that he lives safely past the age when he is an easy catch for such as coyotes and bobcats and horned owls."

While I was speaking, Frosty put on a good show. But he didn't know he was the star before one of the largest crowds ever to gather at Big Basin. He was too busy wrapping his arms around my neck and hugging me and trying to undo the black tie I wore as part of my state park uniform. Out front, my audience was held as if under a spell—but not, I'm sure, by what I was telling them.

I went on: "Raccoons are called the 'bear's little brother,' but they are not closely related to the bear family. They really are closer to the panda of Asia and the ring-tailed cat of our own West. They live anywhere from the creeks and ponds of the lowlands and foothills up into the lower edge of the pine forests and down to the edge of the sea. You can find their babylike hand and foot prints in the winter snows sometimes—and almost any time along the streams of the canyons."

By now I was having a time talking, and the audience was having a time keeping their minds on what I was trying to say. Frosty had climbed up onto one of my shoulders and was sitting with a leg on each side of my neck. One of his hands gripped a fistful of my hair; the other ran a finger round and round in my ear. Just try to give a talk with this going on! But so far, Frosty was so busy he hadn't noticed the camp-fire and the sea of faces out there. So I went on:

"Raccoons eat almost anything, animal or vegetable. They like to fish in creeks, ponds, and marshes and search for frogs, small animals, birds and their eggs, crickets, and wild berries. They—"

Suddenly a log in the campfire popped, setting off a foun-tain of sparks. Frosty saw it all. I knew he was staring at the flames and the sea of faces looking out of the darkness at him, because he stopped poking around in my ear. Everyone in the audience knew he saw them, too. After a moment they began to talk among themselves quietly but excitedly. Frosty had the full attention of well over fifteen hundred people.

"Now," I thought, "this is the moment. Here is the biggest audience Frosty will ever have. What will he do? Will he go tearing out there to hug them?" I had to be ready to move fast.

I might as well have saved myself all that worry. Instead of going wild over the roaring fire and more public than most of us get in a whole lifetime, Frosty all at once became shy and ducked his head down behind mine to hide. Reaching his arms over my ears and around to my face, he gripped a cheek in each hand and pulled himself tight against me. Then, holding on for dear life, he buried his face in the hair on the back of my head. The world had got too big for him.

As I talked on, I patted his feet and legs and tried to let him know that all was well, that there was nothing to fear. Perhaps my voice speaking on quietly helped, too. Anyway, I could feel him relax—enough so that pretty soon one of his hands moved from my cheek to my eyebrow, pulling it down so that it closed one eye. At this the crowd almost forgot itself and laughed aloud. A moment later, it sighed a long, admiring "Aw-w-w-w" when Frosty peeked out at them very shyly. And as I talked on, he peeked at his public again and again, always ducking back quickly afterwards, as if he couldn't bear to look. Frosty had stage fright.

Ending my talk, I said, "This big park, like nearly all vacation spots in our mountains and valleys where there are streams or ponds, is filled with raccoons. These raccoons are friendly. They like people and their things. They'll come to visit you if you invite them.

"How do you invite them? Go back to your camps and cabins after campfire and light your lanterns, maybe even turn on your car lights for a while; get out your loaves of bread and your cookies and candy. Then take a spoon or something and beat on your frying pans and pie tins. The Big Basin raccoons will wonder what's up, and they'll hurry to your lights to find out. All of a sudden you'll look up and see one—maybe three or four—out there at the edge of your circle of light, peering around one of the big trees or through the bushes at you."

By this time all the campers around the campfire were talking among themselves in low tones—planning what they would do later in the evening. By the orange glow of the flames, their eyes shone with eager interest. I said to Frosty, "I think we're making friends, little man." He answered by letting go of my eyebrow and grabbing my nose instead.

I finished my talk with: "Enjoy the raccoons tonight and every night. But let's all remember that Big Basin is their home and that we are guests in that home."

So a good many campers saw their first raccoon that night. They saw him as something very real and understandable— and adorable. The park was filled with love and goodwill toward our forest friends.

When campfire ended, almost all the campers went back to their tents, lighted their lanterns, and banged spoons on kettles and frying pans to see if they really could coax some of the raccoons into their camps. The evening wasn't the quietest one on record in Big Basin, but none has ever been any happier or any more fun, for raccoons came from everywhere. They climbed up from streams; they climbed down from hollow oaks; they crawled out from under park houses.

Just as I had said, they peered from behind the trees and bushes and sniffed the air to find out if these city people smelled right. And if their noses didn't wrinkle up as if they were smelling something long dead, a camper knew he had passed the test. He could now be sure he wasn't giving off any bad odor born of fear or hate.

In almost no time, then, the raccoons edged closer until they were inside the circle of light, their eyes gleaming out of the black mask they all wore.

The campers handed over their best. Into the soft, baby-like hands of our beloved bandits went birthday cake, candles and all. Into those hands went the juicy, red watermelon and the bunches of grapes from the Great Central Valley. As it turned out, the raccoons, not the campers, smacked their lips over the sacks of apricots and peaches, the cream puffs, and the Palm Springs dates.

And what did the campers do when they finally got around to eating? They just opened a can and crunched on the stale rolls the raccoons had refused.

Open House didn't make the front pages of the newspapers, but it was a big hit. Afterwards, for all nights to follow, for years to come, whole families of raccoons deserted the park garbage cans in droves and accepted invitations right and left—thanks to one tiny, scared Frosty.

AUTHOR

"I must be part raccoon," Harriett E. Weaver says to explain why raccoons seem to appear wherever she goes. Her love of raccoons began when she was eight years old and was given a book about a raccoon.

Harriett Weaver was born in Burlington, Iowa, and lived there for much of her childhood. Her family moved to Denver, Colorado, and later to southern California, where she graduated from high school and the University of California at Los Angeles.

After college, on a trip to northern California, she drove through a grove of giant trees—the Big Basin Redwoods State Park. She was so impressed by the redwood forest and its wildlife that for the next twenty summers, she returned there to serve as the only woman on California's state park ranger crews. During the winters, she taught in elementary and junior high schools. In 1971, she was selected as Honorary Lifetime Ranger by the California State Park Rangers' Association.

Miss Weaver has written many magazine articles and three books on redwood forests and their wildlife. This story is taken from *Frosty: A Raccoon to Remember*. Her recent book for children, *Beloved Was Bahamas*, is the story of a Black Angus steer.

READING MAPS

A map is a drawing that shows all or part of the earth's surface. Almost everyone uses a map at one time or another. Travelers use maps to find out where they are and where they want to go. Pupils often use maps in their study of history and geography to locate such things as cities, states, countries, and continents.

But maps may be used to show many things besides the location of a place. For example, a map can answer such questions about a state as: How does it compare in size with other states? Does it lie on the coast or inland? Does it have any major rivers flowing through it? What is its capital city? A map provides a great deal of information about its subject, but the amount of information that you can learn from any map depends on your ability to read that map.

Obviously it would be impossible to draw a map of a country, state, or even a city the same size as that place really is; therefore, the area shown on a map must be drawn in a much smaller size. In order to be accurate, a map must be drawn to **scale.** Scale means the relation between the actual size of something and its size in a picture or model. Look at the map of the state of Iowa on the next page. Notice that the scale of that map is shown at the lower left-hand corner. The scale is shown by means of a bar on which distances have been marked off. You can see that the scale is labeled *Scale of Miles,* so the distances marked 50, 100, and 150 on the scale represent distances of 50 miles, 100 miles, and 150 miles on the earth's surface.

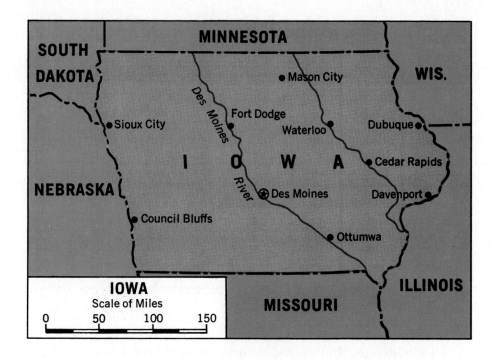

IOWA
Scale of Miles
0   50   100   150

A map's scale makes it possible for you to determine the real distance on the earth's surface between any two points shown on that map. Suppose, for example, you want to use the map of Iowa to find what the distance is between the cities of Waterloo and Cedar Rapids. One good way to do this is to lay a piece of paper flat on the map with one edge of the paper touching the two points that represent Waterloo and Cedar Rapids. Then mark the paper at each of those points like this:

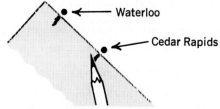

Waterloo

Cedar Rapids

Then place the edge of the paper just under the scale of miles like this:

Scale of Miles
0   50   100   150

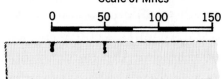

Notice that the first mark, at the left, is placed directly under the **0** mark on the scale. By looking directly above the second mark, you can determine from the scale the distance between Waterloo and Cedar Rapids. You can see the scale shows that the distance between those two cities is about 50 miles. Use that method now to find the approximate distance between Des Moines and Davenport on the same map.

Some maps have a different kind of scale. Look at the scale shown on the map of Kansas on the next page. That scale shows that 1 inch on the map equals 88 miles on the earth's surface. If you want to find the distance between any two points on the map, simply use a ruler to measure the number of inches between the two points and multiply that number by 88. For example, the distance on the map between Hutchinson and Topeka is 1½ inches. By multiplying 1½ by 88, you will find that the approximate distance between those two cities is 132 miles. Use that method now to find the approximate distance between the cities of Liberal and Kansas City.

It is easy to find direction on a map. On most maps, north is toward the top of the map, south is toward the bottom, east is toward the right side of the map, and west is toward the left side. On some maps there is a picture of a compass, called a compass rose, or an arrow which tells you where north is located on the map.

Through the use of **map symbols,** many kinds of information can be shown on a single map. Map symbols are used to stand for natural features of the land such as rivers and mountains. Symbols are also used to stand for features made by people, such as cities and railroads. Most maps have a **key,** or **legend,** that explains what each symbol on the map represents.

Look at the legend shown on the map of Kansas. You can see that it shows three different symbols for cities. One symbol stands for the state capital, another for cities having a population over 100,000, and the third for other important cities and towns. Can you decide what city is the capital of Kansas?

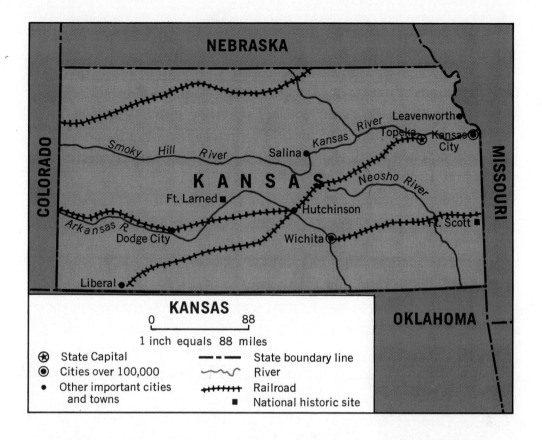

What is one city that has a population over 100,000? What is one other important city that does not have a population over 100,000?

Find the symbol in the legend that represents state boundary lines. Can you find the boundary line between Kansas and Nebraska? What are the names of the other states that border Kansas?

The maps of Iowa and Kansas used in this lesson are **political maps.** Political maps show political divisions of the earth's surface, such as countries and states.

Maps that show landforms such as mountains, hills, and plains are called **physical maps.** The map of the United States shown on the next page is a physical map. Notice that different colors are used to show what the surface of the land is like. The map legend shows what kind of landform is represented by each color. What kind of land is represented by the green areas on the map? By the dark brown areas?

Political maps and physical maps are only two of the many different kinds of maps which give special or general information about the parts of the earth's surface that they show. Whenever you use any map, first read its title to determine what the map is showing. Then see if the map has a legend. If it does, study it carefully to learn what each of the symbols used on the map represents. The map's scale is usually shown in the legend. Even if a map does not have a legend, its scale is usually shown somewhere on the map. When you know what the map is showing, what its scale is, and what all the map symbols mean, you should be able to read that map easily.

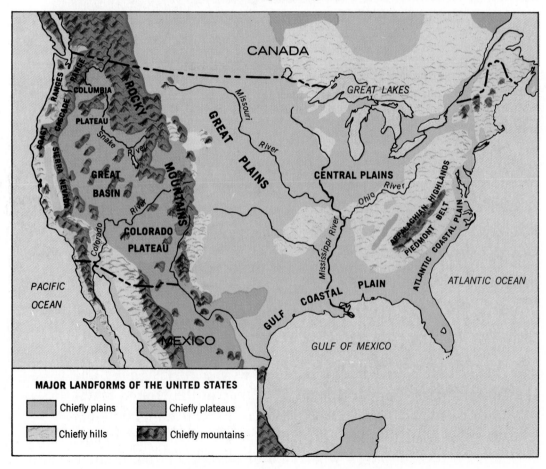

MAJOR LANDFORMS OF THE UNITED STATES

Chiefly plains

Chiefly hills

Chiefly plateaus

Chiefly mountains

Discussion

Help your class answer these questions:

1. What does a map's scale tell you?
2. What is the approximate distance in miles between Liberal, Kansas and Kansas City, Kansas?
3. How can you tell direction on a map?
4. How does a map's legend, or key, help you to read that map?
5. What are the names of the states that border Kansas? What are the names of two rivers that flow through Kansas?
6. What is a political map? What is a physical map?

On your own

Use the three maps shown in this lesson to help you answer the questions that follow. Copy the number of each question on a sheet of paper, and then write your answer to it.

1. What is the approximate distance in miles between Council Bluffs, Iowa and Des Moines, Iowa?
2. What is the approximate distance in miles between Hutchinson, Kansas and Leavenworth, Kansas?
3. What are the names of two cities shown on the map of Kansas that have a population over 100,000?
4. What cities are connected to Hutchinson, Kansas by railroad?
5. Near what cities shown on the map of Iowa does the Des Moines River flow?
6. Are most of the mountains and plateaus in the United States located in the eastern, central, or western part of the country?
7. Is the land in the central part of the United States mostly hills, plains, or mountains?

Checking your work

If you are asked to do so, read aloud some of your answers. Check your paper as others read their answers. If you made a mistake in any, be sure to find out why it was a mistake.

THE COMPUTER TRIUMPHS AGAIN

by Clem Philbrook

The problem with the Red Sox was not that they had the worst coach in the whole Tom Thumb League, for Miss Carmody was a very fine coach. The problem was that every boy on the team thought he should be a pitcher. Instead of paying attention to the position he was playing during a game, each boy was thinking about what he would do if he were pitching. Then Ollie had his brainstorm. His father was a computer programmer, and one of the things a computer could do was to process aptitude tests and select the best person for a particular job. So Ollie had his father make up a baseball aptitude test for the team to take. Perhaps the computer could figure out the best position for each player on the team.

The computer put Ollie exactly where he was—behind home plate. Barney was best suited to first base, Mike to second, Herbie to shortstop, and Billy to third base—the same positions they were already playing. There was a change in the outfield. Tony Girard went from center to left field, Art Finnegan from left to right and Larry Donovan from right to center. But that was it. Everything else stayed the same. Dusty was still the first-line pitcher, with Tony second, and Art to back them up.

Ollie's father read the computer results before practice on Friday afternoon. The questionnaires had contained multiple choice items, such as: *(1) Infielders are more important than outfielders, (2) Pitchers are more important than catchers, (3) The coach is the most important member of a team.* The boys circled *Agree, Neutral,* or *Disagree.* Then there were items like: *A. Usually calm and passive, B. Usually active and energetic.*

"The questionnaires gave us profiles of you as individuals," Mr. Scruggs explained. "We learned your interests and personality characteristics. The computer then selected your position for you according to the data you gave."

When he had finished, Miss Carmody faced them, hands on hips. "Well, you asked for it, gang. The Red Sox have been data-processed by the latest in computer equipment. Let's hope you will now quit crabbing and settle down to business."

Ollie's father grinned. "Anybody want to question my computer?"

"How can you argue with a computer?" Barney wailed. "If it says I'm a first baseman, then I must be a first baseman."

"Yeah, I'll buy that," Mike agreed, "and I've got a lot to learn about my position too."

Herbie drove his right fist into his glove with a loud smack. "Hey, Coach," he said grimly, "how about giving us a few pointers?"

Miss Carmody was quick to take advantage of the situation. "Don't think I won't," she assured him. "You all have a lot to learn about baseball. Fundamental things, like making the right play in the blink of an eye. If you hesitate, you are lost. This is a game of split-second timing."

She paused to let this sink in. "There is one thing you want to watch out for—chatter from the other team. They are trying to rattle you, so you will hesitate that all-important fraction of a second, or will make the wrong play. You will have to close your ears to all this and learn to make the right play instinctively, guided by the teammate nearest you."

She smiled. "There is only one way to learn how to do that—practice. We are going to drill and drill and drill, and then drill some more, until making the right move will be automatic. There's no time like the present, so take your positions."

She picked up a bat and walked to home plate. "I want a lot of chatter out there. Try your best to confuse the man who gets the ball. Dusty, you throw them in. Let's go!"

She squared off at the plate. "Man on first, one out," she called. On the first pitch, she hit a slow bounder back at Dusty.

"Go to second with it, go to second!" Billy Young hollered.

"Hold it, hold it," Herbie Snell advised. "Too late all around!"

"Play the batter!" Barney Sawyer counseled.

Dusty fielded the ball and threw to second. Miss Carmody shook her head. "Wrong move, Dusty. On a hard hit ball, you have a chance for the force play. On a slow hit ball, you don't stand a chance of nailing the runner at second. Always go to first with it."

On the next pitch, Miss Carmody lined one to left field. "Tying run on second, one away!" she sang out.

Coming in fast, Tony Girard took the ball on the first bounce and threw to home. Dusty was in line with the throw. "Cut it off, Dusty!" Mike Turner called. "Let it go!" Ollie shouted. Dusty cut it off.

"That ties up the old ballgame," Miss Carmody told him. "It was a perfect strike to home plate. If you're not in a position to use your own judgment, then listen to your catcher."

She gave Dusty a rest on the next one and hit a high fly to short right field. Mike Turner and Art Finnegan both scrambled for it. "I got it, I got it!" Art yelled.

"It's all yours, Art," Barney Sawyer advised from first.

At the last moment, Mike peeled off and let Art take it. "That's the spirit out there," Miss Carmody said. "Now you're making sense. You infielders, always let the outfielder take it when possible. He's charging the ball, while you're going away from it. And always—I repeat, always—call it loud and clear. The infielder nearest the catch directs the play. Don't listen to anyone else."

That was the beginning of better things. On the next few plays, they started to click. What followed was the liveliest practice session of the year. Oh, they were not suddenly transformed from Willowdale's worst team into the best, Ollie realized. But there was a real change in their attitudes.

Even Sir Winston, Ollie's dog, seemed to sense their mood. For the first time he stayed awake and watched the action, barking his approval.

"I begin to see a glimmer of hope," Miss Carmody said, as practice drew to a close. "At least you are trying."

"You certainly are," Mr. Scruggs agreed heartily. "You are probably the most trying baseball team in the state."

Miss Carmody smiled as the team gathered in a circle around her. "Seriously, I'm proud of you, boys, and I have a strong hunch you will give a good account of yourselves in tomorrow's game against the Yankees."

"We'll be right here to help you," Deedee said. "We have some new baseball cheers, haven't we, Elmira?"

"Har de har har," Dusty said. "What do you know about baseball?"

"Oh, we know a lot about baseball," Deedee laughed.

"Yes, we read up on it," Elmira chimed in. "Tell me, Deedee, why does it take longer to go from second base to third than it does from first base to second?"

Deedee's brown eyes sparkled. "Because there's a *short stop* in between."

They covered their mouths and burst into laughter. Ollie cringed. Dusty held his nose.

When they subsided, Deedee winked at Elmira. "Tell the boys what baseball stockings are, Elmira."

Elmira beamed. "Why certainly, Deedee. Baseball stockings are stockings with runs in them!"

Ollie glanced disgustedly at Dusty as the girls covered their mouths again and burst into fresh gales of laughter.

Not a girl or a boy was grinning Saturday afternoon, though. The boys were determined to make good when Mr. Scruggs called, "Play ball!" They even looked as though they meant business. Uniforms had been altered, cleaned, and pressed. The boys wore them with pride.

No one was more determined to make good than Ollie. He had spent two hours the night before and all that morning studying *How to Play Baseball*. He had read the chapters on pitching many times before, but this was the first time he had really concentrated on the chapters on catching. They had been an eye-opener, too. Gosh, the catcher was just about the most important man on the whole team! He had never realized it until then, even though Miss Carmody had told him so many times. Now, at long last, he knew it was true.

To begin with, the catcher really ran the team. He was in a position to see everything that went on. It was up to him to direct many plays. He should tip off the pitcher when a runner was threatening to steal. The other players, too, depended on him for advice, such as the number of outs and the proper play to make. To coin a phrase, a catcher must be right on the ball, Ollie decided.

"Ho, ho, what do you know," he sang out, as he started the ball on a final trip around the horn, "the Red Sox are ready to go-go-go!"

Yankee lead-off man Ed Smith smirked as he strolled up to the plate. "Hey, hey, what do you say," he answered, "the Yankees will beat you guys today!"

Sir Winston growled at him.

Ed's smirk disappeared as Dusty whistled a couple of smokers past him. The third pitch he lined between first and second base. Barney and Mike both went for the ball, and Mike came up with it. Dusty showed he had been doing his homework too. He remembered that a pitcher should cover first on hits to his left. A scowling Ed Smith was out by a stride.

"The way to go in there, gang," Ollie chirped. "Nobody gets to first."

"Two up, two down," Barney chattered as Rex Noyes moved in, a mean look on his face. Rex tapped the plate with the tip of his bat and squared off.

Five pitches later he had worked Dusty up to a full count. On the next one, Rex hit a screamer to Herbie at short. It was too hot to handle and Herbie juggled it. When he finally got a grip on it, his peg to Barney was wide.

But suddenly Ollie popped out of nowhere to take the wild throw. He had remembered that when there was no runner in scoring position, a catcher should back up throws to first base. Rex was held to a single, when two bases seemed assured. Sir Winston noted Ollie's pleased grin and yipped his approval.

"Heads up baseball, Ollie!" Miss Carmody cried.

Ollie felt a warm glow of pride. Hey, this was good. It was kind of nice to do something right, for a change. He signaled Dusty for a low curve ball as Bob Wilson stepped into the box. According to the book, that could make Bob hit a grounder to the infield.

Sure enough, he did. After taking a called strike, he golfed a low one to Barney at first base. Yankee base runner Rex Noyes could not tell whether Barney would take it on the fly or on a pickup, so he hesitated with a short lead. Barney fielded the ball on the first bounce, stepped on the bag, then tagged Rex for a double play before he could break for second.

An organized cheer went up from the Red Sox side of the field: "Big dog, little dog, floppy-eared pup. Come on, Red Sox, let's chew 'em up!" Deedee and Elmira were doing their stuff. Deedee executed a sprightly cartwheel, and Elmira tried to follow suit. She fell on her back with a thud.

"That was a real smart move, Barney," Miss Carmody said as they came in to the bench. "If you had thrown to second instead of tagging Rex, he could have returned to first and been safe, since the force was removed."

"Yeah, I know," Barney said with a grin. "I read the rule book all morning. As I said, if that computer calls me a first baseman, then a first baseman I'm going to be."

Ollie clapped his hands together. "And a winning ball club this is going to be," he said. "Let's go out there and pile up a few runs."

Herbie Snell swept off his cap and made a low bow. "Your wish is my command, O Sire."

As lead-off man, Herbie was not normally a heavy hitter. He was so charged up, however, that he proceeded to pick up a bat and belt one over the right-field fence.

"Not so fast, not so fast," Ollie reprimanded him as he came trotting in from the round tripper. "You're supposed to save those home runs until we load the bases."

"Sorry, Sire," Herbie apologized with a long face. "I'll try to do better the next time."

It was a long inning for the hapless Yankees. Visibly shaken by the Red Sox's unexpected display of smart baseball, they could not seem to put a good play together. Miss Carmody was experimenting with the batting order. Billy Young followed Herbie to the plate and rapped out a single. Then Larry Donovan hit a slow bounder at Yankee pitcher, Bob Wilson, who went for the double play. His throw to second was not

in time, and both men were safe. Mike worked Bob for a base on balls, and Ollie stepped up to the plate.

"Swing, bat man," Deedee and Elmira chanted.

"Over the fence, chum," Herbie chided him. "As you said, we need the home runs when the bases are loaded."

Ollie did not waste much time. On the second pitch, he stepped into the ball with a clean, level swing, met it solidly with the fat of the bat and kept on going in a full follow-through. He straightened up in time to see the ball drop from sight behind the center-field fence. Caught up in all the excitement, Sir Winston was barking himself hoarse.

That was the second of five home runs. Bob Wilson was shelled from the mound. The Yankees finally rallied in the last two innings, but they were too late with too little. Final score: Red Sox, 13; Yankees, 11.

Coach Carmody called her team together after the customary three cheers had been given. "That was more like it," she said. "If you keep playing that brand of ball, we may stand a chance." She smiled at Ollie's father, who had just joined them. "I think we all owe a vote of thanks to Mr. Scruggs. It was not easy to make out that questionnaire and process the data."

A rousing "yeaaa" was heard for Mr. Scruggs, which he acknowledged with a broad grin. "Believe me, it was well worth it," he told them. "Never have I seen such a change in a team. I predict that you will win the Willowdale Tom Thumb League Championship, because you have been scientifically selected by a computer. Data-processing will triumph again."

"What's this all about?" demanded Nosy Newman, elbowing his way through the group. If anyone ever could smell out news, Nosy could. He covered sports for the weekly *Courier*. He also covered births, deaths, social, business, crime, and all other news. He was tall and hawklike, with dark eyes behind horn-rimmed glasses.

He peered at Mr. Scruggs. "What were you saying about data-processing?"

Mr. Scruggs and Miss Carmody exchanged glances. Finally Miss Carmody shrugged and spread her hands. "Oh well, I guess you might as well know. Some of my players felt they were placed in the wrong positions. Mr. Scruggs offered to devise a questionnaire—an aptitude test, of sorts—which the boys filled out. The data was then fed into one of Mr. Scruggs's computers, which analyzed each player and suggested what position he was best suited for."

Nosy whipped out his notebook and pencil. "And it really worked!" he squeaked. "What a story! What a miracle! What an idea!" He frowned at Miss Carmody. "And whose idea was it, by the way—yours or Big Ollie's?"

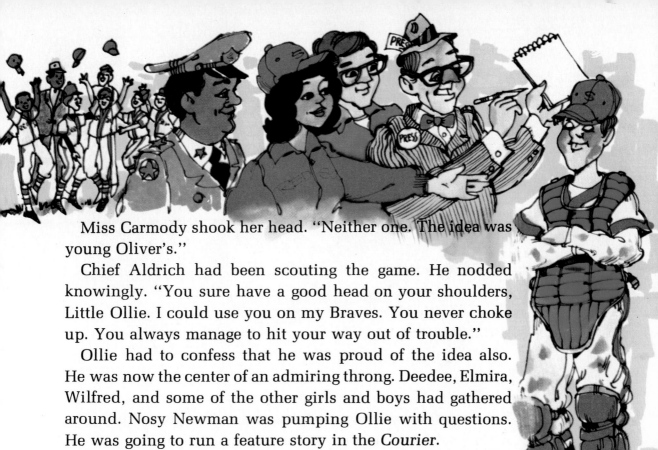

Miss Carmody shook her head. "Neither one. The idea was young Oliver's."

Chief Aldrich had been scouting the game. He nodded knowingly. "You sure have a good head on your shoulders, Little Ollie. I could use you on my Braves. You never choke up. You always manage to hit your way out of trouble."

Ollie had to confess that he was proud of the idea also. He was now the center of an admiring throng. Deedee, Elmira, Wilfred, and some of the other girls and boys had gathered around. Nosy Newman was pumping Ollie with questions. He was going to run a feature story in the *Courier*.

Yes, Ollie decided, he was proud of his idea. It had turned out to be a blockbuster. Best of all, it had enabled the Red Sox to break out of their slump.

AUGHOR

AUTHOR

Clem Philbrook is interested in all sports, especially skiing, fly fishing, and baseball. The selection you have just read is from his book *Ollie's Team and the Baseball Computer.* While Mr. Philbrook was working on the book, he once wrote, "I decided I needed to bring myself up to date on junior baseball. Consequently, I have been attending Little League games like mad—and enjoying them. In fact, I got so carried away the other night that I instinctively fielded a ball thrown my way, thereby disrupting the game!"

Mr. Philbrook was born in Oldtown, Maine. After attending schools in Maine, he worked at various jobs. He is presently writing full time in northern New Hampshire.

GIRLS CAN, TOO!

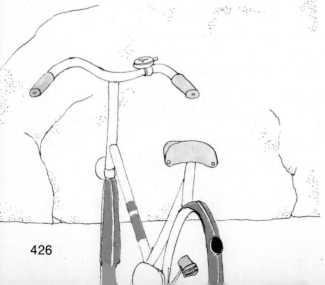

Tony said: "Boys are better!
  They can . . .
      whack a ball,
      ride a bike with one hand,
      leap off a wall."

I just listened
  and when he was through,
I laughed and said:

  "Oh, yeah! Well, girls can, too!"

Then I leaped off the wall,
  and rode away
With his 200 baseball cards
  I won that day.

Lee Bennett Hopkins

COMPUTERS - GIANT BRAINS?

by MALCOLM WEISS and ANITA SOUCIE

Does a computer really think?

News item: Recently, two computers battled it out over the chessboard. Things were nip and tuck for a while. Then finally one computer won. The people who arranged the game said their computer could win a second round—with a little work.

Are computers "brainy"? The above news item might lead you to believe so. But people who work with computers say: "GIGO!"

GIGO stands for *Garbage In, Garbage Out.* In other words, if you put wrong information into the computer, you will automatically get wrong results out of it. This does not necessarily happen with the human brain.

For example, take the 17th-century Italian scientist Galileo (gal-uh-lee′oh). He was taught that the heavier an object is the faster it falls. Books said so. But Galileo thought the books and the men were wrong. Through careful experiments, he proved them wrong.

Computers do not think up new ideas in this way. On the other hand, modern computers can do routine jobs much faster than people can. They can make millions of calculations in one second. A person would take years to do this much work!

What's the difference between human thinking and computer "thinking"? Let's take another look at the chess-playing computers mentioned earlier. Suppose these machines could "think" ahead for five moves at a time. If that were true, said a scientist, one move would take years. Here's why:

Chess is an extremely complicated game. There are 400 possible ways of playing the first two moves. After that, the number of possible moves grows rapidly into thousands and millions of choices.

Human players do not consider all these choices. They do not have time to. More important: in order to play a good game, they do not *have* to.

The human player only looks at a few of the possible choices—those that he or she judges to be best. A good player's judgments will often turn out to be correct. But the computer would have to try all the possibilities.

How does the human brain make judgments? Scientists are not sure. We do not as yet know much about how the brain thinks.

But scientists do know how computers "think."

The working parts of a computer are much like tiny electric switches. Like the switches in your home, they can turn either on or off. But a computer's switches, called relays, can turn on or off hundreds of millions of times each second.

The computer can "think" only in such on-or-off patterns. The patterns are a kind of simple code. Information and instructions are translated into this code and then fed into the computer on cards or tape.

It may seem strange that such a code can hold so much information. But think of the Morse code. This code also uses only two symbols, a dot and a dash. You can think of them as representing either "on" or "off." It takes 26 simple patterns of dots and dashes to stand for all the letters of our alphabet.

A computer can try out hundreds of millions of such patterns in one second. It can also store them in its "memory."

In order for the chess-playing computers to find the best moves, they had to search through all the moves stored in their "memory." As we have seen, this search goes on at incredible speed. Yet the computers in the chess match sometimes took several hours to make a move. Human chess players may be slow, but not that slow.

The computer's "memory" is huge, but it cannot cover all the possible moves in chess. When its "memory" runs out, the computer's instructions "tell" it to pick out any move that does not break the rules of the game. That is where the judgment of the human player has the edge on the machine.

The instructions fed into a computer are called a *program*. The people who prepare the instructions are called *programmers*. A program must tell the computer what to do at each step. It must tell the computer how to use the information stored in its "memory," the information fed into it beforehand. Nothing can be left to the imagination because the computer doesn't have any imagination.

"Stupid" as the computer may be, its fast "thinking" makes it a valuable tool in modern life.

from

BEN *and* ME

A New and Astonishing *LIFE* of
BENJAMIN FRANKLIN
As written by his Good Mouse
AMOS *, , ,*
Lately Discovered, Edited
& Illustrated by

**ROBERT
LAWSON**

The manuscript for BEN AND ME, *a part of which is reprinted on the following pages, was sent to me by an architect friend. While altering an old Philadelphia house, workmen uncovered a small chamber beneath a bedroom hearthstone. This tiny room, for such it appeared to be, was about eighteen inches square. It contained various small articles of furniture, all of the Colonial Period. In one of these, a secretary desk, was found a manuscript book, the leaves of which, about the size of postage stamps, were covered with minute writing.*

With the aid of a powerful reading glass, the architect had managed to decipher the writing.

Scarce able to believe that such a remarkable document could be other than some ancient hoax, he sent it to various authorities for their opinions.

Scientists of the Brownsonian Institute have assured him that their analyses of the paper and ink prove them definitely to be of Early American manufacture, and that the writing was most certainly done with a quill pen of that period.

More startling still was the report from officials of the National Museum of Natural History, stating that, incredible as it might seem, there could be no possible doubt that the handwriting was that of a mouse!

Since the recent death of my lamented friend and patron Ben Franklin, many so-called historians have attempted to write accounts of his life and his achievements. Most of these are wrong in so many respects that I feel the time has now come for me to take pen in paw and set things right.

All of these ill-informed scribblers seem astonished at Ben's great fund of information, at his brilliant decisions, at his seeming knowledge of all that went on about him.

Had they asked me, I could have told them. It was *ME*.

For many years I was his closest friend and adviser and, if I do say it, was in great part responsible for his success and fame.

Not that I wish to claim too much. I simply hope to see justice done, credit given where credit is due, and that's to me — mostly.

Ben was undoubtedly a splendid fellow, a great man, a patriot, and all that; but he was undeniably stupid at times, and had it not been for me — well, here's the true story, and you can judge for yourself.

I was the oldest of twenty-six children. My parents, in naming us, went right through the alphabet. I, being first, was **A**mos, the others went along through **B**athsheba, **C**laude, **D**aniel — and so forth down to the babies: **X**enophone, (zen′oh-fohn) **Y**sobel, (iz′uh-bel) and **Z**enas (zee′nahs).

We lived in the vestry of Old Christ Church on Second Street, in Philadelphia — behind the paneling. With that number of mouths to feed, we were, naturally, not a very prosperous family. In fact we were really quite poor — as poor as church mice.

But it was not until the Hard Winter of 1745 that things really became desperate. That was a winter long to be remembered for its severity. Night after night, my poor father would come in tired and wet with his little sack practically empty.

We were driven to eating prayer books. When those gave out, we took to the Minister's sermons. That was, for me, the final straw. The prayer books were tough, but those ser-mons!

Being the oldest, it seemed fitting that I should go out into the world and make my own way. Perhaps I could in some way help the others. At least, it left one less to be provided for.

So, saying farewell to all of them—my mother and father and all the children from Bathsheba to Zenas—I set forth on the coldest, windiest night of a cold and windy winter.

Little did I dream, at that moment, of all the strange people and experiences I should encounter before I ever returned to that little vestry home! All I thought of were my cold paws, my empty stomach—and those sermons.

I have never known how far I traveled that night, for, what with the cold and hunger, I must have become slightly delir-ious. The first thing I remember clearly was being in a kitchen and smelling *CHEESE!* It didn't take long to find it. It was only a bit of rind and fairly dry, but how I ate!

Refreshed by this, my first real meal in many a day, I be-gan to explore the house. It was painfully bare—clean, but bare. There was very little furniture, and that was all hard and shiny. There were no soft things or dusty corners where a chap could curl up and have a good warm nap. It was cold too, almost as cold as outdoors.

Upstairs were two rooms. One was dark, and from it came the sound of snoring. The other had a light, and the sound of sneezing. I chose the sneezy one.

In a large chair close to the fireplace sat a short, thick, round-faced man, trying to write by the light of a candle. Every few moments he would sneeze, and his square-rimmed glasses would fly off. Reaching for these, he would drop his pen. By the time he found that and got settled to write, the candle would flicker from the draft. When that calmed down, the sneezing would start again, and so it went. He was not accomplishing much in the way of writing.

Of course, I recognized him. Everyone in Philadelphia knew the great Doctor Benjamin Franklin, scientist, inventor, printer, editor, author, soldier, statesman, and philosopher.

He didn't look great or famous that night, though; he just looked cold—and a bit silly.

He was wrapped in a sort of dressing gown, with a dirty fur collar, and on his head was perched an odd-looking fur cap.

The cap interested me, for I was still chilled to the bone, and this room was just as bleak as the rest of the house. It was a rather disreputable-looking affair, that cap; but in one side of it I had spied a hole—just about my size.

Up the back of the chair I went, and under cover of the next fit of sneezes, in I slid. What a cozy place *that* was! Plenty of room to move about a bit, just enough air, such soft fur, and such warmth!

"Here," said I to myself, "is my home. No more cold streets, or cellars, or vestries. HERE I stay."

At the moment, of course, I never realized how true this was to prove. All I realized was that I was warm, well fed, and—oh, so sleepy!

And so to bed.

I slept late the next morning. When I woke, my fur-cap home was hanging on the bedpost, and I in it.

Dr. Franklin was again crouched over the fire attempting to write, between fits of sneezing and glasses-hunting. The fire, what there was of it, was smoking, and the room was as cold as ever.

"Not wishing to be critical—" I said. "But, perhaps, a bit of wood on that smoky ember that you seem to consider a fire might—"

"*WASTE NOT, WANT NOT,*" said he, severe, and went on writing.

"Well, just suppose," I said, "just suppose you spend two or three weeks in bed with *pewmonia*—would that be a waste or—"

"It would be," said he, putting on a log, "whatever your name might be."

"Amos," said I. . . . "And then there'd be doctors' bills—"

"*BILLS!*" said he, shuddering, and put on two more logs, quick. The fire blazed up then, and the room became a little better, but not much.

"Dr. Franklin," I said, "that fireplace is all wrong."

"You might call me Ben—just plain Ben," said he. "What's wrong with it?"

"Well, for one thing, most of the heat goes up the chimney. And for another, you can't get *around* it. Now, outside our church there used to be a Hot-chestnut Man. Sometimes, when business was rushing, he'd drop a chestnut. Pop was always on the lookout, and almost before it touched the ground, he'd have it in his sack—and down to the vestry with it. There he'd put it in the middle of the floor, and we'd all gather round for the warmth.

"Twenty-eight of us it would heat, and the room as well. It was all because it was *OUT IN THE OPEN*, not stuck in a hole in the wall like that fireplace."

"Amos," he interrupted, excited, "there's an idea there! But we couldn't move the fire out into the middle of the room."

"We could if there were something to put it in, iron or something."

"But the smoke?" he objected.

"PIPE," said I, and curled up for another nap.

I didn't get it, though.

Ben rushed off downstairs, came back with a great armful of junk, dumped it on the floor, and was off for more. No one could have slept, not even a dormouse. After a few trips, he had a big pile of things there. There were scraps of iron, tin, and wire. There were a couple of old warming pans, an iron oven, three flatirons, six potlids, a wire birdcage, and an anvil. There were saws, hammers, pincers, drills, nails, screws, bolts, bricks, sand, and an old broken sword.

He drew out a sort of plan and went to work. With the clatter he made, there was no chance of a nap so I helped all I could, picking up the nuts and screws and tools that he dropped—and his glasses.

Ben was a fair terror for work, once he was interested. It was almost noon before he stopped for a bit of rest. We looked over what had been done and it didn't look so bad— considering.

It was shaped much like a small fireplace set up on legs, with two iron doors on the front and a smoke pipe running from the back to the fireplace. He had taken the andirons out of the fireplace and boarded that up so we wouldn't lose any heat up the chimney.

Ben walked around looking at it, proud as could be, but worried.

"The floor," he said. "It's the floor that troubles me, Amos. With those short legs and that thin iron bottom, the heat—"

"Down on the docks," said I, "we used to hear the ship-rats telling how the sailors build their cooking fires on board ship. A layer of sand right on the deck, bricks on top of that, and—"

"Amos," he shouted, "you've got it!" and rushed for the bricks and sand. He put a layer of sand in the bottom of the affair, the bricks on top of that, and then set the andirons in.

It looked pretty promising.

"Eureka!" he exclaimed, stepping back to admire it—and tripping over the saw. "Straighten things up a bit, Amos, while I run and get some logs."

"*Don't* try to run," I said. "And by the way, do you come through the pantry on the way up?"

"Why?" he asked.

"In some ways, Ben," I said, "you're fairly bright, but in others you're just plain dull. The joy of creating may be meat and drink to you, but as for me, a bit of cheese—"

He was gone before I finished, but when he came back with the logs, he did have a fine slab of cheese, a loaf of rye bread, and a good big tankard of ale.

We put in some kindling and logs and lit her up. She drew fine, and Ben was so proud and excited that I had to be rather sharp with him before he would settle down to food. Even then he was up every minute, to admire it from a new angle.

Before we'd finished even one sandwich, the room had warmed up like a summer afternoon.

"Amos," said he, "we've done it!"

"Thanks for the WE," I said. "I'll remember it." And then I dozed off.

When I woke up, the room was sizzling warm. Ben was happily writing, as usual, and I went over to see what was going on. So far he had written, with a lot of flourishes:

An Account of the New Pennsylvania Fireplaces, Recently Invented by Doctor Benjamin Franklin, Wherein Their Construction and Their . . .

"Ben," I said, "we'll have to come to an understanding. Do you recollect your exact words when it worked?"

"Why yes, I do," he admitted, very prompt. He was always fair, Ben was, just overenthusiastic about himself. "As I remember, those words were, 'Amos, we've done it!'"

"Exactly," said I, "'*We've* done it!' 'We' means two: you *and* me. Now let's get things straight, Ben. Fame and honors are nothing to me—cheese is. Also there's my family to consider, twenty-five brothers and sisters in a cold vestry, and hungry. I can be a great help to you. I've proved that. Now what do you propose?"

He looked pretty thoughtful, and I could feel a quotation

coming on. Finally it did. *"THE LABORER IS WORTHY OF HIS HIRE,"* he said.

"I don't labor," I said, "I think. And maxims don't fill empty stomachs. That's not a bad one, itself. Be specific."

Well, we talked it over for some time, and Ben was very reasonable about the whole affair—generous too. I think that being comfortably warm, for once, helped that.

We finally made the following Agreement:

Twice a week, rain or shine, he promised to have delivered to the vestry:

> 1 two-ounce piece best quality CHEESE,
>
> 1 one-inch slice RYE BREAD, fresh,
>
> 88 grains unhulled WHEAT.

For myself I was to have as home or domicile to me and my heirs, to have and to hold forever without let or hindrance, with daily subsistence and clothing, in addition thereto:

> 1 FUR CAP.

On my part,
I was faithfully to give
and perform to him, Benjamin
Franklin, advice, aid, assistance, and succor, at all times
and under all conditions, and with him constantly to abide,
till death did us part, so help me . . . .

Ben wrote it all up neat with lots of flourishes, Latin
phrases, and seals. Then we both signed it and shook hands
on the bargain.

He was fine about the whole thing and never used a single
maxim. I must say he lived up to it, too. Not once in all the
rest of his life did that bread, cheese, and wheat fail to reach
the vestry twice a week, regular as clockwork.

After that we sat around for a while, basking in the warmth,
and I couldn't help thinking how my fortunes had changed
in a short twenty-four hours. Here I was in a snug, comfortable home, my family well provided for, with a good friend
and an interesting future.

I felt so much at peace with the world that when Ben fi-
nally asked, "Amos, what shall we call this affair?" I said,
"My friend, the credit is all yours. WE hereby call it the
FRANKLIN Stove."

ABOUT THE AUTHOR

Robert Lawson was trained as an artist and for years illustrated magazines, greeting cards, and books by well-known authors. He was forty-six before he himself wrote a book— *Ben and Me,* part of which you have just read. Encouraged by its success, he continued writing and eventually was author and illustrator of thirteen other books. Both his stories and his pictures reveal his sense of humor and love for animals, and much of the fascination of books like *Ben and Me* comes from seeing the world through the eyes of animals.

Until his death in 1957, Mr. Lawson and his wife lived in Westport, Connecticut. Their home, called Rabbit Hill, provided the setting and title for one of his award-winning books. Typical of Robert Lawson was this sign in his driveway: "Please drive carefully on account of small animals."

BOOKS TO ENJOY

LAST NIGHT I SAW ANDROMEDA *by Charlotte Anker*

After her parents' divorce, Jenny tries to impress her scientist father with her new interest in fossils she has found. She and the boy next door also become involved with snakes and astronomy.

TUCK EVERLASTING *by Natalie Babbitt*

What if you could live forever at the same age? The Tuck family's knowledge of how to do this leads to some danger-filled adventures in a fantasy world.

INDIAN PAINTBRUSH *by Edna Walker Chandler*

A girl who is part Sioux and part Mexican has problems identifying with her companions on the Sioux reservation where she lives.

SUPERSUITS *by Vicki Cobb*

With unusual detail, this book describes the special clothes needed for living in space, deep under the sea, and in extreme cold and heat.

ESKIMO CRAFTS AND THEIR CULTURAL BACKGROUNDS *by Jeremy Comins*

This "how-to" book includes many helpful directions for reproducing pieces of Eskimo art, such as sculpture, masks, stencils, scrimshaw, and ookpiks (owl-like furry dolls).

THE WHIM-WHAM BOOK *by Duncan Emrich*

Here is a funny, fascinating collection of Americana — superstitions, customs, proverbs, jokes, and odds and ends.

COUSINS AND CIRCUSES *by Lucy J. Sypher*

In a frontier town in North Dakota, Lucy has a series of lively summer adventures, highlighted by a five-day drive to see a big three-ring circus.

Currents

Currents

STORIES

PLAY

ARTICLES

The TRIAL of PETER ZENGER

by Paul T. Nolan

Characters

NARRATOR

PETER ZENGER

ANNA ZENGER, *his wife*

MRS. ZENGER, *Peter's mother*

CATHIE ZENGER, *Peter's sister*

TWO WOMEN

FRANCIS HARISON, *the Governor's writer*

JAMES ALEXANDER

SHERIFF OF NEW YORK

TWO CONSTABLES

RICHARD BRADLEY, *Attorney General*

ANDREW HAMILTON, *defense attorney*

CHIEF JUSTICE JAMES DELANCEY

JUSTICE FREDERICK PHILIPSE

MEMBERS OF THE JURY

Copyright © 1973 by Plays, Inc. Reprinted from *Plays, the Drama Magazine for Young People*, Boston, Mass. 02116

SCENE 1

BEFORE RISE: NARRATOR *enters and speaks to audience.*

NARRATOR: I publish a small local paper called the *Weekly Chronicle*, and it's a good business to be in. My father got me started, and I've been in it all my life. I can print exactly what I please in my paper—take up the local issues or even national ones. No one censors what I print. No one tells me what I can or can't say. (*Gestures to audience*) That wasn't always the case for newspapers. As a matter of fact, our traditional right to a free press began way back in 1734, all because of the courage of a man named Peter Zenger, who ran a little print shop in New York. (NARRATOR *exits.*)

TIME: *1734*

SETTING: *Peter Zenger's printing shop in colonial New York. There is a table on the left, with sheets of newsprint on it, and there are two chairs beside the table.*

AT RISE: *Stage is dimly lighted. Spotlight comes up on* PETER ZENGER *holding up sheet of newsprint and reading it critically.* ANNA ZENGER *enters.*

ANNA (*Calling*): Peter! Where are you?

PETER: Here I am, Anna.

ANNA (*Joining him at table*): Is it finished, Peter?

PETER (*Nodding*): It's ready to be printed. (*Showing* ANNA *newsprint*) This is the first issue of our *Journal*. We're making history, Anna.

ANNA: I'm glad for you. You're a good printer, Peter. I have always said so.

PETER (*Pointing to newsprint*): See what it says here? (*Reading*) "Printed by John Peter Zenger." It's a good thing to see one's name on one's own work.

ANNA (*Looking at newsprint*): It *is* a good thing. Our *Journal* also says that Governor Cosby is an idiot and a tyrant. I don't think that such opinions will please Governor Cosby. This is very strong language, Peter, very strong.

PETER: There are times when only strong language will do. You know that I just print the *Journal*. Perhaps *I* would not say things that way if I were the writer, but it's the truth. And it's a good thing to publish the truth, Anna.

ANNA: But no one else's name appears in the *Journal*. One would think that you had written it all.

PETER: The well-known lawyer James Alexander writes most of the paper. You know that. Everyone knows that.

ANNA: I don't see his name. I see only strange names like Cato, Philo-Patrias, Thomas Standby. No such people live in New York.

PETER: Anna, you know that if Mr. Alexander were to sign his real name, the Governor could arrest him. He uses a pen name.

ANNA: Ah, but you use your real name. Why don't you use a pen name, Peter?

PETER: Anna, this paper is our chance to have our own little business. I want people to know that I have printed it. (*Impatiently*) Don't you want me to be successful, Anna?

ANNA: Don't I work with you, Peter? Don't I set the type and pound the proofs and crank the press? Yes, and make the ink? (*Staunchly*) I want you to be the best printer in all America.

PETER: I'm not complaining, Anna. You're a better printer than I am. But ever since we began talking about starting the *Journal*, you have seemed — forgive me for saying this — you have seemed to be against me.

ANNA: No, Peter, I have never been against you.

PETER: Anna, someone must stand up and tell Governor Cosby that we don't want to be robbed, cheated, and insulted! We came to this new world so that we might work and be free. But now this governor comes to strip us of everything. (*Takes sheet of newsprint*) Listen to this and tell me if it is not the truth. (*Reads*) "A Governor turns rogue, does a thousand things for which a small rogue would have deserved a halter. Because it is difficult to be protected against him,

449

it is prudent to obey him in order to save oneself. A Governor does all he can to chain you, and it being difficult to stop him, it becomes prudent to help him put on the chains!" That's the truth, Anna. People have to join in his unlawful ways in order to keep their liberty. Look at what he has done to our courts. Our Royal Governor is a jailer, and he's making all of us his prisoners. (*Earnestly*) Is it not the truth, Anna? If I'm wrong, tell me.

ANNA: It's the truth, Peter. But the Governor can arrest you and send you to jail for printing this!

PETER (*Patiently*): Mr. Alexander has told me a hundred times the chance I'm taking. I know that I may be sent to jail. Truth and freedom are worth the chance.

CATHIE ZENGER (*Calling from off-stage*): Peter! Anna!

MRS. ZENGER (*Calling from off-stage*): John Peter! (*Entering with* CATHIE) Peter! Anna! I've just heard the most awful thing in the marketplace.

PETER (*Alert*): Yes, Mama? What have you heard? Is it some-

thing that I can print in the *Journal?*

CATHIE: Then what I heard is true, John Peter. You *are* publishing a newspaper!

MRS. ZENGER: Oh, Peter, people say that Governor Cosby won't like it.

CATHIE: Don't you know the Governor is opposed, John Peter?

PETER: I don't know, little sister. I don't know what the Governor opposes. Our Governor Cosby likes so few things in our colony that it's difficult to say whether or not he will like my *Journal*.

MRS. ZENGER: Peter, it's a dangerous thing to offend those in high office.

PETER: It's also a dangerous thing for those in high office to offend the people. I'm doing Governor Cosby a service by letting the *Journal* tell him so.

CATHIE: Peter, don't cause trouble.

PETER: I'll try *not* to cause trouble.

MRS. ZENGER: That's a good son. Then you won't print this paper?

PETER: No, Mama, it's because I don't want trouble that the

Journal must be published. And I will be a good son if this paper makes our New York a better village in which to live. That's my only desire.

MRS. ZENGER: Anna, you're his wife. He'll listen to you. Tell him not to do this foolish thing.

ANNA: I can't do that, Mama. I'm helping him. New York needs such a paper.

MRS. ZENGER: There's already one paper, Mr. Bradford's *Gazette*. Surely, in a village as small as New York, we don't need two papers.

ANNA: The *Gazette* isn't a paper for the people. It's just the voice of the Governor. The *Journal* will publish for the people. And it will publish the truth.

MRS. ZENGER (*Shaking her head*): There will be trouble, Anna. Great trouble.

PETER: Try not to worry, Mama. This is something that I must do. And we have known trouble before, have we not? (*Spotlight goes out.* PETER, ANNA, CATHIE *and* MRS. ZENGER *exit. There is a pause to indicate passage of time, and then spotlight comes up on the right on* TWO WOMEN, *who are carrying shopping baskets.*)

1ST WOMAN: Another of Zenger's *Journals* was published today.

2ND WOMAN: I didn't think the Governor would let him continue. Each week the paper grows bolder. . . .

1ST WOMAN: And Governor Cosby grows angrier. The paper won't last much longer. It's said that the *Journal* is even causing the Governor trouble with the lords in London.

2ND WOMAN: Lewis Morris, one of our most prominent citizens, has gone to London to protest the Governor's tampering with the courts.

1ST WOMAN: It would be better for Peter Zenger if Mr. Morris had stayed here. Peter will need all the help he can get when the Governor moves against him. Last week, he ordered a copy of the *Journal* to be burned at the public hanging place.

2ND WOMAN: I feel sorry for Anna.

1ST WOMAN: And for Peter's mother.

2ND WOMAN: And for Peter.

1ST WOMAN: Poor little Peter. What can one small man do

against such powerful enemies? (*Spotlight goes out. Two Women exit. There is a pause to indicate passage of time. Then spotlight comes up on the left on* James Alexander *and* Peter Zenger. *They are standing at printing press, talking.* Alexander *holds sheaf of papers.*)

Alexander (*Handing papers to* Peter): And, Peter, remember to be careful when you set the type. Some of these sentences will be completely misunderstood if the type is scrambled.

Peter: I shall be careful, Mr. Alexander. These are good words. (*Reading*) "The liberty of the press is a subject of the greatest importance, and in which every individual is as much concerned as he is in any other part of liberty." (*Looking up*) Mr. Alexander, do you think many people care about the liberty of the press? I know they say they do, but even my old friends are a little frightened to speak to me in public now.

Alexander: Perhaps not many know that they are concerned, yet. But they will. They will.

(*Strongly*) All people want to be free, and they cannot be free unless they know the facts. (*Pauses*) Peter, this article is going to cause you trouble. Maybe, great trouble.

PETER: I suppose it might. (*Slowly*) I suppose it might. (FRANCIS HARISON, *the Governor's writer, enters suddenly at left.*)

HARISON: Aha! I see that I have caught the two principal plotters together. (*Swaggers up to the men*)

ALEXANDER: Plotters, Harison? Have you a charge to make against me and my friend Mr. Zenger?

HARISON (*In smug tone*): No. Not yet. No charge. But I know what I know.

ALEXANDER (*Sharply*): Hah! What would a spaniel dog like you know, except to run and fetch for your master and sit up and beg? Oh, yes, and to bark at your betters. That's all that you know.

HARISON (*Angrily*): You go too far, sir!

ALEXANDER: I would go much farther to avoid the sight of you.

HARISON: There's no need to say more. I know what you think of me, sir. I read the *Journal!*

ALEXANDER: Then you read a better paper than the one you write for.

HARISON: What! Do you mean you read the *Gazette*, sir?

ALEXANDER: I read it for punishment. But it's much better to wrap the fish in. (PETER *turns to hide smile.*)

HARISON: Since you read our paper, did you like what the *Gazette* said about the enemies of our good Governor Cosby being "seditious rogues"?

ALEXANDER: I was pleased the author could spell the words.

HARISON: I wrote that!

ALEXANDER: Then I am also surprised. I didn't know you could spell your own name, Harison.

HARISON (*Turning his back on* ALEXANDER; *to* PETER): And you, Master Zenger, what do you think of my proposal that the name Zenger be used as a synonym for *liar?*

PETER (*Calmly*): I think you know even less about the Dutch language than the English. Zenger does not mean "liar," Mr. Harison.

HARISON: No, it means "fool"! (*Furiously*) I am here to warn you, Zenger, to stop these attacks on the Governor! And this is the last warning you are going to get. Good day to both of you! (*He turns and stamps offstage, as* ANNA *enters.*)

ANNA: The Governor's dog has a loud bark.

ALEXANDER: And sharp teeth, too. Peter, perhaps we had better stop. Mr. Morris seems to be doing little good in England. We cannot fight on alone much longer. (*Sadly*) Why should you go to jail for no purpose? Perhaps the *Journal* should stop.

PETER: If you say the *Journal* is to stop, it will stop, Mr. Alexander. I cannot do the writing without you, I know.

ALEXANDER: It's up to you, Peter. I will continue to work for justice in what ways I can. But it is you, Peter, whom the Governor has warned. It is you who will receive the full force of his attack. Harison was sent here to warn you.

PETER: Anna, what do *you* think?

ANNA: It's like picking up a stray dog on the streets. One does not need to do it, but once a person has adopted the stray,

one has a responsibility. The *Journal* is like that stray dog, and I wouldn't want to give it up now.

PETER (*Smiling*): Thank you, Anna, thank you! (*To* ALEXANDER) It's not easy for me to print this paper in the face of such powerful opposition. I'm not a brave man; I want only to do my work, eat my bread, and be with my family. But if I were to stop printing the *Journal* now, because I am frightened, I'd be no man at all.

ANNA: You *are* a brave man, Peter. It takes great courage to make a stand, in spite of your fear.

ALEXANDER: And the time is coming when you will need all your courage. It may come sooner than we know. I have heard rumors. . . . (*Spotlight dims.* ANNA *and* ALEXANDER *exit.* PETER *remains onstage, at table, where he begins to work busily on papers. Spotlight goes out, then comes up on the right on* SHERIFF *and* TWO CONSTABLES.)

SHERIFF: If he's not alone, we'll wait.

1ST CONSTABLE: Why wait? No one can stop us. We're on the Governor's business.

2ND CONSTABLE: We're not afraid of being stopped. But this business must remain private. You were told that. Don't you ever listen?

1ST CONSTABLE: I did listen. I just don't understand. Why should a public arrest be kept quiet?

SHERIFF: Both of you be quiet! Don't say a word. Now, follow me, and do what I say. (SHERIFF *starts to cross stage, followed by* TWO CONSTABLES. *Spotlight crosses to* PETER, *working at table, and comes up full.* PETER *looks up, startled, as* SHERIFF *points to him.*) You there. Are you John Peter Zenger, the printer?

PETER: Why, Sheriff, you know I am. A hundred times you have seen me in the streets of New York.

SHERIFF: Just answer the question yea or nay. This is official business.

PETER: Yea, I am John Peter Zenger.

SHERIFF: Then, John Peter Zenger, I have a warrant for your arrest. (*Takes paper from coat and reads it*) "It is ordered that the Sheriff for the City of New York" (I am that man) "do forthwith take and apprehend John Peter Zenger" (you are that man) "for printing and publishing several seditious libels." That means lies!

PETER: The *Journal* prints no lies.

SHERIFF: Do not interrupt!

PETER (*Loudly*): The *Journal* prints no lies.

SHERIFF (*Seriously*): It makes no difference if what you have printed is the truth. It is enough that you have printed materials that are offensive to the Governor. (*Firmly*) The greater the truth, the greater the libel. That is the law. (*Pauses*) Now, where was I? Oh, yes. It says that these libels were in your newspaper. (*Continues reading*) "These libels have in them many things that can anger and upset the people of this province. These materials can inflame people's minds with contempt for His Majesty's government, thus greatly disturbing the peace thereof." Do you understand?

PETER: I understand, but I would like to consult a lawyer.

SHERIFF: You do not need a lawyer until you are charged. Now, I charge you. (*Reading*) "The Sheriff is to take the said John Peter Zenger and commit him to the prison or common jail of the said city and county." Now you are charged, and now you will come with us.

PETER: May I now seek the services of a lawyer?

SHERIFF: The warrant says "forthwith." We have no time for you to find a lawyer.

PETER: May I not even bid my wife goodbye?

SHERIFF: No. You may speak to no one.

PETER: May I write a letter? A short one?

SHERIFF (*Impatiently*): No, and no more questions. All right, Constables, he will come with us. (Two CONSTABLES *move up to* PETER, *and each takes one of his arms. They lead him to the right, followed by* SHERIFF.)

ANNA (*Calling from offstage*): Peter! Peter! (PETER *turns his head and looks back as* CONSTABLES *lead him off the stage.* SHERIFF *follows them off. A moment later,* ANNA *enters left.*) Peter! (*She looks around, puzzled; then goes to table slowly, speaking to herself.*) Peter? Has it happened? Has it finally happened? (*She stands alone at table as spotlight goes out. Curtain.*)

SCENE 2

BEFORE RISE: *Spotlight comes up on* TWO WOMEN, *carrying shopping baskets. They slowly cross stage, talking.*

1ST WOMAN: So, finally, Peter is getting his trial today.

2ND WOMAN: If you can call it a trial. He doesn't stand much chance.

1ST WOMAN: It is better than being in jail without a trial.

2ND WOMAN: They just dragged him off at night. Wouldn't even let him tell Anna where he was going, I've heard.

1ST WOMAN: For seven days, he was not permitted to talk to anyone. It was terrible for Anna.

2ND WOMAN: And a lot of good it did for Mr. Alexander to see him! Justice Delancey set Peter's bail so high it would have taken him ten years to raise the money.

1ST WOMAN: Anna has been so brave! During these nine long months that Peter has been in jail, she has kept publishing the *Journal.*

2ND WOMAN: If the Governor thought that keeping Peter in jail would silence the *Journal,* he must now be disappointed.

1ST WOMAN: But if Peter is sent back to jail after the trial for a long time, can she go on?

2ND WOMAN: And Peter *will* go back to jail. Governor Cosby's two hired judges are going to try the case.

1ST WOMAN: Even the Court Clerk is the Governor's man.

2ND WOMAN: Yes—that Harison! He's a bad one.

1ST WOMAN: And what does Peter have? Just an old lawyer from Philadelphia—Andrew Hamilton. He must be seventy years old.

2ND WOMAN: What could they do? The Governor won't allow Mr. Alexander to argue cases in New York now.

1ST WOMAN: But an old man— how can he help Peter?

2ND WOMAN: Andrew Hamilton was once a fine lawyer. I've heard of him.

1ST WOMAN: Once! Once! Once!

All he is now is an old lawyer from Philadelphia.

2ND WOMAN (*Shaking her head*): Poor Peter.

1ST WOMAN (*Also shaking head*): Poor Anna.

2ND WOMAN: Poor New York. (*They exit and spotlight goes out.*)

* * *

TIME: *1735.*

SETTING: *Courtroom. Upstage center is the Judge's bench, and in front of it, at one side, is a small table for Clerk of the Court. On the left is a table for Attorney General, and on the right, a table for defense attorney. To right and at an angle is the jury box—two rows of six chairs each.*

AT RISE: PETER, ANNA, *and* JAMES ALEXANDER *are sitting at defense table on the right.* SHERIFF, TWO CONSTABLES, *and Attorney General* RICHARD BRADLEY *are sitting at table left.* JURY MEMBERS *sit in jury box.* HARISON *sits at Clerk's table. Judges* JAMES DELANCEY *and* FREDERICK PHILIPSE *sit at bench, upstage center.* ANDREW HAMILTON *is addressing the jury, standing in front of jury box.*

HAMILTON: Gentlemen of the Jury. This is a case of libel. But some larger questions must be considered. It is natural; it is a privilege—I will go further—it is a *right* that all free people have—to complain publicly when they are hurt by power that is used badly. They have a right to warn their neighbors against wrongs or open violence of those in authority.

RICHARD BRADLEY (*Rising*): Your Honors, I protest. Mr. Hamilton goes too far. I don't like his liberties. (*Sits*)

HAMILTON: Surely, Mr. Attorney General, you can have no objections to what I have said thus far. You do not favor wrongs and violence, do you?

BRADLEY: Your entire speech sounds dangerously close to treason, sir.

HAMILTON: Only if you apply what I have said to the present government. Now, I do not. Everyone agrees that we are governed by the best of kings, our good King George. Also, I believe that it is the will of the Crown that all people, without respect to their station in life, be accorded common justice. So I am here to argue for John Peter Zenger. The laws of England know no exceptions. Those in authority are not free from observing the rules of justice.

BRADLEY: Your Honors, again Mr. Hamilton has suggested that the Governor has abused his power! I must protest.

CHIEF JUSTICE DELANCEY: Indeed, Mr. Hamilton, it would appear that you are going too far. Don't you agree, Justice Philipse?

PHILIPSE: Oh, I do. I do. Indeed I do.

HAMILTON: Your Honors, this is a dangerous example you are setting. Let us say that I am walking through the streets of New York and happen to be reading aloud a book of history of ancient times. Suppose I am reading that the leaders caused the people to err, and that they destroyed the people? If I were overheard reading this history, would I be accused of treason? Would the Attorney General have me arrested for libel because he would understand me to mean it thus: "The leaders of this

people (he means the Governor and Council) cause them (he means the people of New York) to err . . ."?

DELANCEY (*Angrily*): That is quite enough, Mr. Hamilton. I do not know how you run your courts in Philadelphia, but here in New York, we know well enough what is meant. We'll have no more of it.

HAMILTON: Your Honors, if I am not permitted to reason for my client, what am I permitted to do?

DELANCEY: You may present the case. Did Mr. Zenger print the scandalous, false libel, or did he not? That is the only question in this case.

HAMILTON: I do not even know what is meant by the words, *scandalous, false libel.* Your Honors will not permit us to examine what words my client has printed to determine if they are scandalous or false. Your Honors, if my client were accused of stealing a plopple——

PHILIPSE (*Interrupting*): A plopple! What is a plopple? I have never heard the word *plopple* before.

HAMILTON: Exactly, Justice Philipse. You have asked the right question. When one is accused of a crime, it is necessary to know what that crime is. Before we can determine if Mr. Zenger has committed libel, we must know if a libel has been committed.

PHILIPSE: But I still don't know what a plopple is.

DELANCEY: The learned gentleman from Philadelphia made a trap for you, and you fell into it. There is no such thing as a plopple.

PHILIPSE: Oh! Oh, I see. It was an example. (MEMBERS OF THE JURY *laugh.*)

BRADLEY: Your Honors, Mr. Hamilton has gone very much out of the way to make himself and the people merry. But his examples have nothing to do with the case. All the jury has to decide is that Mr. Zenger printed and published harmful libels that reflect on the Governor and the men of this government. Zenger has confessed he did the printing, and there can be no doubt the matter is harmful. So there should be no doubt that the jury will

find the defendant guilty and leave the sentencing of the criminal to the Court.

DELANCEY: I quite agree, Mr. Bradley. It seems quite clear to me that since Mr. Zenger has admitted that he did the printing, the jury can find no verdict but guilty.

HAMILTON: Your Honor, does the jury have the right to give what verdict it sees fit?

DELANCEY: I see no reason for the jury to have any doubt. . . . But yes, Mr. Hamilton, the jury has that right. Now are you ready to let the jury speak?

HAMILTON: Your Honor, I would like to speak to the jury for the last time.

DELANCEY: Very well. But limit yourself to this case.

HAMILTON: I shall, Your Honor. (*He turns to look at* ZENGER, *then goes to address the* JURY.) Gentlemen of the Jury, freemen of New York. John Peter Zenger here, whom many of you know, is a simple, hard-working and law-abiding man. During the long time that I have worked with him on this case, I have grown quite fond of him. He is a gentle man, and his good wife,

Anna, is a gentle woman. (*Changes pace, speaking more quickly*) But, Gentlemen of the Jury, something more important than Peter Zenger is on trial here today. The harm done to this man means more than a personal hurt. It can mean a loss of liberty that will affect our country—our new, struggling, hopeful country. (*Intensely*) Gentlemen of the Jury, I ask you to think about this: How will you live in this province if no one may speak the truth for fear of being arrested for libel?

BRADLEY (*Jumping to his feet*): Your Honors, Mr. Hamilton goes too far!

HAMILTON (*To* BRADLEY): I do not think so. (*To* JURY) Gentlemen of the Jury, experience should warn us that when our neighbor's house is on fire, ours is in danger.

BRADLEY: Your Honors, is Mr. Hamilton to speak forever? We have all grown weary with this talk. (*Sits*)

HAMILTON: Not as weary as my client has grown at being kept from speaking out. If weariness is an issue in this

court, think of the weariness of a wife and mother waiting for the return of her husband.

BRADLEY: Your Honors, the Court, too, is very sorry for Mrs. Zenger—sorry that she did not warn her husband more strongly.

ANNA (*Rising*): I did not warn him at all. I encouraged him, and I would do it again.

DELANCEY: What is this? A woman speaking in this court without permission? Is this what all this talk of liberty is coming to? (*To* ANNA, *sharply*) Woman, you are not to speak in this court. Do you understand?

ANNA: But, Justice Delancey, the Attorney General has said——

DELANCEY: I said that you are to sit down and be quiet! If you speak again, I'll have you removed from the courtroom. (ANNA *sits*.) Now, Mr. Hamilton, have you finished?

HAMILTON: I have but a sentence or two more, Your Honor.

DELANCEY (*Curtly*): Well, make them brief. The Court has other business besides that of a poor printer.

HAMILTON (*To* JURY): It is, Gentlemen of the Jury, not the cause of one poor printer, nor of New York alone, that I plead. No. In this trial may be the beginning of a rule of law that will affect every person in all of the colonies. The cause I plead is the cause of liberty. Today, if you decide in favor of my client, you will give all people the right to speak and write the truth.

DELANCEY: Are you quite finished, Mr. Hamilton?

HAMILTON: I am now content, Your Honor, to leave justice to the jury. (*Sits at table.*)

DELANCEY: Well, I am not. You have so twisted the issues that I must speak. (*Turns to* JURY) Gentlemen of the Jury, Mr. Hamilton hopes, no doubt, to make you disregard my instructions. I will, therefore, first point out that Mr. Zenger has already confessed to the printing of the alleged libels. Your verdict should simply acknowledge that you heard that confession. As to whether the words that Mr. Zenger printed were libel or not, that is a matter for the Court— not you—to decide. Justice Philipse will tell you that I have spoken the law.

PHILIPSE: Indeed you have—indeed you have. The very law.

DELANCEY: Mr. Hamilton has also appealed to your hearts. The Court is not without sympathy for this poor printer and his wife. In fact, if Mr. Zenger were to rise and admit his full guilt—and give the Court his promise not to err again—the Court would, upon the verdict of the jury, be likely to show a goodly amount of mercy. (*He pauses and looks at* PETER.) Well, Mr. Zenger?

HAMILTON: Your Honor, may I speak to my client in private?

DELANCEY: It is not usual, but in the interest of mercy, the Court will consent. We will have a brief recess.

HAMILTON: Thank you, Your Honor. (*He leads* PETER *to the right; others hold their positions.*) Peter, do you understand what has happened?

PETER: I'm not sure that I do, Mr. Hamilton.

HAMILTON: The Court is willing to free you, with just a warning, perhaps, if you will agree to admit your guilt and publish no more articles in the *Journal.*

PETER: Do you think I should do this?

HAMILTON: I don't know, Peter. I don't know. If the jury finds you guilty, you may be sent to prison for many years. It will be hard, Peter, hard for you and hard for Anna.

PETER: Will the jury find me guilty?

HAMILTON: I can't tell. The Judge has told them they have no choice. They may be afraid that by voting for you, they will anger the Governor and bring his wrath down on them. What has been done to you has made many of them afraid.

PETER: I see.

HAMILTON: Then you understand what your choice is?

PETER: I understand, and I have made my decision.

HAMILTON: Well, don't tell me. Tell the Court. (*They return to the table.*)

DELANCEY: Well, Mr. Zenger, have you decided to accept the mercy of the Court?

PETER: May I speak to the whole Court, Your Honor?

DELANCEY: Yes, but make it brief.

PETER (*Rising*): Gentlemen of the Jury, members of the Court: Mr. Hamilton has

I miss my wife, my children, my friends. I thank the Court for its offer of mercy. But I cannot say what is not true! (*Passionately*) I did not publish libels! What I published was the truth. I will not promise to avoid the truth in the future! (*Judges half rise, shocked*.) Mr. Hamilton has told me that the jury is likely to decide against me. If so, Gentlemen (*Nodding to* JURY), I understand. I will not blame you. But I will not judge myself guilty when I am innocent; I will not sell my right to be free and honest in order to remain a prisoner out of prison.

DELANCEY (*Angrily*): Have you quite finished, Mr. Zenger?

PETER: Yes, Your Honor, and I thank you for what you have tried to do for me.

DELANCEY: Then the jury will now be dismissed to decide upon its verdict. I again direct you, Gentlemen, that your verdict need not determine if a libel was committed, merely if Mr. Zenger published the material. And to that question, there can be but one answer. The jury is now dismissed. (JURY

explained to me that if I admit guilt and promise to print no more, I may be allowed to breathe the free air again. It is a pleasing prospect. I have, during these long months in prison, grown to hate bars.

MEMBERS *huddle together, talking rapidly among themselves.*) What is going on here? I said the jury was dismissed.

1ST JUROR: Your Honor, must we be dismissed?

DELANCEY: Of course! You must come to a verdict.

2ND JUROR: But we already have, Your Honor.

DELANCEY: And is it unanimous? Do you all agree?

3RD JUROR: We do, Your Honor.

DELANCEY: Very well, the Court will hear the verdict. (*To* HARISON) Master Clerk, will you poll the jury?

HARISON (*Rising; to* JURY): Gentlemen, will each of you tell me privately your vote—guilty or not guilty—and I will record it. (*Takes paper and pencil and crosses to jury box. Each* JUROR *speaks to* HARISON, *who marks paper. Then he writes a note on paper and takes it to* DELANCEY. *All watch anxiously.*)

DELANCEY (*Taking paper from* HARISON): Is this the verdict?

HARISON: Yes, Your Honor.

DELANCEY: Mr. Attorney General, would you come here, please. (BRADLEY *goes up to bench.*)

ANNA (*Rising*): What is their verdict?

DELANCEY: Quiet in this courtroom! (ANNA *sits.* DELANCEY *and* BRADLEY *confer for a moment.* BRADLEY *returns to his seat.*) The Attorney General has requested that the jury be polled publicly. It shall be done. Clerk, poll the jury, and each member of the jury will answer publicly. (HARISON *starts to rise as* 1ST JUROR *stands.*)

1ST JUROR (*Quickly*): I vote not guilty!

2ND JUROR (*Rising*): Not guilty!

3RD AND 4TH JURORS (*Rising*): Not guilty.

OTHER JURORS (*Rising*): Not guilty.

DELANCEY (*Furiously*): You will wait until the Clerk calls your names!

1ST JUROR: We will wait, Your Honor, but it won't change our verdict.

DELANCEY (*Rising and looking at* BRADLEY): Very well. This Court has found John Peter Zenger not guilty. The jury is dismissed.

JURORS (*Ad lib*): Hurrah! Zenger is freed! Hurrah!

DELANCEY (*Banging gavel*): Quiet

in this courtroom! It becomes more and more obvious that you men have no notion of court justice. Cheering in a courtroom! This behavior is as outrageous as your verdict.

HAMILTON: Your Honor, there is a precedent for the jury voicing its satisfaction. In a case in London . . .

DELANCEY: And, Mr. Hamilton, I've had all the lectures on law I want from you. Court is adjourned! (*To* PHILIPSE) Well, Justice Philipse, the trial is over. Now we must report the result to the Governor. (*He rises and turns upstage.*)

PHILIPSE (*Following him*): Oh, dear. Oh, dear. I'm afraid *our* trial has just begun. (DE-LANCEY *and* PHILIPSE *exit, followed by* BRADLEY, CON-STABLES *and* SHERIFF. HARI-SON *watches unhappily as* JURORS *gather around* PETER, *congratulating him.*)

JURORS (*Ad lib*): Congratulations, Peter! You're a free man now!

HARISON *turns and exits. One by one,* JURORS *exit, talking happily to each other.* PETER *turns to* ANNA, *embraces her, then shakes* ALEXANDER'S *hand. Finally,* PETER *goes up to* HAMILTON, *who is standing alone at table, right.*)

PETER: Mr. Hamilton, I will never be able to tell you how much I owe you.

HAMILTON: No, Peter, let me tell you what I owe you. Let me tell you what all free people owe you. A century from now, two centuries from now, people will still speak of you and what your courage has done this day. Peter, you have won a great battle for freedom. Freedom of the press was born today.

PETER: Freedom of the press! Those are big words.

HAMILTON: And from today on, they are not only words. With your courage today, Peter, with your insistence that all people have the right to speak the truth, to hear the truth, to write the truth, and to read the truth, you have made Truth a respectable citizen of our land. In years to come, when journalists name the greats of their profession, John Peter Zenger will lead all the rest. (*Curtain.*)

Eat-It-All Elaine

I went away last August
To summer camp in Maine,
And there I met a camper
Called Eat-it-all Elaine.
Although Elaine was quiet,
She liked to cause a stir
By acting out the nickname
Her camp-mates gave to her.

The day of our arrival
At Cabin Number Three
When girls kept coming over
To greet Elaine and me,
She took a piece of Kleenex
And calmly chewed it up,
Then strolled outside the cabin
And ate a buttercup.

Elaine, from that day forward,
Was always in command.
On hikes, she'd eat some birch-bark.
On swims, she'd eat some sand.
At meals, she'd swallow prune-pits
And never have a pain,
While everyone around her
Would giggle, "Oh Elaine!"

One morning, berry-picking,
A bug was in her pail,
And though we thought for certain
Her appetite would fail,
Elaine said, "Hmm, a stinkbug."
And while we murmured, "Ooh,"
She ate her pail of berries
And ate the stinkbug, too.

The night of Final Banquet
When counselors were handing
Awards to different children
Whom they believed outstanding,
To every *thinking* person
At summer camp in Maine
The Most Outstanding Camper
Was Eat-it-all Elaine.

Kaye Starbird

An Impossible Choice

by William Stevenson

Jackie Rhodes is the daughter of an English game warden in Kenya, East Africa. She believes that Kamau, her pet galago, or bush baby, will not be allowed to travel on the ship with her when the Rhodes family goes back to England. She decides, therefore, to return Kamau to his native home in the wild over a hundred miles from the coast. For the journey, she enlists the help of her old friend Tembo Murumbi, an African headman from the interior plains who is her father's former assistant. Before setting out, Jackie and Tembo borrow a canoe in order to catch some fish to eat on the way.

They paddled the borrowed outrigger canoe beyond the river's mouth, turning eastward along the coast a short way. Tembo, who could not swim, had lost some of his dislike of the sea and watched eagerly as the girl steered them above the coral. There was a rope, weighted with a rock, that served as an anchor. This she lowered until it lodged in the coral.

"We must not stay long," he warned.

"Ten minutes," she promised, snapping on the goggles and taking a speargun. "There are many fish here, and easy to catch."

"Perhaps I could try?"

"Of course!" Her eyes lit up. "You can hang onto the canoe's side and rest your feet on the coral."

She picked up a speargun and showed him how to use it. As so often happened, she found Swahili a hard language in which to explain anything mechanical. And yet it forced a simple explanation that made her think more clearly.

It was a simple device. Tembo saw that there was a light piece of nylon fishing line that fastened the harpoon to the swimmer to prevent the escape of an injured fish. His love of the hunt was aroused, and he fingered the gun with lively curiosity.

"Let's go!" Jackie picked up the second harpoon and lowered herself over the side of the canoe. Tembo followed her and found that he could balance on the coral by leaning against one of the canoe's outriggers.

"What about Kamau?" he shouted, catching sight of the bush baby creeping out of his basket.

But Jackie was already stalking a flat, diamond-shaped creature moving slowly across a bed of sand. It was a sand-gray plaice, propelling itself with the graceful movements of a large bird. She sighted along the speargun and fired. Her eyes, magnified by the goggles, gleamed triumphantly. The little harpoon, still fastened to her wrist by the line, had pinned the fish to the sea bed.

She surfaced, took a deep breath, and dived to get the speared fish.

"It is small but good to eat," she said, swimming back to the canoe and tossing the fish into the bottom.

She caught sight of Kamau, who was squatting on the prow. His ears were pinned back and he was looking at the fish with clear distaste, uttering an unhappy cry that sounded like the twanging of a guitar string.

"Will he be safe?" asked Tembo.

"Yes," Jackie said. "He fears water."

She dived back under the sea.

Tembo squinted at the bush baby. He seemed to be frozen to his perch, and it was not likely that he would move. Holding the outrigger with one hand, Tembo sank below the sea's surface, peering through the goggles Jackie had given him.

Almost at once a large sea bass, a grouper, swam lazily into his view, its huge mouth wide open.

Tembo lifted his head and gulped a great lungful of air. When he ducked under again, the grouper had swum so close that it seemed enormous. Shakily he aimed the speargun and fired.

To his surprise and delight, the harpoon struck the grouper. The fish seemed to become fiery red and turned tail in a flash, almost jerking the harpoon line from Tembo's hand. He staggered back, astonished by the weight of its pull. The

grouper thrashed back and forth on the end of the line and then dived for a hole in the coral.

The man's excited shouts now brought Jackie splashing to his side. She yelled instructions to keep the line taut and dived for the hole.

He saw her sink slowly down the side of the coral, saw the grouper peer at her from the darkness of the hole, and then watched in horror as an unspeakably horrible creature like a fat and wart-ridden snake reared up from a nearby hole.

Tembo tried to cry a warning but water clogged his throat. He caught his breath and ducked once more underwater. His hand gripping the outrigger shook violently.

The girl had thrust her arm into the grouper's hiding place. Gripping it by the gills, she hauled the struggling fish into open water.

Behind her the creature that looked like a snake swam clear from its hole. It was a good five feet in length, with a crinkly, green head and jaws sewn with teeth. The body was smooth and scaleless, and it moved in jerks through the silence of the sea's depths. Tembo forgot his fear of the sea and prepared to plunge from the coral.

He had pushed away from the outrigger and with his head once again under water, he glanced back at the canoe.

He was horrified to see Kamau struggling beside it. The bush baby was paddling with hands and feet, but each time he kicked against the canoe, he floated away from it. Already the weight of water in his fur was dragging him below the surface.

Tembo glanced from the bush baby to the girl. She had turned to face her attacker and seemed to be warding it off with her speargun. He turned back to Kamau, whose struggles were getting plainly weaker.

The choice was an impossible one. If he tried to help the girl, Tembo would have to leave the bush baby to drown. If he saved the bush baby, he would use up crucial seconds in which the girl could lose her battle.

She had plunged the speargun into the snapping jaws that seemed to be striking for her legs. She was a few feet below water, swimming on her back, her fingers still fastened in the grouper's gills.

Tembo launched himself awkwardly toward the canoe and made a wild grab for the bush baby. He was not prepared for the awful feeling of having no firm support beneath his feet. With his free hand he somehow discovered the upper edge of the canoe's side and holding onto it, he scooped Kamau out of the water and tossed the half-conscious bush baby into the boat.

When he turned back to Jackie, he saw that she had poked the speargun straight down her attacker's throat. The jaws snapped tight on the wooden shaft. At once the rest of the body coiled like a spring. The girl heaved away the speargun and its awful victim and kicked frantically for the surface.

She was still gasping as she swam alongside Tembo.

"I hate those things," she said, coming to rest on the coral. Seeing the look on Tembo's face, and interpreting it wrongly, she said: "It's all right. It was a moray eel. They don't often

attack or bite like that." She spat. The salt water in her mouth reminded her of the eel.

Tembo said: "The bush baby—"

She let go of the grouper. "What's happened?" The fish slapped the water with its tail and sank from sight, trailing the harpoon line.

"He's in the boat, baba. He fell in—"

She pulled one of the outrigger poles and swung the canoe until she could scramble into it. The bush baby lay sprawled in the bottom, eyes closed, in a pool of water.

She fell on hands and knees beside him. "Kamau!" Her voice was almost a shriek. She lifted the tiny body and saw water dribble from the half-closed mouth. He seemed lifeless.

The girl raised him to her lips. His fur had turned into stiff little spikes, showing an alarmingly small body with a rat's tail. She pursed her lips and held her mouth to his, blowing gently between the bared teeth. After thus breathing carefully into Kamau's mouth so that she filled the water-logged lungs, she pressed gently with hands cupped around his tiny chest and then listened to the gentle bubbling hiss of air that emerged. She did this several times, holding him nearly upside down.

Slowly he began to breathe again. A few seconds passed, and his eyelids fluttered.

"He lives," said Tembo.

The girl was shivering. Kamau was gasping now, his body shaking. She placed him on the hot planks of the canoe and ran worried fingers through his matted fur.

"How did this happen?"

Tembo was shocked by the anger in her eyes. "I don't know, baba."

"You must have rocked the canoe!" she accused him.

Tembo clamped his mouth shut.

"I should never have trusted you alone with him!" Jackie said, and she began to cry.

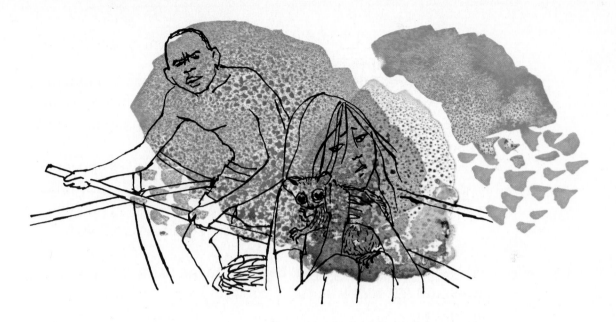

The man moved slowly to the prow of the canoe and hauled in the stone-weighted rope. "We must go quickly," he said quietly. "Forget the fish."

The sun was already high. He began paddling back to the river mouth, his face expressionless, eyes narrowed to slits as he watched for other fishermen. The girl lay in the bottom of the boat, still stroking the reviving bush baby.

They moved into the river, the canoe wrapped in silence. Sometimes the girl glanced back at the man in the stern, paddling with a smooth, steady rhythm. He avoided her eyes.

Kamau stirred and sat up weakly. He blinked owlishly at the girl and examined his arms and legs. He looked like a toothbrush, his fur still spikey, his tail bedraggled. He began cautiously to groom himself, combing the fur with the long nail on each of his little fingers. He chuckled as he did this, now and again glancing up at the girl.

She said, her face turned away from Tembo: "He seems fully recovered."

"I am glad," said the man.

"Perhaps I spoke too hastily," said the girl. "Forgive me."

"Of course, baba." But Tembo's voice was noncommittal.

"I lost my head," said the girl.

"It is understandable."

"I was very upset. It was no reason to be rude." Suddenly she turned and stretched out her hand, resting it lightly on the man's knee. "To save the bush baby you must have had to swim?"

A smile appeared on his face and around his eyes appeared a thousand small wrinkles of laughter. He said, "Swim! Like a camel!"

"Tembo, I'm truly sorry for what I said. Was it awful—*swimming?*"

She started to laugh too. Between them, the tension melted away and left a new sense of comradeship. "It was terrible," he told her.

As Jackie and Tembo go deeper into Africa with Kamau, they come face to face with many other kinds of African wildlife, most of them equally as unfriendly as the moray eel. The book THE BUSH BABIES *tells the whole story of the three travelers' unusual adventures.*

AUTHOR

William Stevenson has lived in Africa, Hong Kong, India, and Malaysia. He began telling children's stories about Asian and African wildlife to his family to fill the evenings when they were in remote parts of the world. His two sons and two daughters had bush babies among their pets, including the real Kamau, who accompanied Mr. Stevenson's daughter Jackie from Kenya to Scotland and then to Malaya.

Mr. Stevenson has written books for children and for adults; he has been a news correspondent, a pilot, and a film-maker, all of which have enabled him to travel and to learn about animals.

Mr. Stevenson was born and grew up in England and now lives in Canada.

IN TIME of SILVER RAIN

by Langston Hughes

In time of silver rain
The earth
Puts forth new life again,
Green grasses grow
And flowers lift their heads,
And over all the plain
The wonder spreads
    Of life,
    Of life,
    Of life!

In time of silver rain
The butterflies
Lift silken wings
To catch a rainbow cry,
And trees put forth
New leaves to sing
In joy beneath the sky
As down the roadway
Passing boys and girls
Go singing, too,
In time of silver rain
    When spring
    And life
    Are new.

The Memory of Beauty

by Hanako Fukuda

In Japan, more than two hundred years ago, a lonely little boy grew up to be a great man. His name was Yataro Kobayashi. Yataro had been left motherless at an early age, and his father, though kind, was often too busy to take notice of him. Yataro's best friend was his grandmother, who helped him to find pleasure and happiness in the beauty of the earth and its creatures.

Yataro's village school was taught by a well-known haiku poet, and as Yataro began to compose his own haiku and to express his deepest feelings in them, the master sensed that his shy pupil had a gift for writing poetry.

Then Yataro's grandmother died, his father remarried, and Yataro had to leave school to do heavy work in the fields and take care of a small stepbrother. But another important change in Yataro's drab life, an exciting change for him, was still to come.

Yataro's father thought much and deeply about his son. He said nothing, but deep in his heart he knew that Yataro would one day be a truly fine poet. But he needed training. What should be done?

While the father pondered, Yataro's life continued in the same way—work, loneliness, friendship with the creatures of meadow and sky. There were moments of happiness, but they were fragile and fleeting, like the sudden breeze that made the field poppies nod. Happiness and beauty seemed brief and fleeting. Did nothing beautiful remain for long? The birds' songs were so sweet and so short! Flowers blossomed only a few days before they lost their freshness. Small creatures were so easily hurt. Nothing stayed the same. Leaves fell from the trees. The clouds in the sky appeared and disappeared. The brook was always moving, never pausing.

Yataro thought much about this mystery of life. The beauty of the earth, his mother, his grandmother, comfort, happiness—how quickly they vanished! Even the fireflies lingered but a moment. Beauty was gone too soon.

The first firefly
Swept away, leaving—
The wind in my hand.

One evening his father came to him. "I have made arrangements for you to go to Edo (now Tokyo)," he said. "A friend of mine is setting out late tonight. He will take you there and help you to find a job and a place to live. I can only send you with my blessings and a little food, my son."

Yataro was speechless.

"Something in my heart tells me it is best to do this," his father continued. "Forgive me that I have been a poor father to you, my motherless child! The spirits of your mother and your grandmother speak to me in my dreams. They tell me you will find your true way in Edo. My own heart tells me you are a poet. It is a hard life, but you will become a good poet."

Thus it was decided.

The new life in Edo was not an easy one for fourteen-year-old Yataro. Before leaving the city, his father's friend had found a job for him in the household of a rich family. Now Yataro was entirely on his own.

The boy had much to do and many things to discover in the weeks that followed. The rich family was not unkind to him, but no one was kind, either. As long as Yataro did his work, nobody cared about him. He had many duties. In time, he learned to help in the formal garden; sometimes he looked after the younger children of the household. Often he was busy running errands for the master of the house. Every errand taught him something new about the big city.

Edo was so large that Yataro wondered if he would ever find its edges. There was a great bustle all of the time, many people making much traffic in the narrow streets. Everywhere were houses! Houses in rows, crowded together like rice grains. Houses with great parks around them and gardens, pools, trees, and walls to keep the others out. Houses on top of hills, houses running up and down hillsides. Houses as elegant and beautiful as the ladies Yataro sometimes saw riding in handsome rickshas. Houses poor and little and thin, like many of the poor people on the street, like Yataro himself.

Life was exciting, and it was always interesting to young Yataro, but it was not really happy. It was very hard to make friends. His simple country manners did not attract people. In time, he left the rich family and drifted from job to job. Sometimes he was without any work at all.

When the weather was cold, Yataro often had to look for shelter for the night. Few people would trust strangers enough to take them in. Few people had enough room for themselves. How many were the times when Yataro had to beg for lodgings!

"Go away, boy," someone would say.

"Have you money to pay for the room?" another would ask.

"I am sorry. I have no room to give you."

Sometimes Yataro would go to the temple to sleep. He would even live there for short intervals, in some small corner where no one would come to chase him away.

In the summer there were hundreds and hundreds of insects in Edo. For many, it was great sport to take nets and to go forth in the daytime to collect them. Everyone wanted to catch some of the beautiful dragonflies that flew about. Best of all was to catch a singing insect, like a cricket. Oh, in the daytime insects were fun! But at night they came and stung one and crawled over one's bed. It was at such times that Yataro missed having a bed of his own.

> *Rubbing my hands together,*
> *I ask for a small corner*
> *Of the mosquito net.*

Whenever Yataro did have a job and a place to live, he was usually too poor to afford things of comfort for himself. Even if he could pay for a room and for enough food to make a

small meal, he might have to eat it in the dark because he could not afford a candle.

> *How cold it is,*
> *Eating supper by the light*
> *Of the next room.*

In the midst of his poverty and loneliness, Yataro found solace in expressing himself by trying to write haiku. There were haiku schools and haiku clubs in the city, but he could not afford to attend them. Besides, he felt sure that the pupils and club members would not want a poor young man who had no fine city manners nor good clothes.

However, he managed to find some cast-off brushes and to buy some cheap paper. Then he found materials to make his own ink. When the light was good in his candleless room, or when he huddled against the wall of a temple in the daytime, he would try to compose haiku and to write them down as well as he could. And in one poem after the other, he expressed his great homesickness.

> *I'll try not to . . . but*
> *I can't help thinking*
> *Of my old home.*

But life was not entirely bleak. Indeed, there were many causes for happiness. Sometimes Yataro even enjoyed himself. When the weather was fair, he could wander in the city and the parks and admire the beauties of Edo. He loved the celebration of New Year's Day. In Edo, New Year's was the traditional day for flying kites; it was the beginning, too, of the kite-flying season. Kites were made in many wonderful shapes and colors. Many kites were square, but others were the shapes of animals or had pictures painted on them. Some were so big that it took many people running fast and pulling the kites after them to make them fly into the air. This was always an exciting time! Some kites cost much money, but some cost only a penny. That first New Year's in Edo, Yataro bought himself a kite and joined with the others who were flying theirs high into the sky. Yataro's kite was not large, and it was not special—only a little square of bright yellow paper, with a blue tail. It had cost only a halfpenny. But it flew as gaily as all the others, and Yataro's good spirits soared with it.

The New Year's Day:
Even the halfpenny kite
Flies in the Edo sky.

Quickly the years went by. Although he did not make any close friends, Yataro did find many others who wrote haiku, and he was accepted by them. More and more, he gathered the courage to write about the things he felt, and more and more, his haiku were recognized by fellow poets.

After a time, Yataro came to be considered by many as a poet of promise. He was even invited to join one of the best haiku clubs in Edo, the Nirokuan Club, and he attended the Nirokuan School. His haiku were among the best. But he had suffered too much, and for too long, to become proud.

When, finally, he had become well known among the poets of Edo, he decided to change his name to Issa. It was the custom for a poet to take another name. Yataro chose the name because he was a humble man and *Issa* means "a cup of tea," which is very common and humble.

"Why call yourself such a common, such a comical name?" he was asked many times.

"It is good enough for me," he would reply. "If I can become as well known and as well loved for the simple beauty and comfort of my poems as tea is known for its warmth and comfort, I shall be happy." And so it was that

from that time on, to the very end of his life, Yataro was called Issa.

In due time it even came to pass that Issa was made president of the Nirokuan Haiku Club! It was the greatest honor of his life. But this honor did not last very long.

Some of the members of the Nirokuan School were proud and difficult persons. They thought haiku should be written only in certain definite ways, in very special, elegant, flowery language. It irritated them that Issa wrote about everyday things and used everyday words and expressions.

"Cup of Tea he may call himself," they grumbled to each other, "but his writing is too common. It isn't proper. It isn't dignified. He disgraces our school."

Whenever any of them tried to tell Issa to change his ways, he simply would not listen. "I write as I feel and as seems honest and true to me," he would retort. "I write poems that simple people can enjoy."

The members were truly horrified by Issa's words. "We must cherish our tradition," they shouted.

"If you think we should follow only tradition, then I'd better resign as president," said Issa sadly. "I cannot live honestly if I cannot speak my own true feelings in my poetry."

And so it was that Issa was president of the club for only a short time. Indeed, after that, he no longer associated with the Nirokuan School. He was in disgrace. None of the respectable poets would have anything to do with him.

"It is my destiny to travel a lonely path," Issa told an old Buddhist priest one day. He often stayed with the priests in the temple. They had come to know him as a homeless young man. They liked his poetry, even if others laughed at it, but they tried to persuade him to be more tactful with others.

"I cannot go against my own way," Issa told the priest. "I have decided to leave Edo."

"Where will you go, and what will you do?" asked the man. "You have no profession or skills. Poets cannot earn a living unless they run a school. If you have fallen out with your fellow poets, no pupils will come to your school."

"I will wander, as many poets do," said Issa. "I know now that I prefer a simple life of poverty and solitude to a busy life among those who will not accept me as I am."

So Issa left Edo. He began to wander all over Japan, marveling at new sights, new sounds. Often he would return to Edo. Sometimes he would find odd jobs; at other times he might earn a little money teaching the writing of haiku to a few students. Always he remained poor. More often than not, his home was a simple hut, but there everyone was sure of a welcome—grownups and children, and even cats, frogs, crickets, sparrows, and flies.

To a cricket he said,

> *Cricket, my boy,*
> *Take care of my house*
> *While I am gone.*

Issa laughed at this idea because there was nothing of value in his house that could not be well guarded by a lowly, little cricket.

In his wanderings Issa met many people and saw many places. He turned each experience into a poem. In the forest, where he spent much time, he came to know the deer. He wrote,

> *The sleeping little fawn*
> *Shakes off the butterfly*
> *And sleeps again.*

Thinking of his childhood home always made him sad. In his journeys throughout Japan, Issa was gratified to find that most children were happy. They had happy homes, something he had not known since his grandmother died. He had really always been alone, inside himself, since that day of sorrow. As the years went by, Issa came to understand loneliness and to realize that to be lonely is less terrible than never to be alone and never to be at peace. In loneliness he could look into his mind and heart and find much to rejoice in.

I have nothing at all
But this peacefulness, quietness,
And this coolness.

Perhaps it was because of his memories of his mother, his grandmother, and his father that Issa decided to return to his home village. Perhaps that is why he came to be sitting there under a tree with some children one summer day.

"Are you an orphan?" asked the children, who had been listening to his story.

"Yes, I am," he said. "But the earth is my mother now, and her creatures are my family."

But the children looked puzzled. They didn't quite understand what he meant.

"Is the world always so sad?" asked a little girl.

"The world is not at all sad," answered Issa. "It is we who are sad because there is so much that we do not understand."

"But you said that lovely things are fleeting. That is sad," a boy told him.

"No—it is only true. Lovely things can never be lost; they remain in our memories, where they live forever. Only in our minds can we own things. And there is nothing more worth owning than the memory of beauty and the ideas of truth."

The first firefly
Swept away, leaving—
The wind in my hand.

Hanako Fukuda's full-length biography of Issa, from which this story was taken, is called WIND IN MY HAND, *and it is based on Issa's diary. The author selected and translated into English the many lovely haiku of Issa's that appear in the biography. In translating them, however, she could not keep the seventeen-syllable form in which Issa wrote them, but she kept as close as she could to the original poems.*

AUTHOR

Hanako Fukuda became especially interested in the poet Issa in her youth when she spent many summers at his birthplace, Kashwabara. She was born in Tokyo, Japan, and spent her early school years there. She went to Canada to study at the Toronto Conservatory of Music and returned to Japan to teach music. Some years later, she moved to the United States and continued her education at San Diego State College and the University of Southern California, where she received her Ph.D in music education. Dr. Fukuda not only writes and translates haiku but is an accomplished musician as well. She now lives in California.

Ellen Swallow

founded ecology . . .

On an October day in 1973, scientists, teachers, and people from government met along Boston's Charles River to honor ecology and the scientist who founded it—Ellen Swallow. Born in Dunstable, Massachusetts, in 1842, Ellen Swallow was the first woman to enter the Massachusetts Institute of Technology. In 1873, she became the first woman to earn a chemistry degree. The Institute did not allow her to do further study because she was a woman; however, she did become the first woman to teach there.

When she was a student, she began to test the water in certain rivers of Massachusetts. These tests were the beginning of the environmental sciences, or studies of our surroundings, that we have today. Ecology, the study of relationships between living things and environment, is among these sciences. Ellen Swallow also found ways to test air, soils, food, and the ways that cities and factories get rid of waste.

Ellen Swallow did not stop there. In the field of education, she worked for women's rights. She found ways to encourage scientific study by women.

In 1876, she conducted a study of groceries, which led to the first state food laws. She opened the New England Kitchen in 1890 to feed the poor and to educate them in proper diet. She helped people in schools, hospitals, and factories to serve the proper foods, and she taught people how to eat wisely at home.

Meanwhile, Ellen Swallow never stopped studying the relationship between people and nature. She had hoped that these studies would be the most important part of her human ecology movement. Ellen Swallow believed that there is a relationship between people's health, their states of mind, and the purity of the environment. The leading scientists of the day felt that people could and should change nature as they wished. Ellen Swallow, who warned about a coming environmental crisis, was called a troublemaker. She died in 1911, and her work on improving the environment was ignored until the mid-1960's. Then people began talking about what she felt was most important: respect for the earth.

and Rachel Carson

brought it to our attention.

Many experts feel that the current ecology movement exists because of the public pressure that was brought about by Rachel Carson's book *Silent Spring,* which was published in 1962. In *Silent Spring,* Rachel Carson claimed that the chemicals used by people to kill pests and to kill weeds could upset the "balance of nature."

As a child, Rachel Carson had two loves: writing and studying nature. Later she would use both to make her points. She earned a Master's Degree from Johns Hopkins University in Baltimore, Maryland, and in 1935, was hired by the U.S. Bureau of Fisheries as an aquatic biologist. Soon she began to publish beautifully written science articles and books about the sea. In 1951, her book *The Sea Around Us* was published, and she won the National Book Award for it.

Though captivated by the sea, Rachel Carson had yet another area of interest. She had long worried that the wide use of DDT as an insect killer would harm the birds who needed insects for food. Her studies proved her fears to be right. Massachusetts had sprayed an area heavily with a DDT-based compound to kill mosquitoes. The mosquitoes were killed, but so were many birds. In some areas where spraying was done, new generations of robins were unable to have any young. Ms. Carson feared that, as insects became able to resist DDT, people would have to use stronger and stronger chemicals in order to control the insects.

In making her findings known, Rachel Carson ran into a huge obstacle. People did not think the subject was important enough, so she decided to write *Silent Spring.* It was a success, and people became concerned about their environment. Government studies were begun and action was taken. Ms. Carson died in 1964, but not before she had made us aware of our need for ecological study.

RECOGNIZING IMPORTANT STORY ELEMENTS

As you watch a movie that tells a good story about people, do you learn who the story characters are and decide what kind of person each of them is? Do you notice when and where the story takes place? Do you wonder from time to time what will happen next and how things will turn out? Probably you do all these things so that you will enjoy the movie as much as you can.

As with watching a movie, you will find stories you read more entertaining if you watch for three important things: the **characters**—the people or animals in the story; the **setting**—the place and time in which the story takes place; and the **plot**—the plan for the events in the story. In some stories, there will also be a fourth thing, a **theme**—a message that the author wants to share with you.

In "The Tunnel," the characters are Thomas Small, his parents, and his twin brothers. Thomas is the main character because the story is mainly about something that happened to him. In the story from *Ben and Me*, there are two main characters. There are usually other characters besides the main characters in a story too. They are called minor characters, and often one of them is just as interesting as the main character. Who is the main character in "Flight to Freedom"? Who are the minor characters?

Every story happens at some time and at some place. The setting of a story is the combination of the time and the place in which the events occur. The setting of "The Computer Triumphs Again" is Willowdale, a town in the United States, in the present day. Amos, the mouse in the story from *Ben and Me*, tells you when and where the story takes place: Philadelphia in 1745. Do you remember what the setting for *Damon and Pythias* is?

The plot of a story is the plan for the things that are to happen in the story. The author builds the plot by telling what the characters do, what they say, and what happens to them.

Good authors have many ways of getting you interested in the plot as soon as you begin to read their stories. Sometimes, near the beginning of a story, things are said and done to make you think of one or more questions you want answered. Just after you started to read "The Cherub and My Sainted Grandmother," you probably asked yourself this question: *Will Maggie be able to break the pony for the Hagens?* With this question in your mind, you read the story to get the answer.

Sometimes the author lets you know early in the story that the plot includes a character with a problem to be solved or to overcome. In the story from *Call It Courage*, for example, you learn that Mafatu has a problem—a strong fear of the sea. You read the story to find out if Mafatu was able to overcome his fear.

Sometimes an author will provide hints here and there in the story to show how the plot is going to turn out. At other times, an author will deliberately keep you in suspense until the end of the story. For instance, in "Expedition from Arreol," you learn only at the very end that Rob delivered his message in time to save the visitors from Arreol.

In addition to a plot, a story may have a theme. This is a message that the author particularly wants to share with you. The plot of "Purim Jester" can be told simply. Ella has her heart set on playing Queen Esther in the Purim play and is bitterly disappointed to be chosen to play the jester instead. After some encouragement from her family, she decides to make the best of it and ends by captivating the audience. The theme, or underlying message, that this story contains is that a willingness to try to overcome disappointment may lead to success; therefore, a person should not give up or quit if disappointment comes. The message is one that can be applied to many different situations and people, not just to those in the story "Purim Jester." In some stories, it may not be easy to discover the theme; an author rarely comes right out and tells what the underlying message of a story is.

How can you pay attention to the characters and the setting in order to enjoy a story more? As you read about the people in a story, think whether each of them is a person you would like to have as a friend or a neighbor. Make pictures in your mind of the characters, the setting, and the events. The more you do this, the more real the people, the places, and the actions in the story will seem to you.

Paying attention to the plot will also help you enjoy a story. When you think of questions to be answered or problems to be solved, watch carefully for any hints the author gives you as you read along. Try to decide how you would solve a particular problem that a story character has if you were in the same situation. After you have decided what you would do, you will be eager to find out if the character solves the problem in the same way.

Since the theme, or the message, of a story is usually not stated directly by the author, you may have to think carefully about the question *What message is the author trying to give me?* in order to get the theme. Perhaps that message will solve one of your problems or teach you something that will help you.

Discussion

Help your class to answer each of the following questions:
1. Tell what each of the following terms means as it relates to stories: characters, setting, plot.
2. What is meant by the theme that a story may contain?
3. Who are the main characters in "A Flying Tackle"?
4. What is the setting for "An Impossible Choice"?
5. What would you say to explain briefly the plot of "Keplik, the Match Man"?
6. What do you think the theme of "The Cherub and My Sainted Grandmother" is?

On your own

On a sheet of paper, write the number of each question that follows and then your answer to it. If you cannot remember the right part of any one of the stories, you may look at it again to refresh your memory.

1. Who is the main character and who are the minor characters in "A Horse for Reg"?
2. Who is the main character and who are the minor characters in "The Great Penobscot Raid"?
3. What is the setting for "Federico Discovers the Sea"?
4. What is the setting for "Open Gate to Freedom"?
5. What is the plot of the story "A Secret for Two"?

Checking your work

If you are asked to do so, read aloud one or more of your answers. Listen while other boys and girls read their answers, and compare your answers with theirs. If you made a mistake in any of your answers, find out why it is a mistake.

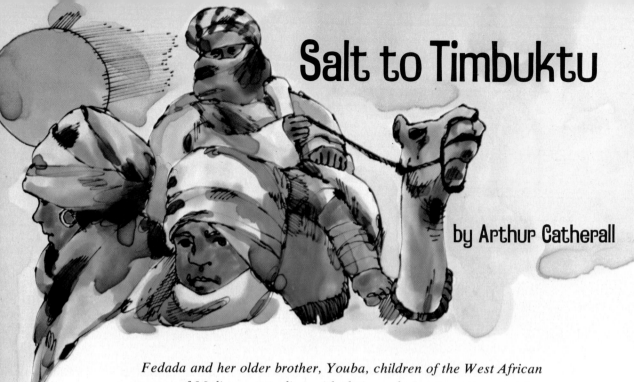

Salt to Timbuktu

by Arthur Catherall

Fedada and her older brother, Youba, children of the West African country of Mali, are traveling with their uncle in a caravan carrying salt across the desert from Taoudenni to Timbuktu. Their camel, Tamerouelt, has recently given birth to a baby, whom the delighted children named Amr'r. A kind old man called Omar El Hassim, also in the caravan, helps them strengthen Amr'r's legs so that the little camel can keep up with the caravan, and Omar treats Amr'r's cut foot.

Then desert raiders attack, and in the confusion the two children, the old man, and their camels become separated from the caravan and are left behind in the desert with little food and water. To make matters worse, Omar and the camel Tamerouelt have been wounded in the raid. Now the little group faces the almost impossible task of catching up with the caravan or finding the next water hole by themselves.

All three sat staring at each other until Fedada abruptly rose to her feet. "I shall light a small fire and make tea with the water we have left," she said briskly to Omar. "While the water is boiling, I will look to your wound. My brother can search where the caravan was resting, in case someone has left behind a gerba of water or anything else that might be useful. Is that a good idea?"

Youba looked in surprise at his sister. Among desert people, it was not the custom for girls to make suggestions when important things

502

were being spoken of. Perhaps the old man would think Fedada impudent. He was relieved when Omar El Hassim chuckled approvingly and said, "Boy, you have a sister who talks with wisdom. Do you agree with what she says?"

Youba could only nod, and he wandered off to search each of the tiny campsites in case something of value had been left behind. Fedada examined the bullet wound in Omar El Hassim's leg. They could not spare water to wash the wound, but when she looked inquiringly at the old man, he said, "It is a clean wound. The bullet went right through. Bind it with a rag. In a week or ten days it will have healed."

Since he did not seem too worried about it, Fedada did as he suggested, tearing a strip of cloth from the bottom of her dress to use as a bandage. Then she lit a fire and carefully drained every drop of water from the gerba into their kettle. She was dismayed to discover how little water they had.

By the time the tea had been made, Youba was back. He carried a gerba, a small sack of millet, some dates, and a bundle of feed for their camels. As he laid the gerba down, he said triumphantly,

"We are lucky. There is enough water here for another day, perhaps even longer if we are careful."

He sat down and watched Fedada pour the tea. After they had finished drinking, and Fedada had carefully cleaned the glasses with sand, Youba said, "I think we should start south, now, sir. If we follow the tracks of the caravan, they will surely lead us to the next water hole. Since you are injured and cannot walk, we will put our food and the gerba on Tamerouelt, which my sister will ride. You can ride your own camel. I will walk. It will be no hardship, for I have walked since we left Taoudenni."

"And my salt?" the old man asked. "What of that? By good fortune, the raiders must have thought it not worth halting for my poor baggage. Yet those six blocks are all I have. They cannot be left behind."

"The salt must be left behind, sir," Youba said firmly. "We have only the two camels. Can your camel carry you *and* the salt? It would be too much, and I know Tamerouelt cannot carry your salt and my sister."

"But I could walk," Fedada suggested.

"No. Even if you walked, the salt would be too heavy for her. Not only is she limping, but she is also feeding Amr'r. You could not expect her to have the strength to do so many things. The salt must be left."

"No! That will be left behind only if I stay behind." There was no gentleness in Omar El Hassim's voice. "If I had a son in Timbuktu who would offer me a corner in his house and give me food, then I would leave the salt. But there is no one to welcome me to the place where I was born. If I leave my salt behind—then I shall return to Timbuktu a penniless beggar. I could not face a life of sitting at the street corner, begging from those who pass by."

"But we can take you only if you ride Tamerouelt and your own camel carries the salt," Youba protested. "That would mean my sister would have to walk. If we do this, we may never reach the next water hole. You must know, sir, that even a little wind can blow sand into footprints. Tracks that are a day or so old can be lost forever. Is it not better to leave the salt than stay here to die?"

Omar El Hassim turned to Fedada, and there was a wishful

note in his voice when he said, "Fedada, you will not leave me, I know. I have seen goodness in your eyes from the first day I looked on you. Speak to your brother. We must believe that the tracks to the water hole will remain to guide us. You will not leave an old man to die alone in this sand."

Fedada turned to her brother, but Youba was angry. He grabbed the riding saddle lying by the side of Tamerouelt and swung it onto the camel's creamy back. Without looking at the old man, he said angrily, "There are three laws for those who walk the desert, sir. One—you must see that your camel is strong and drinks his fill of water before you leave the oasis. The second law is that you must carry a full gerba for yourself; and the third is that you must know where the next water hole lies. We cannot keep any of those laws. We have one good camel, and three people. If I had not found this gerba, we would have no water at all now. And most important, we do not know where the next water hole lies."

"But if we follow the tracks of the caravan," Fedada urged, "they will lead us to water."

"We might do that if we leave the six slabs of salt behind," Youba said sharply. "For then you could ride Tamerouelt—and you are not heavy. Omar El Hassim could ride his camel, and so we might hurry, before the wind rises and wipes out the tracks."

"Then you will not take me," the old man said gently.

"Only a fool would take you!" The anger in Youba's voice made it rise almost to a shout. He was going to say more, but his glance rested for a second on Amr'r. He was feeding, eagerly taking in his mother's rich milk. Then Youba remembered how much Omar El Hassim had done for the baby camel. He had saved Amr'r not once but several times.

Suddenly Youba was ashamed. Turning to the old man, he said, "Sir, perhaps I am a fool, but I cannot leave you here. Come, my sister, help me lift him on Tamerouelt's back. It means you will have to walk all the time."

"I can do that," Fedada said. "It is best to do, my brother; I know we will not be sorry."

They helped Omar El Hassim onto Tamerouelt, then loaded the six slabs of salt onto the old man's camel. It was a mangy-looking beast, and twice it tried to bite Youba as he tightened the ropes that held the slabs of salt in place.

"Strike it hard on the nose," the old man suggested. "That is the way to show you are its master."

Youba grunted, but he did not strike the camel. He called both beasts to their feet, and the march south began. They passed a place where vultures were feeding on one of the salt camels that had died from a stray bullet. Fedada screwed up her face in disgust as the horrible-looking birds of prey flapped noisily into the air, only to return to their feasting as soon as the two adult camels and little Amr'r had gone by.

Through the rest of the sun-scorched day, they walked steadily south. Youba had to slow down Omar's camel, for Tamerouelt was limping badly and could not keep up. Little Amr'r, too, needed attention. The rag on his injured foot kept working loose, and Fedada grew quite expert at re-tying it.

Only Omar's big, raw-boned working camel protested when they stopped to allow Amr'r to feed. And once that salt-laden beast had flopped to the sand, he

did not want to get up again. It was slow going all day, and their speed was less than two miles an hour.

Toward sundown, when they were almost too weary to continue, there was a sudden gust of hot wind that stirred up a fog of sand for a minute or so. The wind died down almost at once, but it made Fedada, Youba, and Omar El Hassim turn and look worriedly to the east.

They had left the sand dunes behind more than an hour earlier and were now crossing an almost flat plain. Winds had scoured most of the sand away, and they were marching across yellow earth, baked hard by the heat. Only in the hollows was there any sand, and they had to watch every patch of it for the footprints of the caravan. On the hard yellow earth, it was impossible to see tracks of any kind.

Two minutes after the first gust of wind, a second came and swirled sand about. This gust lasted longer than the other. Omar El Hassim groaned. Youba shot a quick glance at his sister, but he said nothing.

It was Fedada who said what the other two were thinking, "My brother, had we not better unload the camels and make ready? There will be more wind, and maybe a real sandstorm."

"Perhaps we could hurry and get ahead of the wind," Omar suggested. "Men who cross the desert regularly tell me that the sandstorms are sometimes only a few miles wide."

His suggestion brought a sad laugh from Youba, who asked, "Can we fly like the vultures, sir? Can we make Tamerouelt walk quicker? She is a brave one to walk at all. Little Amr'r, too, limps as badly as his mother.

And my sister is very tired—though she pretends not to be. We cannot hurry, so we must stop and unload. This place will do as well as any other. See, the wind is coming even now."

He pointed to what looked like a wall of smoke in the distance.

Calling the camels to kneel, they unloaded the salt and built the six slabs into a wall. Together they helped Omar El Hassim behind the shelter the slabs made. While Fedada was scooping a comfortable place for herself behind the old man, Youba haltered the two camels. He did not halter Amr'r. The young camel would not leave his mother; of that he was sure.

By the time Youba had finished, the wind was blowing in savage gusts, driving before it a fog of gritty sand. No one could have stood for long in that wind-blasted yellow fog. It was impossible to see more than a dozen yards, and the sand would have peeled the skin from a person's face in minutes.

The camels were kneeling, their long necks outstretched, their nostrils closed to the merest slits so that they could take in air, but not sand. Youba hurriedly threw himself down by his sister and drew his cloak over his head.

Howling like a demon, the wind blew at hurricane speed for minutes on end, then would die down to no more than a whisper. In those quiet moments it seemed as if it had lost its strength, but then, with a scream, it would come again, sand-laden and hot. The sand spread everywhere. Despite the cloaks with which they covered their faces, Omar, Fedada, and Youba had sand on their eyelids, their lips, even in their nostrils.

The wind built sand up against the protecting salt slabs, then spilled over the top. It covered all of them with a layer several inches thick, adding to their discomfort; it was like a covering of blankets, making them hotter and hotter.

Fedada soon drifted off into an uneasy sleep, but Youba could not sleep. A nagging doubt about the decision to bring Omar El Hassim along kept bothering him. The old man had helped them with Amr'r, but should they have risked their lives for Omar? If they had not agreed to carry the salt, as well as its owner, they might have covered much more distance—might even have escaped the path of the sandstorm. If they had, they could have continued walking through the night and might have caught up with the caravan. Youba was sick

508

with worry. They seemed to have done so many wrong things.

Of one thing he was certain: They were very short of water, and after a sandstorm the wells were sometimes covered over. Then, only someone who had spent a lifetime crossing and recrossing the desert could hope to find water.

Despite his fears, Youba could not keep awake after an hour or so. The wind did not sound so wild now that they were covered by a layer of sand, and he fell into a doze. When he awoke a few hours later, his heart was beating fast, and he had a feeling there was some terrible danger near.

Taut nerved, and with every muscle tense in case he had to leap up and run for his life, he lay and listened. Only after a few minutes did he realize that he had wakened in terror because of the silence. The wind had dropped. Under the drifted sand he could not hear even a whisper.

Shaking himself clear of the sand, he blinked at the blue sky above him. The night had gone and the day was at least an hour old. The desert was as quiet as it usually was, with not a breath of wind moving. Wiping sand from his eyelashes, Youba looked south.

When he had looked in that direction just before the sandstorm began, the way ahead had been flat, yellow earth with, here and there, patches of soft sand, broken by the footprints of people and camels—showing the way the caravan had gone.

It was different now. The hard-baked, yellowish earth was covered by millions of tiny ripples of sand. They stretched ahead like the waves of an ocean, and there was not a footprint of any kind to be seen. The tracks they had been following, their guide to the next water hole, had all disappeared. The sand had filled them in, then covered them over. The trail had vanished.

Slowly, Youba turned and scraped away the sand that covered Fedada. She woke and sat up, brushing yellow dust from her face, then pushing back her head covering so that she could shake some of the fine sand from her hair.

"What now, my brother?" she asked, rising, then kneeling again to scrape the covering of sand from Omar El Hassim. "Shall we drink tea before we move on?"

Youba stared south for a few moments before replying. Then he said quietly, "We can drink tea, my sister, but where we shall move to from here I do not know. Look at the way we have to go. There is no track of any kind. The sand has covered everything."

Fedada looked, and there was a quiver in her voice when she said bravely, "I will light a fire while you waken the old man. He will know. He is old, and years bring wisdom."

"I can waken him," Youba agreed, "and he will be glad of tea; but I do not think he can help us. If you remember, he said he had not been over this desert since he was a boy. How can he know where the wells are? He will be like a blind beggar, leading other blind beggars."

Fedada bent over and looked at the old man. His eyelids were fluttering a little, and she waited for him to waken. Then, to her surprise, one eye opened a fraction, but it closed again.

Fedada moved back a few paces but never took her eyes off the old man. She had a sudden feeling that he was awake but was pretending to be asleep. Why he should do this she could not imagine; but after a few moments she thought she had guessed the answer. He must be trying to give her and Youba a chance to drink their tea and then leave him.

Turning to her brother, she said, "Youba, waken him. We must not stay here any longer than necessary. We should march before the heat becomes greater than we can bear."

Youba slipped to his knees beside the old man and began shaking him, first gently, then more vigorously. Fedada watched Omar El Hassim's face all the time. She saw his lips tighten, and she was sure then that he was only pretending to be asleep.

Youba, however, could get no response at all from the old man. Finally the boy rose, saying sadly, "I think he is dying, Fedada. Perhaps we should save his two glasses of tea. Later we shall need every drop of liquid that we can get. And while he lies there that way, he cannot drink."

"No, he is not dying, my brother," Fedada said urgently. "He is just pretending, so that we will use the water and leave him to die. Lift him up. Once the tea is at his lips, he will drink. I know he will."

A few moments later Omar El Hassim was lifted into a sitting position. His eyes remained closed, though Youba could feel the muscles of the old man's upper arms tense, proving that he was not asleep.

Fedada put the glass of hot sweet tea to his mouth. The old man drew back as if it were poison, but Fedada moved the glass to his mouth again and tilted it so that the tea was wetting his lips.

She had guessed right. That first taste of tea was a strong temptation to Omar. Lifting a hand, he steadied the glass and gulped the hot liquid.

His eyes opened, and he looked at Youba and Fedada. He did not swallow the tea but held it in his mouth, enjoying the sweetness and the wetness on his parched tongue. It was a beautiful feeling, but he had to swallow, and a moment later the tea was gone.

"There is more," Youba urged, nodding to his sister to put the glass to the old man's lips again. "It will give you strength."

Omar shook his head sadly.

"Old men do not need to drink tea as younger ones do. Already I feel better. I have been thinking. . . ." He stopped talking when Fedada pressed the glass to his lips again. Giving her a smile, he finished what was left of the tea.

"That was good, but I must drink no more. I have something important to say."

"There is another glass of tea for you," Fedada urged, but Omar shook his head and waved a hand to keep her from picking up the little kettle.

"Listen to me, both of you. I know we are lost and that there is very little water. I know, too, that a limping camel walks too slowly. Take my camel and come back for me when you have found water."

Youba gave Fedada a long, questioning look, but she shook her head "No."

Rising, Youba went to get Tamerouelt and ordered the camel to kneel. Then, with Fedada helping him, the boy lifted the old man onto the camel's back.

Fedada gave Omar six dates, and apologized because she could not give him more. "We shall eat again the next time we stop," she promised.

Omar put a date into his mouth and began to chew. Now that he was back in the saddle, he wanted to live. The glass of tea had given him a little strength, and more courage. To Youba he said, "That camel of mine I bought from a man who had walked it from Timbuktu to Taoudenni for seven years. Twice each year he carried salt on the beast. It must know the way to the water holes. Let it lead."

Fedada's eyes brightened, but clouded again when Youba reminded the old man, "You are forgetting, sir, that your camel is without a rider now and that a camel goes forward only when it has a rider or when a man pulls on its lead rope. I can lead the camel toward the midday sun, for I know Timbuktu lies that way. Whether I can find the next well, I cannot know."

Omar nodded in agreement, but despite his exhaustion and the pain of his wound, he managed a little smile as he said, "When a camel needs water, my son, neither a rider nor a lead rope is necessary. If he is really thirsty, and if he knows where the water hole lies—he will walk."

Through the blistering heat they marched, halting at midday while Amr'r drank of his mother's milk. It was best to stop during the worst heat of the day. Youba did what he could to see that Omar El Hassim rested.

While Fedada lit a small fire and made some tea, using water from the gerba her brother had found,

Omar insisted on first massaging Amr'r's legs, then examining the injured foot.

After the fiercest heat of the day they continued south, and the sun seemed to dry up every drop of moisture from their bodies. They tried to eat a few dates, but swallowing was difficult.

Twice during that time, Youba almost shrieked with joy at the sight of what he thought was a lake with palm trees ahead. But each time he realized within seconds that it was only a mirage— and it faded very quickly.

Then, toward the end of the afternoon, he swung around at a call from his sister. He was just in time to help Fedada prevent Omar El Hassim from falling heavily from the saddle. Gently they eased the old man to the ground. His eyes were closed, and he had apparently fainted.

They wet his lips with a few drops of their precious water, and after a minute or so, he recovered enough to open his eyes, look up at them, and whisper, "It is the leg wound. You will have to leave me. Each time my leg strikes against the camel's side, it hurts terribly. You must go on and come back after you have found water."

"We cannot leave you, sir," Youba protested. "We may not find water until tomorrow. Then, how would we find you? If we stay here for a little while—"

"No, you must go now," Omar insisted. "As for finding me, if you leave some firewood, I will light a little fire when darkness comes. The desert is very flat here, and a fire will be seen for miles. Take my camel, but leave the salt. The camel will walk better with you than with me, for I am heavier than you."

"Sir, we cannot go on without you!" Fedada exclaimed.

Youba added his reason why they could not do as the old man suggested: "If we leave you, and you light a fire, it might be seen by the raiders."

Omar shook his head. "If the raiders came, they would find nothing worth stealing. I have no jewels. You must go. I am an old man, old enough to be your grandfather. Were you not taught that it is not polite to disobey the wishes of an old man?"

"We were taught that, sir," Fedada agreed, "but it would not be right to leave you. If you were our grandfather—would we leave you?"

"How happy I would be if I had grandchildren like you," Omar said sadly. Then, brightening, he went on, "I was wrong when I insisted that we should bring along my salt. It has delayed us. But now I am going to insist that you go. Those who help themselves . . . Aih! See, the camels are on their way to water. Even they know that time is too precious to waste. Follow them, or it will be too late."

Fedada and Youba turned in sudden panic at the old man's words, and Youba scrambled to his feet. Omar was right. His big, scrawny-looking camel was striding south, and because Tamerouelt's lead rope was tied to him, she had to follow. Little Amr'r was trotting obediently behind his mother. The three camels were already some distance away.

Yelling for them to halt, Youba began to run; but he was tired, and the camels had been walking for several minutes. After a minute the boy had to stop. He was weaker than he had imagined, and the camels were walking briskly, even the lame Tamerouelt and the slightly limping Amr'r.

Returning to where Fedada was kneeling by Omar, Youba agreed they would have to leave him. They gave him matches and some sticks, then turned without a word to follow their camels.

For three miles they struggled to catch up, but hardly gained a yard. Then the camels began to increase their lead. Finally brother and sister were forced to depend on the camel tracks. Tired and despairing, they walked on until they came to the beginning of a gorge. Its rocky sides were already beginning to cast long shadows, for the sun was dropping toward the western horizon. In less than an hour night would be on them.

Youba and Fedada paused at the entrance to the gorge, looking down. It was as if some long-dead giant had scooped a deep channel from the desert itself. The rocky walls were pink, and at the top where the rays of the setting sun lit them, they glowed as if on fire. The entrance was like the neck of a bottle, but inside, the gorge widened quickly. Large rocks littered its floor, and there was a strange eeriness about the place.

Fedada clutched at her brother's sleeve as Youba pointed to camel tracks between the rocks. Putting their fears aside, the two of them walked into the gorge. They could feel cool air moving past them, here where the sun could not reach. Then, farther down where the gorge was widest, they saw the three camels, and at once their fears were forgotten.

Tamerouelt and the other camel were kneeling by a rocky pool, their long necks outstretched, while little Amr'r stood patiently by his mother's side. He knew that when she had drunk her fill, there would be rich milk for him.

"They are drinking," Fedada whispered. "My brother, they have found water."

Youba and Fedada walked slowly forward. The camels had done it, Youba thought. They had found water. As soon as he and his sister had satisfied their own thirsts and refilled the almost empty gerba, they could go back for Omar El Hassim. Neither he nor Fedada spoke, for they were too filled with joy.

Although Fedada and Youba found water, their troubles were far from over. You can find out what else happens to them if you read the book CAMEL CARAVAN *by Arthur Catherall.*

AUTHOR

Arthur Catherall, who was born in England, remembers writing his first story at the age of eight. Now he has had over a thousand stories and more than a hundred books published in a number of countries. In search of exciting things to write about, he has traveled to many parts of the world.

Mr. Catherall has sailed on small trawlers in the Arctic and Atlantic Oceans, traveled in the Far East, and walked across Norway, Sweden, and Finland. Before writing *Camel Caravan*, he crossed the Atlas Mountains to get to the Sahara Desert, and he knows what it is like to be very thirsty and have an empty water bottle.

He finds that being a good listener has helped him to be a writer as much as his adventures have helped him.

Mr. Catherall enjoys climbing, camping, and sailing. When he is not traveling, he lives in Lancashire, England.

Camels: Ships of the Desert
by Roger Caras

The two-humped camel, or Bactrian camel, comes from Central Asia. It stands about six feet at the shoulder and weighs as much as three-quarters of a ton. Not quite so tall as its one-humped cousin, or dromedary, nor quite so speedy, it is more gentle and much easier to ride.

There are still small groups of wild Bactrian camels left in remote regions, but there are probably many more in captivity than in the wild. The Bactrian camel is becoming a vanishing animal.

The camel that is used by the desert people of Africa is the dromedary. There probably are not any wild dromedaries left except those that have escaped from their owners. Originally, they probably came from Arabia, but they have been transported all over the world. They are used in Australia and were once used in the American Southwest, where wonderful legends grew up about them.

The story that camels can store huge quantities of water in their stomachs is not true. Although they can last without water for longer periods of time than most animals, they certainly cannot go without it for very long. After a few days, they start to lose both weight and strength rapidly. If they are without enough food for long, their humps get soft and start to droop.

Camels have been called "ships of the desert" because, like ships, they are used to carry cargo. That is so, but there is another way in which they seem like ships. They roll fiercely as they move along, and if you happen to be riding one, it is quite possible that you will get terribly seasick—many, many miles from the nearest sea.

The dromedary is not very pleasant. When it is in a bad mood, it has the habit of spitting at the nearest person, and it might bite the person as well.

Despite their nasty manners, the dromedaries are very useful and are good companions to have on a desert crossing. They will eat kinds of plants that other animals could not possibly live on. They will drink any kind of water, even salt water, will carry great loads over long distances, and will tolerate terrible weather.

MATT HENSON: A TRUE EXPLORER

by Pat Robbins

Often children from very poor families grow up with a desire for adventure that takes them to far places. A few come home to honor and glory. Many—like Columbus—die poor and must wait for history books to bring them fame.

Such a man was Matt Henson. His name often comes up when explorers gather, but not too many young people know about him.

A year after the Civil War ended, a baby was born in Charles County, Maryland, on a farm called Nanjemoy. The parents, former slaves, named the boy Matthew Alexander Henson.

Matthew left the farm at the age of eleven for Washington, D.C., where he lived with an aunt, worked, and went to school. Two years later he walked to Baltimore and shipped as a cabin boy on a schooner bound for China. For five salty years Matt tasted adventure. Back home and settled into a porter's job in a Washington hat shop, he probably found life dull.

Then one day a Navy lieutenant came into the shop. The two men talked, perhaps of far places. The lieutenant saw something special in the porter and hired him for a surveying job in Nicaragua. The lieutenant was Robert E. Peary, who was to become Admiral Peary, one of the world's greatest explorers.

For twenty years, Henson shared the thrills and dangers of seven Arctic expeditions as Peary tried again and again to reach the North Pole. The former Maryland farm boy learned to blaze a trail, handle sled dogs, build igloos and sleds, and speak many Eskimo languages.

Eskimos called him *Marri Palook*, which means "dear little Matthew." Peary called him "my most valuable companion."

In April, 1909, Peary made his famous last dash to the Pole. The party had come within 133 miles of their goal, but a spring thaw was closing in fast. A small group would have to race over cracking ice. Peary chose Henson and four Eskimos, Ootah, Ooqueah, Seegloo, and Egingwah, to go with him.

As Henson later described it: "Peary said we'd reached the do-or-die part. And really you didn't know whether you'd get back or not. I decided to take a chance. Of course, I went up there to stick with him."

Henson took charge of one dog team and broke trail. Peary followed. On April 6, they reached the top of the world and planted an American flag. Henson led the Eskimos in three rousing cheers.

Peary came home to fame, but Henson lived most of his eighty-eight years unknown, working as a parking-lot attendant and then as a customs clerk. Toward the end of his life, he began to receive some attention. He was made an

honorary member of the Explorers Club. He received medals from the government and learned societies. He was invited to visit the White House. Now a tablet in the Maryland State House honors him as "Co-Discoverer of the North Pole."

Henson never became bitter over his lack of fame, perhaps because he had the outlook of a true explorer. Peary once said that true explorers work not for any hope of rewards or honor, but because the thing they have set themselves to do is part of their very being.

SKILL LESSON

RECOGNIZING ELEMENTS
OF AUTHOR'S STYLE

You know that the characters in a story are one of the important story elements. Have you noticed how an author tells you what kind of person a character is? The author may describe the character fully for you, or the author may give you clues to a character's personality through what the character says or does. For instance, if a character is described as always frowning, the frowns may be a clue that he or she is a worrier. Different authors use different ways of showing a character's personality. These are the ways the author has of building **character development**.

One of the things Evelyn Sibley Lampman wants you to know about Shad, the main character of "Indian Boy Joins Sentinel Staff," is that he is hard working and reliable. But she does not simply say that about him. Instead, she uses different ways to provide character development for Shad. First, she has Mrs. Hicks say, "It's high time somebody but me sees what a good, dependable worker Shad is." The author helps you see what a good worker Shad is through the conversation of a minor character. After Shad discovers that he needs to know the alphabet to keep his job, he says, "I'll try hard. . . . I promise to work at it." Then he thinks that "Somehow, some way, he had to learn. . . ." What do Shad's thoughts tell you about him? Having told you what another character thinks of

Shad and what Shad thinks, Ms. Lampman shows you how hard he is willing to work by telling how he concentrates at every chance on learning the alphabet. By using these different ways to show Shad's character, the author helps you understand Shad better and causes you to care about what happens to him. Character development is one of the very important elements of an author's style—his or her individual way of writing.

Authors use other elements of style to give you important information in a story. Armstrong Sperry tells you why Mafatu, the main character of "Call It Courage," is afraid by using a **flashback**. A flashback interrupts a story to tell you something that happened before the events in the story or to give you background information. By using flashbacks, an author can give you facts that help you understand the feelings or actions of a character in the main part of the story. In "Call It Courage," you learn through a flashback that when Mafatu was a small child, he and his mother were swept out to sea and caught in a storm. His mother saved him, but she died. What does this flashback tell you about Mafatu's feelings? The flashback not only tells you why Mafatu is afraid of the sea, but it also tells you something else that is important to the story: that the sea can be very dangerous.

Authors often use **sensory words** as an element of style in a story to help you hear, see, feel, smell, or taste the same things

that the characters do. Such words can make a story seem very real. In "Open Gate to Freedom," László Hámori draws you into the story by using sensory words. You hear with Latsi how the cornstalks "rustled" and "crackled . . . like thunder" as he moved through the cornfield. You see with him the "dazzling searchlight" and the "flood of light" that hunted for him. You feel with him the coarse lumps of earth that meant he had reached the minefield, and you feel his heart pound or thump and his knees tremble. Can you think of other sensory words that the author used? Having shared Latsi's experiences through sensory words, you are able to imagine more clearly his relief when he finally reaches freedom.

Authors use many elements of style to make their stories interesting. Being aware of some of these elements will help you find greater enjoyment in reading and help you understand better what you read.

Discussion

Help your class answer each of the following questions:
1. What is meant by an author's style?
2. What are some elements of an author's style?
3. What are some ways an author develops characters?
4. Why does an author use a flashback?
5. How do sensory words help you?

On your own

On a sheet of paper, write the number of each question that follows and then your answer to it:

1. What is the part of "A Flying Tackle" from the last para-graph on page 243 through the second complete paragraph in the second column on page 248 called?

2. What do you learn from those pages about Maria's reasons for wanting to rescue the mining engineer herself?

3. What are some sensory words on page 326 of "Call It Courage" that help you see, hear, and feel what Mafatu did as he left his home island?

4. Reread pages 415–417. How does the author of the story show that Miss Carmody is a good coach?

Checking your work

If you are asked to do so, read aloud one or more of your answers. Listen while other boys and girls read their answers, and compare your answers with theirs. If you made a mistake in any of your answers, find out why it is a mistake.

THE LITTLE LIZARD'S SORROW

by Vo-Dinh

There is in Viet-Nam a certain species of small lizard only three inches long with webbed feet and a short, round head. They are often seen indoors, running swiftly on the ceiling or walls, making little snapping cries that sound like "Tssst . . . tssst!" Suppose that you drop an egg on the kitchen floor; the kind of sound you would make then, with the tip of your. tongue between your teeth, is like the cry of these harmless, funny little lizards—sounds of mild sorrow, of genuine shock but somehow humorous regret, that seem to say,"Oh, if only I had been . . . If only I had known . . . Oh, what a pity, what a pity . . . Tssst! Tssst!"

There was once a very rich man whose house was immense and filled with treasures. His land was so extensive that, as the Viet-Namese say, "Cranes fly over it with outstretched wings," for cranes do so only over very long [...] Wealth breeding van- [...] he rich man's greatest [...] vas beating other rich [...] game he himself had invented. One player would announce one of his rare possessions; the other would counter the challenge by saying that he, too —if he really did—owned such a treasure. "A stable of fifty buffalos," one man would say. The other would reply, "Yes, I also have fifty of them." It was then his turn to announce, "I sleep in an all-teak bed encrusted with mother-of-pearl." The first player would lose if he slept on simple cherry planks!

One day, a stranger came to the rich man's house. Judging from his appearance, the gatekeeper did not doubt that the visitor was a madman. He wanted, he said, to play the famous game with the mansion's master. Yet, dressed in clothes that looked as if they had been mended hundreds of times and wearing broken straw sandals, the stranger appeared to be anything but a wealthy man. Moreover, his face was gaunt and pale as if he had not had a good meal in days. But there was such proud, quiet dignity to the stranger that the servant did not dare shut the gates in his face. Instead, he meekly went to inform his master of the unlikely visitor's presence. Intrigued, the man ordered that the pauper be ushered in.

Trying to conceal his curiosity and his surprise, the rich man offered his visitor the very best chair and served him hot, perfumed tea.

"Well, stranger, is it true that you have come here to play a game of riches with me?" he began inquiringly.

The visitor was apparently unimpressed by the rich surroundings, giving them only a passing, casual look. Perfectly at ease, sipping his tea from a rare porcelain cup, he answered in a quiet though self-assured voice, "Yes, sir, that is if you, too, so wish."

"Naturally . . . naturally." The rich man raised his hand in a sweeping motion. "But, may I ask, with your permission, where you reside and what is your honorable occupation?"

The stranger was amused. "Sir, would you gain any to know about these? I came here simply to play your game; only, I have two conditions, if you are so generous as to allow them."

"By all means! Pray, tell me what they are," the rich man readily inquired.

The visitor sat farther back on the brocaded chair, his voice soft and confidential. "Well, here they are. A game is no fun if the winner does not win anything and the loser does not lose anything. Therefore, I would suggest that if I win, I would take everything in your possession — your lands, your stables, your servants, your house and everything contained in it. But if you win—" Here the stranger paused, his eyes narrowed ever so slightly, full of humorous malice, "If you win, you would become the owner of everything that belongs to me." The stranger paused again. "What belongs to me, sir, you will have no idea of. I am one of the most fortunate men alive, sir. . . . And besides that," he added, "I would remain in this house to serve you the rest of my life."

For a long moment, the rich man sat back in silence. Another long moment went by; then the rich man spoke: "That's agreed. But, please tell me your other condition."

Eyes dreamy, the stranger looked out of the window. "My second condition, sir, is not so much a condition as a request. I hope you would not mind giving me, a visitor, an edge over you. May I be allowed to ask the first question?"

The rich man thought for a long second, then said, "That is also agreed. Let's begin."

"Do I really understand that you have agreed to both my conditions?" the stranger asked thoughtfully.

Something in the visitor's manner and voice hurt the rich man's pride. He was ready to stake his very life on this game that he himself had created. There was no way out. "Yes," he said. "Yes, indeed I have. Now tell me, please, what do you have that I have not got?" The stranger smiled. Reaching to his feet, he took up his traveling bag, a coarse cotton square tied together by the four ends. Opening it slowly, ceremoniously, he took out an

object and handed it to his host without a word. It was an empty half of a coconut shell, old and chipped, the kind poor people use as a container to drink water from.

"A coconut-shell cup!" the rich man exclaimed. One could not know whether he was merely amused or completely shattered.

"Yes, sir, a coconut-shell cup. A *chipped* shell cup. I use it to drink from on my wanderings. I am a wanderer," the visitor said quietly.

Holding the shell between his thumb and his forefinger and looking as if he had never seen such an object before, the rich man interrupted, "But, but you don't mean that I do not have a thing like this?"

"No, sir, you have not. How could you?" the stranger replied.

Turning the residence upside down, the man and his servants discovered odds and ends of one thousand and one kinds, but they were unable to produce a drinking cup made from a coconut shell. In the servants' quarters, they found a few such cups, but they were all brand new, not chipped. The servants of such a wealthy man would not drink from a chipped cup. Even a beggar would throw it away.

"You see, sir," the stranger said to the rich man once they were again seated across the tea table, "you see, I am a wanderer, as I have said. I am a free man. This cup here is several years old and my only possession besides these poor clothes I have on. If you do not think me too immodest, I would venture that I treasure it more than you do all your collections of fine china. But, from this day, I am the owner and lone master of all that belongs to you."

Having taken possession of the rich man's land, houses, herds and all his other treasures, the stranger began to give them away to the poor and needy people.

Then, one day, taking up his old cotton bag, he left the village and no one ever saw him again.

As for the once rich man, it is believed that he died of grief and regret and was transformed into this small lizard. Curiously, one sees him scurrying about only indoors. Running up and down the walls, crossing the ceiling, staring at people and furniture, he never stops his "Tssst, Tssst." Children are very fond of him, for he looks so harassed, so funny.

But, oh, such sorrow, such regret, such self-pity.

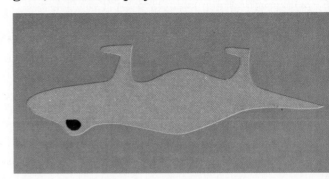

AUTHOR

Vo-Dinh, a Viet-Namese artist and author, was born in Hue, the former imperial capital of Viet-Nam. He was educated in Hue and in Paris, France, and is a professional artist whose work includes paintings, woodcuts, and illustrations for books. Among the books that he has written is a collection of animal folktales from Viet-Nam, *The Toad is the Emperor's Uncle,* from which this story was taken. Of these tales he has said, "By the age of ten, like all other Viet-Namese children, I knew a number of my country's folktales. Now, years later, I still remember them most vividly."

Vo-Dinh now lives in Pennsylvania with his wife and two daughters.

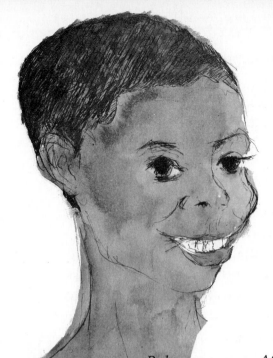

MY FRIEND IN AFRICA

By Frederick Franck

Bolo, a young African boy, had suffered from an ulcer on his foot for several weeks. Then one day Dr. Franck, a dentist at Dr. Albert Schweitzer's hospital in Lambaréné, came through the village where Bolo lived. He saw the ugly sore on the boy's foot and persuaded Bolo and his parents that Bolo should return with him to the hospital. But once at the hospital, Bolo became a problem because he refused to stay in bed.

The story you are about to read is true, and it is just a small part of the book MY FRIEND IN AFRICA. *The story was written and illustrated by Dr. Frederick Franck, the dentist who brought Bolo to the hospital.*

One morning Dr. Schweitzer came into the ward. With him was a tall boy a little older than Bolo. Dr. Schweitzer looked around as if he were searching for someone. "Where is 'the-boy-who-will-not-stay-put?'" he demanded.

Everyone laughed, but Bolo ducked his head. Then, without waiting for an answer, the Old Doctor and the tall boy went straight to Bolo's bed.

The white-haired doctor looked thoughtfully at Bolo.

"What is your great trouble with that bunk?" he asked solemnly.

Bolo said, "There is so much I want to see outside."

"H'm," said the Doctor. "Well, perhaps that is a good enough reason for driving my orderlies crazy." Then he introduced the tall boy at his side. "This boy is Darri. He has come to visit you."

Darri and Bolo smiled at each other. The Old Doctor smiled at them both and went away.

"He has so much to do," Darri said. "All day long someone wants him: doctors and nurses and patients, and visitors, too. People come from over the sea to talk to him and look at the Hospital."

Bolo said, "I like him, and I like the Hospital, but I do not like being a patient. I thought it would be fun, but it isn't. I want to get up and see things."

The older boy sat on the foot of the bed, cross-legged. Bolo sat at the head, hugging his knees.

"I was in bed here a long, long time," Darri said. "I was so sick I didn't mind being in bed. Sometimes I think I was so sick I didn't know *where* I was."

Bolo was startled. He had never seen anyone so sick as that. Then he noticed Darri's arms for the first time. They were so thin they looked like sticks, Bolo thought.

"Was what happened to your arms your sickness?" he asked.

"Yes," said Darri. "But the English doctor here stopped the sickness and saved my life. They said he had to work very hard to make me well."

"Do you feel bad about your arms?" Bolo thought he would feel terrible if they were *his* arms.

The older boy said, "Yes, at first I couldn't do anything with my arms. I couldn't even hold anything in my hands, but now I can. See?" And he picked up a wooden stool and lifted it from one side of the bunk to the other.

Suddenly he scowled so fiercely that Bolo wondered
what was the matter. "You must do what the doctors tell
you, Bolo!" Darri exclaimed. "Don't you want to have a
good leg instead of a bad one?"

"Of course I do!"

"Don't you want to get outside? I could take you all
around the Hospital and show you all the animals. Wouldn't
you like that?"

"Yes, of course," said Bolo. "That is just what I want to
do!"

"Then you must stay on your bunk. I heard the doctors
say your foot will heal if you give it a chance. But when
you get up and move around, you keep it from healing.
You are a silly boy if you keep yourself in here when you
could be getting outside soon!"

It really wasn't long after that when Bolo heard a cheerful
voice saying, "Bolo, you can get up today." What an exciting

announcement! Bolo bounced out of his bunk. Then he bounced back again, fearfully. "Are you sure?"

He was worried because it was his friend the dentist who brought him the good news. "You are not a foot doctor, you are a tooth doctor. Are you sure it is all right for me to get up now?"

Dr. Frederick was certain. "I have checked with all kinds of doctors," he said. "You have been so good that your foot is healing nicely. I will show you how to use a stick to help you walk, and then you may go out. Darri will be here soon to go with you."

"Outdoors, outdoors!" sang Bolo. Never had he wanted anything so much, and never had the world seemed so pleasant. The Hospital was the finest place, and the doctors were the greatest people—in all Africa!

After that happy day, Bolo said two important things to himself every night before he fell asleep. "I love the Hospital. Some day I will be a doctor here." Sometimes he added, "I hope a boy like me could become a doctor. . . ."

He had always taken animals for granted, but here in the Hospital he began to see them in a new way.

Any animal that happened to come to the Hospital, from the jungle or with people, was welcome, and it could stay forever if it wanted to. So there were nearly as many animals about as there were people. The Old Doctor did not take them for granted. He seemed to love the animals just as much as he did people, people of his own family. It made Bolo think.

All the doctors and nurses at the Hospital soon discovered that Bolo had learned to love animals and that animals loved him. Before long, the doctors were calling on Bolo whenever any creature, wild or tame, needed looking after.

"Bolo, watch over that dog Bumble today. I think he is not very well."

"Bolo, don't let Petite, the cat, run around today or she

will hurt her bad foot again. And see that she doesn't tear off the bandage."

"That white-faced monkey has to be fed carefully for a while. Tell Bolo. He'll take good care of the little creature."

Bolo was delighted. He looked after the lively animals, as well as the sick ones. He checked up every morning on the ducks and the chickens, the goats and the sheep, and the pelicans and parrots. He visited the wild boars in their fenced-in yard, and the graceful, soft-eyed antelopes in theirs.

He talked to the tame stork and the sleepy-looking owl that had once been patients and were now pets. He had more than a dozen dogs and cats of all kinds, a young chimpanzee, and a monkey to play with.

He called all of them by name—Mombambra, the stork; Fritzli, the chimp; Tecla, the wild boar; Jackie, the toucan; and all the dogs and cats. Sometimes a little parade went up or down one of the Hospital streets, Bolo with a white-nosed monkey on his shoulder and Fritzli at his heels, grabbing at his ankle with every step. Then a dog or two followed, and perhaps a goat.

When the dogs were not around, a shy young antelope followed Bolo wherever he went. The antelope limped from a broken leg, and Bolo limped because of his healing foot. Bolo would hold out his hand, and the antelope would stop to be petted and stroked by the boy.

The patients and their families and the doctors and nurses were amazed at the sight. People in Africa usually are not so friendly with animals.

Early one morning, Bolo was going to call on the wild boars when he heard a big voice booming his name.

"Bolo! Bolo!"

That was Dr. Schweitzer's voice! Bolo was so surprised he didn't answer. He just stared up the street toward the sound of the voice. What could it mean, the great Doctor,

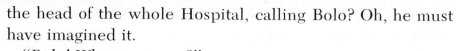

the head of the whole Hospital, calling Bolo? Oh, he must have imagined it.

"Bolo! Where are you?"

Then Bolo believed his ears. He moved faster than he had ever moved before. Half hopping, half hobbling, he hurried up the Hospital street.

There was Dr. Schweitzer outside the Pharmacy, the building where much of the Hospital work was done. With him was the tooth doctor who was already Bolo's great friend, Dr. Frederick from America.

There were a nurse and two men of Bolo's own people. And there was a monkey. No, it was a baby gorilla.

The nurse was holding the little animal, and it was bleeding badly. Dr. Schweitzer and Dr. Frederick were talking angrily about people with guns, and Bolo realized that the little gorilla had been shot.

Bolo's eyes grew wide and his mouth made a big circle. He sucked in his breath when the little gorilla cried out with pain.

Bolo could almost feel what the animal felt. He felt great anger, too, that such a little animal had been hurt.

The gorilla cried again, and Bolo pushed into the group around Dr. Schweitzer.

"There you are, Bolo," said the Doctor. "You are the one who is so good with animals. Come and help me take care of this poor fellow. We must get the bullet out."

Bolo's eyes grew even wider, and for a moment he was frightened.

"I do not . . . I do not know how," he stammered.

"I know how!" said the Old Doctor gruffly. "I will take out the bullet and you will hold the gorilla on the operating table. Then you can care for him afterward. Come now! Be a man! You will see blood more than once in your life. I want you to help me."

With the little gorilla in his arms, the Doctor went off to the operating room in the Pharmacy. Bolo squared his shoulders and followed. "After all, if I want to be a doctor . . ." he mused.

The next day a bandaged gorilla baby sat on Bolo's lap under a palm tree, eating its dinner from a spoon and holding tight to one of Bolo's hands.

People stopped to talk when they saw the pair. "Look. Bolo has a new patient."

Dr. Frederick came by and asked how the patient was doing. "Is he eating well? Let me know if he needs a tooth filled!"

Bolo laughed. "I will. But you can draw a picture of him any time." Dr. Frederick drew pictures when he was not treating people's teeth. Around the Hospital, everyone called him "the-tooth-doctor-who-draws." Bolo thought the drawings were beautiful, especially the drawings of animals.

"I'll give you the first picture I do of your new friend," Dr. Frederick promised. "Have you given him a name, Bolo?"

"I am just giving him one now," said Bolo. "I think I will name him Peter."

"Peter is a funny name for a gorilla!"

"It is a *good* name," Bolo insisted, frowning. "It is just as good as Percival is for a pelican, or Mombambra is for a stork!"

Dr. Frederick laughed. "You are right. It certainly is. Well, Peter seems to like you very much. But what will you do when he grows big? You cannot hold him on your lap then. After he is grown, he could crush your bones with a friendly hug, you know."

Bolo knew that. He had often heard tales of what a huge gorilla could do to a person. Yet Peter could not go back to the jungle if he stayed at the Hospital very long. An animal raised among people does not know how to live in the jungle anymore. It is killed soon by the wilder animals that have always lived there.

"I will think of something to do," Bolo said, "before Peter gets too big to stay here." He stroked the gorilla's head with the back of his hand.

Peter looked very sad and serious, as if he understood the problem.

AUTHOR

In 1959 Dr. Frederick Franck set up a dental clinic for Dr. Albert Schweitzer at Schweitzer's hospital in Lambaréné, Africa. There Dr. Franck and his wife spent three summers treating people who came hundreds of miles for dental care. During that time, Dr. Franck, who is an excellent artist, made hundreds of drawings of the people and things he saw there. He also wrote three books about his experiences in Africa: *African Sketchbook, My Friend in Africa,* and *My Days with Albert Schweitzer.* Dr. Franck and his wife still continue to write to Bolo, the boy you just read about. Bolo went on to study at a college in Africa. Holland-born Dr. Franck has degrees in medicine, dentistry, and art. He now has written sixteen books and devotes all his time to writing, drawing, and art.

HINKY-PINKY

For example:

A.	A skinny young horse is a: *bony*	*pony.*
B.	Alaska is a: *great*	*state.*
C.	The skinny one of two is a: *thin*	*twin.*

Now you finish these:

1.	A seafood platter is a: *fish*	XXXX
2.	A gritty sweet is a: *sandy*	XXXX
3.	A tiny insect is a: *wee*	XXXX
4.	Lucky numbers are: *seven*	XXXX
5.	A great baseball team is a: *fine*	XXXX
6.	A happy dog is a: *jolly*	XXXX
7.	Colored lemonade is a: *pink*	XXXX
8.	A sixth-month satellite is a: *June*	XXXX
9.	A sixty-minute rain is an: *hour*	XXXX

Now try these yourself:

10.	Noah's unlighted boat is a:	XXXX
11.	A happy father is a:	XXXX
12.	A girl from Switzerland is a:	XXXX
13.	Skinny James is:	XXXX

FROM THE WIND IN THE WILLOWS

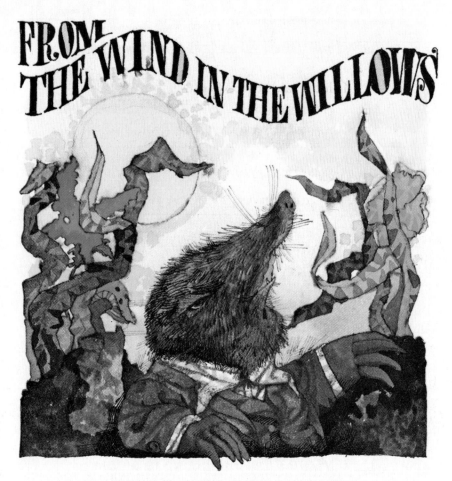

by KENNETH GRAHAME

The mole was very busy cleaning his dark little home which, of course, was deep underground. But something kept calling him from above. It was spring! The Mole could not resist the call so he said, "Hang the spring cleaning!" and dug himself a tunnel up, up, and up until his little snout finally broke through the surface of the ground and into the sunlight. The Mole strolled across the meadows enjoying the sunshine, the birds, the flowers, and all of the other delights of spring. It all seemed too good to be true. Suddenly, he found himself standing on the bank of a river. The Mole who had never seen a river before was quite fascinated by it. As he stood on the bank marveling at the river, he spied a small brown face with whiskers looking at him from a hole in the opposite bank of the river. The face belonged to Water Rat.

THE RIVER BANK

"Hullo, Mole!" said the Water Rat.

"Hullo, Rat!" said the Mole.

"Would you like to come over?" inquired the Rat presently.

"Oh, it's all very well to *talk*," said the Mole, rather pettishly, he being new to a river and riverside life and its ways.

The Rat said nothing, but stooped and unfastened a rope, hauled on it, and then lightly stepped into a little boat which the Mole had not observed. It was painted blue outside and white within, and was just the size for two animals. The Mole's whole heart went out to it at once, even though he did not yet fully understand its uses.

The Rat sculled smartly across and made fast. Then he held up his forepaw as the Mole stepped gingerly down. "Lean on that!" he said. "Now then, step lively!" and the Mole to his surprise and rapture found himself actually seated in the stern of a real boat.

"This has been a wonderful day!" said he, as the Rat shoved off and took to the sculls again. "Do you know, I've never been in a boat before in all my life."

"What?" cried the Rat, open-mouthed. "Never been in a—you never—well, I—what have you been doing, then?"

"Is it so nice as all that?" asked the Mole shyly, though he was quite prepared to believe it as he leaned back in his seat and surveyed the cushions, the oars, the rowlocks, and all the fascinating fittings, and felt the boat sway lightly under him.

"Nice? It's the *only* thing," said the Water Rat solemnly, as he leaned forward for his stroke. "Believe me, my young friend, there is *nothing*—absolutely nothing—half so much worth doing as simply messing about in boats. Simply messing," he went on dreamily, "messing — about — in — boats; messing——"

"Look ahead, Rat!" cried the Mole suddenly.

It was too late. The boat struck the bank full tilt. The dreamer, the joyous oarsman, lay on his back at the bottom of the boat, his heels in the air.

"—about in boats—or *with* boats," the Rat went on composedly, picking himself up with a pleasant laugh. "In or out of 'em, it doesn't matter. Nothing seems really to matter, that's the charm of it. Whether you get away, or whether you don't; whether you arrive at your destination or whether you reach somewhere else, or whether you never get anywhere at all, you're always busy, and you never do anything in particular; and when you've done it, there's always something else to do, and you can do it if you like, but you'd much better not. Look here! If you've really nothing else on hand this morning, supposing we drop down the river together and have a long day of it?"

The Mole waggled his toes from sheer happiness, spread his chest with a sigh of full contentment, and leaned back blissfully into the soft cushions. *"What* a day I'm having!" he said. "Let us start at once!"

"Hold hard a minute, then!" said the Rat. He looped the painter through a ring in his landing-stage, climbed up into his hole above, and after a short interval reappeared staggering under a fat, wicker luncheon basket.

"Shove that under your feet," he observed to the Mole, as he passed it down into the boat. Then he untied the painter and took the sculls again.

"What's inside it?" asked the Mole, wriggling with curiosity.

"There's cold chicken inside it," replied the Rat briefly; "cold-tonguecoldhamcoldbeefpickled-gherkinssaladfrenchrollscresssand-widgespottedmeatgingerbeerlemon-adesodawater——"

"O stop, stop," cried the Mole in ecstasies. "This is too much!"

"Do you really think so?" inquired the Rat seriously. "It's only what I always take on these little excursions, and the other animals are always telling me that I'm a mean beast and cut it *very* fine!"

The Mole never heard a word he was saying. Absorbed in the new life he was entering upon, intoxicated with the sparkle, the ripple, the scents, the sounds, and the sunlight, he trailed a paw in the water and dreamed long waking dreams. The Water Rat, like the good fellow he was, sculled steadily on and forebore to disturb him.

"I like your clothes awfully, old chap," he remarked after some half an hour or so had passed. "I'm going to get a black velvet smoking suit myself someday, as soon as I can afford it."

"I beg your pardon," said the Mole, pulling himself together with an effort. "You must think me very rude; but all of this is so very new

to me. So—this—is—a—River!"

"*The* River," corrected the Rat.

"And you really live by the river? What a jolly life!"

"By it and with it and on it and in it," said the Rat. "It's brother and sister to me, and aunts, and company, and food and drink, and (naturally) washing. It's my world, and I don't want any other. What it hasn't got is not worth having, and what it doesn't know is not worth knowing. Lord! the times we've had together! Whether in winter or summer, spring or autumn, it's always got its fun and its excitements. When the floods are on in February, and my cellars and basement are brimming with drink that's no good to me, and the brown water runs by my best bedroom window; or again when it all drops away and shows patches of mud that smells like plum cake, and the rushes and weeds clog the channels, and I can potter about dry-shod over most of the bed of it and find fresh food to eat, and things careless people have dropped out of boats!"

"But isn't it a bit dull at times?" the Mole ventured to ask. "Just you and the river, and no one else to pass a word with?"

"No one else to—well, I mustn't be hard on you," said the Rat with forbearance. "You're new to it, and of course you don't know. The bank is so crowded nowadays that many people are moving away altogether. O no, it isn't what it used to be, at all. Otters, kingfishers, dabchicks, moorhens, all of them about all day long and always wanting you to *do* something—as if a fellow had no business of his own to attend to!"

"What lies over *there?*" asked the Mole, waving a paw towards a background of woodland that darkly framed the water meadows on one side of the river.

"That? O, that's just the Wild Wood," said the Rat shortly. "We don't go there very much, we river-bankers."

"Aren't they—aren't they very *nice* people in there?" said the Mole a trifle nervously.

"W-e-ll," replied the Rat, "let me see. The squirrels are all right. *And* the rabbits—some of 'em, but rabbits are a mixed lot. And then there's Badger, of course. He lives right there in the heart of it; wouldn't live anywhere else, either, if you paid him to do it. Dear old Badger! Nobody interferes with *him.* They'd better not," he added significantly.

"Why, who *should* interfere with him?" asked the Mole.

"Well, of course—there—are others," explained the Rat in a hesitating sort of way. "Weasels—and stoats—and foxes—and so on. They're all right in a way—I'm very good friends with them—pass the time of day when we meet, and all that—but they break out sometimes, there's no denying it, and then—well, you can't really trust them, and that's the fact."

The Mole knew well that it is quite against animal-etiquette to dwell on possible trouble ahead, or even to allude to it; so he dropped the subject.

"And beyond the Wild Wood again?" he asked. "Where it's all blue and dim, and one sees what may be hills or perhaps they mayn't, and something like the smoke of towns, or is it only cloud drift?"

"Beyond the Wild Wood comes the Wide World," said the Rat. "And that's something that doesn't matter, either to you or me. I've never been there, and I'm never going, nor you either, if you've got any sense at all. Don't ever refer to it again, please. Now then! Here's our backwater at last, where we're going to lunch."

Leaving the main stream, they now passed into what seemed at

first sight like a little landlocked lake. Green turf sloped down to either edge, and brown snaky tree roots gleamed below the surface of the quiet water. Ahead of them the silvery shoulder and foamy tumble of a weir, arm-in-arm with a restless dripping mill wheel that held up in its turn a grey-gabled mill house, filled the air with a soothing murmur of sound, dull and smothery, yet with little clear voices speaking up cheerfully out of it at intervals. It was so very beautiful that the Mole could only hold up both forepaws and gasp, "O my! O my! O my!"

The Rat brought the boat alongside the bank, made her fast, helped the still-awkward Mole safely ashore, and swung out the luncheon basket. The Mole begged as a favor to be allowed to unpack it all by himself. The Rat was very pleased to indulge him, and to sprawl at full length on the grass and rest, while his excited friend shook out the tablecloth and spread it, took out all the mysterious packets one by one, and arranged their contents in due order, still gasping, "O my! O my!" at each fresh revelation. When all was ready, the Rat said, "Now, pitch in, old fellow!" and the Mole was indeed very glad to obey, for he had started his spring-cleaning at a very early hour that morning, as people *will* do, and had not paused for bite or sup; and he had been through a very great deal since that distant time which now seemed so many days ago.

"What are you looking at?" said the Rat presently, when the edge of their hunger was somewhat dulled, and the Mole's eyes were able to wander off the tablecloth a little.

"I am looking," said the Mole, "at a streak of bubbles that I see traveling along the surface of the water. That is a thing that strikes me as funny."

"Bubbles? Oho!" said the Rat, and chirruped cheerily in an inviting sort of way.

A broad glistening muzzle showed itself above the edge of the bank, and the Otter hauled himself out and shook the water from his coat.

"Greedy beggars!" he observed, making for the provender. "Why didn't you invite me, Ratty?"

"This was an impromptu affair," explained the Rat. "By the way — my friend Mr. Mole."

"Proud, I'm sure," said the Otter, and the two animals were friends.

"Such a rumpus everywhere!" continued the Otter. "All the world seems out on the river today. I came up this backwater to try and get a moment's peace, and then stumbled upon you fellows! At least—I beg pardon—I don't exactly mean that, you know."

There was a rustle behind them, proceeding from a hedge wherein last year's leaves still clung thick, and a stripy head, with high shoulders behind it, peered forth on them.

"Come on, old Badger!" shouted the Rat.

The Badger trotted forward a pace or two, then grunted, "H'm! Company," and turned his back and disappeared from view.

"That's *just* the sort of fellow he is!" observed the disappointed Rat. "Simply hates Society! Now we shan't see any more of him today. Well, tell us *who's* out on the river?"

"Toad's out, for one," replied the Otter, "in his brand-new wager-boat, new togs, new everything!"

The two animals looked at each other and laughed.

"Once, it was nothing but sailing," said the Rat. "Then he tired of that and took to punting. Nothing would please him but to punt all day and every day, and a nice mess he made of it. Last year it was house-boating, and we all had to go and stay with him in his houseboat, and pretend we liked it. He was going to spend the rest of his life in a houseboat. It's all the same, whatever he takes up, he gets tired of it, and starts on something fresh."

"Such a good fellow, too," remarked the Otter reflectively, "but no stability—especially in a boat!"

From where they sat they could get a glimpse of the main stream

across the island that separated them. Just then a wager-boat flashed into view, the rower—a short, stout figure—splashing badly and rolling a good deal, but working his hardest. The Rat stood up and hailed him, but Toad—for it was he—shook his head and settled sternly to his work.

"He'll be out of the boat in a minute if he rolls like that," said the Rat, sitting down again.

"Of course he will," chuckled the Otter. "Did I ever tell you that good story about Toad and the lock-keeper? It happened this way. Toad . . ."

An errant Mayfly swerved unsteadily across the current in the excited fashion affected by young bloods of Mayflies seeing life. A swirl of water and a "cloop!" and the Mayfly was visible no more.

Neither was the Otter.

The Mole looked down. The voice was still in his ears, but the turf whereon he had sprawled was clearly vacant. Not an Otter to be seen, as far as the distant horizon.

But again there was a streak of bubbles on the surface of the river.

The Rat hummed a tune, and the Mole recollected that animal-etiquette forbade any sort of comment on the sudden disappearance of one's friends at any moment, for any reason or no reason whatever.

"Well, well," said the Rat, "I suppose we ought to be moving. I wonder which of us had better pack the luncheon basket." He did not speak as if he was frightfully eager for the treat.

"O, please let me," said the Mole. So, of course, the Rat let him.

Packing the basket was not quite such pleasant work as unpacking the basket. It never is. But the Mole was bent on enjoying everything, and although just when he had got the basket packed and strapped up tightly, he saw a plate staring up at him from the grass, and when the job had been done again, the Rat pointed out a fork which anybody ought to have seen, and last of all, behold! the mustard pot, which he had been sitting on without knowing it—still, somehow, the thing got finished at last, without much loss of temper.

The afternoon sun was getting low as the Rat sculled gently homewards in a dreamy mood, murmuring poetry-things over to himself, and not paying much attention to Mole. But the Mole was very full of lunch, and self-satisfaction, and pride, and already quite at home in a boat (so he thought), and was getting a bit restless besides. Presently he said, "Ratty! Please, *I* want to row, now!"

The Rat shook his head with a smile. "Not yet, my young friend," he said. "Wait till you've had a few lessons. It's not so easy as it looks."

The Mole was quiet for a minute or two. But he began to feel more and more jealous of Rat, sculling so strongly and so easily along, and his pride began to whisper that he could do it every bit as well. He jumped up and seized the sculls, so suddenly, that the Rat, who was gazing out over the water and saying more poetry-things to himself, was taken by surprise and fell backwards off his seat with his legs in the air for the second time, while the triumphant Mole took his place and grabbed the sculls with entire confidence.

"Stop it, you *silly* fool!" cried the Rat, from the bottom of the boat. "You can't do it! You'll have us over!"

The Mole flung his sculls back with a flourish, and made a great dig at the water. He missed the surface altogether, his legs flew up above his head, and he found himself lying on the top of the prostrate Rat. Greatly alarmed, he made

a grab at the side of the boat, and the next moment—Sploosh!

Over went the boat, and he found himself struggling in the river.

O my, how cold the water was, and O, how *very* wet it felt. How it sang in his ears as he went down, down, down! How bright and welcome the sun looked as he rose to the surface coughing and spluttering! How black was his despair when he felt himself sinking again! Then a firm paw gripped him by the back of his neck. It was the Rat, and he was evidently laughing—the Mole could *feel* him laughing, right down his arm and through his paw, and so into his—the Mole's—neck.

The Rat got hold of a scull and shoved it under the Mole's arm. Then he did the same by the other side of him and, swimming behind, propelled the helpless animal to shore, hauled him out, and set him down on the bank, a squashy, pulpy lump of misery.

When the Rat had rubbed him down a bit and wrung some of the wet out of him, he said, "Now, then, old fellow! Trot up and down the towing-path as hard as you can till you're warm and dry again, while I dive for the luncheon basket."

So the dismal Mole, wet without and ashamed within, trotted about till he was fairly dry, while the Rat plunged into the water again, recovered the boat, righted her and made her fast, fetched his floating property to shore by degrees, and finally dived successfully for the luncheon basket and struggled to land with it.

When all was ready for a start once more, the Mole, limp and dejected, took his seat in the stern of the boat. As they set off, he said in a low voice, broken with emotion, "Ratty, my generous friend! I am very sorry indeed for my foolish and ungrateful conduct. My heart quite fails me when I think how I might have lost that beautiful luncheon basket. Indeed, I have been a complete fool and I know it. Will you overlook it this once and forgive me, and let things go on as before?"

"That's all right, bless you!" responded the Rat cheerily. "What's a little wet to a Water Rat? I'm more in the water than out of it most days. Don't you think any more about it. Look here! I really think you had better come and stop with me for a little time. It's very plain and rough, you know—not like Toad's house at all—but you haven't seen that yet; still, I can make you comfortable. I'll teach you to row and to swim, and you'll soon be as handy on the water as any of us."

The Mole was so touched by his kind manner of speaking that he could find no voice to answer him, and he had to brush away a tear or two with the back of his paw. But the Rat kindly looked in another direction, and presently the Mole's spirits revived again. He was even able to give some straight back talk to a couple of moorhens who were sniggering to each other about his bedraggled appearance.

When they got home, the Rat made a bright fire in the parlor, and planted the Mole in an armchair in front of it, having fetched down a dressing gown and slippers for him, and told him river stories till suppertime. Very thrilling stories they were, too, to an earthdwelling animal like Mole. Stories about weirs, and sudden floods, and leaping pike, and steamers that flung hard bottles—at least bottles were certainly flung, and *from* steamers, so presumably *by* them; and about herons, and how particular they were whom they spoke to; and about adventures

down drains, and night fishings with Otter, or excursions far afield with Badger. Supper was a most cheerful meal. But very shortly afterwards, a terribly sleepy Mole had to be escorted upstairs by his considerate host, to the best bedroom, where he soon laid his head on his pillow in great peace and contentment, knowing that his new-found friend the River was lapping the sill of his window.

The Mole and the Water Rat became great friends and shared many adventures together with Toad, Badger, and Otter. You can share these adventures with them by reading the rest of Kenneth Grahame's THE WIND IN THE WILLOWS.

ABOUT THE AUTHOR

Kenneth Grahame was born in Edinburgh, Scotland, in 1859. He was brought up in England by his grandmother after losing his parents as a boy. He was a good student and yearned to go to college but, for lack of money, had to go to work instead. From his first position as a clerk, he eventually rose to a high post in London's Bank of England.

Long days at work, plus many hours spent enjoying the outdoors, left Kenneth Grahame little time for writing. However, one of the few books he did write—*The Wind in the Willows*—is considered a masterpiece and made him famous. You have just read part of its opening chapter, "The River Bank." The book grew out of bedtime stories that Mr. Grahame made up for his young son, Alastair, affectionately nicknamed "Mouse." Although it was intended for children, it has delighted readers of all ages ever since its publication in 1908.

In that same year, poor health forced the author to give up his bank work and most of his writing. After his only son died tragically at the age of twenty, Mr. Grahame retired to a village beside the River Thames in southern England and lived quietly there until his death in 1932.

BOOKS TO ENJOY

THE CAT SITTER MYSTERY by Carol Adorjan
Beth's cat-sitting duties while the people next door are away convince her that their house is haunted.

GOOD-BY TO STONY CRICK
by Kathryn Borland and Helen Speicher
When his family moves to Chicago from the hills of Kentucky, Jeremy faces a lonely new life.

A PRIVATE MATTER by Kathryn Ewing
A girl gradually tries to adopt an elderly neighbor as her new father after her parents' divorce.

THE GOLDEN VENTURE by Jane Flory
Minnie stows away in her father's covered wagon in order to go to the California gold rush with him. This is the start of some challenging and unusual adventures.

RECYCLOPEDIA by Robin Simons
This unique guidebook shows you how to see and use recycled materials in new ways — as games, crafts, and science equipment.

THURSDAY'S CHILD by Noel Streatfeild
Plucky Margaret Thursday plans an escape from the orphanage where she has lived since infancy.

THEY LOVED THE LAND by Bennett Wayne
Here are short biographies of four people who helped make us aware of the importance of conservation and ecology — Rachel Carson, John James Audubon, Luther Burbank, and John Muir.

GLOSSARY

Some of the words in this book may have pronunciations or meanings you do not know. This glossary can help you by telling you how to pronounce those words and by telling you the meanings with which those words are used in this book.

You can find out the correct pronunciation of any glossary word by using the special spelling after the word and the pronunciation key at the bottom of each left-hand page.

The pronunciation key below is a full one that shows how to pronounce each consonant and vowel in a special spelling. The pronunciation key at the bottom of each left-hand page is a shortened form of the full key.

FULL PRONUNCIATION KEY

CONSONANT SOUNDS

b	bib	k	cat, kick, pique	t	tight
ch	church	l	lid, needle	th	path, thin
d	deed	m	am, man, mum	*th*	bathe, this
f	fast, fife, off,	n	no, sudden	v	cave, valve, vine
	phase, rough	ng	thing	w	with
g	gag	p	pop	y	yes
h	hat	r	roar	z	rose, size,
hw	which	s	miss, sauce, see		xylophone, zebra
j	judge	sh	dish, ship	zh	garage, pleasure,
					vision

VOWEL SOUNDS

ă	pat	ī	by, guy, pie	o͞o	boot, fruit
ā	aid, they, pay	î	dear, deer,	ou	cow, out
â	air, care, wear		fierce, mere	ŭ	cut, rough
ä	father	ŏ	pot, sorry	û	firm, heard, term,
ĕ	pet, pleasure	ō	go, row, toe		turn, word
ē	be, bee, easy,	ô	alter, caught,	yo͞o	abuse, use
	leisure		for, paw	ə	about, silent, pencil,
ĭ	pit	oi	boy, noise, oil		lemon, circus
		o͝o	book	ər	butter

STRESS MARKS

Primary Stress ′
bi•ol′o•gy (bī ŏl′ə jē)

Secondary Stress ′
bi′o•log′i•cal (bī′ə lŏj′ĭ kəl)

Pronunciation key and word meanings adapted from *The American Heritage School Dictionary*, published by American Heritage Publishing Co., Inc., and Houghton Mifflin Company.

ab•do•men (ăb′də mən) *or* (ăb dō′-) *n.*
1. In human beings and other mammals, the front part of the body from below the chest to about where the legs join, containing the stomach, intestines, and other organs of digestion. 2. The major rear section of the body of an insect.

a•brupt•ly (ə brŭpt′lē) *adv.* In a way that is unexpected; sudden: *to change abruptly.* —**a•brupt′** *adj.*

ab•sorb (ăb sôrb′) *or* (-zôrb′) *v.* 1. To take in; soak up: *A sponge absorbs moisture.* 2. To occupy the full attention of: *completely absorbed by her work.*

a•bun•dance (ə bŭn′dəns) *n.* A great amount or quantity; a plentiful supply.

a•ca•cia (ə kā′shə) *n.* Any of several mostly tropical trees with feathery leaves and clusters of small, usually yellow flowers.

ac•cu•mu•late (ə kyōō′myə lāt′) *v.* **ac•cu•mu•lat•ed, ac•cu•mu•lat•ing.** To gather together; pile up; collect: *Snow has begun to accumulate on the road.*

ad•journ (ə jûrn′) *v.* 1. To bring (a meeting or session) to an official close, putting off further business until later: *I move that the meeting be adjourned. There is a motion to adjourn.* 2. To come to an official close; break up: *The legislature adjourned in July.*

ad•min•is•tra•tion (ăd mĭn′ĭ strā′shən) *n.* 1. The act of governing or directing. 2. Management: *business administration.* 3. The officials who manage an institution or organization: *the school administration.*

ag•i•ta•tion (ăj′ĭ tā′shən) *n.* 1. The act of violently shaking or stirring up. 2. Great emotional disturbance or excitement. 3. Energetic action to arouse public interest in a cause.

air•strip (âr′strĭp′) *n.* A flat, clear area that can serve as an airfield, usually only temporarily or in emergencies.

al•cove (ăl′kōv′) *n.* A small room opening on a larger one without being separated from it by a wall.

al•fal•fa (ăl făl′fə) *n.* A plant with cloverlike leaves and purple flowers, grown as feed for cattle and other livestock.

al•leged (ə lĕjd′) *adj.* Stated to be as described but not so proved: *the alleged kidnaper of the child.*

al•ler•gic (ə lûr′jĭk) *adj.* Having a disorder in which exposure to a substance causes a reaction that may include itching, difficulty in breathing, sneezing, watering of the eyes, and shock.

al•lude (ə lōōd′) *v.* **al•lud•ed, al•lud•ing.** To refer to indirectly; mention casually or in passing.

an•te•lope (ăn′tə lōp′) *n., pl.* **an•te•lope** or **an•te•lopes.** 1. Any of various swift-running, often slender, long-horned animals of Africa and Asia. 2. An animal similar to a true antelope, especially the pronghorn of western North America.

an•ti•sep•tic (ăn′tĭ sĕp′tĭk) *adj.* Capable of destroying very small organisms, such as bacteria that produce disease. —*n.* An antiseptic substance or agent.

an•vil (ăn′vĭl) *n.* A heavy block of iron or steel, with a smooth, flat top on which metals are shaped by hammering.

anx•ious (ăngk′shəs) *or* (ăng′-) *adj.* 1. Having a feeling of uneasiness; worried: *The mother was anxious about her child.* 2. Marked by uneasiness or worry: *anxious moments.* 3. Eagerly earnest or wishing: *anxious to begin.*

ap•pa•ri•tion (ăp′ə rĭsh′ən) *n.* 1. A ghost. 2. An eerie sight.

ă pat/ā **pay**/â care/ä father/ĕ **pet**/ē be/ĭ pit/ī pie/î fierce/ŏ pot/ō go/ô paw, for/oi oil/ōō book/
ōō boot/ou **out**/ŭ cut/û fur/*th* the/th thin/hw which/zh vision/ə ago, item, pencil, atom, circus

ap•pren•tice (ə prĕn'tĭs) *n.* **1.** A person who works for another without pay in return for instruction in a craft or trade. **2.** Any beginner.

a•quat•ic (ə kwăt'ĭk) *or* (ə kwŏt'-) *adj.* **1.** Of or in water. **2.** Living or growing in or on the water: *aquatic mammals; aquatic plants.* **3.** Taking place in or on the water: *aquatic sports.*

ar•ray (ə rā') *n.* **1.** An orderly arrangement. **2.** An impressive display or collection: *a fine array of talent.* **3.** Clothing or finery. —*v.* **1.** To arrange or draw up, as troops. **2.** To dress up, especially in fine clothes; adorn: *She was splendidly arrayed in red velvet.*

as•a•fet•i•da (ăs'ə fĕt'ĭ də) *n.* A plant substance with a very unpleasant odor, formerly used in medicine.

as•sault (ə sôlt') *n.* **1.** A violent physical or verbal attack: *an assault upon the enemy walls.* **2.** The way of beginning an activity: *Edison's greatest skill was his organized assault on a problem.* —*v.* To attack violently.

au•di•to•ri•um (ô'dĭ tôr'ē əm) *or* (-tōr'-) *n., pl.* **au•di•to•ri•ums** *or* **au•di•to•ri•a** (ô'dĭ tôr'ē ə) *or* (-tōr'-). A large room or building designed for a big audience.

bac•te•ri•a (băk tîr'ē ə) *pl. n.* The less frequently used singular is **bac•te•ri•um** (băk tîr'ē əm). Very small one-celled organisms often considered to be plants, although they usually lack green coloring.

Bac•tri•an camel (băk'trē ən). A two-humped camel of central and southwestern Asia.

bail¹ (bāl) *n.* Money supplied for the temporary release of an arrested person and guaranteeing his or her appearance for trial.

bail² (bāl) *v.* To remove (water) from a boat by repeatedly filling a container and emptying it: *bail with a coffee can.*

bam•boo (băm bōō') *n.* **1.** A tall, tree-like tropical grass with hollow, jointed stems. **2.** The strong, woody stems of this plant, used for building, window blinds, fishing poles, etc.

ban•dan•a *or* **ban•dan•na** (băn dăn'ə) *n.* A large, colorful handkerchief.

bar•ra•cu•da (băr'ə kōō'də) *n., pl.* **bar•ra•cu•das** *or* **bar•ra•cu•da.** A sea fish with a long, narrow body and very sharp teeth, found mostly in tropical waters.

ba•salt (bə sôlt') *or* (bā'sôlt') *n.* A hard, dense, dark rock formed by volcanic action.

bass (bās) *n.* **1.** The lowest range of musical tones. **2.** The lowest singing voice in the range of men's voices. **3.** A man having such a voice. **4.** A part written in the range of this voice. **5.** An instrument having low tones.

beam (bēm) *n.* **1.** A long, rigid piece of wood or metal used to support or strengthen a structure. **2.** The widest part of a ship. **3.** Light projected into space, as by a flashlight. —*v.* **1.** To send (a radio signal) in a beam. **2.** To send off light; shine. **3.** To smile broadly.

beck•on (bĕk'ən) *v.* **1.** To signal (someone) to come, as by nodding or waving: *The astronomer beckoned us over to look through her telescope.* **2.** To seem attractive to or to seem to attract: *A garden bench beckons the weary.*

be•drag•gled (bĭ drăg'əld) *adj.* Wet, drenched, messy, etc.

bent (bĕnt). Past tense and past participle of **bend.** —*adj.* **1.** Curved or crooked: *a bent nail.* **2.** Having made a firm decision; determined: *a woman bent on traveling around the world.*

bet•ter (bĕt'ər) *adj.* Comparative of **good.** Used to indicate a higher degree of excellence or quality. —*n.* **1.** The superior of two: *Both of you are good at this, but which is the better?* **2. betters.** One's superiors: *Don't interrupt your betters.*

bill·ing (bĭl′ĭng) *n.* The order in which performers' names are listed in programs and advertisements and on theater marquees: *The two actors share top billing.*

blaze¹ (blāz) *n.* **1.** A brightly burning fire. **2.** Any bright or direct light: *the blaze of day.* **3.** A brilliant or striking display. —*v.* **blazed, blaz·ing. 1.** To burn brightly. **2.** To shine or shimmer brightly, as with light or heat.

blaze² (blāz) *n.* **1.** A white spot on the face of a horse or other animal. **2.** A mark cut on a tree to indicate a trail. —*v.* **blazed, blaz·ing.** To indicate (a trail) by marking trees with cuts.

bleak (blēk) *adj.* **bleak·er, bleak·est. 1.** Exposed to the winds; barren and unsheltered: *a bleak hillside.* **2.** Cold and harsh: *a bleak wind.* **3.** Gloomy; somber; dreary: *bleak thoughts.* —**bleak′ly** *adv.* —**bleak′ness** *n.*

blind (blīnd) *adj.* **blind·er, blind·est. 1.** Without the sense of sight; sightless. **2.** Performed without the use of sight: *blind flying.* **3.** Hidden or screened from sight: *a blind intersection.* —*n.* **1.** Something that shuts out light or hinders vision: *windows protected by solid wood blinds.* **2.** A shelter for concealing hunters or observers of animals. —*v.* **1.** To deprive of sight. **2.** To dazzle.

boar (bôr) *or* (bōr) *n.* **1.** A male pig. **2.** Also **wild boar.** A wild pig with dark bristles.

bo·ni·to (bə nē′tō) *n., pl.* **bo·ni·to** or **bo·ni·tos.** An ocean fish related to the tuna, caught for food and sport.

bow¹ (bō) *n.* **1.** A weapon used to shoot arrows. **2.** A knot tied with a loop or loops at either end.

bow² (bou) *v.* To bend (the body, head, or knee) in greeting, agreement or respect. —*n.* A bending of the body or head, as when showing respect or accepting applause.

bow³ (bou) *n.* The front section of a ship or boat.

brack·ish (brăk′ĭsh) *adj.* **1.** Slightly salty and not fit to drink: *brackish lake water.* **2.** Bad-tasting.

bro·cade (brō kād′) *n.* A heavy cloth with a rich, raised design woven into it, often with threads of silver, gold, or colored silk. —*v.* **bro·cad·ed, bro·cad·ing.** To weave with a raised design. —**bro·cad′ed** *adj.: brocaded gowns.*

bronc (brŏngk) *n. Informal.* A small wild or half-wild horse; a bronco.

Bud·dhist (boo′dĭst) *or* (bood′ĭst) *adj.* **1.** Of or having the beliefs said to have been put forward by the Indian philosopher Gautama Siddhartha, who was titled Buddha. **2.** Of the religion or the people who follow Buddhist beliefs.

bush baby. A small primate, the galago. See **galago.**

bus·tle (bŭs′əl) *v.* **bus·tled, bus·tling.** To hurry or cause to hurry busily and excitedly. —*n.* A stir of activity; commotion.

butt (bŭt) *v.* **but·ted, but·ting, butts. 1.** To hit or push with the head or horns. **2.** To join at the end or ends.

cal·cu·la·tion (kăl′kyə lā′shən) *n.* **1.** The act, process, or result of finding or determining (an answer or result) by using mathematics. **2.** The act, process, or result of making an estimate of. —**cal′cu·late** *v.*

cap·size (kăp′sīz′) *or* (kăp sīz′) *v.* **cap·sized, cap·siz·ing.** To overturn: *A huge wave capsized our boat. The ship capsized in the storm.*

ă pat/ā pay/â care/ä father/ĕ pet/ē be/ĭ pit/ī pie/î fierce/ŏ pot/ō go/ô paw, for/oi oil/oo book/ oo boot/ou out/ŭ cut/û fur/*th* the/th thin/hw which/zh vision/ə ago, item, pencil, atom, circus

cap•ti•vate (kăp′tə vāt′) *v.* **cap•ti•vat•ed, cap•ti•vat•ing.** To fascinate or charm with wit, beauty, intelligence, etc. —**cap′ti•vat′ing** *adj.: a captivating story.* —**cap′ti•va′tion** *n.*

car•a•van (kăr′ə văn′) *n.* **1.** An expedition of merchants, pilgrims, etc., traveling together, especially through desert regions. **2.** Any file of vehicles or pack animals.

car•i•bou (kăr′ə bōō′) *n., pl.* **car•i•bou** or **car•i•bous.** A deer of arctic regions of North America, with large, spreading antlers from the heads of both the males and females.

cast (kăst) *or* (käst) *v.* **cast, cast•ing. 1.** To throw: *cast a fishing line.* **2.** To assign a certain role to. **3. a.** To form (an object) by pouring a melted or soft material into a mold and allowing it to harden: *The artist cast her sculpture in bronze.* **b.** To pour (a material) in forming an object in this way. —*n.* **1.** The act of throwing. **2.** The actors in a play or movie. **3.** An impression formed in a mold: *a cast in plaster of a face.*

cav•i•ty (kăv′ĭ tē) *n., pl.* **cav•i•ties. 1.** A hollow or hole. **2.** A hollow area within the body: *the abdominal cavity.* **3.** A hollow area in a tooth, caused by decay.

cen•sor (sĕn′sər) *n.* A person who has the power to remove or prevent publication of material considered harmful in literature, news, letters, etc. —*v.* To remove material from or prevent the publication of: *censor a news story.*

cer•e•mo•ni•al (sĕr′ə mō′nē əl) *adj.* Of a ceremony. —**cer′e•mo′ni•al•ly** *adv.*

cer•e•mo•ny (sĕr′ə mō′nē) *n., pl.* **cer•e•mo•nies. 1.** A formal act or set of acts performed in honor or celebration of an occasion, such as a wedding, funeral, etc.: *a wedding ceremony; the ceremony of hoisting the flag.* **2.** Formality: *He was welcomed with great ceremony.*

cham•ber (chām′bər) *n.* **1.** A private room in a house, especially a bedroom. **2.** A room in which a person of high rank receives visitors. **3. chambers.** A judge's office in a courthouse.

cham•pi•on (chăm′pē ən) *n.* **1.** Someone or something acknowledged as the best of all, having defeated others in competition. **2.** A person who fights for or defends a cause, movement, etc.: *a champion of freedom.*

chan•nel (chăn′əl) *n.* **1.** The depression or cut in the earth through which a river or stream passes. **2.** A part of a river or harbor deep enough to form a passage for ships. **3.** A band of radio-wave frequencies reserved for broadcasting or communication: *a television channel.*

char•ter (chär′tər) *n.* **1.** A written document from a ruler, government, etc., giving certain rights to the people, a group, or an individual. **2.** The hiring or renting of a bus, aircraft, boat, etc., for a special use. —*v.* **1.** To grant a charter to; establish by charter: *Congress chartered the bank for twenty years.* **2.** To hire or rent by charter: *The travel club chartered a plane.*

chef (shĕf) *n.* A cook, especially the chief cook of a large kitchen staff, as in a restaurant.

civ•ics (sĭv′ĭks) *n.* (*used with a singular verb*). The study of how local and national government works and of the rights and duties of citizens.

clin•ic (klĭn′ĭk) *n.* **1.** A training session for medical students in which they observe while patients are examined and treated. **2.** A medical center, usually associated with a hospital or medical school, that is mainly for patients who do not stay overnight.

cock•pit (kŏk′pĭt′) *n.* The part of an airplane where the pilot and copilot sit.

coin•age (koi′nĭj) *n.* **1.** The process of making coins: *the coinage of silver.* **2.** Metal coins in general. **3.** The invention of new words.

col•lide (kə līd′) *v.* **col•lid•ed, col•lid•ing. 1.** To strike or bump together with violent, direct impact: *The planes collided in midair.* **2.** To disagree strongly; clash.

com•bus•tion (kəm bŭs′chən) *n.* **1.** The process of burning. **2.** A chemical change, especially a combination with oxygen, that goes on rapidly and produces light and heat.

com•mis•sion (kə mĭsh′ən) *n.* The act of granting authority to someone to carry out a certain job or duty. —*v.* To grant a commission to: *They commissioned the artist to paint a portrait.*

com•mit (kə mĭt′) *v.* **com•mit•ted, com•mit•ting. 1.** To do, perform, or be guilty of: *commit a crime.* **2.** To put in a certain condition or form, as for future use: *She committed the secret code to memory.*

com•pose (kəm pōz′) *v.* **com•posed, com•pos•ing. 1.** To make up; form: *This flower is composed of many petals.* **2.** To make or create by putting parts or elements together: *An artist composes a picture by arranging forms and colors.* **3.** To create (poetry, music, etc.). **4.** To make calm, controlled, or orderly. **5.** To arrange or set (type or matter to be printed).

com•pound (kŏm′pound′) *n.* **1.** Something consisting of a combination of two or more parts, ingredients, etc.: *The fragrance filling the bakery shop was a compound of fresh bread, apple pie, and chocolate.* **2.** A chemical substance that consists of atoms of at least two different elements combined in definite proportions.

con•ceal (kən sēl′) *v.* To keep from being seen, noticed, or known; hide: *A bank of clouds concealed the setting sun.*

conch (kŏngk) *or* (kŏnch) *n., pl.* **conchs** (kŏngks) or **conch•es** (kŏn′chĭz). **1.** A tropical sea animal related to the snails, having a large, often brightly colored spiral shell. **2.** The shell of such an animal.

con•di•tion (kən dĭsh′ən) *n.* **1.** A state of being; the way something or someone is. **2. a.** A state of general health or fitness. **b.** Readiness for use; working order. **3.** A disease or ailment. **4.** Something stated as necessary or desirable; a requirement; provision: *She let me borrow the book on the condition that I return it in a week.* —*v.* To put into good or proper condition; make fit.

con•fi•den•tial (kŏn′fĭ děn′shəl) *adj.* **1.** Told in trust that (the matter) will be kept secret: *confidential information.* **2.** Entrusted with private matters: *a confidential secretary.* **3.** Showing a feeling of trust or intimacy: *He told about the problem in a confidential voice.* —**con′fi•den′tial•ly** *adv.*

con•tempt (kən tĕmpt′) *n.* **1. a.** A feeling that someone or something is inferior and undesirable: *The unfriendly club members treated outsiders with contempt.* **b.** The condition of being regarded in this way. **2.** Open disobedience to a court of law or to Congress.

con•tra•dict (kŏn′trə dĭkt′) *v.* **1.** To express the opposite of (a statement): *What you say now contradicts what you said before.* **2.** To declare to be untruthful or untrue: *She contradicted her sister.*

con•vict (kən vĭkt′) *v.* To find or prove guilty of an offense, especially in a court of law. —*n.* (kŏn′vĭkt′). Someone who has been found guilty of a crime and sentenced to prison.

ă pat/ā pay/â care/ä father/ĕ pet/ē be/ĭ pit/ī pie/î fierce/ŏ pot/ō go/ô paw, for/oi oil/ŏŏ book/ ōō boot/ou out/ŭ cut/û fur/*th* the/th thin/hw which/zh vision/ə ago, item, pencil, atom, circus

cor•al (kôr′əl) *or* (kŏr′-) *n.* **1.** A hard, stony substance formed by many skeletons of tiny sea animals massed together. It is often white, pink, or reddish. **2. a.** One of the tiny animals that form this substance. **b.** A mass of this substance, often branched or rounded in shape.

cor•po•ral (kôr′pər əl) *or* (-prəl) *n.* A non-commissioned officer in the military, ranking below a sergeant.

cov•ey (kŭv′ē) *n., pl.* **cov•eys.** A group or small flock of partridges, grouse, or other birds.

da•ta (dā′tə) *or* (dăt′ə) *or* (dä′tə) *pl. n.* The less frequently used singular is **da•tum** (dā′təm) *or* (dăt′əm) *or* (dä′təm). **1.** Information, especially when it is to be analyzed or used as the basis for a decision. **2.** Numerical information suitable for processing by computer.

daw•dle (dôd′l) *v.* **daw•dled, daw•dling. 1.** To take more time than necessary; linger: *No one dawdled over lunch.* **2.** To move slowly and aimlessly; loiter: *She saw him dawdling along the other side of the street.* —**daw′dler** *n.*

DDT. A powerful insecticide that is also poisonous to human beings and animals. It remains active in the environment for many years.

de•bate (dĭ bāt′) *n.* **1.** A discussion of the arguments for and against something. **2.** A formal contest in which two teams argue for opposite sides of an issue. —*v.* **de•bat•ed, de•bat•ing. 1.** To present or discuss arguments for and against (a question, proposal, etc.). **2.** To consider and try to decide: *I was debating what to do.* **3.** To call into question; argue about: *The wisdom of that decision is still debated.* **4.** To engage in a formal public argument over an issue or issues.

de•ci•pher (dĭ sī′fər) *v.* **1.** To change (a message) from a code to ordinary language; decode. **2.** To read or interpret (something hard to understand or not clearly written or printed).

de•ject•ed (dĭ jĕk′tĭd) *adj.* Low in spirits; depressed. —**de•ject′ed•ly** *adv.*

de•lir•i•ous (dĭ lîr′ē əs) *adj.* **1.** In a temporary state of mental confusion resulting from high fever, poisoning, or shock. **2.** In a state of uncontrolled excitement or emotion.

des•ert[1] (dĕz′ərt) *n.* A dry, barren region, often covered with sand, having little or no vegetation. —*adj.* Uninhabited: *a desert island.*

de•sert[2] (dĭ zûrt′) *v.* **1.** To reject by leaving; abandon. **2.** To leave (the army or an army post) illegally and with no intention of returning: *He deserted his post just before the attack.*

de•spair (dĭ spâr′) *n.* **1.** Utter lack of hope: *She cried out in despair.* **2.** Someone or something that causes grief or mental pain: *He was the despair of his family.* —*v.* To lose all hope.

des•per•ate (dĕs′pər ĭt) *or* (-prĭt) *adj.* **1.** In a critical or hopeless situation and thus ready to do anything. **2.** Having an urgent need for something: *desperate for food.* **3.** Nearly hopeless; critical; grave: *Things look desperate.* **4.** Undertaken in critical or nearly hopeless circumstances: *desperate measures; a last desperate attempt.* —**des′per•ate•ly** *adv.*

des•per•a•tion (dĕs′pə rā′shən) *n.* Despair or extreme action resulting from it: *reach the point of desperation.*

dev•il (dĕv′əl) *n.* **1.** A spirit of evil; a demon. **2.** A person who is daring, clever, or full of mischief. **3.** A printer's devil. See **printer's devil.**

de•vour (dĭ vour′) *v.* **1.** To swallow or eat up greedily: *Hungry campers devoured all the food.* **2.** To destroy. **3.** To take in greedily with the senses or mind: *devouring every book about judo.*

dex·ter·i·ty (dĕk stĕr′ĭ tē) *n.* **1.** Skill in the use of the hands or body. **2.** Mental skill; cleverness.

di·a·lect (dī′ə lĕkt′) *n.* A regional variety of a language, distinguished from other varieties by pronunciation, vocabulary, etc.: *Cockney is a dialect of English.* —**di′a·lect′al** *adj.*

dig·ni·ty (dĭg′nĭ tē) *n., pl.* **dig·ni·ties. 1.** The condition of being worthy or honorable: *a certain dignity in every human being.* **2.** The respect and honor that go with an important position. **3.** A stately or poised manner.

din·gy (dĭn′jē) *adj.* **din·gi·er, din·gi·est. 1.** Dirty; soiled; grimy: *a dingy coat.* **2.** Drab; dirty: *a dingy room.*

dis·mal (dĭz′məl) *adj.* **1.** Causing gloom or depression; dreary: *a dismal fog.* **2.** Feeling or showing gloom: *a face as dismal as three days of rainy weather.*

dis·rep·u·ta·ble (dĭs rĕp′yə tə bəl) *adj.* **1.** Lacking a good reputation; not respectable. **2.** Not respectable in appearance or character: *His manner of dress was casual to the point of being disreputable.*

dom·i·no (dŏm′ə nō′) *n., pl.* **dom·i·noes** or **dom·i·nos. . 1.** A small, rectangular block, the face of which is divided into halves, each half blank or marked by one to six dots. **2. dominoes** (*used with a singular verb*). The game played with a set of these pieces.

dor·sal (dôr′səl) *adj.* **1.** Of, toward, on, in, or near the back of an animal. **2.** Having to do with the main fin on the back of a fish or sea mammal.

dote (dōt) *v.* **dot·ed, dot·ing. 1.** To show excessive fondness or affection: *Her aunt doted on her.* **2.** To be foolish or feeble-minded, especially in old age.

draw (drô) *v.* **drew** (drōō), **drawn** (drôn), **draw·ing. 1. a.** To pull or move (something) in a given direction or to a given position: *draw the belt through the loops.* **b.** To cause to move, as by pulling. **2. a.** To pull out; remove. **b.** To take out: *draw swords.* **3.** To cause to flow: *draw water.* **4.** To take in (air or water): *She drew a breath.* **5.** To represent (figures or pictures); sketch. **6.** To reach (a conclusion) from evidence at hand.

drows·i·ly (drou′zĭ lē) *adv.* In a sleepy manner. —**drows′y** *adj.*

drum·head (drŭm′hĕd) *n.* A piece of calfskin or other material stretched across one or more open ends of a drum, on which a musician beats, either with the hands or with sticks.

dry·shod (drī′shod′) *adj.* With dry shoes or feet.

ear·phone (îr′fōn′) *n.* A device that changes electrical signals into sound that can be heard, made to be worn near or in contact with the ear.

eaves (ēvz) *n.* (*used with a plural verb*). The part of a roof that forms the lower edge and projects beyond the walls.

ebb (ĕb) *v.* **1.** To flow or fall back, as the tide does after reaching its highest point. **2.** To fade or fall away; weaken; fail: *The hooked fish struggled more and more weakly as its strength ebbed.*

e·col·o·gy (ĭ kŏl′ə jē) *n.* **1.** The science of the relationships between living things and their environment. **2.** The relationship between living things and their environment.

ec·sta·sy (ĕk′stə sē) *n., pl.* **ec·sta·sies.** A state of intense emotion, especially of joy or delight.

ef·fec·tive·ly (ĭ fĕk′tĭv lē) *adv.* In a way that produces the desired effect or result. —**ef·fec′tive** *adj.*

ă pat/ā pay/â care/ä father/ĕ pet/ē be/ĭ pit/ī pie/î fierce/ŏ pot/ō go/ô paw, for/oi oil/ŏŏ book/
ŏŏ boot/ou out/ŭ cut/û fur/*th* the/th thin/hw which/zh vision/ə ago, item, pencil, atom, circus

el (ĕl) *n. Informal.* An elevated railway; a railway on a raised structure that allows people walking and in vehicles to pass under it.

e·la·tion (ĭ lā′shən) *n.* An intense feeling of happiness or joy: *the elation that a musician or an athlete feels after a good performance.*

eld·er (ĕl′dər) *adj.* A comparative of **old,** used only of persons who are relatives: *her elder sister.* —*n.* **1.** An older person. **2.** An older, influential person of a tribe, community, etc.

em·phat·ic (ĕm făt′ĭk) *adj.* **1.** Expressed or performed with emphasis, or with special force or feeling: *an emphatic shake of the head.* **2.** Bold and definite in expression or action: *an emphatic person.*

en·coun·ter (ĕn koun′tər) *n.* A chance or unexpected meeting: *an encounter with a bear in the woods.* —*v.* To meet or come upon, especially unexpectedly: *encounter many new words in a book.*

en·gi·neer (ĕn′jə nîr′) *n.* A person who works in the practical application of scientific principles to practical ends, especially someone having had special training at the college level or beyond.

en·try (ĕn′trē) *n., pl.* **en·tries. 1. a.** The inclusion of an item in a diary, register, list, or other record. **b.** An item thus entered. **2.** A word, phrase, or term entered and defined in a dictionary or encyclopedia.

en·vi·ous (ĕn′vē əs) *adj.* Expressing a feeling of discontent and resentment aroused by the abilities, qualities, or achievements of another, with a strong desire to have them for oneself: *I am envious of your achievements. She had an envious look on her face.* —**en′vi·ous·ly** *adv.* —**en′vi·ous·ness** *n.*

en·vi·ron·ment (ĕn vī′rən ment) *or* (-vī′ərn-) *n.* Surroundings and conditions that affect natural processes and the growth and development of living things: *Fish and birds, like all living things, are adapted to living in special places within their environment.* —**en·vi′ron·ment′al** *adj.: Environmental studies help to save wildlife.*

err (ûr) *or* (ĕr) *v.* **1.** To make a mistake or error; be incorrect: *He erred when he said that pollution wasn't a problem.* **2.** To stray from the proper or moral way.

er·rant (ĕr′ənt) *adj.* **1.** Roving, especially in search of adventure; wandering. **2.** Mistaken; wrong; straying from the right course.

es·cort (ĭ skôrt′) *v.* To accompany to give protection or guidance or to pay honor: *Police escorted the President during the parade. I escorted them home.*

et·i·quette (ĕt′ĭ kĭt) *or* (-kĕt′) *n.* Rules of correct behavior among people, in society, in a profession, etc.: *court etiquette; military etiquette.*

ex·cru·ci·at·ing (ĭk skroo′shē ā′tĭng) *adj.* Intensely painful; agonizing: *excruciating pain in her left hand; an excruciating headache.*

ex·cur·sion (ĭk skûr′zhən) A short, brief journey, especially a tour made for pleasure with a group; an outing.

ex·haus·tion (ĭg zôs′chən) *n.* **1.** An act or example of exhausting, especially the complete using up of a supply. **2.** A condition in which someone or something is drained of energy, strength, or vitality: *nervous exhaustion.*

ex·pe·di·tion (ĕk′spĭ dĭsh′ən) *n.* **1.** A trip made by an organized group of people with a definite purpose: *a map-making expedition; an expedition to the South Pole.* **2.** A group making such a trip: *The expedition finally arrived.*

ex·ten·sive (ĭk stĕn′sĭv) *adj.* Large in area, amount, etc.; vast: *She owns extensive stretches of land near the ocean.*

fal·ter (fôl′tər) *v.* **1.** To lose strength of purpose or action; hesitate: *Her determination faltered.*

felt (fĕlt) *n.* A smooth, firm cloth made by pressing and matting wool, fur, or other fibers together instead of weaving them.

fer·ret (fĕr′ĭt) *n.* A North American animal, similar to a weasel, with yellowish fur and dark feet.

fetch (fĕch) *v.* To go after and return with; get: *Shall I fetch your bags for you?*

fig·u·rine (fĭg′yə rēn′) *n.* A small ornamental figure made of wood, porcelain, glass, etc.; a statuette.

fil·a·ment (fĭl′ə mənt) *n.* **1.** A fine wire that is enclosed in a light bulb and gives off light when heated by electric current. **2.** Any fine or slender thread, strand, fiber, etc.

firm[1] (fûrm) *adj.* **firm·er, firm·est. 1.** Not giving way under pressure; solid; hard: *firm ground.* **2.** Not changing; fixed: *I have a firm belief.* —**firm′ly** *adv.* —**firm′ness** *n.*

firm[2] (fûrm) *n.* A business, especially one consisting of a partnership of two or more persons.

flank (flăngk) *v.* To be placed or situated at the side of: *Two chairs flanked the couch.*

fledg·ling, also **fledge·ling** (flĕj′lĭng) *n.* **1.** A young bird that has just grown its flying feathers and is learning to fly. **2.** Any beginner.

flour·ish (flûr′ĭsh) *or* (flŭr′-) *v.* **1.** To grow well; thrive. **2.** To wave vigorously or dramatically. —*n.* **1.** An act or example of waving something vigorously or dramatically: *a flourish of a sword.* **2.** An added, decorative touch: *His handwriting has many flourishes.*

fools·cap (fo͞olz′kăp′) *n.* Writing paper in large sheets about 13 inches wide and 16 inches long.

for·bear (fôr bâr′) *v.* **for·bore** (fôr bôr′) *or* (-bōr′), **for·borne** (fôr bôrn′) *or* (-bōrn′), **for·bear·ing.** To hold back; refrain: *forbear from replying.*

for·bear·ance (fôr bâr′əns) *n.* Patience, tolerance, or restraint: *The leader appealed to her restless group for more time and forbearance.*

for·mi·da·ble (fôr′mĭ də bəl) *adj.* **1.** Inspiring fear, dread, or alarm: *a formidable weapon; a formidable threat.* **2.** Admirable.

fran·tic (frăn′tĭk) *adj.* Very excited with fear, anxiety, etc.; desperate: *a frantic mob scene; a frantic scream.* —**fran′ti·cal·ly** *adv.*

frig·ate (frĭg′ĭt) *n.* **1.** Any of various fast-sailing square-rigged warships built between the 17th and the mid-19th centuries. **2.** An antisubmarine ship. **3.** A frigate bird.

frigate bird. A tropical sea bird with long, powerful wings and dark feathers.

frol·ic (frŏl′ĭk) *n.* **1.** Gaiety; merriment. **2.** A gay, carefree time or entertainment. —*v.* To behave playfully; romp.

fu·gi·tive (fyo͞o′jĭ tĭv) *adj.* Running or having run away, as from the law or justice: *a fugitive convict.* —*n.* A person who flees; a runaway; refugee.

ful·fill (fo͝ol fĭl′) *v.* **1.** To make come true. **2.** To carry out: *ordered to fulfill the terms of a contract.* **3.** To measure up to; satisfy: *fulfilling all needs.*

fur·row (fûr′ō) *or* (fŭr′ō) *n.* **1. a.** A long, narrow, shallow trench made in the ground by a plow or other tool. **b.** Any rut or groove similar to this: *furrows cut in the dirt road by water.* **2.** A deep wrinkle in the skin, as on the forehead. —*v.* To make furrows in.

ă pat/ā pay/â care/ä father/ĕ pet/ē be/ĭ pit/ī pie/î fierce/ŏ pot/ō go/ô paw, for/oi oil/o͝o book/
o͞o boot/ou out/ŭ cut/û fur/*th* the/th thin/hw which/zh vision/ə ago, item, pencil, atom, circus

gab•ble (găb′əl) *n.* Rapid, unconnected, and unclear speech.

ga•la (gā′lə) *or* (găl′ə) *or* (gä′lə) *adj.* Festive; suitable to celebration: *There will be a gala dance on the last night of the voyage.* —*n.* A festive occasion or celebration.

gal•a•go (găl′ə gō′) *n.* Any of several small African primates having dense, woolly fur, large, round eyes, prominent ears, and a long tail. Also called "bush baby."

garb (gärb) *n.* Clothing or way of dressing: *sailors' garb.* —*v.* To clothe or dress: *The judge was garbed in robes.*

gauge (gāj) *n.* **1.** A standard or scale of measurement. **2.** Any of a number of instruments used in making or showing measurements: *a pressure gauge.*

gaunt (gônt) *adj.* **gaunt•er, gaunt•est.** Thin and bony; haggard; emaciated: *a gaunt face.*

gav•el (găv′əl) *n.* A small wooden mallet used by a person in authority to signal for attention or order.

ge•ra•ni•um (jĭ rā′nē əm) *n.* A plant with rounded leaves and showy clusters of red, pink, or white flowers, often grown as a potted plant.

ger•ba (gĕr′bə) *n.* A goatskin bag used in North Africa to carry water.

ges•ture (jĕs′chər) *n.* **1.** A motion of the hands, arms, head, or body used while speaking or in place of speech to help express one's meaning: *The speaker used dramatic gestures.* **2.** An outward show of something, such as courtesy or friendship. —*v.* **ges•tured, ges•tur•ing.** To motion, signal, or point, using a gesture or gestures.

gid•di•ness (gĭd′ē nĕs) *n.* The state or condition of having a lightheaded or whirling sensation; dizziness. —**gid′dy** *adj.*

gill (gĭl) *n.* The breathing organ by means of which fish and certain other water animals take oxygen from the water.

gin•ger•ly (jĭn′jər lē) *adv.* Cautiously; carefully; warily: *I walked over to the brown horse and patted it gingerly.*

gla•cier (glā′shər) *n.* A large mass of slowly moving ice, formed from snow packed together by the weight of snow above it.

glare (glâr) *v.* **glared, glar•ing.** **1.** To stare fiercely or angrily: *glared with fury.* **2.** To shine intensely; dazzle: *A hot sun glares down on the dunes.* —*n.* **1.** A fixed, angry stare. **2.** A very strong and blinding light.

gorge (gôrj) *n.* **1.** A deep, narrow passage with steep, rocky sides, as between mountains. **2.** The throat or gullet.

gout (gout) *n.* A disease in which hard deposits form in joints, especially of the big toe, causing swelling and pain.

gran•deur (grăn′jər) *or* (-jŏŏr) *n.* Awe-inspiring greatness; splendor.

grat•i•tude (grăt′ĭ tōōd) *or* (-tyōōd′) *n.* Appreciation or thankfulness, as for something received or kindness shown.

hai•ku (hī′kōō) *n.* A poem of a three-line, seventeen-syllable form that often points to something in nature. The form originated in Japan.

half•pen•ny (hā′pə nē) *n.* A British coin worth half of a penny.

hal•ter (hôl′tər) *n.* **1.** A device of rope or leather straps that fits around the head or neck of an animal, such as a horse, and can be used to lead or secure it. **2.** A rope with a noose used for execution by hanging.

har•ass (hăr′əs) *or* (hə răs′) *v.* To bother or torment with repeated interruptions, attacks, etc.: *harass a speaker with whistles and shouts.* —**har′ass•ment** *n.*

har•poon (här pōōn′) *n.* A spear with a rope attached and a barbed head that is hurled by hand or shot from a gun, used in hunting whales and large fish. —*v.* To strike, kill, or take with a harpoon. —**har•poon′er** *n.*

hi·me·ne (hē′mə nā) *n.* **1.** A gathering place for men in a Polynesian village. **2.** A native song or hymn of Polynesia.

hin·drance (hĭn′drəns) *n.* **1.** Something or someone that makes difficult or prevents the action or progress of something; an obstacle. **2.** An act of interfering or a condition of being interfered with: *unable to proceed without hindrance.*

hoax (hōks) *n.* A trick or action intended to deceive others, often in the form of a practical joke, false report, etc., that fools the public. —*v.* To deceive or cheat by a hoax.

hol·low (hŏl′ō) *adj.* **hol·low·er, hol·low·est.** **1.** Having or consisting of a space or opening inside: *a hollow log.* **2.** Shaped by or as if by scooping out; bowl-shaped. —*n.* **1.** An opening, space, or indentation in or within something. **2.** A small valley. —*v.* To make or become hollow. —**hol′low·ly** *adv.*

hon·or·a·ble (ŏn′ər ə bəl) *adj.* **1.** Deserving honor or respect: *an honorable occupation.* **2.** Having or showing a strong sense of what is right or just: *an honorable person.*

hon·or·ar·y (ŏn′ə rĕr′ē) *adj.* Given or holding as an honor, without the fulfillment of the usual requirements: *an honorary college degree.*

hov·er (hŭv′ər) *or* (hŏv′-) *v.* **1.** To fly, soar, or float as if hanging from something: *Hummingbirds hover over the flowers they feed on.* **2.** To remain or linger close by.

hum·ble (hŭm′bəl) *adj.* **hum·bler, hum·blest.** **1. a.** Having or showing feelings of humility rather than of pride; modest; meek. **b.** Expressed in a modest spirit: *humble thanks.* **2.** Of low social or political rank: *a humble clerk of the court.*

hum·mock (hŭm′ək) *n.* A low mound or ridge, as of earth or snow.

hy·dran·gea (hī drān′jə) *or* (-jē ə) *or* (-drăn′-) *n.* A shrub with large, rounded clusters of white, pink, or blue flowers.

im·mac·u·late (ĭ măk′yə lĭt) *adj.* **1.** Perfectly clean: *an immaculate coat.* **2.** Free from fault or error.

im·mense (ĭ mĕns′) *adj.* Of great, often immeasurable, size, extent, degree, etc.: *immense rocks; an immense span of time.* —**im·mense′ly** *adv.*

im·pact (ĭm′păkt′) *n.* The action of one body striking against another; collision: *Neither car had been traveling fast at the time of impact.*

im·pend·ing (ĭm pĕn′dĭng) *adj.* Likely or due to happen soon.

im·per·a·tive (ĭm pĕr′ə tĭv) *adj.* **1.** Expressive of a command or order: *an imperative manner.* **2.** Urgently necessary. —*n.* A command or order.

im·pose (ĭm pōz′) *v.* **im·posed, im·pos·ing.** **1.** To place (a burden) on someone. **2.** To set type or plates (for printing) on a stone or metal slab.

im·promp·tu (ĭm prŏmp′tōo) *or* (-tyōo) *adj.* Not prepared beforehand; not rehearsed: *an impromptu lecture.*

in·cred·i·ble (ĭn krĕd′ə bəl) *adj.* **1.** Unbelievable: *an incredible excuse.* **2.** Astonishing; amazing: *She runs with incredible speed.*

in·dif·fer·ence (ĭn dĭf′ər əns) *or* (-dĭf′rəns) *n.* **1.** Lack of concern or interest. **2.** Lack of importance; insignificance: *a matter of indifference.*

in·dulge (ĭn dŭlj′) *v.* **in·dulged, in·dulg·ing.** **1.** To yield to the desires of; pamper: *indulge a child.* **2.** To allow oneself some special pleasure: *indulge in an ice-cream soda.*

ă pat/ā pay/â care/ä father/ĕ pet/ē be/ĭ pit/ī pie/î fierce/ŏ pot/ō go/ô paw, for/oi oil/ŏŏ book/
ōō boot/ou out/ŭ cut/û fur/*th* the/th thin/hw which/zh vision/ə ago, item, pencil, atom, circus

in·nate (ĭ nāt′) or (ĭn′āt′) adj. **1.** Possessed from birth; inborn: *an innate instinct.* **2.** Existing as a basic, seemingly inborn, characteristic: *an innate love of learning.* —**in·nate′ly** adv.

in·spect (ĭn spĕkt′) v. To examine carefully and critically, especially for flaws.

in·stal·la·tion (ĭn′stə lā′shən) n. **1.** The act or process of setting into place: *the installation of telephones.* **2.** A system of machinery or other equipment set up for use. **3.** A military base or camp.

in·stinc·tive·ly (ĭn stĭngk′tĭv lē) adv. In a way that suggests the natural tendency or impulse that leads a person or animal to behave in a certain way. —**in·stinc′tive** adj.

in·tel·li·gence (ĭn tĕl′ə jəns) n. **1.** The capacity to learn, think, understand, and know; mental ability. **2.** Information; news, especially secrets about an enemy.

in·ter·val (ĭn′tər vəl) n. **1.** A period of time between two events: *an interval of rest before returning to work.* **2.** A space between two points or objects: *Pierce the meat at one-inch intervals.*

in·tox·i·cat·ed (ĭn tŏk′sĭ kā′tĭd) adj. **1.** Drunk or in a condition resembling drunkenness. **2.** Highly excited; elated; overjoyed.

in·tri·cate (ĭn′trĭ kĭt) adj. Having a complicated structure, pattern, etc.

is·let (ī′lĭt) n. A very small island.

jan·gle (jăng′gəl) v. **jan·gled, jan·gling.** To make or cause to make a harsh, metallic sound.

jeer (jîr) v. To shout or shout at in a mocking way. —n. A loud mocking shout of disapproval. —**jeer′ing** adj.: *jeering voices.*

jeop·ard·ize (jĕp′ər dīz′) v. **jeop·ard·ized, jeop·ard·iz·ing.** To expose to loss or injury; endanger: *jeopardize one's health.*

kin (kĭn) n. **1.** A person's relatives; family. **2.** Fellow members of a group or kind: *Beagles and their kin are hound dogs.* —adj. Related: *The moose is kin to the elk, another large deer.*

lac·quer (lăk′ər) n. A liquid material that can be applied to a surface, drying to leave a glossy finish. —v. To coat with lacquer. —**lac′quered** adj.: *a lacquered tray.*

lady-in-waiting. pl. **ladies-in-waiting.** A lady of a court appointed to attend a queen or princess.

la·goon (lə goon′) n. A body of water, usually connecting with the ocean and bounded by sandbars or coral reefs.

landing-stage. A dock; a pier.

leaf (lēf) n., pl. **leaves** (lēvz). **1.** A usually thin, flat, green plant part attached to a stem or stalk. **2.** A leaflike part, such as a petal. **3.** One of the sheets of paper forming the pages of a book, magazine, notebook, etc.

leg·end (lĕj′ənd) n. **1.** A story of uncertain truthfulness handed down from earlier times. **2.** An explanatory caption or note under a map, chart, etc.

let[1] (lĕt) v. **let, let·ting.** To grant permission to; allow: *She let him continue.*

let[2] (lĕt) n. Obstacle; something standing in the way of progress: *free to investigate without let or hindrance.*

li·bel (lī′bəl) n. **1.** A written or printed statement that unjustly damages a person's reputation or exposes him or her to ridicule. **2.** The act or crime of making such a statement.

lib·er·ty (lĭb′ər tē) n., pl. **lib·er·ties.** **1.** Freedom from confinement or forced labor. **2.** Freedom of action, belief, or expression. **3.** A legal right to take part in a certain kind of action without control or interference: *the civil liberties protected by the Bill of Rights.* **4.** Often **liberties.** A bold or disrespectful course of action: *take liberties.*

lin·ger (lĭng′gər) v. **1.** To remain in a place longer than usual, as if reluctant to leave. **2.** To be slow in acting.

Lip·pi·zan (lĭp′ət sän′) n. A horse of a breed that is trained for shows.

lithe (līth) adj. **lith·er, lith·est.** Smooth and graceful in motion. —**lithe′ly** adv.

lunge (lŭnj) n. A sudden, forceful movement forward; a plunge: *The fielder made a lunge for the ball.* —v. **lunged, lung·ing.** To make a sudden, forceful movement forward.

mal·ice (măl′ĭs) n. The desire to harm others or to see others suffer; ill will; spite.

man·gy (mān′jē) adj. **man·gi·er, man·gi·est.** Having many bare spots; shabby: *a mangy old fur coat.*

man·sion (măn′shən) n. A large, stately house.

man·u·script (măn′yə skrĭpt′) n. A handwritten or typewritten book, paper, article, etc.

mar·ble (mär′bəl) n. **1.** Any of several rocks, often having irregularly colored marks due to impurities. It is used in buildings and in making ornaments. **2. a.** A little ball made of a hard substance such as glass. **b. marbles** (*used with a singular verb*). A game played with such balls.

mas·quer·ade (măs′kə rād′) n. **1. a.** A dance or party at which masks and fancy costumes are worn. **b.** The costume worn. **2.** Any disguise or false pretense.

ma·ter·ni·ty (mə tûr′nĭ tē) n. The state of being a mother. —*adj.* Connected with pregnancy and childbirth: *a maternity dress; maternity care.*

max·im (măk′sĭm) n. A brief statement of a basic principle or rule of conduct.

mech·a·nism (měk′ə nĭz′əm) n. **1.** A machine or mechanical device. **2.** The arrangement of connected parts in a machine.

mil·let (mĭl′ĭt) n. **1.** A grass grown for its edible seeds and for use as hay. **2.** The white seeds of this plant, widely used as a food grain.

mill·race (mĭl′rās′) n. The fast-moving stream of water that drives a mill wheel.

min·er·al (mĭn′ər əl) n. **1.** Any natural substance that has a definite chemical and physical structure. **2.** Any substance, such as granite or other rock, composed of a mixture of minerals. **3.** Any substance that is not of plant or animal origin.

min·ute[1] (mĭn′ĭt) n. **1.** A unit of time equal to 1/60 of an hour or 60 seconds. **2. minutes.** An official record of the events or doings at a meeting.

mi·nute[2] (mī nōōt′) *or* (-nyōōt′) *or* (mĭ-) adj. **1.** Exceptionally small; tiny. **2.** Marked by close examination or careful study of small details.

mi·rage (mĭ räzh′) n. An optical illusion, or imagined sight, in which water that is not really there and upside-down reflections of distant objects are seen. It is caused by changes that occur as light passes between layers of hot and cold air.

mis·sion·ar·y (mĭsh′ə něr′ē) n., pl. **mis·sion·ar·ies.** A person sent to do religious or charitable work in some territory or foreign country.

mo·rale (mə răl′) n. The state of a person's or group's spirits, as shown in confidence, cheerfulness, and willingness to work toward a goal.

mo·ray (môr′ā) *or* (mōr′ā) *or* (mə rā′) n. Any of several tropical ocean eels that have sharp teeth and can be dangerous to swimmers.

ă pat/ā pay/â care/ä father/ĕ pet/ē be/ĭ pit/ī pie/î fierce/ŏ pot/ō go/ô paw, for/oi oil/ŏŏ book/
ŏŏ boot/ou out/ŭ cut/û fur/*th* the/th thin/hw which/zh vision/ə ago, item, pencil, atom, circus

mor•tal•ly (môr′tl ē) *adv.* **1.** In a deadly or fatal manner. **2.** To the point of death: *mortally wounded.*

mount¹ (mount) *v.* **1.** To climb; ascend: *mounted the stairs; mounting to the top of the hill.* **2.** To grow higher; increase: *The death toll mounted.* **3.** To get up on (a horse or other animal). —*n.* A horse or other animal for riding.

mount² (mount) *n.* A mountain.

mul•ti•col•ored (mŭl′tĭ kŭl′ərd) *adj.* Having many colors.

muz•zle (mŭz′əl) *n.* **1.** The nose and jaws of certain animals, such as a dog or horse. **2.** A leather or wire device fitted over an animal's snout to prevent biting or eating. —*v.* **muz•zled, muz•zling. 1.** To put a muzzle on (an animal). **2.** To prevent (someone) from expressing an opinion.

naught (nôt) *pron.* Nothing: *There were no trees, no shrubs, no grasses, naught but bare rocks.* —*n.* Zero; the digit 0.

nav•i•gate (năv′ĭ gāt′) *v.* **nav•i•gat•ed, nav•i•gat•ing. 1.** To plot and control the course of (a ship or aircraft). **2.** To follow a planned course on, across, or through.

nec•tar (nĕk′tər) *n.* **1.** A sweet liquid in certain flowers, used by bees in making honey. **2.** In Greek mythology, the drink of the gods. **3.** Any delicious drink.

neu•tral (nōō′trəl) *or* **(nyōō′-)** *adj.* Not joined with, supporting, or favoring any side in a war, dispute, or contest.

news•print (nōōz′print′) *or* **(nyōōz′-)** *n.* The kind of cheap, thin paper, made from wood pulp, on which newspapers are printed.

non•com•mit•tal (nŏn′kə mĭt′l) *adj.* Not indicating how one feels or what one thinks or plans to do.

non•de•script (nŏn′dĭ skrĭpt′) *adj.* Lacking in distinctive qualities and thus difficult to describe.

numb (nŭm) *adj.* **numb•er, numb•est. 1.** Unable to feel or to move normally: *toes numb with cold.* **2.** Stunned, as from shock. **3.** Slow in responding or understanding; stupid. —*v.* To take away the power to feel or move normally; stiffen: *a wind that numbed our hands and cheeks.* —**numbed** *adj.*

ob•sti•nate (ŏb′stə nĭt) *adj.* Stubborn; resistant to argument or reason.

of•fi•cial (ə fĭsh′əl) *adj.* **1.** Of an office or post of authority: *official duties.* **2.** Coming from an authority: *an official document.* —*n.* A person in a position of authority. —**of•fi′cial•ly** *adv.*

orange stick. A stick of wood used to care for hands and fingernails.

or•a•tor (ôr′ə tər) *or* **(ōr′-)** *n.* **1.** A person who delivers a formal speech. **2.** A person skilled in public speaking.

or•der•ly (ôr′dər lē) *adj.* **1.** Well arranged or managed; neat. **2.** Without violence; peaceful. —*n., pl.* **or•der•lies.** An attendant in a hospital.

Or•lon (ôr′lŏn′) *n.* A trademark for a synthetic fiber that is used in fabrics.

out•rig•ger (out′rĭg′ər) *n.* **1.** A long, thin float attached to the side of a seagoing canoe by projecting poles as a means of preventing it from capsizing. **2.** A canoe having such a float.

out•wit (out wĭt′) *v.* **out•wit•ted, out•wit•ting.** To get the better of with cleverness; to fool.

o•ver•se•er (ō′vər sē′ər) *n.* A person who watches over and directs workers.

o•zone (ō′zōn′) *n.* A poisonous, blue, unstable gaseous form of oxygen.

pact (păkt) *n.* A formal agreement; a treaty.

paint•er¹ (pān′tər) *n.* A person who paints.

pain•ter² (pān′tər) *n.* A rope attached to the bow of a boat, used for tying up.

pal·i·sade (păl/ĭ sād/) *n.* A fence of stakes forming a defense barrier.

pan·da·nus (păn dā/nəs) *n., pl.* **pan·da·nus·es.** A palmlike tropical tree with large prop roots and narrow leaves that yield a fiber used in weaving mats and other articles.

pan·ic (păn/ĭk) *n.* A sudden, overwhelming terror. —*adj.* Of panic: *a panic reaction.* —*v.* **pan·icked, pan·ick·ing, pan·ics. 1.** To be affected with panic: *The troops panicked and fled.* **2.** To cause panic in.

par·a·lyze (păr/ə līz/) *v.* **par·a·lyzed, par·a·lyz·ing. 1.** To make unable to feel or move. **2.** To make helpless or motionless: *paralyzed by fear.*

parch (pärch) *v.* To make or become very dry, especially with intense heat: *A constant south wind parched the earth.* —**parched** *adj.: a parched throat; parched corn.*

pa·re·u (pä/rā ōō/) *n.* A piece of cloth worn in Polynesia that wraps around the body and is like a skirt or loincloth.

peev·ish·ness (pē/vĭsh nĕs) *n.* The state or condition of being annoyed. —**peev/ish** *adj.*

pel·i·can (pĕl/ĭ kən) *n.* A large, longbilled, web-footed bird of warm regions, having under its lower bill a large pouch used for holding the fish it has caught.

pen·sion (pĕn/shən) *n.* A sum of money paid regularly as a retirement benefit.

per·cus·sion (pər kŭsh/ən) *n.* **1.** The striking together of two bodies, especially when it creates noise. **2.** A sound, vibration, or shock produced in this way.

percussion instrument. A musical instrument in which sound is produced by striking, as a drum or piano.

per·fid·i·ous (pər fĭd/ē əs) *adj.* Disloyal; treacherous; betraying of trust.

per·il·ous (pĕr/ə ləs) *adj.* Full of danger; hazardous. —**per/il·ous·ly** *adv.*

pike (pīk) *n., pl.* **pike** or **pikes.** A large freshwater fish with a narrow body and a long snout, often caught for sport.

pitch (pĭch) *v.* **1.** To throw; hurl; toss. **2.** To set at or as if at a given level, musical key, etc.: *He pitches his voice high to be heard in the crowd.* —**pitch in.** To set to work with energy, especially in cooperation with others. —*n.* **1.** An act of pitching. **2.** The quality of a musical tone or other sound by which it is judged to be high or low.

plague (plāg) *n.* **1.** Anything that causes much suffering or trouble. **2.** A very contagious, usually deadly, disease. —*v.* **plagued, pla·guing. 1.** To cause misery or trouble in or for. **2.** To annoy; bother.

plaice (plās) *n., pl.* **plaice** or **plaic·es.** A large flatfish related to the flounders, used as food, especially in Europe.

pon·der (pŏn/dər) *v.* To think or consider carefully and at length: *She pondered over the decision.*

por·ce·lain (pôr/sə lĭn) *or* (pōr/-) *n.* **1.** A hard, white, translucent material made by baking a fine clay at a high temperature and glazing it with one of several variously colored materials. **2.** An object or objects made of this material.

pot·ter (pŏt/ər) *v.* To keep oneself busy with aimless activity or trivial tasks; putter.

pra·line (prä/lēn) *or* (prā/lēn) *n.* A crisp candy made of pecans or other nuts and boiled brown sugar.

prej·u·dice (prĕj/ə dĭs) *n.* **1.** A strong feeling about some subject, formed unfairly or before one knows the facts; a bias. **2.** Hostility toward members of a group, race, religion, or nationality other than one's own.

ă pat/ā pay/â care/ä father/ĕ pet/ē be/ĭ pit/ī pie/î fierce/ŏ pot/ō go/ô paw, for/oi oil/ōō book/
ōō boot/ou out/ŭ cut/û fur/*th* the/*th* thin/hw which/zh vision/ə ago, item, pencil, atom, circus

press (prĕs) *v.* **1.** To push against; bear down on. **2.** To form into a desired shape by force. —*n.* **1.** Any of various machines used to put pressure on something. **2.** A machine that transfers printed matter onto sheets of paper by contact with an inked surface; a printing press. **3. a.** Printed matter as a whole, especially newspapers and magazines. **b.** The people, as editors and reporters, involved in preparing such publications.

pres·tige (prĕ stēzh′) *or* (-stēj′) *n.* Importance or status in the eyes of others, gained through success or fame.

pre·sum·a·bly (prĭ zoo′mə blē) *adv.* By assuming reasonably; probably.

prey (prā) *n.* **1.** An animal or animals hunted or seized by another for food. **2.** Someone or something helpless against attack. —**bird of prey.** A bird that seizes other animals for food.

prickly pear. 1. A cactus with flat, spiny stems, showy, usually yellow flowers, and egg-shaped, bristly, but often edible fruit. **2.** The fruit of such a cactus.

prim·i·tive (prĭm′ĭ tĭv) *adj.* Of or in an early stage of development: *a primitive form of life.*

prin·ci·pal (prĭn′sə pəl) *adj.* First or foremost in rank, degree, importance, etc.; chief.

printer's devil. A person who is working for a printer while learning the printing trade; a printer's apprentice.

priv·i·lege (prĭv′ə lĭj) *n.* A special right, benefit, permission, etc., granted to or enjoyed by an individual, class, or group.

proc·ess (prŏs′ĕs′) *or* (prō′sĕs′) *n.* A series of steps, actions, or operations used in making something or bringing about a result. —*v.* **1.** To put through a given series of steps: *process an application.* **2.** To prepare or treat by means of some process.

pro·file (prō′fīl′) *n.* **1.** A side view of an object, especially of the human head. **2.** A piece of writing, especially a biographical sketch.

pro·hi·bi·tion (prō′ə bĭsh′ən) *n.* A law or order that forbids or prevents one from doing something.

prom·i·nent (prŏm′ə nənt) *adj.* **1.** Projecting outward; bulging or jutting: *prominent brows.* **2.** Highly noticeable. **3.** Well-known; leading: *a prominent writer; a prominent career in public service.* —**prom′i·nent·ly** *adv.*

prompt (prŏmpt) *adj.* **prompt·er, prompt·est.** **1.** On time. **2.** Done without delay. —*v.* **1.** To urge (someone) to some action. **2.** To assist by supplying a forgotten word, a cue, or another reminder: *prompt an actor.*

pro·pel·lant, also **pro·pel·lent** (prə pĕl′ənt) *n.* A fuel or explosive charge used to cause (a vehicle, rocket, body, etc.) to move or continue in motion.

pros·pect (prŏs′pĕkt′) *n.* **1.** Something presented to the eye; a scene; view. **2.** Something expected or foreseen; an expectation: *hurried home with the prospect of a good dinner.*

pros·trate (prŏs′trāt′) *adj.* Lying flat: *a sleeper prostrate on the floor.*

pro·trude (prō trood′) *v.* **pro·trud·ed, pro·trud·ing.** To stick out from a surface; project: *Curly hair protruded from the edges of his cap.*

prov·en·der (prŏv′ən dər) *n.* **1.** Dry food, such as hay, for livestock; feed. **2.** *Informal.* Any food.

prov·ince (prŏv′ĭns) *n.* **1.** A part; division; region. **2.** A political subdivision of a country: *Alberta is a province of Canada.* **3. the provinces.** The outlying areas of a country away from the capital.

pru·dent (prood′nt) *adj.* Having or showing good judgment; sensible.

pub·lic·i·ty (pŭ blĭs′ĭ tē) *n.* **1.** Information given out, as to the press, as a means of attracting public notice to a person or thing. **2.** Public notice directed toward a person or thing.

punt (pŭnt) *n.* A long flat-bottomed boat with squared ends for use in shallow waters, propelled with a long pole. —*v.* To propel (a boat) with a pole.

Quak·er (kwā′kər) *n.* A member of the Society of Friends, a religious group. The word "Quaker" is not used officially by the Friends.

ques·tion·naire (kwĕs′chə nâr′) *n.* A printed form with a series of questions, used to gather information.

rap·ture (răp′chər) *n.* Overwhelming delight; joy that carries one away; bliss.

rash (răsh) *adj.* **rash·er, rash·est.** Too bold or hasty; reckless. —**rash′ly** *adv.*

re·bel (rĭ bĕl′) *v.* **re·belled, re·bel·ling.** **1.** To refuse loyalty to an established government or ruling authority or to oppose it by force. **2.** To resist or oppose openly any authority based on law or custom. —*n.* **reb·el** (rĕb′əl). A person who rebels.

reed (rēd) *n.* Any of several tall, hollow-stemmed grasses or similar plants that grow in wet places.

reef (rēf) *n.* A strip or ridge of rock, sand, or coral that rises to or close to the surface of a body of water.

re·flec·tive·ly (rĭ flĕk′tĭv lē) *adv.* Thoughtfully.

ref·u·gee (rĕf′yŏŏ jē′) *n.* A person who flees, especially from his or her country, to find safety.

re·fuse[1] (rĭ fyŏŏz′) *v.* **re·fused, re·fus·ing.** **1.** To decline to do (something). **2.** To decline to accept; turn down.

ref·use[2] (rĕf′yŏŏs) *n.* Worthless matter; waste.

re·in·force·ment (rē′ĭn fôrs′mənt) *or* (-fōrs′-) *n.* **1.** The act or process of making stronger by or as if by adding extra support to: *reinforcement for a bridge.* **2.** Something that strengthens. **3.** *Often plural.* Military units sent to add strength to units already sent.

re·mote (rĭ mōt′) *adj.* **re·mot·er, re·mot·est.** **1.** Located far away: *a remote Arctic island.* **2.** Distant in time: *the remote past.* —**re·mote′ly** *adv.*

ren·dez·vous (rän′dā vŏŏ′) *or* (-də-) —*v.* **ren·dez·voused** (rän′dā vŏŏd′) *or* (-də-), **ren·dez·vous·ing** (rän′dā vŏŏ′ĭng) *or* (-də-), **ren·dez·vous** (rän′dā vŏŏz′) *or* (-də-). To meet together or cause to meet together at a certain time and place.

rep·ri·mand (rĕp′rĭ mănd′) *or* (-mänd′) *n.* A severe scolding. —*v.* To scold or rebuke severely.

re·prov·ing·ly (rĭ prŏŏv′ĭng lē) *adv.* In a scolding way. —*v.* **re·prove.**

re·search (rĭ sûrch′) *or* (rē′sûrch′) *n.* Careful study of a given subject, field, or problem: *scientific research; medical research.* —*v.* To do research on.

re·sent·ment (rĭ zĕnt′mənt) *n.* Bitterness or indignation over something that is thought to be uncalled-for or unfair.

re·sist (rĭ zĭst′) *v.* To work against; try to stop; oppose (an enemy, attack, etc.): *resist an attack. The people resisted with all their might.*

res·pite (rĕs′pĭt) *n.* **1.** A short interval of rest or relief. **2.** A postponement or delay.

re·spond (rĭ spŏnd′) *v.* **1.** To make a reply; answer. **2.** To react in a particular or desired way to an action: *The patient responded to treatment.*

rev·e·la·tion (rĕv′ə lā′shən) *n.* **1.** Something revealed, or made known, especially something surprising. **2.** The act of revealing.

ă pat/ā pay/â care/ä father/ĕ pet/ē be/ĭ pit/ī pie/î fierce/ŏ pot/ō go/ô paw, for/oi oil/ŏŏ book/ ŏŏ boot/ou out/ŭ cut/û fur/*th* the/th thin/hw which/zh vision/ə ago, item, pencil, atom, circus

re·vive (rĭ vīv′) *v.* **re·vived, re·viv·ing.** **1.** To bring back or return to life or consciousness: *revive a drowning person.* **2.** To bring back or give vigor or strength to (something): *The music revived my spirits.*

rick·sha (rĭk′shô′) *n.* A small two-wheeled carriage of the Orient, drawn by one or two persons.

ridge (rĭj) *n.* **1.** A long, narrow peak or crest of something: *the ridge of a wave; the ridge of a roof.* **2.** A long, narrow formation of raised land; a long hill or chain of mountains.

ridge·pole (rĭj′pōl′) *n.* The highest horizontal timber in a roof, to which the ends of the rafters are attached.

rogue (rōg) *n.* **1.** A person who tricks or cheats others; a scoundrel; rascal. **2.** An animal, especially an elephant, that lives by itself rather than with its herd and that has become wild and dangerous.

role (rōl) *n.* **1.** A character played by an actor in a dramatic performance; a part. **2.** The usual or proper function of a person, thing, etc.

rol·lick·ing (rŏl′ĭ kĭng) *adj.* High-spirited and full of fun: *a rollicking cowboy song.*

rous·ing (rou′zĭng) *adj.* **1.** Stirring; inspiring: *a rousing call to action.* **2.** Energetic; vigorous: *a rousing dance tune.*

rou·tine (rōō tēn′) *n.* A series of activities performed regularly; standard or usual procedure. —*adj.* Not special; ordinary: *a routine day.*

ruf·fi·an (rŭf′ē ən) *or* (rŭf′yən) *n.* A tough or rowdy fellow.

rum·pus (rŭm′pəs) *n.* A noisy disturbance; disorderly clamor.

sab·o·tage (săb′ə täzh′) *n.* The deliberate destruction of property or disruption of work by enemy agents or as a protest. —*v.* **sab·o·taged, sab·o·tag·ing.** To damage, destroy, or defeat by sabotage.

sanc·ti·ty (săngk′tĭ tē) *n.* The quality of being saintly, holy, or sacred.

sar·cas·ti·cal·ly (sär kăs′tĭ klē) *adv.* In a way that is sharply mocking.

sat·el·lite (săt′l īt′) *n.* **1.** A celestial body of relatively small size and mass that travels in an orbit around a planet: a moon. **2.** Any of various objects launched to orbit a celestial body.

scale (skāl) *n.* **1.** A series of marks placed at fixed distances, used for measuring. **2. a.** The relationship between the actual size of something and the size it is when represented on a model, map, drawing, etc.: *a scale of 1 inch to 50 miles.* **b.** A line with marks showing the actual dimensions of something represented on a map, plan, drawing, etc. **3.** A rising or falling series of musical tones that includes all tones that are used in some key, or system of tones.

scan·dal·ous (skăn′dl əs) *adj.* **1.** Causing a public disgrace: *scandalous behavior.* **2.** Containing gossip that is intended to harm: *scandalous talk.*

scath·ing (skā′thĭng) *adj.* Extremely severe or harsh: *scathing criticism.*

schoo·ner (skōō′nər) *n.* A fore-and-aft-rigged sailing vessel with two or more masts.

scourge (skûrj) *n.* A cause of widespread suffering.

scram·ble (skrăm′bəl) *v.* **scram·bled, scram·bling.** **1.** To move hurriedly or in a disorganized manner: *She scrambled over the stone wall.* **2.** To struggle or move about eagerly or urgently in competition with others.

scruff (skrŭf) *n.* The back of the neck or the loose skin there; the nape.

scull (skŭl) *n.* **1.** An oar used for rowing a boat from the stern. **2.** A kind of short-handled oar. **3.** A small, light racing boat. —*v.* To propel (a boat) with a scull or sculls.

sculp·tor (skŭlp′tər) *n.* An artist who sculptures.

sculp·ture (skŭlp′chər) *n.* **1.** The art of making figures or designs that have depth, as by carving wood, chiseling stone, or casting metal. **2. a.** A work of art created in this way. **b.** All such works of art or a group of such works: *African sculpture.* —*v.* **sculp·tured, sculp·tur·ing.** To shape (stone, metal, wood, etc.) into sculpture.

scut·tle (skŭt′l) *v.* **scut·tled, scut·tling.** To move with quick little steps; scurry: *Just then a crab scuttled between two rocks.*

seal (sēl) *n.* **1.** An instrument, such as a ring with a design cut into it, used to stamp an impression in wax or other soft material. **2. a.** The impression made, especially one used as an official mark of authority. **b.** A small disk of wax or paper bearing such a mark. **3.** A fitting that makes a tight closing. —*v.* **1.** To put a seal onto as a mark of genuineness. **2.** To close with or as if with a seal.

sea urchin. Any of several sea animals having a soft body enclosed in a thin, round shell covered with spines.

se·di·tious (sĭ dĭsh′əs) *adj.* Of or engaged in conduct or language that causes others to rebel against the authority of the state. —**se·di′tion** *n.* —**se·di′tious·ly** *adv.*

self-im·posed (sĕlf ĭm pōzd′) *adj.* Placed (a responsibility or difficulty) upon oneself; voluntarily taken on.

sen·nit (sĕn′ĭt) *n.* A braided cord or fabric made of braided rope yarns.

se·quoi·a (sĭ kwoi′ə) *n.* Either of two very large cone-bearing evergreen trees, the **giant sequoia** of the mountains of southern California or the redwood of northern California.

se·rene·ly (sə rēn′lē) *adv.* In a way that is peaceful and untroubled.

set¹ (sĕt) *v.* **set, set·ting. 1.** To put; place: *set the package on the table.* **2.** To place in a firm or unmoving position. **3.** To become hard or rigid; harden: *Some concrete sets very quickly.*

set² (sĕt) *n.* **1.** A group of matching or related things. **2.** A structure on the stage of a theater, designed to represent the place where the action of a play or scene occurs.

se·vere (sə vîr′) *adj.* **se·ver·er, se·ver·est. 1.** Stern; strict: *a severe law; severe terms.* **2.** Intense and serious; extreme: *a severe storm.*

shat·ter (shăt′ər) *v.* **1.** To break suddenly into many pieces, as with a violent blow; smash. **2.** To disrupt suddenly, as with a loud noise. **3.** To destroy beyond hope of repair; ruin: *shattered his hopes.*

she·nan·i·gans (shə năn′ĭ gənz) *pl. n.* Playful tricks or pranks; mischief.

shift·less (shĭft′lĭs) *adj.* Lacking ambition or purpose; lazy.

siege (sēj) *n.* **1.** The surrounding and blockading of a town or fortress by an army bent on capturing it. **2.** A prolonged period, as of illness.

sig·nif·i·cant·ly (sĭg nĭf′ĭ kənt lē) *adv.* In a way that is full of meaning: *He looked significantly at the bakery, saying, "I certainly am hungry, Dad."* —**sig·nif′i·cant** *adj.*

sin·ew (sĭn′yōō) *n.* **1.** A tendon. **2.** The connective tissue which connects muscles to bones.

sin·gle-prop (sĭng′gəl prŏp) *adj. Informal.* Having only one propeller: *A single-prop plane.*

slew (slōō) *v.* To turn or twist sideways.

slith·er (slĭth′ər) *v.* To move along by gliding, as a snake does.

ă pat/ā pay/â care/ä father/ĕ pet/ē be/ĭ pit/ī pie/î fierce/ŏ pot/ō go/ô paw, for/oi oil/ōō book/
ōō boot/ou out/ŭ cut/û fur/*th* the/th thin/hw which/zh vision/ə ago, item, pencil, atom, circus

smart (smärt) *adj.* **smart•er, smart•est.** **1.** Mentally alert; bright: *a smart woman.* **2.** Sharp and quick. —*v.* To cause to feel a stinging pain: *My leg began to smart from the hornet's sting.* —*n.* A stinging pain.

smol•der (smōl′dər) *v.* To burn and produce heat, some smoke, and no visible flame.

sniv•el (snĭv′əl) *v.* **sniv•eled** or **sniv•elled, sniv•el•ing** or **sniv•el•ling.** **1.** To complain or whine tearfully. **2.** To run at the nose, especially while crying.

snooze (snōōz). *Informal.* *v.* **snoozed, snooz•ing.** To take a light nap; doze. —*n.* A light nap.

snor•kel (snôr′kəl) *n.* A breathing tube used by skin divers, consisting of a plastic tube curved at one end and fitted with a mouthpiece.

sod (sŏd) *n.* Grass and soil forming the surface of the ground.

sol•emn•ly (sŏl′əm lē) *adv.* In an impressive way; seriously. —**sol′emn** *adj.*

so•lo (sō′lō) *n., pl.* **so•los.** A musical composition or passage for a single voice or instrument, with or without accompaniment.

span (spăn) *n.* **1.** The distance between two points, lines, objects, etc. **2.** A section of a bridge that extends from one point of vertical support to another.

spasm (spăz′əm) *n.* **1.** A sudden, involuntary contraction of a muscle or group of muscles. **2.** Any sudden burst of energy, activity, etc.

spec•ta•cle (spĕk′tə kəl) *n.* **1.** A public performance or display. **2.** A marvelous sight. **3.** A scene that is regrettably seen by the public: *They lost control and made a spectacle of themselves.*

spell (spĕl) *v.* **spelled** or **spelt** (spĕlt), **spell•ing.** **1.** To name or write in order the letters forming (a word or part of a word). **2.** To be the letters of; form (a word or part of a word). **3.** To mean; signify: *The way she looked at us spelled trouble.*

spon•ta•ne•ous (spŏn tā′nē əs) *adj.* Happening or arising without apparent outside cause. —**spon•ta′ne•ous•ly** *adv.*

spontaneous combustion. The breaking into flame of a mass of material, such as oily rags or damp hay, as a result of heat generated by the slow combining of a substance with oxygen.

sput•ter (spŭt′ər) *v.* **1.** To spit out in short bursts, often with a spluttering sound, as when excited. **2.** To make a coughing noise: *The engine sputtered and died.* **3.** To speak in a hasty or confusing manner; stammer.

squad•ron (skwŏd′rən) *n.* **1.** Any of various military units. **2.** Any group of people or animals: *squadrons of flies.*

star•dom (stär′dəm) *n.* The status of an actor or other performer known as a star, or leading performer.

star•tle (stär′tl) *v.* **star•tled, star•tling.** **1.** To cause to make a sudden movement of surprise or alarm. **2.** To fill with sudden surprise.

staunch•ly (stônch′lē) *or* (stänch′lē) *adv.* In a way that is firm in supporting or defending; loyally. —**staunch** *adj.*

ster•ile (stĕr′əl) *adj.* Free from bacteria that cause disease: *a sterile bandage.*

stern[1] (stûrn) *adj.* **stern•er, stern•est.** **1.** Telling or seeming to tell others to obey or do their duty; severe: *a stern lecture on table manners.* **2.** Strict: *stern discipline.* —**stern′ly** *adv.*

stern[2] (stûrn) *n.* The rear end of a ship or boat.

stoat (stōt) *n.* A weasel, the ermine, especially when its fur is brown.

store (stôr) *or* (stōr) *n.* **1.** A place where merchandise is offered for sale; a shop. **2.** A stock or supply reserved for future use. —*v.* **stored, stor•ing.** To put away for future use.

stout (stout) *adj.* **stout•er, stout•est.** **1.** Determined, bold, or brave. **2.** Strong, sturdy, or solid. **3.** Bulky in figure: *a stout man.*

strain (strān) . v.   **1.** To pull, draw, or stretch tight. **2.** To work to the greatest possible degree: *strain your eyes. The oxen strained with all their might.* **3.** To injure by overworking: *strain a muscle.* **4.** To force or stretch beyond a proper limit: *strain a point.*

stran·gu·la·tion (străng′gyə lā′shən) n. The act of strangling, or choking, or the condition of dying from choking.

stretch (strĕch) v.   **1.** To lengthen or widen by pulling: *stretch a rubber band.* **2.** To become or be able to become lengthened or widened. —n. An unbroken expanse of space or time.

stride (strīd) v. **strode** (strōd), **strid·den** (strĭd′n), **strid·ing.** To walk vigorously with long steps. —n. A long step.

strife (strīf) n. Bitter conflict or struggle.

strive (strīv) v. **strove** (strōv), **striv·en** (strĭv′ən) or **strived, striv·ing. 1.** To exert much effort or energy. **2.** To struggle.

struc·tur·al (strŭk′chər əl) adj.   Of the way in which parts are arranged, constructed, or put together to form a whole. —**struc′tur·al·ly** adv.

strut (strŭt) n.   **1.** A stiff, self-important gait.   **2.** A bar or rod used to brace a mechanical structure against forces applied from the side. —v. **strut·ted, strut·ting. 1.** To walk with a strut. **2.** To brace or support with a strut or struts.

sub·or·bit·al (sŭb ôr′bĭt əl) adj. Having to do with less than one orbit, or path around a celestial body such as a planet.

sub·sis·tence (səb sĭs′təns) n. The act, condition, or means of getting food and maintaining life: *daily subsistence from the soil.*

suc·cor (sŭk′ər) n.   Assistance or help in time of distress.

suf·frage (sŭf′rĭj) n.   The right to vote.

surf (sûrf) n.   The waves of the sea as they break upon a shore or reef. —v. To ride on a surfboard.

sur·vey (sər vā′) or (sûr′vā′) v.   **1.** To look over the parts of; view broadly: *surveyed the neighborhood from a rooftop.*   **2.** To examine; investigate: *surveyed the damages from the storm.* **3.** To find the measure of (land) by measuring angles and distances.

sur·vey·ing (sər vā′ĭng) n.   The measurement and description of a region, part, or feature of the earth, as used for marking boundaries or mapmaking.

sus·pend (sə spĕnd′) v.   **1.** To cause to hang down from a place of attachment. **2.** To support without a prop or resting place; cause to float: *For an instant the acrobat seemed to suspend herself in midair.*

sus·tain (sə stān′) v.   **1.** To support from below; hold or prop up.   **2.** To keep alive; supply with needed nourishment: *the grasses that sustain antelope.*

Swa·hi·li (swä hē′lē) n.   A Bantu language of eastern and central Africa, widely used in trade and as a general means of communication.

swiv·el (swĭv′əl) v. **swiv·eled** or **swiv·elled, swiv·el·ing** or **swiv·el·ling.** To turn or rotate.

syn·thet·ic (sĭn thĕt′ĭk) adj.   Artificial; made by people: *synthetic rubber; synthetic fabrics.*

tam·a·risk (tăm′ə rĭsk′) n.   **1.** A shrub or tree of warm regions, having small, scalelike leaves and clusters of pink flowers.   **2.** *Informal.* A tamarack, or larch tree; a tall, cone-bearing tree that sheds its needles every year.

ă pat/ā pay/â care/ä father/ĕ pet/ē be/ĭ pit/ī pie/î fierce/ŏ pot/ō go/ô paw, for/oi oil/ŏŏ book/
ŏŏ boot/ou out/ŭ cut/û fur/*th* the/th thin/hw which/zh vision/ə ago, item, pencil, atom, circus

tam•per (tăm′pər) *v.* To interfere or to bring about an improper situation in a harmful manner.

tank•ard (tăng′kərd) *n.* A large drinking cup, usually having a handle and a hinged cover.

ta•pa (tä′pə) *n.* A paperlike cloth made in the islands of the Pacific Ocean by pounding the inner bark of a kind of mulberry tree.

ta•per (tā′pər) *v.* To make or become gradually thinner toward one end: *a candle tapering to a point.*

taut (tôt) *adj.* **taut•er, taut•est. 1.** Pulled or drawn tight: *sails taut with wind.* **2.** Strained; tense: *his taut and angry face.* —**taut′ly** *adv.* —**taut′ness** *n.*

tax•i (tăk′sē) *n., pl.* **tax•is** or **tax•ies.** A taxicab. —*v.* **1.** To be transported by taxi. **2.** To move slowly over the surface of the ground or water before takeoff or after landing, as an aircraft does.

tech•nique (tĕk nēk′) *n.* A method by which a complicated task is accomplished, as in a science or art.

temp•ta•tion (tĕmp tā′shən) *n.* Something that tempts, or is inviting or attractive.

ten•don (tĕn′dən) *n.* A band of tough tissue that forms a connection between a muscle and a bone.

thatch (thăch) *n.* Plant stalks or leaves, such as straw, reeds, or palm fronds, used to make or cover a roof.

thick•et (thĭk′ĭt) *n.* A dense growth or clump of shrubs, small trees, underbrush, etc.

this•tle•down (thĭs′əl doun′) *n.* The silky, fluffy material attached to the seeds of a thistle plant, by means of which the seeds float through the air.

throng (thrông) *or* (thrŏng) *n.* A large group of people or things crowded together.

throt•tle (thrŏt′l) *n.* A valve in an engine by which the flow of fuel is controlled.

thwart (thwôrt) *v.* To prevent from taking place. —*n.* A seat across a boat, on which the rower sits.

tim•pa•ni (tĭm′pə nē) *pl. n.* A set of kettledrums.

tou•can (tōō′kăn′) *or* (-kän′) *n.* A tropical bird with brightly colored plumage and a very large bill.

trans•con•ti•nen•tal (trăns′kŏn tə nĕn′tl) *or* (trănz′-) *adj.* Spanning or crossing a continent: *a transcontinental flight.*

trans•fer (trăns fûr′) *or* (trăns′fər) *v.* **trans•ferred, trans•fer•ring. 1.** To move from one place, person, or thing to another. **2.** To move from one job, school, or location to another. **3.** To move (a pattern, design, or set of markings) from one surface to another: *Trace the design, then transfer it to the leather.*

trans•form (trăns fôrm′) *v.* To change markedly in form or appearance: *The witch transformed the men into mice.*

treach•er•y (trĕch′ə rē) *n., pl.* **treach•er•ies.** Willful betrayal of trust; treason.

trea•son (trē′zən) *n.* Betrayal of one's country, especially by giving aid to an enemy in wartime or by plotting to overthrow the government.

trill (trĭl) *n.* A fluttering or tremulous sound, as that made by certain birds; a warble.

tri•umph (trī′əmf) *v.* To be victorious; win; be greater in strength. —*n.* **1.** The instance or fact of being victorious; success. **2.** Great joy coming from victory: *a cry of triumph.*

trove (trōv) *n.* Something of value discovered or found.

trust fund. Money, real estate, etc., belonging to one person but managed for his or her benefit by another.

ty•rant (tī′rənt) *n.* **1.** A ruler who exercises power in a harsh, cruel manner; an oppressor. **2.** Any tyrannical or despotic person.

un•in•hab•it•ed (ŭn′ĭn hăb′ĭ tĭd) *adj.* Not inhabited; not lived in or on.

un•pro•voked (ŭn′prə vōkt′) *adj.* **1.** Not provoked or prompted. **2.** Not having aroused the anger of.

ur•gent (ûr′jənt) *adj.* Calling for immediate action or attention; pressing: *a problem of an urgent nature.*

ven•ture (vĕn′chər) *n.* An undertaking, course of action, etc., that involves risk or uncertainty. —*v.* **ven•tured, ven•tur•ing. 1.** To risk; stake. **2.** To dare to say; express at the risk of denial, criticism, etc.: *venture an opinion.* **3.** To travel, engage in a course of action, undertake a project, etc., despite danger and fear; dare.

ve•ran•da or **ve•ran•dah** (və răn′də) *n.* A roofed porch or balcony.

ver•min (vûr′mĭn) *n., pl.* **ver•min.** Any of various insects or small animals, such as cockroaches or rats, that destroy things, annoy people and animals, and can harm one's health.

ves•sel (vĕs′əl) *n.* **1.** A ship, large boat, or similar craft. **2.** A hollow container, as a bowl, pitcher, jar, or tank.

ves•try (vĕs′trē) *n., pl.* **ves•tries. 1.** A room in a church where vestments and holy objects are kept. **2.** A meeting room in a church.

vi•brate (vī′brāt′) *v.* **vi•brat•ed, vi•brat•ing.** To move or cause to move back and forth rapidly.

vi•rus (vī′rəs) *n., pl.* **vi•rus•es.** A tiny particle capable of producing a disease.

vis•i•bil•i•ty (vĭz′ə bĭl′ĭ tē) *n.* **1.** The fact, condition, or degree of being able to be seen. **2.** The greatest distance over which it is possible to see without help from instruments under given weather conditions.

wa•ger-boat (wā′jər bōt′) *n.* A light racing boat used in contests between single scullers, or rowers.

ward (wôrd) *n.* **1.** A section of a hospital devoted to the care of a particular group of patients: *a maternity ward.* **2.** A large hospital room shared by a number of patients: *a four-bed ward.*

war•i•ly (wâr′ĭ lē) *adv.* In an alert and watchful manner: *She stepped warily across the old boards of the porch.* —**war′y** *adj.* —**war′i•ness** *n.*

wart-rid•den (wôrt′rĭd′n) *adj.* Covered with warts or with bumps similar in appearance to warts.

wa•ter ou•zel (wô′tər ōō′zəl) *n.* A small bird that dives into swift-moving streams and feeds along the bottom.

weir (wîr) *n.* A dam placed across a river or canal.

whee•dle (hwēd′l) *or* (wēd′l) *v.* **whee•dled, whee•dling.** To get by pleading, flattering, etc.: *He wheedled a promise out of me.*

wist•ful•ly (wĭst′fəl lē) *adv.* In a way that is full of a sad yearning; wishfully. —**wist′ful** *adj.* —**wist′ful•ness** *n.*

witch•craft (wĭch′krăft′) *or* (-kräft′) *n.* Magic as practiced by witches; sorcery.

with•er (wĭth′ər) *v.* **1.** To dry up or cause to dry up from lack of water; shrivel: *The flowers withered in the vase.* **2.** To fade or disappear: *His anger withered away.*

with•ers (wĭth′ərz) *pl. n.* The highest part of the back of a horse or similar animal, between the shoulder blades.

wit•ti•cism (wĭt′ĭ sĭz′əm) *n.* A cleverly worded, amusing remark.

Yo•sem•i•te National Park (yō sĕm′ə-tē) An area of 1,183 square miles in east-central California.

ă pat/ā pay/â care/ä father/ĕ pet/ē be/ĭ pit/ī pie/î fierce/ŏ pot/ō go/ô paw, for/oi oil/ŏŏ book/
ŏŏ boot/ou out/ŭ cut/û fur/*th* the/th thin/hw which/zh vision/ə ago, item, pencil, atom, circus

BCDEFGHIJ-D-85432101/79